The Vikings in the Hebrides

This book is dedicated to

Mary Davis

without whom
it would not exist

The Vikings in the Hebrides

Niall Sharples

Windgather Press is an imprint of Oxbow Books

Published in the United Kingdom in 2025 by
OXBOW BOOKS
81 St Clements, Oxford OX4 1AW

and in the United States by
OXBOW BOOKS
1950 Lawrence Road, Havertown, PA 19083

© Windgather Press and the author 2025

Paperback Edition: ISBN 978-1-914427-39-8
Digital Edition: ISBN 978-1-914427-40-4 (epub)

A CIP record for this book is available from the British Library

All rights reserved. No part of this book may be reproduced or transmitted in any form or by any means, electronic or mechanical including photocopying, recording or by any information storage and retrieval system, without permission from the publisher in writing.

Printed in the United Kingdom by Short Run Press
Typeset in India by DiTech Publishing Services

For a complete list of Windgather titles, please contact:

United Kingdom
OXBOW BOOKS
Telephone (0)1226 734350
Email: oxbow@oxbowbooks.com
www.oxbowbooks.com

United States of America
OXBOW BOOKS
Telephone (610) 853-9131, Fax (610) 853-9146
Email: queries@casemateacademic.com
www.casemateacademic.com/oxbow

Oxbow Books is part of the Casemate group

Cover: Viking sword hilt. National Museum of Scotland. Discovered at Kildonnan, Eigg (https://www.flickr.com/photos/dun_deagh/7845756908/, dun_deagh, CC-BY-2.0); South Uist Machair (https://www.flickr.com/photos/timniblett/201266026/, Tim Niblett, CC-BY-2.0)

The Publisher's authorised representative in the EU for product safety is Authorised Rep Compliance Ltd., Ground Floor, 71 Lower Baggot Street, Dublin D02 P593, Ireland.
www.arccompliance.com

Contents

List of figures   vii
Acknowledgements   xix

1. Bornais, the Vikings and the Outer Hebrides   1
   Introduction – green porphyry   1
   Viking settlement in the Hebrides   5
   Excavations at Bornais and Cille Pheadair   9
   Chronology and structure   15
   Landscape   20
   Vegetation   28
   Animals   29
   Conclusion   32
2. Before the Vikings   35
   Introduction – a bone die   35
   The wheelhouse   37
   The occupation of the wheelhouse   40
   Wheelhouses in the Western Isles   44
   Brochs   48
   Reconstruction and abandonment   52
   A crisis   58
   The appearance of 'individuals'   66
   The 'Little Ice Age'   69
   The Picts   70
   A burial at Cille Pheadair   75
   Conclusion   78
3. The Viking colonisation of the Outer Hebrides   83
   Introduction – the burial at Cnip   83
   The history   86
   The archaeology   90
   Viking treasure   111
   The Cille Bharra cross slab   114
   The agricultural economy   116
   Conclusion   121

4.	The Kingdom of Man and the Isles	127
	Introduction – a find of Ringerike art	127
	The history	130
	Archaeology and the Kingdom of Man	132
	A high-status residence on mound 2	134
	The agricultural economy	166
	Size and status	168
	Church and Thing	173
	Conclusion	177
5.	Scots and Gaels	183
	Introduction – the Lewis chessmen	183
	The history	187
	The archaeology	188
	A Late Norse hall	189
	'Peasant' houses	198
	A comb-maker's workshop	204
	Red deer	211
	Kilns	212
	Crops and the agricultural economy	215
	Animals and the agricultural economy	216
	Castle and church	217
	Conclusion	220
6.	The origin of the clans	223
	Introduction	223
	The history	225
	The settlement evidence	226
	Climate and plague	233
	Castle and church	235
	Conclusion	239
Bibliography		242
Index		248

List of figures

1.1	Two fragments of green porphyry from Bornais, South Uist.	1
1.2	A large fragment of green porphyry on the Capitoline Hill, Rome, Italy.	2
1.3	A portable altar of the late twelfth century from Cologne, with a green porphyry tile at its centre. © Sarah Luginbill, July 2019.	4
1.4	A location map of the western seaboard of Scotland, showing the Viking and Norse sites mentioned in the text.	6
1.5	Excavations at Bornais mound 2 during the summer of 2004.	7
1.6	Excavations at Cille Pheadair showing how close the sea was to destroying the main house exposed by the excavations.	7
1.7	An aerial view of the complex of churches and chapels at Howmore, South Uist. © Historic Environment Scotland.	8
1.8	A contour survey of the settlement mounds at Bornais, South Uist, showing the areas excavated between 1994 and 2004.	10
1.9	The first season of excavation at Bornais mound 2, 1994. © Mike Parker Pearson.	11
1.10	A geophysical survey of the northern part of the settlement at Bornais. The rectangular enclosure that forms the most visible feature of the survey is a walled enclosure, created to pen sheep in the nineteenth century. The concentrations of high magnetic anomalies indicate concentrations of midden and stone walls that define settlement mounds 2, 2A, 2B and 3.	12
1.11	A view of the eroding beach at Cille Pheadair, South Uist. This was taken after the excavations had been completed, and when coastal erosion had removed over 80% of the settlement area.	13
1.12	Excavations at Bornais in 2004 looking east across the excavated area of mound 2A.	14
1.13	Excavating the floor of a Middle Norse house (House 2) at Bornais.	15
1.14	The three main phases of occupation on mounds 2 and 2A at Bornais.	18
1.15	A satellite image of the Western Isles. Licensed under the Creative Commons Attribution-ShareAlike 3.0 IGO license.	20
1.16	A simplified geological map of the western seaboard of Scotland. Licensed under the Creative Commons Attribution-ShareAlike 3.0 IGO license.	21

1.17	A view north along the coastline of Lewis. In the foreground is Barvas machair, the largest area of machair in Lewis. © Crown Copyright: HES.	22
1.18	The ice scoured mountains of Harris. © G F Geddes.	23
1.19	The Sound of Harris looking across the island of Ensay to Pabbay and in the distance St Kilda. © G F Geddes.	23
1.20	An aerial view of the promontory of Rubha Ardvule, South Uist. © Crown Copyright: HES.	24
1.21	A view of the machair plain of South Uist from the isle of Orosaigh.	24
1.22	A crop of barley growing on the machair plain of South Uist.	25
1.23	An aerial view across Lochboisdale, an important port in one of the east facing sea lochs of South Uist. © Crown Copyright: HES.	26
1.24	An aerial view of the Bishop's Islands south of Barra. In the foreground is Berneray and behind this Mingulay. © Crown Copyright: HES.	27
2.1	The parallelopiped die from Bornais mound 1.	35
2.2	Exposing the remains of a Late Iron Age wheelhouse on Bornais mound 1.	36
2.3	A simplified plan of the wheelhouse on Bornais mound 1. The east side is fairly well documented in the archaeological record, but the west side is largely conjectural with only the worn sill stones of the entrance to provide a clue to the location of the west wall.	37
2.4	Excavating the burnt roof timbers of the wheelhouse on Bornais mound 1.	38
2.5	An experimental reconstruction of a small wheelhouse at Old Scatness, Shetland. The photograph shows the entrance to two of the cells with their corbelled stone vaults and the timber roof that covers the central part of the house.	39
2.6	The whale bone axe and a view of it *in situ* when it was lodged between two of the burnt timbers of the wheelhouse roof; it lies just below the left-hand side of the scale.	41
2.7	The distribution of stone cobble tools on the floor of the wheelhouse with insets showing the stone tools that comprised cluster A and cluster F during excavation. The clusters adjacent to the wall of the house also included bones which are clearly visible in the photo of cluster F.	42
2.8	An outline of the floor layer from the original and the rebuilt wheelhouse showing the distribution of the objects found. The objects on the top are all burnt, whereas those on the bottom are unburnt.	43

2.9	An unusual iron and antler comb showing the incised decoration on one side. This object was heavily burnt and fragmented, and was associated with the primary occupation of the wheelhouse.	44
2.10	Plans of a selection of excavated wheelhouses from the Western Isles. A) Cnip, B) A'Cheardach Bheag, C) Allt Chrisal, D) A'Cheardach Mhor, E) Sollas.	45
2.11	A view of the excavation of the wheelhouse at A'Cheardach Bheag in 1956. © Courtesy of HES. Papers of Dr Horace Fairhurst, archaeologist, Glasgow, Scotland.	46
2.12	A plan of the settlement mounds adjacent to the broch at Dun Vulan highlighting in red those with definite Middle Iron Age occupation.	47
2.13	A general view of the broch at Carloway, Isle of Lewis.	49
2.14	The remnants of the staircase of the broch at Dun Vulan, South Uist. These were truncated by the sea, and the passage into the interior of the broch is filled with earth and occupation debris.	50
2.15	An aerial view of the broch of Dun Torcuil, North Uist, showing its location and the stone causeway leading out to the artificial island on which it was built. © Historic Environment Scotland.	51
2.16	The distribution of Middle Iron Age settlements on South Uist.	52
2.17	The parallelopiped die and decorated astragalus found on mound 1, Bornais.	53
2.18	A view of the remains of the rebuilt wheelhouse on mound 1, Bornais.	54
2.19	A plan and photograph of the hearth in the rebuilt wheelhouse, showing the arrangement of cattle metapodials at the east end.	54
2.20	Excavating the hearth metapodials and adjacent floor layers. The hearth metapodials are pushed into the orange sand which represents the burnt down roof.	55
2.21	Cleaning the central hearth in the rebuilt wheelhouse on Bornais mound 1.	55
2.22	A Roman brooch from the wheelhouse at Kilpheder (Cille Pheadair), South Uist. © National Museums Scotland.	58
2.23	A section through the sand layers infilling the hollow above the wheelhouse floors. It shows a series of charcoal-rich layers surrounded by the windblown sand that was slowly infilling the hollow.	59
2.24	Weaving combs and weaving tablets from the charcoal layers filling the abandoned house. Note the wear marks around the holes at the corners of the weaving tablets.	60

2.25	Drawn sections through the abandoned deposits in the wheelhouses at Kilpheder (Cille Pheadair), A'Cheardach Bheag and A'Chearadach Mhor (from top to bottom).	61
2.26	A composite antler comb and two pins from the Late Iron Age occupation of Bornais mound 2.	63
2.27	A view of a badly robbed Pictish house at the Udal, North Uist. © IAC, Udal Archives.	64
2.28	A plan of the Pictish house at Bostadh on Lewis. © Tim Neighbour.	65
2.29	The fragmentary remains of an elaborate Late Iron Age comb from The Udal. © IAC, Udal Archives.	67
2.30	A selection of metalworking debris from a settlement at Loch Olibhat, including moulds for hand pins, brooches and decorated discs, crucibles and bar moulds. © Ian Armit.	68
2.31	A comparison of the large well-made vessel from the early first millennium wheelhouse on Bornais mound 1 with a smaller rather crudely made vessels found in the later first millennium deposits on Bornais mound 2.	69
2.32	The Pictish symbol stone from Benbecula in the National Museum Scotland. © National Museums Scotland.	73
2.33	An aerial view of the island of North Rona and a detail of the settlement complex which includes the Early Christian Oratory in the enclosure in the centre of the image. © Historic Environment Scotland.	74
2.34	John Raven excavating the Pictish burial surrounded by the kerb of the square cairn at Cille Pheadair. © Mike Parker Pearson.	76
3.1	The Cnip peninsula on the west coast of Lewis; a Viking cemetery was found in the large erosion scar at the far end. © Crown Copyright: HES.	84
3.2	A pair of brooches and a necklace of glass beads from the Viking burial at Cnip on the Isle of Lewis. © National Museums Scotland.	85
3.3	A reconstructed view of the town of Dublin in the Viking period. © National Museum of Ireland	87
3.4	The Hostage Stone from Inchmarnock, Argyll. It is thought to depict a Viking with his captured slave. © National Museums Scotland.	88
3.5	A view of the Viking burial pit on the South Dorset Ridgeway during excavation; a cluster of detached skulls lies in front of the two excavators.	91
3.6	Two broken Pictish symbol stones from Portmahomack, Easter Ross. © National Museums Scotland.	92
3.7	The distribution of Viking graves in Scotland and northern England.	93

3.8	The Aird a'Mhorain peninsula on the south side of the Sound of Harris. The Viking settlement of the Udal lies in the middle distance just inland of the small tidal islet. © Crown Copyright: HES.	94
3.9	A schematic plan showing a sequence of houses at the Udal that begins with a jelly baby house of the eighth century, is followed by a Viking house of the ninth to tenth century, and sealed by a fourteenth-century house. © IAC, Udal Archives.	95
3.10	A large whale bone object which can be interpreted as a 'scutcher' used to break up flax stalks as part of the process of making linen textiles. This was found in a small pit on Bornais, mound 1.	97
3.11	The ogham inscribed plaque found on the surface of Bornais mound 1.	97
3.12	A coin of the Norwegian king Olaf Kyrre (the Peaceful) from Bornais mound 1.	98
3.13	A plan of the three superimposed houses on Bornais mound 2.	98
3.14	The west end of House 1 on Bornais, mound 2. The two upper photos show the house floor before and after it was excavated. The drawings below these show the extent of the floor layer, the structural features below this, and then the pits which were dug as a foundational act.	99
3.15	An overall plan of Bornais House 1, showing the excavated areas at the two gable ends.	100
3.16	A photo of a collection of finds exposed in the fill of a pit in House 1. The finds included a horn core, a cattle metapodial and a whale bone chopping board.	100
3.17	The lead cross from the floor of Bornais House 1.	102
3.18	Examples of the large ceramic and steatite vessels from the floor of Bornais, House 1.	103
3.19	Two pins including a pig fibula pin with an incised spiral decoration which came from the sand deposits infilling Bornais, House 1.	105
3.20	A possible iron candlestick from the sand deposits infilling Bornais, House 1.	106
3.21	The distinctive brown streaks indicating ard cultivation in the windblown sand at the base of Bornais, mound 2A.	107
3.22	A cross section through a hearth built into the cultivation soil of Bornais, mound 2A.	107
3.23	A selection of finds from the cultivation soil on Bornais, mound 2A; including a glass gaming counter, two whetstones, a stone spindle whorl broken during production, the side plate of a composite comb, two bone pins, tweezers and the copper alloy ring from a ring headed pin.	108

xii *List of figures*

3.24	A view of the early house at Cille Pheadair during excavation. © Mike Parker Pearson.	109
3.25	The excavation of a Viking longhouse at Drimore, South Uist. © Crown Copyright: HES.	111
3.26	The silver hoards from Dibidale and Stornoway Castle on the Isle of Lewis. © Museum nan Eilean.	112
3.27	The hoard of gold rings from Oronsay. © National Museums Scotland.	113
3.28	The Viking gravestone from Cille Bharra. © Society of Antiquaries of Scotland.	115
3.29	Barley cultivated and stacked to dry on the machair plain of South Uist.	117
3.30	A diagram showing the variation in the different crops recovered from the early Norse deposits on mound 2 (BB) and mound 2A (GA) at Bornais.	118
3.31	A photo of the fish bones recovered from careful sieving and sorting of one of the soil samples from Bornais. The large white bone is a Saithe otolith, but the other bones are mostly from herring.	119
3.32	The relative percentages of cattle, sheep, pig and red deer bones from Bornais, mound 2 and 2A, showing the changes through time.	121
4.1	A photograph of the antler cylinder decorated with a Ringerike beast from the floor of Bornais, House 2.	127
4.2	A drawing of the antler cylinder decorated with a Ringerike beast from the floor of Bornais, House 2.	128
4.3	Great beasts in Viking art. Bornais is 2 and it is compared to the much larger images on the memorial stones of 1. Tullstorp, Skåne, Sweden; 3 Stora Ek, and 4. Norra Åsarp, Västergötland, Sweden.	129
4.4	The broken head of a bone pin from Cille Pheadair decorated with a Ringerike knot.	130
4.5	A map of South Uist showing the location of settlement mounds producing Norse ceramics, the possible early church sites, fortifications and administrative boundaries (based on information in Raven 2005).	133
4.6	A photograph of House 2 from the east during excavation.	135
4.7	A plan of House 2 showing its relationship with the underlying House 1. Note the reuse of the northeast gable wall of House 1 as an entrance passage wall in House 2.	136
4.8	The excavation of the entrance to House 2 showing the large whale bone rib that lay in the infilling sand.	137
4.9	A view of the internal wall on the north side of House 2.	138

List of figures xiii

4.10	The pit below the floor of House 2 containing Cardiff University student Katherine Adams.	139
4.11	A plan of House 2 showing the pits that lay below the house floor.	140
4.12	A plan of the interior of House 2 showing the extent of the ash layers that define the central aisle.	140
4.13	Simplified plans of Viking longhouses from the North Atlantic: A) Bornais House 1; B) Bornais House 2; C) Cille Pheadair; D) Snjáleifartóttir, Iceland; E) Niðri á Toft, Faroes; F) Granastaðir 9, Iceland; G) Oma, Norway; H) Aðalstræti, Iceland; I) Hofstaðir, Iceland.	141
4.14	A section through the ash layers that define the central aisle of Bornais House 2.	142
4.15	A selection of unusual finds from the floor of House 2 including a decorative fragment of amber cross, a fragment of an early Norse comb, a lead pendant, two clipped silver coins, a folded section of gold strip, a fragment of green porphyry, and a blue glass bead.	143
4.16	Four of the more elaborately carved bone pinheads from the House 2 floor.	144
4.17	The copper alloy stick pins from Bornais; those from the floor of House 2 have a triangle next to the pinhead.	144
4.18	An Early Norse comb from the floor of House 2.	144
4.19	Two Middle Norse combs from the floor of House 2.	145
4.20	A comb from the floor of House 2.	146
4.21	Two decorated antler tines.	146
4.22	The drinking horn held by a queen in the Lewis chess set. © National Museums Scotland.	147
4.23	A selection of iron knives from House 2.	148
4.24	A photograph of an iron knife (6030) before cleaning and conservation showing the vestigial remains of the wooden handle on the left side.	148
4.25	Two broken whetstones from the floor of House 2. These were imported from Norway; that on the right is of Eidsborg schist and that on the left purple phyllite.	149
4.26	A selection of the complete spindle whorls recovered from all the occupation periods at Bornais.	149
4.27	A selection of bone and copper alloy needles from Bornais House 2.	150
4.28	Two bone needle cases from the floor of Bornais House 2	150
4.29	A flexible iron cauldron handle from the floor of Bornais House 2	151
4.30	A bag of iron scrap, largely holdfasts but including a broken axe.	152
4.31	A drawing of some of the almost complete pots from the floor of Bornais House 2.	152

4.32	A photo of one of the well-preserved pots from House 2 showing the soot-blackened surface that indicates repeated use for cooking on the hearth.	153
4.33	The fragmentary remains of a pot imported from the southwest of England.	153
4.34	A modern replica of a Norse platter that was used to bake a flatbread.	154
4.35	Flotation of the various soil samples recovered from the excavations was a messy process which took place in one of the local farmyards. The process was essential for recovering representative collections of carbonised grains and the small bones that documented the importance of fishing. It also produced a large assemblage of eggshell, pictured on the right, which would otherwise not have been recovered.	155
4.36	A comparison of the density of different categories of material in the peripheral floor layers, the central, ash-covered, aisle and the pit fills of House 2.	155
4.37	The overall distribution of small finds found on the floor of House 2 showing three concentrations of finds.	157
4.38	The distribution of needles and spindle whorls, knives and whetstones and roves and holdfasts on the floor of House 2.	158
4.39	A possible division of Bornais House 2 into four spaces, probably rooms divided by internal walls, showing the position of the five finds clusters in relation to hearth layers.	159
4.40	The spatial organisation of the house at Granastaðir in northern Iceland as suggested by the excavator Einarsson.	160
4.41	The spatial organisation of the house at Aðalstræti in Iceland as suggested by Milek. © Karen Milek.	161
4.42	The occupation of House 500 at Cille Pheadair on South Uist. © Mike Parker Pearson.	163
4.43	The bone cross pendants from Cille Pheadair. The cross on the right came from the north end of the interior of House 500.	164
4.44	A view of the fourteenth-century house at the Udal. © IAC, Udal Archives.	166
4.45	A plan of the Middle Norse kilns and platform on mound 2A with photographs of them during excavation.	167
4.46	Comparative plans of the settlements at Finlaggan, Islay, Bornais, Birsay in Orkney, Jarlshof in Shetland and Ardtornish, Morvern.	171
4.47	A view of Finlaggan, an important settlement on Islay that acted as one of the centres for the MacDonald Lords of the Isles. © Crown Copyright: HES.	172
4.48	A plan of the church at Cill Donnain to the south of Bornais on South Uist. After Fleming and Woolf 1992.	175

List of figures

5.1	A group shot of Lewis chessmen © National Museums Scotland.	183
5.2	A photo of a bishop, a king, a queen and a warder from the Lewis chess set © National Museums Scotland.	185
5.3	A simplified plan of Late Norse House 3 at Bornais, showing its relationship with the Middle Norse House 2.	189
5.4	A view of Bornais Late Norse House 3 from the north during the excavation of the floor.	190
5.5	The east facing entrance passage to the Late Norse House 3.	191
5.6	Excavating floor layers and pits in Late Norse House 3.	192
5.7	The foundation pits at the centre of Late Norse House 3.	192
5.8	A charcoal rich layer at the base of one of the foundation pits of Late Norse House 3.	193
5.9	Three plans of the floor layers in Late Norse House 3 showing the pits and peat ash layers. The earliest floor is on the left the latest on the right.	193
5.10	The distribution of the artefacts found in the early and late floors of Late Norse House 3.	194
5.11	A whale bone comb from the floor of Late Norse House 3.	195
5.12	A continental imitation of a long cross penny made between 1248 and 1270. Found on the floor of Late Norse House 3.	196
5.13	A close up of a section through the ash layers of the central hearth in Late Norse House 3.	196
5.14	The distribution of mammal bones, fish bones and limpet shells showing the density for every half metre square of the floor layers excavated.	197
5.15	Simplified plans of the late Norse houses at Cille Pheadair and Bornais mound 3.	199
5.16	A view of the late Norse house on mound 3, Bornais with Beinn Mhor in the background.	199
5.17	A view of the excavation of the Late Norse house on Bornais mound 3 with the hearth in the foreground.	200
5.18	A reconstruction drawing of the Late Norse house on mound 3.	200
5.19	The Late Norse house at Cille Pheadair during the excavation. © Mike Parker Pearson.	201
5.20	A schematic plan of the last two houses at Cille Pheadair showing their relationship and the contemporary ancillary buildings to the southwest.	203
5.21	Cardiff students excavating the floors of the ancillary building on Bornais mound 2A.	204
5.22	A diagram showing the different stages of antler working that are required to produce a composite comb.	205
5.23	Antler working debris from Bornais mound 2A. On the top, the sections of antler retain the rough outer surface, on the bottom the antler segments have been smoothed and are ready to be incorporated into a comb.	206

xvi List of figures

5.24	A plan of the area excavated on Bornais mound 2A showing the Late Norse structures and the distribution of comb making debris. The inset shows a cluster of debris that probably indicates a bag of material left behind when the workshop was abandoned.	208
5.25	A selection of relatively complete composite combs from the Udal, North Uist. © IAC, Udal Archives.	209
5.26	The two relatively complete 'fish-tailed' combs from Bornais, the comb on the bottom came from mound 2, that on the top from mound 2A.	210
5.27	A selection of gaming pieces from Bornais. Most of these are unfinished and come from the workshop on mound 2A.	211
5.28	Antler gaming pieces from Bornais.	211
5.29	A view of the grain-drying kiln on Bornais mound 3.	213
5.30	Excavating a nineteenth-century kiln at Frobost, South Uist.	214
5.31	Oat stooks on the machair plain of North Boisdale, South Uist.	215
5.32	A view of Kisimul Castle from the pier at Castlebay, Barra.	218
6.1	A general view of the tomb of Alasdair Crotach in the church at Rodel, Harris. © Crown Copyright: HES.	224
6.2	A detail showing the castle, bishop and hunting scene in the tomb of Alasdair Crotach. © Crown Copyright: HES.	224
6.3	A plan of the final house at Cille Pheadair showing the later shelters built into the northeast and southwest corners of the house. © Mike Parker Pearson.	228
6.4	The impressions of cattle hoof prints pressed into the abandoned floor of House 3 and filled with white windblown sand.	229
6.5	A view of the shelter built into the south end of Bornais House 3 after it had been abandoned.	229
6.6	A plan of the shelter at the south end of Bornais House 3 showing the ashy floor layer extending out of the entrance.	230
6.7	Two of the smaller shelters built after the settlement had been largely abandoned, that on the left was built against the west wall of Bornais House 3, that on the right is built in the northeast corner of the final house in mound 2A.	231
6.8	A plan and two views of the shelter built into the northwest corner of the kiln on Bornais mound 3. It was built as the kiln filled up with windblown sand.	232
6.9	The Northern Hemisphere (NH) temperature anomaly (relative to the 1990 level) from a wide variety of paleoclimate proxies: the black line is the mean value, and the colors give the uncertainty probability distribution. The blue dots are the instrumental record. The dashed lines mark the start	

	and end of the Little Ice Age (LIA) defined by the (NH) temperature anomaly level -0.16 degrees Celsius. Lockwood *et al.* 2017 and Owens *et al.* 2017.	233
6.10	A view of the tower in Dùn Èistean at Ness, Lewis. © Rachel Barrowman.	236
6.11	A plan of the buildings on the stack at Dùn Èistean, Ness, Lewis. © Rachel Barrowman.	237
6.12	Plans of a variety of unusual castles and modified duns probably built in the fifteenth and sixteenth centuries.	238
6.13	The unmortared stone castle of Dun Raouill in Loch Druidibeg, South Uist, an isolated building only accessible by boat. © Crown Copyright: HES.	239
6.14	Dun an Sticar in North Uist showing the substantial stone causeway leading out to the dun.	239
6.15	The church at Rodel, Harris. © Denys Pringle.	240

Acknowledgements

This book represents the culmination of a project which began in 1990 when Mike Parker Pearson asked me to become involved in fieldwork on the island of South Uist in the Outer Hebrides. I am immensely grateful for his invitation as I found the fieldwork on the island immensely pleasurable and the analysis and writing that followed stimulating and, though to a lesser extent, enjoyable. Mike has also been very supportive during the writing of this book allowing me to freely use the results of his excavations at Cille Pheadair and reading and editing the final text.

The fieldwork could not have been undertaken without the support of a large number of islanders who made us very welcome on the island. Permission to excavate was provided by the Bornais Grazing Committee through Ewan Steele, South Uists Estates (who owned the island at the time of our excavations) through Tim Atkinson and Scottish Natural Heritage through Mary Harman. During the fieldwork we received invaluable support from the members of Comann Eachdraich Uibhist a Deas, Kathy Bruce, the late James MacDonald and the late Calum MacDonald, the late Alasdair MacIntyre, the late Gill MacLean, the late Neil MacMillan, the late Effie Macmillan and Robert Tye. Mrs K. Frazer, Mrs M. MacIsaac, Mr and Mrs A.J. MacKinnon, Mrs M.K. Morrison and Col H. Massey kindly provided accommodation for the excavation personnel.

Financial support for the project was provided by Cardiff University, Historic Scotland and laterally Historic Environment Scotland. Noel Fojut, Rod McCullagh, Lisa Brown, Rebecca Jones, Kevin Grant and Kirsty Owen have all provided invaluable support. The excavations at Bornais could not have been undertaken without the skill and experience of the various supervisors: Katherine Adams, Jerry Bond, Mark Brennand, Dave Brewer, Nicola Collins, Luke Craddock-Bennett, Oliver Davis, Sam Emmett, Mike Hamilton, Rachel Jackson, Suzi Reeve, Alex Rowe, Katinka Stentoft, Katy Stronach, Chris Swanson, Kate Waddington, Nick Wells, and Dave Wyatt. There were many Cardiff University students and volunteers who participated in the dig and I am grateful to every one of them. The environmental processing undertaken on the island and in Cardiff was an amazing effort set up by Helen Smith and Jacqui Mulville and undertaken with the help of Rachel Ballantyne, Yvonne Cunningham, Sarah Housley, Ruaraidh McKay, Fiona Morris, Kelly Reed, Rachel Smith, Frances Taylor, Rhiannon Thomas and Mark Ward.

This book and the associated detailed excavation reports could not have been written without the contributions of all the specialists who have worked on the Bornais material over the last thirty years. Their contributions are fully documented in the excavation reports, but they need to be mentioned and thanked for their contribution to this synthesis as without them it would not have been possible to write it. They are Julia Best, Julie Bond, Chris Bronk Ramsey, Abby Carter, Judy Cartledge, Ben Cartwright, Emmanuelle Casanova, Dana Challinor, Ann Clarke, Sue College, Gordon Cook, Lucy Cramp, Anna Davies-Barrett, Duncan Brown, Mary Davis, Ian Dennis, Sally Evans, Richard Evershed, Amanda Forster, Katherine Forsyth, Peter Forward, Clara Freer, Ian Freestone, Rowena Gale, Jacob Griffiths, Mark Hall, Kirsty Harding, Tom Horne, Clare Ingrem, Jennifer Jones, Alan Lane, Matt Law, Jan Light, Phil MacDonald, Richard Madgwick, Pete Marshall, Karen Milek, Jacqui Mulville, Tamsin O'Connell, Amelia Pannett, Phil Parkes, James Peake, Adrienne Powell, Mark Redknap, Clare Riley, Alex Rowe, Dale Serjeantson, Andrea Smith, Helen Smith, Rachel Smith, Rachel Stevens, John Summers, Nigel Thew, Helen Wickstead, Gareth Williams and Tim Young.

The illustrations were provided by various organisations and individuals. The original site drawings were brought to a publication standard by Ian Dennis and Kirsty Harding and the photographs by John Morgan and Mark Lodwick. A large number of photographs were provided by Historic Environment Scotland thanks to Mindy Lynch and by the National Museums Scotland thanks to Margaret Wilson, with a little help from Adrian Maldonado. Thanks, are also due to Rachel Barrowman for images of Dùn Èistean, Beverley Ballin Smith for images from the Udal archive. Denys Pringle for his picture of Rodel church and Sarah Luginbill for the Cologne altar. Mike Parker Pearson gave permission to use several images from his work at Cille Pheadair. Tim Neighbour allowed me to use a plan of his excavations at Bostaidh. Kirsty Harding worked hard to bring the final illustrations up to an acceptable publication standard. Karen Milek allowed me to use her illustration of the spatial organisation of the house at Aðalstræti in Iceland.

This text would not have achieved its present form without significant help from Mary Davis, Karen Godden, Mike Parker Pearson and John Raven.

CHAPTER ONE

Bornais, the Vikings and the Outer Hebrides

Introduction – green porphyry

The village of Krokees lies in the middle of Laconia, a region in the Peloponnese in Greece. Immediately to the north lies the city of Sparta, the great military city state of Classical Greece, and to the west of this lies Mystras, a Medieval hill city dominated by a Frankish fortress. Mystras became an important political and cultural centre for the eastern Mediterranean in the thirteenth and fourteenth centuries, effectively the capital city of the Byzantine Empire after Constantinople fell to the Ottomans in 1453.

What have these distant lands to do with the Outer Hebrides? One of the most surprising discoveries during the excavations at Bornais in South Uist were two fragments of stone that are of such a distinctive nature (Fig. 1.1) that we can confidently state that they came from quarries a couple of kilometres south of Krokees. The stones are small fragments, and one appears to be the corner of a rectangular tile approximately 14 mm thick. Their identification is secured by their distinctive appearance: their dark green matrix contains light green inclusions with an elongated rectangular shape. The scientific term for these rocks is a porphyritic metabasalt, though I will refer to this as green porphyry, and they are a unique feature of the volcanic rocks that characterise the Peloponnese in Greece.

FIGURE 1.1. Two fragments of green porphyry from Bornais, South Uist.

So, we can be certain that these small fragments from South Uist travelled many thousands of kilometres (over 6300 km in a direct line) to get here from Greece, though we can only speculate on how and when this journey took place and what it signified. It would be nice to think that the Kingdom of Man and the Isles had diplomatic ties with the Frankish principality of Achae, or even the succeeding Despotate of Morea, both of which were based in the town of Mystras in the Peloponnese and ruled the region from the twelfth to fourteenth centuries at the same time as the Kingdom of Man and the Isles, but this seems very unlikely. A more protracted and complex life history seems a more appropriate explanation for the movement of these fragments.

This green porphyry appears as boulders in the relatively unfertile soils and drift deposits of the low hills to the south of Krokees, and when I visited in October 2023, I could see small boulders and numerous fragments eroding from a road cutting. These were not the attractive highly coloured pieces that we recovered at Bornais, as their burial in the iron rich soils gives them a rusty red coating that masks their original colouring. Nevertheless, the pale inclusions are clear enough and, when the fragments are broken, the green colour is visible and dramatic. This is an attractive material when freshly broken or polished and it is a durable material which does not easily break, wear or tarnish when exposed. This hardness makes it a difficult material to work but it can be flaked, sawn and ground, and polishing highlights the vivid colours that are its principal attraction.

This type of porphyry was appreciated in prehistory as an exceptional stone and, by the second millennium BC, it was being actively quarried and large pieces were being shaped and moved to the nearby centres of the Mycenaean and Minoan civilisations; both the Late Bronze Age centres at Mycenae in the Peloponnese and Knossos in Crete have fragments incorporated into some of the principal important spaces in these towns. Porphyry was exploited throughout the Classical era, but its exploitation appears to really have taken off with the Roman occupation of the Peloponnese. The Romans made extensive use of coloured stones from all over the empire to decorate high-status buildings, particularly in Rome (Fig. 1.2). Fragments of green porphyry were routinely used with other coloured stones to create complex mosaic floors (*opus sectile*). These floors then became popular in the early churches of Late Antiquity,

FIGURE 1.2. A large fragment of green porphyry on the Capitoline Hill, Rome, Italy.

and green porphyry continued to be used in this manner throughout the Middle Ages. Large tiles of green porphyry can be seen in St Peter's in the Vatican and in the Hagia Sofia in Istanbul (Constantinople).

It is possible that the Bornais pieces started off life in this manner, quarried by Roman slaves and shipped to Rome to be incorporated as a tile in an important high-status building in the Imperial capital. However, this would have been just the first stage of their life. The status of the porphyry appears to have been transformed by its presence in the Holy City and, for some pieces, their association with the early Church gave them a sanctity that transcended their decorative function. In the early Medieval period pilgrims from Christian communities at the western extremities of Europe began to visit Rome and fragments of this distinctive stone were collected and brought back to their homelands. The stone seems to have been particularly popular in Ireland where numerous fragments of green porphyry have been recovered by archaeologists. However, these pieces are also known in Scotland and England, though in smaller numbers, and there are a few fragments from Norway and Iceland where they are associated with historic churches.[1]

The precise reasons for the collection of these fragments of green porphyry is unclear but various suggestions have been made. In discussing some examples from southwest Scotland, Cormack suggested that they could be used as portable altars to administer the Catholic mass, as relic covers to decorate shrines, as raw materials for the manufacture of jewellery, or simply as souvenirs and mementos of a trip to Rome. Their use as altars is a favoured explanation because many are broken pieces of rectangular tiles.

Portable altars were a critical feature of the early Church and were required for the correct execution of the mass. During this ritual the chalice and the paten had to be placed on the stone surface of an altar that had been blessed by a bishop or an abbot, and normally contained a relic. Portable altars were used for outdoor masses but might also be used to celebrate mass in the homes of housebound individuals, and the Vatican Archives contain records of indulgences provided for the use of portable altars. One was granted to Roderick MacLeod of Lewis in June 1405 and there is another to Alexander, Lord of the Iles, and Jacobella his wife in October 1433. Clearly, portable altars were available to the Hebridean elite in the late Medieval period, and there is no reason to assume they were not available to the inhabitants of Bornais in the twelfth and thirteenth centuries.

The examples that have survived in continental Europe tend to be prestigious objects and take two standard forms: the tablet and the box. Both had a flat surface where a stone tile was set in a frame, made of wood in the simplest forms but more rarely of silver, bronze and gold. The metal frames often incorporated elaborate decoration (Fig. 1.3) which depicted important biblical scenes. Several surviving examples from the tenth to twelfth centuries have a green porphyry tile in the centre, and this stone clearly had a religious significance that transcended its decorative characteristics.

FIGURE 1.3. A portable altar of the late twelfth century from Cologne, with a green porphyry tile at its centre. © Sarah Luginbill, July 2019.

Many of the Irish, Scottish and English fragments of green porphyry from the first millennium AD were found in ecclesiastical locations, such as Whithorn in southwest Scotland, Armagh and Downpatrick in Ireland and Jarrow in England, and the general assumption is that they are the fragmented remains of portable altars. However, there are also considerable numbers found in later Norse contexts in Scotland and Ireland, and Scandinavian examples include a significant concentration within the town of Sigtuna in Sweden.[2] Many of these fragments came from much less obviously religious contexts and the pieces from Bornais are fairly typical examples; one came from the midden infilling a house and the other came from a house floor.

These fragments could have been looted from churches and other religious establishments in Ireland and Scotland, and historical records document the Viking raids on the important religious centres of Iona and Lindisfarne where these altars could be found. At this time the green porphyry might have been looted because of its attractive and exotic nature rather than its religious significance. However, by the twelfth and thirteenth centuries, when the Bornais pieces were deposited, the occupants of the settlement were Christian, so the religious significance of these fragments is likely to be understood. They could have been circulating simply as a material that had the potential to be made into an attractive decorative object, but it is likely that they retained a sacred significance. The assemblage of green porphyry from Scandinavia includes quite small fragments that are set into wooden altars; examples are known from Hedareds stavkyrka, Vastergotland; Lom Kyrka, Norway; Hvammskirkja, Iceland and Gosmer Kirke, Denmark. The altar from Gosmer Kirke still contains a relic stored in a recess covered by the small fragment of green porphyry.

In this preface I have tried to show how the material recovered by archaeological excavations in the Hebrides can be used to link the islands to larger narratives of European history. The inhabitants of the islands were travelling around the western seaboard of Britain at the turn of the first and second millennia AD and the trading networks they connected with provided contacts with communities linked to both the Mediterranean and Scandinavian worlds. The inhabitants of the Hebrides may have been literate, but sadly history provides no documents that record these individuals and their encounters with the world around them. We have to rely almost entirely on archaeology to give us an insight into the nature of these connections and the beliefs of the individuals who occupied the houses and lived in the settlements that can be found throughout the islands.

Viking settlement in the Hebrides

The main aim of this book is to provide an archaeological examination of the Viking colonisation of the Outer Hebrides, or Western Isles of Scotland and to document their transformation as Scandinavians arrived and settled on the islands. For over 300 years the islands were effectively controlled by these Scandinavian invaders, until 1266 when they were sold to the Scottish kingdom. Even after this period there continued to be close contact with the homelands in Scandinavia and the archaeological record of settlement can be traced continuously until the fifteenth century when the demise of the Lords of the Isles seemed to have been a catalyst for major settlement disruption.

The archaeological understanding of the Viking invasion and settlement of the islands comes from recent excavations at two settlements, Bornais and Cille Pheadair (Figs 1.4, 1.5 and 1.6), on the island of South Uist carried out by myself and Mike Parker Pearson. Prior to this work, understanding of this period of the island's history had been little explored and our knowledge was minimal. A further aim of this book is therefore to provide an account of the excavations at these two sites, Bornais in particular, as the evidence recovered has transformed our understanding of this critical period in the history of the islands.[3]

The only previous significant exploration of the historic landscapes of the Western Isles was by Ian Crawford at The Udal in North Uist. He excavated two large settlement mounds that spanned the period from the beginning of the first millennium AD through to the seventeenth century. These excavations were tremendously important and should have provided a good understanding of the pre-Viking Late Iron Age settlement of the seventh and eighth centuries AD as well as the nature of the Viking conquest and the subsequent occupation when the islands were part of the Kingdom of Man and the Isles. Unfortunately, the complexity and richness of the archaeology and the limited resources for writing up the results, meant that Crawford was unable to fully analyse the material he recovered, and the settlement sequence has never been documented. Crawford's interim publications provide only tantalising glimpses of the potential of his discoveries, and it seems unlikely that a full report will ever be written on this important site.[4]

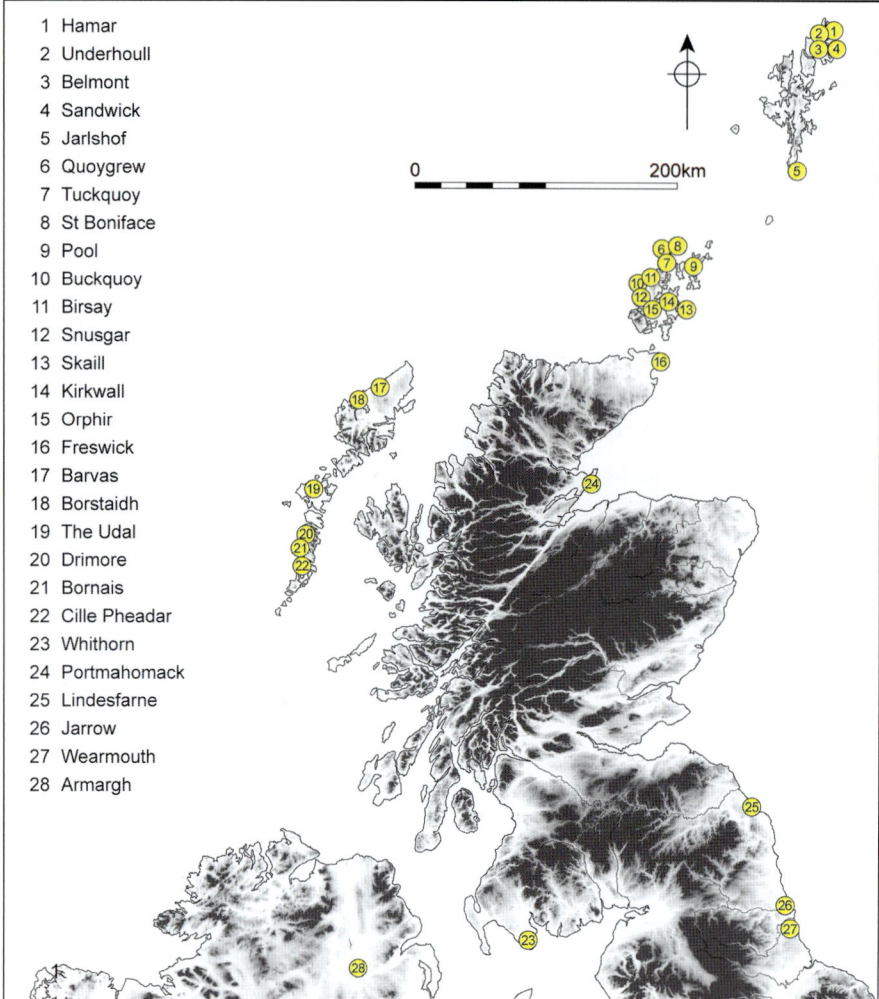

FIGURE 1.4. A location map of the western seaboard of Scotland, showing the Viking and Norse sites mentioned in the text.

1 Hamar
2 Underhoull
3 Belmont
4 Sandwick
5 Jarlshof
6 Quoygrew
7 Tuckquoy
8 St Boniface
9 Pool
10 Buckquoy
11 Birsay
12 Snusgar
13 Skaill
14 Kirkwall
15 Orphir
16 Freswick
17 Barvas
18 Borstaidh
19 The Udal
20 Drimore
21 Bornais
22 Cille Pheadar
23 Whithorn
24 Portmahomack
25 Lindesfarne
26 Jarrow
27 Wearmouth
28 Armargh

There have been other small-scale excavations and discoveries that provide some evidence for the Norse[5] occupation of the islands. A settlement was explored at Barvas in Lewis, though this was on a small scale and the preliminary excavations were never followed up.[6] More extensive excavations at Bostaidh on the island of Bernera, Isle of Lewis were focused on a well-preserved Late Iron Age settlement, an adjacent Norse settlement was examined but it was badly eroded and provided only limited information on the Norse period. There are many other unexcavated settlement mounds identified along the coast of the Western Isles; these are regularly being eroded by the sea and frequently produce finds that date to the Scandinavian occupation of the islands.

There are other discoveries that tell us about the period. Very occasionally rich pagan burials and spectacular collections of precious metal dating to the Viking period have been unearthed. In the Outer Hebrides four metalwork hoards and approximately 15 burials, or potential burials, have been discovered.

FIGURE 1.5. Excavations at Bornais mound 2 during the summer of 2004.

FIGURE 1.6. Excavations at Cille Pheadair showing how close the sea was to destroying the main house exposed by the excavations.

Most of these burials are very imperfectly known as they were discovered in the nineteenth or early twentieth centuries. They mainly provide brief records of exotic artefacts common in Viking graves, and only occasionally was the presence of human remains noted. There is one well-documented and fully reported cemetery at Cnip in Lewis. The first burial at Cnip was discovered in

1979 but it was not until further burials were discovered in the early 1990s that the full significance of this location as a cemetery was realised.[7]

The earliest well-documented hoard was discovered in 1865 when a collection of gold finger-rings was discovered, probably on the small island of Oronsay in Valley Sound, North Uist. There is an earlier record of a coin hoard being found on North Uist in the later part of the eighteenth century, but this has since been lost. In 1938 a hoard of three pieces of 'ring money' and two finger-rings was found at Dibidale on the west coast of Lewis. In 1988–90 a hoard of 37 pieces of hack silver and two coins were found partially contained within a horn core in the grounds of Stornoway Castle, Lewis. As I am writing this book a new hoard of silver has been reported from Barvas on the west coast of Lewis.

The architectural history of the islands is relatively poor. There are a few castles and churches with Medieval origins on the islands but most of these buildings were probably constructed after the fourteenth century and have little connection with the Scandinavian occupation of the islands. The few exceptions are churches but even these are difficult to date. The religious complex at Howmore on South Uist is probably the most important group of early buildings on the islands and the large church at the centre of this complex is generally dated to the thirteenth century (Fig. 1.7). Another church at Cille Donnain on South Uist may be earlier and it has been argued that a twelfth-century date is likely for this distinctive bicameral church. Many other churches have historical evidence for an early creation, but the visible remains suggest that the upstanding buildings were constructed at a later date. The complex of buildings at Cille Bharra is one of these important early centres and an elaborate cross with a runic inscription was found nearby and provides important evidence for

FIGURE 1.7. An aerial view of the complex of churches and chapels at Howmore, South Uist. © Historic Environment Scotland.

Early Norse Christianity and literacy, although the chapel is unlikely to be as early. The only remains of pre-Norse religious buildings are those surviving on the isolated island of North Rona to the north of the Butt of Lewis and on the Shiant islands in the Minch between Harris and Skye.[8]

The historical record for the islands at this time is minimal and heavily dependent on a few sources, the most important of which is the *Chronicles of the Kings of Man and the Isles*.[9] The *Orkneyinga Saga: The history of the earls of Orkney*[10] also has several references to activities in the Western Isles and these islands feature in several other important texts such as the *Saga of King Haakon*. These texts were written down in the thirteenth century and the authors' knowledge of events associated with the Viking conquest of the isles is minimal and problematic. However, from the middle of the twelfth century, details increase, and the sources do seem to give essentially accurate accounts. The records mutually corroborate each other, and the events recorded in them can be confirmed by other, more distant sources from Ireland, England and Iceland. Nevertheless, the references to the Outer Hebrides are very limited even in these later periods and do no more than hint at what life was like in the isles for the vast majority of the population.

All of this material will be discussed in this book but the principal evidence for the Viking colonisation and Norse settlement of the islands now comes from the excavations at Bornais and Cille Pheadair, and one of the main goals for writing this book is to provide a summary of the principal results of these excavations in an easily digestible form that can be appreciated by a wide audience, especially the current inhabitants of the islands who did so much to support our work. It is hoped that in doing so I will also produce a book that will inform visitors who are enchanted by the landscape of these exceptional islands and will want to know more about their history. To help understand the significance of the work undertaken at Bornais and Cille Pheadair, I will now provide an outline history of the excavations at these sites and summarise the archaeological sequences that were revealed.

Excavations at Bornais and Cille Pheadair

The excavations at Bornais and Cille Pheadair were part of a project originally set up by the University of Sheffield to explore the long-term settlement of the southern islands of the Outer Hebrides, and were primarily focused on South Uist, Barra and the Southern Isles. They involved a series of surveys and excavations on a wide variety of sites and landscapes and have been published as large monographs, PhD theses, scientific papers and popular books and articles.[11] Initially the excavations concentrated on the Iron Age archaeology of the islands as this was easily identifiable, and a number of sites were clearly being eroded by the sea and the wind or threatened by development. However, at the end of 1994, after the excavation of the broch at Dun Vulan on South Uist and the wheelhouses at Cill Donnain on South Uist and Allt Chrisal on Barra had been completed, it was decided that a broader research programme was required. We determined that we should

10   *The Vikings in the Hebrides*

aim to understand the settlement sequence throughout the occupation of the islands from the earliest inhabitants, the Mesolithic hunter-gatherers of 8000 years ago, through to the pre-Clearance settlements of the seventeenth and eighteenth centuries AD.

A potentially interesting group of prominent mounds that attracted our attention lay at the centre of the machair plain in the middle of South Uist, close to the promontory on which the broch at Dun Vulan was located. These were the Bornais mounds; three prominent mounds which appeared to indicate prolonged occupation and represent one of the most significant concentrations of settlement activity on the coastal plain of South Uist (Fig. 1.8). The 'machair' is a deposit of windblown shell sand that accumulated against the west coast of the Outer Hebrides. In the Uists it formed a significant extension to the coastal plain that was extensively occupied from the second millennium BC. Erosion is a problem at these mounds and at Bornais it had exposed archaeological deposits and produced distinctive ceramics that dated to the Norse period. The central mound (mound 2) was selected for initial excavation by Mike Parker

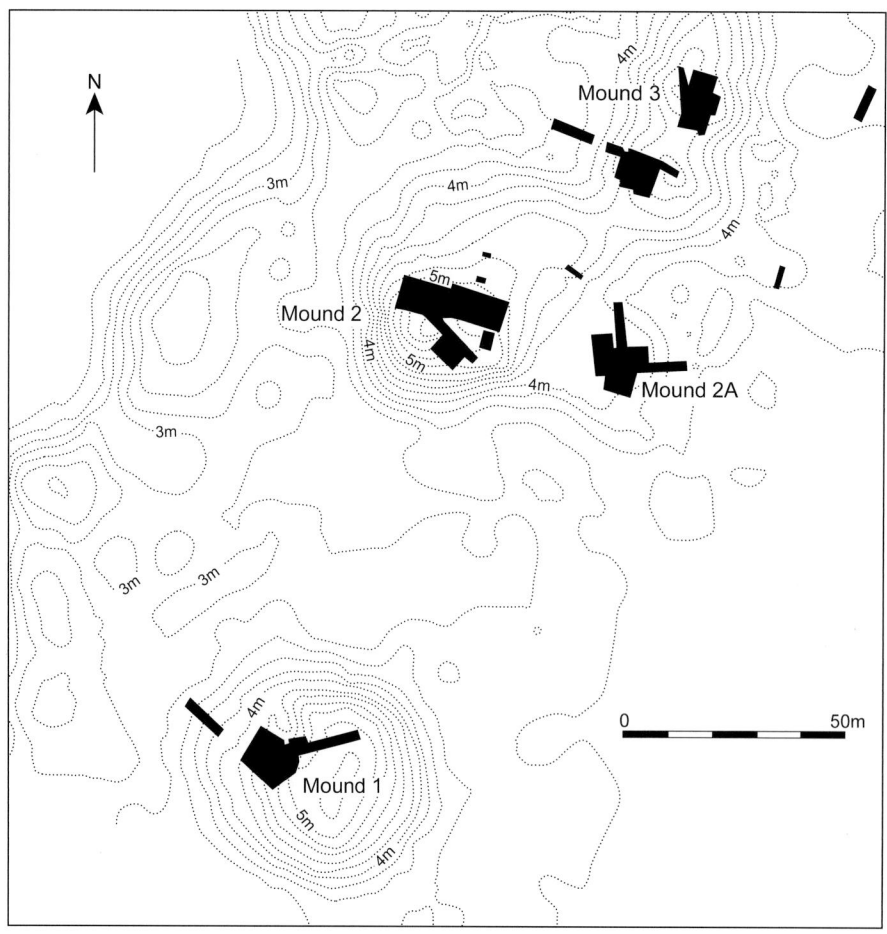

FIGURE 1.8. A contour survey of the settlement mounds at Bornais, South Uist, showing the areas excavated between 1994 and 2004.

FIGURE 1.9. The first season of excavation at Bornais mound 2, 1994. © Mike Parker Pearson.

Pearson as it had produced the Norse ceramics, and a trench 20m by 2m was excavated across its highest point (Fig. 1.9).

The aims of this initial excavation were
- to identify the latest structural phase from the Norse period.
- to locate buildings within the mound.
- to establish the depth of the stratigraphic sequence and, as far as possible, to examine its formation.
- to recover artefact assemblages that would allow us to characterise and to date the sequence of occupation.
- to find out if the apparent discontinuity of occupation noted at the Udal for the beginning of the Viking period was also identifiable here.
- to recover bone and carbonised crop assemblages that would enable comparisons with the earlier assemblages from Dun Vulan.

The excavations proved remarkably successful. A sequence of Norse deposits was revealed that comprised thick midden layers and the structural evidence for several buildings that included the corner of a large, well-built, stone-walled house. The material recovered from this house contained several significant finds including a complete antler comb and pin that suggested a date in the tenth to eleventh centuries.

The following summer the author took over the excavation of Bornais.[12] The main aim for the next two seasons was to characterise the archaeological activity on the two remaining mounds at Bornais, mounds 1 and 3 (see Fig. 1.8), with further work continuing on the central mound (mound 2). The approach taken was similar on all three mounds; an initial trench was cut across each mound, and this was then slightly expanded to clarify the character of any obvious structures that were observed in each trench. These trenches revealed an early settlement on mound 1, which dated back to the fifth and sixth centuries, and buildings dating to the fifteenth century on mound 3 that showed similarities with the Hebridean buildings that characterised the crofting landscape of the nineteenth century. However, the limitation of this excavation strategy was exposed and emphasised by the completion of a geophysical survey of all the mounds, which revealed a wealth of information about the extent and character of the settlement (Fig. 1.10). It was now clear that the settlement area at Bornais

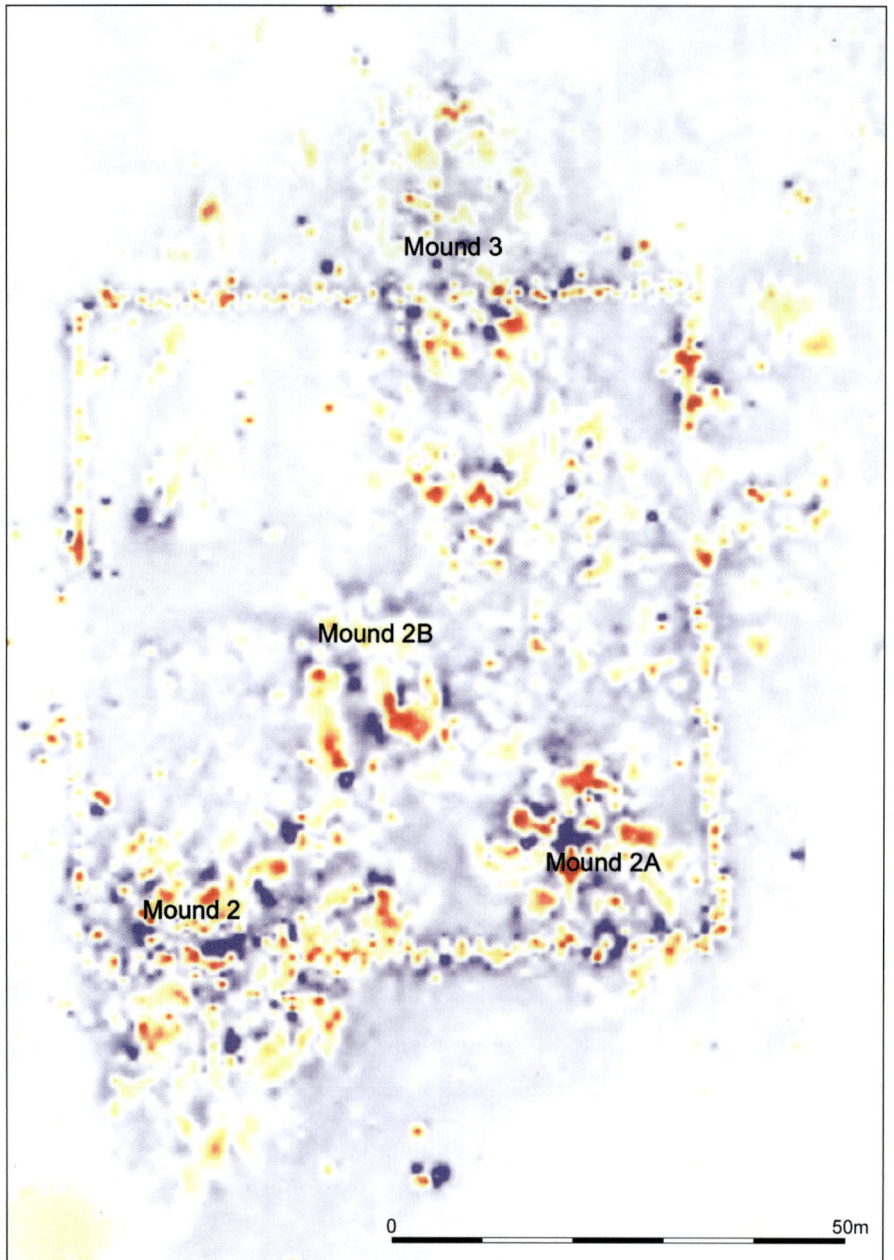

FIGURE 1.10. A geophysical survey of the northern part of the settlement at Bornais. The rectangular enclosure that forms the most visible feature of the survey is a walled enclosure, created to pen sheep in the nineteenth century. The concentrations of high magnetic anomalies indicate concentrations of midden and stone walls that define settlement mounds 2, 2A, 2B and 3.

1. Bornais, the Vikings and the Outer Hebrides

FIGURE 1.11. A view of the eroding beach at Cille Pheadair, South Uist. This was taken after the excavations had been completed, and when coastal erosion had removed over 80% of the settlement area.

was much larger than had previously been thought; two additional foci, labelled mounds 2A and 2B, and several isolated structures scattered around the edge of the mounds were identified. It was now clear that this was a very substantial settlement that needed a much more extensive excavation strategy.

In 1996 a complementary programme of excavations was begun by Mike Parker Pearson on a Norse settlement at Cille Pheadair, a township at the south end of South Uist. This was exposed by catastrophic coastal erosion which characterises the coastline in this area, and it was clear that if excavations were not undertaken immediately, very little of this settlement would survive. When I visited the site in 2005, seven years after the end of the excavation, approximately 90% of the site area had disappeared through coastal erosion (Fig. 1.11). Cille Pheadair, in contrast to Bornais, was a single settlement mound, which allowed for a relatively complete excavation in three seasons (1996 to 1998) and these excavations are fully documented in a substantial publication.

In 1997 the main focus of the work on Bornais continued to be mounds 1 and 3, and an increase in the workforce enabled the exposure of complete buildings on both these mounds. A large area was also opened on mound 2 which emphasised the size and architectural quality of the house originally exposed on this mound. No excavations were carried out at Bornais in 1998.

Work recommenced in 1999, when the excavations ambitiously encompassed work on mounds 1, 2, 2A and 3. The excavation season was expanded to eight weeks and an increased student labour force was recruited. On mound 2, the principal objective was to define the extent of the large house, and to excavate floor levels that would confirm its date. On mound 2A, a large trench uncovered a building that was being badly damaged by modern ploughing. By the end of 1999 we had completed the excavation of the fifth to sixth-century structures on mound 1 and the fifteenth-century house and a kiln on mound 3.

In 2000 the excavations were focused on mounds 2 and 2A, and this remained our focus until the end of the excavations in 2004. Our aim on mound 2 was to examine the large house at its centre. The complete excavation of this

FIGURE 1.12. Excavations at Bornais in 2004 looking east across the excavated area of mound 2A.

house would meet the principal objectives of the overall project, to identify and explore the use of domestic space. The excavation of mound 2A largely avoided the excavation of houses, but instead explored the sequence of middens and cultivation soils that had accumulated around the houses, as this would clarify the chronological span of these settlement mounds (Fig. 1.12).

We originally intended to return and excavate in 2001, but unfortunately an outbreak of foot and mouth disease meant this was not possible, and work was focused on post-excavation analysis. The critical importance of this work became obvious, and a second post excavation season was organised for 2002. The return to the field was delayed until 2003.

By the end of 2000 it was clear that the large house on mound 2 was the middle building in a sequence of three large houses that had been constructed one on top of the other thus creating the 'mound' of mound 2. The main goal of the excavation in 2003 was to excavate the large house, now known as House 2, but to do this we had to completely excavate the later structure, House 3, which covered the east end of House 2. We also had to accurately define the extent of an earlier structure, House 1, which lay underneath House 2. By the end of 2003, most of House 3 had been excavated and the floor of House 2 was exposed and ready for excavation in 2004. The west end of House 1 was defined and excavated, and the presence of Late Iron Age deposits was confirmed and some of these deposits were explored. On mound 2A a series of ancillary structures to the north of the main house sequence were excavated and one of these proved to be a workshop for a comb maker. The full sequence of middens on the northern edge of the mound was also explored and revealed an Early Norse cultivation soil that underlay the occupation deposits that formed the settlement mound.

FIGURE 1.13. Excavating the floor of a Middle Norse house (House 2) at Bornais.

The 2004 season was designed to be the final season of excavation at Bornais. The principal aim was to complete the excavation of the floors of Houses 2 and 3 (Fig. 1.13); any further information on the nature of the earlier House 1 would be a bonus. On mound 2A the main goal was to excavate as much as possible of the cultivation soil at the base of the archaeological sequence. These early deposits were rich in artefacts and animal bone that would provide important evidence for the economy of the settlement immediately after the Viking conquest of the islands.

In conclusion, by the end of the excavations at Bornais
- the extent of the settlement was defined.
- the chronological limits of the settlement were known.
- major changes in the location of the settlement had been defined.
- four houses were completely excavated and a further 11 houses had been identified and partially explored.
- a class of ancillary buildings was identified and six were explored.
- a class of simple shelters was identified and explored.
- the large finds assemblage collected from mounds 2 and 2A included 1,390 iron objects, 153 copper alloy objects, 83 lead objects, six silver coins and one fragment of a silver bar, one fragment of a gold strip, 17 glass beads and two glass objects, 90 pieces of steatite and 1,127 flints, 1,460 pieces of antler, bone or whale bone and 14,416 potsherds weighing 96 kg.
- 333 soil samples were processed to recover 131,070 charred plant macrofossils.
- 17,756 identifiable animal bones, 1,248 identifiable bird bones and over 48,000 fish bones were recovered.

It would have been possible to continue for another 10 years excavating at Bornais and the results would undoubtedly be informative and immensely valuable for understanding not only the Norse settlement of the islands but also the Late Iron Age settlement that preceded this. However, it seemed prudent to bring the excavations to an end. The analysis and interpretation of the material recovered would be a time-consuming process and we did not want to end up with an archive of material that was inaccessible and incomprehensible. In the end it took almost 20 years to produce the final publication. Stopping when we did was a sensible decision and has left plenty of undisturbed archaeological remains for future archaeologists to explore.

Chronology and structure

Chronology is an important issue for any archaeologist and this book is structured into chapters with defined time periods that span roughly a thousand years in total, from the middle of the first millennium AD to the middle of the second millennium AD. The excavations at Bornais and Cille Pheadair included a systematic programme of radiocarbon dating which was innovative for the medieval archaeology examined here. This was necessary due to the lack of historical records for the islands and the very limited incorporation of historically dateable artefacts, such as coins, in the excavated deposits. The archaeology was ideally suited to the development of a detailed radiocarbon chronology as organic materials such as bone and charcoal were very well preserved and were recovered in substantial quantities. This enabled the careful selection of material that was deposited soon after the death of the living organism supplying the carbon to be dated, a key criterion for an accurate radiocarbon date. The stratigraphy of the settlements was also clearly defined, and different phases of the site associated with buildings, floor layers and midden deposits could be ordered into stratigraphic sequences and phases of activity that contained suitable radiocarbon samples. The development of a Bayesian statistical approach by Pete Marshall early in the project's genesis meant that we were able to construct a detailed chronology that could be compared to the historic record with some confidence.[13] The use of Bayesian statistics to analyse the radiocarbon dates has enhanced the precision of the chronology considerably and it is now possible to achieve a historical accuracy for the archaeological evidence that was not previously possible. I am not going to explain the nature of Bayesian statistics, but the key to improving the precision of the dates is the ability to factor in *a priori* knowledge from the relative chronology of the samples dated into the analyses: if you know one sample is earlier than another because of the site's stratigraphy, then this will affect how you assess the statistical accuracy of the date from that sample.

The Bayesian approach is very important for the sites we have excavated in the Western Isles. Both Bornais and Cille Pheadair are exceptionally well-stratified settlements, and the radiocarbon samples came from long sequences which had clear stratigraphic relationships. The quality of the chronology was improved by the preservation conditions, the sampling strategies and the wide range of organic material that could be dated. We tried to deal only with material that we could be certain had not been moved around after death. Due to Historic Environment Scotland's generosity, we have a very large number of radiocarbon dates from Bornais and Cille Pheadair and we are able to speak with confidence about the chronological development of these settlements. We can identify when different houses were constructed and abandoned, how long they were occupied, the length of the gaps in the occupation sequence, and when the settlements were abandoned. The chronologies are not perfect, but they are a significant improvement on what came before and means that we are not guessing about the relationship between archaeology and history.

Following on from this introduction, Chapter 2 considers the period before the Viking incursions and charts the transformations that occurred in the first millennium AD. The first half of the millennium begins with the monumental roundhouse traditions that include the highly visible brochs and wheelhouses, but by the middle of the millennium these were disappearing as the much less monumental cellular buildings of the seventh and eighth centuries appeared.

At Bornais, the fifth to sixth-century occupation of mound 1 includes a ruined wheelhouse which can be compared with other monumental roundhouses known locally from this period. In the middle of the millennium the settlement moved from mound 1 to mound 2 and involved the systematic demolition of the buildings on mound 1. This period of settlement disruption may have been part of a wider phenomenon documented across large areas of Europe that was caused by a major natural disaster. In the succeeding phase, in the seventh to eighth centuries, the islands seem to have become more integrated into the political geography of mainland Scotland. This is most obviously indicated by the increased importance of material culture, in particular the use of ornaments as expressions of personal identity. The seventh and eighth centuries are not well documented at Bornais but settlements such as Bostadh on Lewis have well-preserved houses which will be discussed. The excavations at Cille Pheadair also discovered a distinctive burial which documents the influence of mainland Scottish developments in the islands.

The Scandinavian occupation of the islands has been split into three chapters. The first of these, Chapter 3, is further divided into a period of Viking raids and early Norse settlement. Chapter 4 covers the Middle Norse period when the Outer Hebrides were part of the Kingdom of Man and the Isles. Chapter 5 follows the sale of the islands to Scotland in 1266 and continues until the fourteenth and fifteenth centuries, when the waning power of the Lords of the Isles coincided with the abandonment of the settlements on the machair plain. This period can be referred to as the Scottish period, but I also refer to it as the Late Norse period in Chapter 5. None of these periods are rigorously defined in this book. They are just handy structural devices that are used to order the archaeological evidence from the excavations at Bornais (Fig. 1.14) and Cille Pheadair and can be used to discuss some of the wider social and political changes that occurred between the eighth and fifteenth centuries.

The term 'Viking' is used here to describe a period of raiding that began at the end of the eighth century and lasted throughout the ninth century. This preceded the establishment of settlements with substantial houses and associated middens, such as Bornais, which appeared in the tenth century, and which marked the beginning of the period I refer to as Early Norse. The archaeological evidence for the Viking period is problematic but includes historical evidence of raiding and a scatter of pagan burials along the north and west coasts of Scotland. These burials include an important small cemetery from Cnip on Lewis which contains a high-status female burial with a rich selection of grave goods. New scientific analysis of these burials is providing important information about where these individuals came from and how they moved around the North Atlantic. Settlement in this period is rare and difficult to locate but some of the evidence from the Udal in North Uist suggests that this location may have been occupied very early in the colonisation process. Both Bornais and Cille Pheadair appear to have been established as Norse settlements in the middle of the tenth century, and this seems to be the period when colonisation of the North Atlantic islands was occurring on a major scale. Evidence from

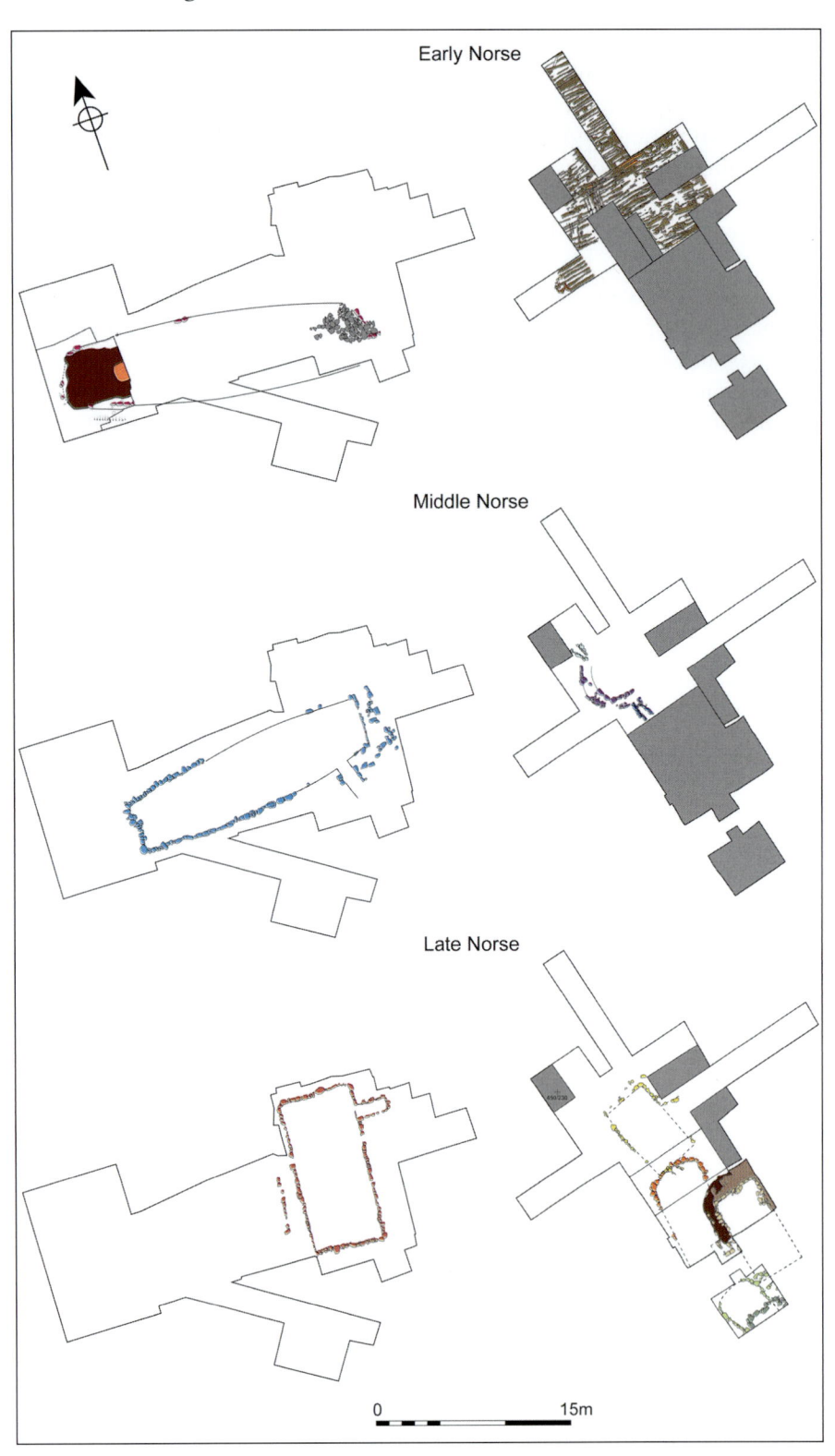

FIGURE 1.14. The three main phases of occupation on mounds 2 and 2A at Bornais.

these early phases at both Bornais and Cille Pheadair provides valuable information on the architecture of the initial settlements and, more importantly, the development of an agricultural economy that could support the increasingly densely occupied coastal plain.

In the second half of the eleventh century, after the defeat of a Scandinavian invasion of England at Stamford Bridge in 1066, there were significant political developments in the Atlantic region. One of the survivors of this battle was Gofraid Croban who established himself in the Isle of Man as the King of Man and the Isles in 1079. He was clearly an influential figure and most of the subsequent Kings of Man and the Isles claimed to be his descendants. During the next two centuries the region appears to have been stable enough for the settlements at Bornais and Cille Pheadair to flourish, and the machair landscapes of the Uists became densely occupied with settlements similar to Cille Pheadair. Bornais seems to stand out as a particularly large settlement with multiple buildings clustered in one area. The house on the main settlement mound (mound 2) at Bornais is also larger and more traditionally 'Scandinavian' in its plan than the house at Cille Pheadair. Both houses have produced large artefactual assemblages that provide an incredible source of information on the economy and lifestyle of the Norse inhabitants of South Uist that will be explored in detail.

The connection with the Isle of Man diminished in the later twelfth century due to the political struggles of the dynasty, and in the middle of the thirteenth century the Kings of Scotland achieved the peaceful transfer of the islands from Norway to Scotland with the Treaty of Perth. This major political change in the history of the islands could have had a major impact on life on the islands. Although change can be observed and will be discussed in Chapter five, the archaeological evidence suggests a great deal of continuity in economic practices and only a gradual evolution in domestic architecture. A regional identity also started to emerge that distinguished the Western Isles from other island groups of Norse descent in the North Atlantic, but important connections to the Scandinavian homelands were retained.

The concluding chapter briefly considers the last 500 years of the Western Isles history. The archaeological record suggests that there was both continuity and disruption in the period immediately after the settlements at Bornais and Cille Pheadair were abandoned. The historical records also suggest a period of instability which was characterised by the return to defensive settlements by the island elite. Several of the island duns were reoccupied in this period and distinctive fortifications were constructed on the cliff coastlines of Lewis and Harris. Nevertheless, the evidence suggests that in the southern isles the domestic architecture that evolved in the thirteenth and fourteenth centuries formed the basis of settlement characteristics that can be recognised in the eighteenth and nineteenth centuries. These late settlements are found in large numbers across the islands and illustrate the destruction caused by the 'Clearances' that formed such a traumatic event in recent history.

Landscape

The Western Isles or Outer Hebrides (Na h-Eileanan Siar) are a discrete group of islands located off the northwest coast of Scotland (Fig. 1.15). The nearest land is the isle of Skye which comes to within 25 km of the east coast of the Outer Hebrides. They are separated from Skye and the mainland by the Minch, a deep channel which existed even during the peak of the last Ice Age. Any animals or people found on the islands had to be able to swim long distances, fly or came across on boats.

There are five main islands: Lewis and Harris (one island divided by a significant mountain range), North Uist, Benbecula, South Uist and Barra. There are a further 10 currently inhabited small islands and a minimum of 50 uninhabited islands, many of which were occupied until relatively recent times. In reality there are innumerable small islands, islets and rocks exposed around the very rugged coastline.[14]

FIGURE 1.15. A satellite image of the Western Isles. Licensed under the Creative Commons Attribution-ShareAlike 3.0 IGO license.

The names of the two main islands of Lewis and Uist, *Ljóðhús* and *Ívist* in Old Norse, are likely to be pre-Norse names in origin as they are unusual and have no obvious meanings in Old Norse. It has been argued they were adopted by early raiders during initial contacts with the indigenous islanders. However, linguistic transfers in the colonisation period of the late eighth and early ninth centuries appear to be minimal as nearly all scholars who have studied the place-names on the islands argue for a complete replacement of the pre-Norse language with Norse terms.[15] The hybrid Norse/Gaelic names that exist today are due to the later replacement of Norse by Gaelic as the language of choice by both the people on the land and their leaders. The complete absence of pre-Norse placenames, other than the two islands, may be partly due to their derivation from a Pictish language that had become extinct by the fourteenth century.

The underlying geology of the islands is Lewisian Gneiss, a metamorphosed igneous rock which is one of the oldest rocks in Europe (Fig. 1.16). The only exceptional areas of geology are some small granite intrusions in Lewis and Harris and a more substantial outcrop of sandstone around the town of Stornoway on the east coast of Lewis. The Lewisian Gneiss is a hard rock which is not easy to quarry or shape. It can be used for building simple but robust structures, but any architectural embellishments would require the importation

FIGURE 1.16. A simplified geological map of the western seaboard of Scotland. Licensed under the Creative Commons Attribution-ShareAlike 3.0 IGO license.

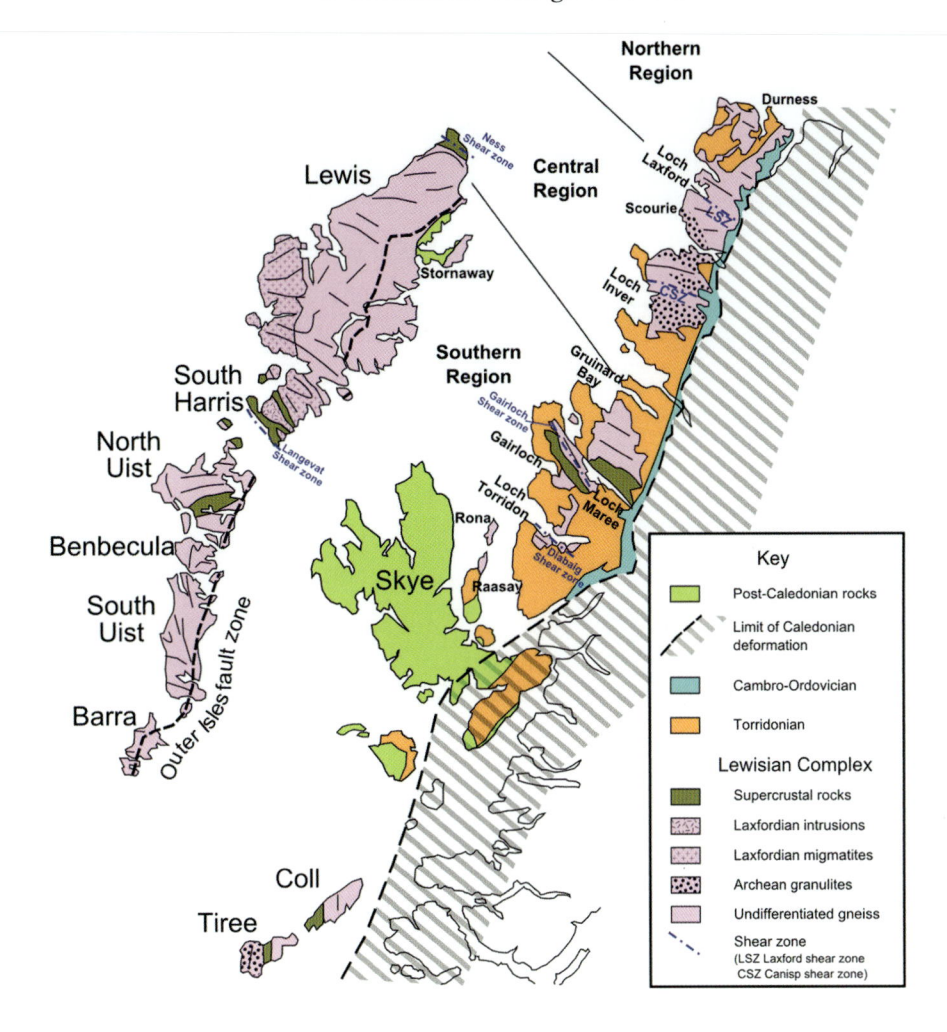

of more tractable stone from mainland Scotland, or the sandstones of the Stornoway area.

The northernmost area of the Outer Hebrides, the Isle of Lewis, is characterised by an extensive, low, flat plateau which is currently covered by peat (Fig. 1.17). Cultivable land is concentrated on the coast around the wide-open bays that characterise much of the west coast, but the most fertile and densely populated landscape occurs around the town of Stornoway, on the east coast, where the low-lying, well-drained soils, based on a slightly more amenable sandstone geology, attracted human settlement. The creation of the town was facilitated by the presence of a large natural harbour which was developed and enhanced as a fishing centre and the main port for the island.

The land rises as you move south towards Harris and the two parts of the island are separated by a range of mountains that, together with the long sea lochs, such as Loch Seaforth (Shiophoirt), made land communications between the north and south difficult. These topographic barriers resulted in the administrative separation of the island; Lewis was included in the county of Ross and

FIGURE 1.17. A view north along the coastline of Lewis. In the foreground is Barvas machair, the largest area of machair in Lewis. © Crown Copyright: HES.

Cromarty, and Harris and the southern islands were included in the county of Inverness-shire. It was only in 1975 that the islands achieved the administrative unity they have today. The highest mountain in the Outer Hebrides is Clisham in north Harris, which reaches 799 m. The interior of Harris is both mountainous and glacially scoured so there is very little scope for agricultural exploitation (Fig. 1.18). Settlement is concentrated on the coast and the west coast has an attractive and fertile coastal plain due to the presence of thick blown sand deposits.

The Sound of Harris separates the island of Harris from the island of North Uist, and is a shallow channel studded with islands, many of which were inhabited until the nineteenth century (Fig. 1.19). The channel is strategically important as it is deep enough to have allowed the longships used by the Vikings and the later Gaelic 'birlinns' easy passage from the Minch to the Atlantic. The Uists and Benbecula have very similar overall topography and are only separated by shallow sea channels that could be crossed at low tide prior to the construction of the road bridges and causeways that now connect the islands. It is likely that for much of prehistory South Uist, Benbecula and North Uist would have formed a single landmass.

The landscape of the Uists is divided into zones aligned roughly north to south and this provides a useful means of considering the different resource areas. These zones are most clearly visible in South Uist, Benbecula and the southern part of North Uist. The north end of North Uist has similar areas of machair and hills but these encircle a large area of low-lying land at the centre of the island which is now covered in thick peat deposits but which in the distant past may have been capable of agricultural exploitation.

FIGURE 1.18. The ice scoured mountains of Harris. © G F Geddes.

FIGURE 1.19. *(below)* The Sound of Harris looking across the island of Ensay to Pabbay and in the distance St Kilda. © G F Geddes.

The waters of the Atlantic coast of the Uists are relatively shallow as an extensive shelf extends some distance to the west. Most of this coastline is defined by a sandy beach but rocky promontories occasionally project beyond the coastal dunes (Fig. 1.20). These promontories can provide shelter and are still used as a summer anchorage for small inshore fishing boats.

The topography around the settlement at Bornais will be described in detail as it is directly relevant to understanding the economy of this settlement and it is also representative of the Uist landscape in general. The shoreline to the west of the Bornais settlement is defined by a coastal dune several metres high that provides a valuable buffer between the sea and the machair plain. This dune is unstable and mobile in the long term, but its current cover of marram grass provides relative stability, and the coastline is not eroding as badly as it is in other areas, such as around the settlement at Cille Pheadair which has no protective coastal dune system.

Immediately behind the coastal dune is the 'machair plain' (Fig. 1.21). This runs down the west coast of the Uists and comprises a sand deposit made up

FIGURE 1.20. An aerial view of the promontory of Rubha Ardvule, South Uist. © Crown Copyright: HES.

FIGURE 1.21. A view of the machair plain of South Uist from the isle of Orosaigh.

of shell and siliceous minerals, which provides a calcareous environment that is markedly different to the peat covered moorlands to the east. The sands formed after the last Ice Age as a result of the submergence of the extensive shallow coastal plain that lay off the west coast of the Uists.[16] The sand is comprised of relict glacial material and large quantities of comminuted shell from the ancient storm-washed shoreline that lay to the west of the glaciers. It is assumed that after the ice melted, there was a fairly rapid rise in sea level up until about 5000–7000 years ago when sea level was probably close to what it is today. This rise in sea level was accompanied by the ancient beach deposits that were constantly carried upwards by currents and tides. Eventually around 4050–3890 BC, there was a massive influx of these shell sand deposits onto the west coast of the Uists, and this probably preceded the final rise in sea level that divided the islands of South Uist, Benbecula and North Uist.

The deposition of this shell sand created an extension to the solid geology of the island which has proved an attractive settlement location for the inhabitants of the island from the Beaker period, about 2300 BC, onwards. In recent years, although the machair has not hosted permanent settlements, it has proved a valuable agricultural landscape. The plain is a relatively well-drained, flat surface and is one of the few areas of the Western Isles that can be extensively cultivated for cereals, barley in the past, but currently black oat and rye (Fig. 1.22). The Uist machair is one of the most agriculturally productive areas of the west coast of Scotland and has been a desirable landscape for farmers throughout the last four millennia.

On the eastern edge of the machair plain is Loch Bornais, one of a disconnected chain of lochs that run along the edge of the machair plain.

FIGURE 1.22. A crop of barley growing on the machair plain of South Uist.

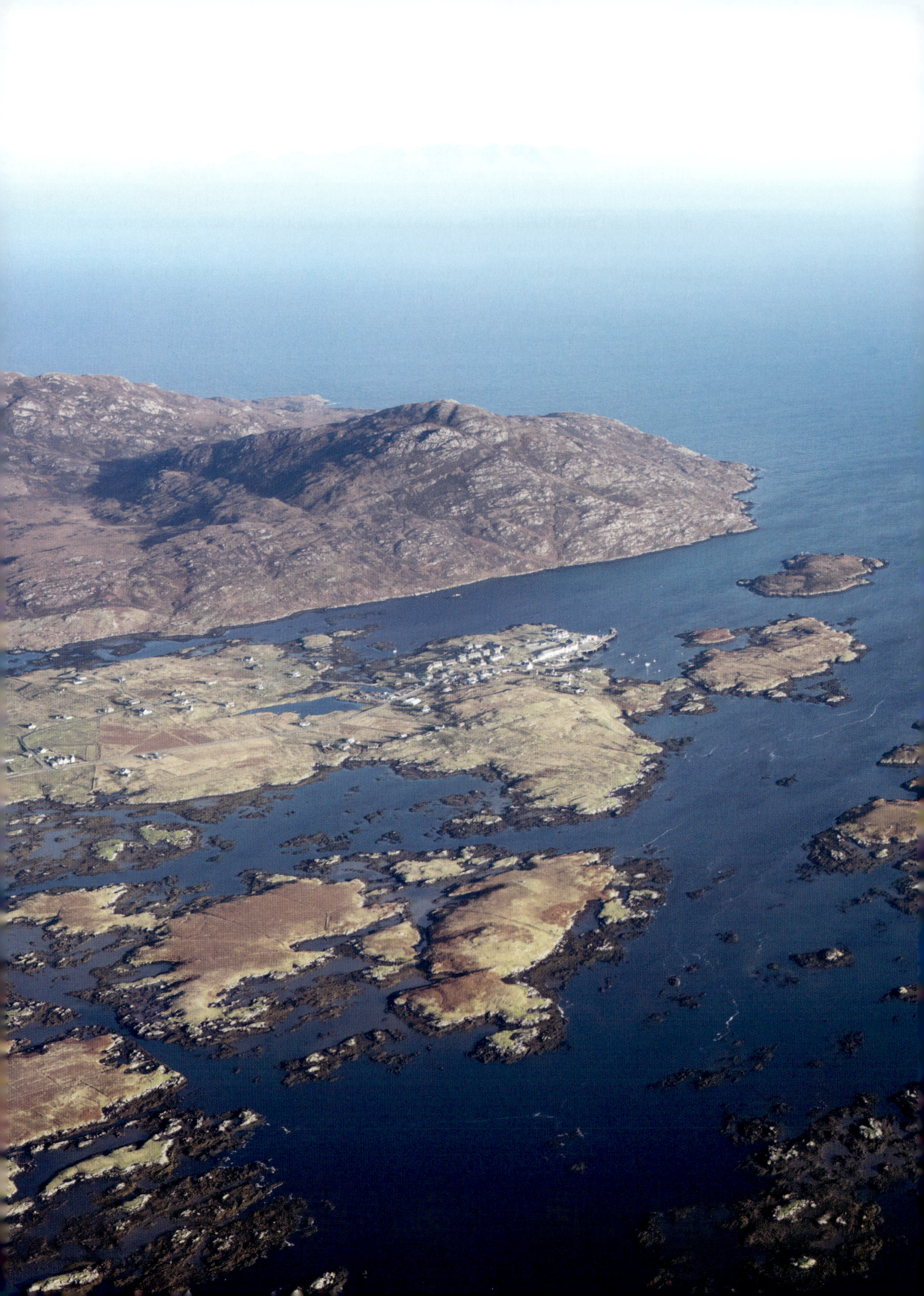

FIGURE 1.23. (*opposite*) An aerial view across Lochboisdale, an important port in one of the east facing sea lochs of South Uist. © Crown Copyright: HES.

The current inhabitants of the township of Bornais occupy the area immediately to the east of the loch. They inhabit a landscape characterised by rock outcrops interspersed between numerous small lochs and boggy ground. Most of this landscape is covered in thick peat deposits but, in the settlement area adjacent to the machair plain, human activity, and the addition of shell sand by both natural and anthropogenic means, has improved the quality of the soils. These areas have been intensively cultivated in the recent past.

Generally, as one moves east the ground rises, initially quite gradually, the lochs become smaller and in the valleys that push into the hills the peat becomes thicker and more extensive. The peat in this area is exploited for fuel but the agricultural potential of the land is limited to summer grazing, and scattered across the area are small seasonally occupied structures known as shielings that were occupied into the early twentieth century. About halfway across the island the land becomes increasingly mountainous; Beinn Mhor, at 608 m, is the highest peak in the Uists.

The mountains drop relatively precipitously to the east coast where there are only small, isolated patches of low-lying ground capable of supporting human settlement. The east coast of South Uist is not characterised by vertical cliffs, and these are not a feature of any of the Uist coastlines. The mountainous spine of the island is penetrated by a sea loch, Loch Aoineart, which stretches westward from the east coast to end just 3 km from the machair plain. A comparable sea loch to the south, Lochboisdale, is the current terminus for the main ferry

FIGURE 1.24. An aerial view of the Bishop's Islands south of Barra. In the foreground is Berneray and behind this Mingulay. © Crown Copyright: HES.

to South Uist (Fig. 1.23) and these sea lochs would always have provided the principal means of access between the islands and the Scottish mainland. Both Lochboisdale and Loch Aoineart would have provided sheltered anchorages for any ships, or fleets of ships, travelling through the Minch.

The channel between South Uist and Barra is more substantial than the channels between the other islands, and it would probably have separated the islands from relatively early in the postglacial period. Barra is a small island only 18 km long and 10 km wide, and the interior is mountainous with a limited amount of agricultural land arranged around the coastline, particularly along the west and north coasts where machair is present.

To the south of Barra are the Bishop's Isles, a group of five large and four small islands (Fig. 1.24). The only one of these currently inhabited is Vatersay which is immediately adjacent to Barra and is now connected to it by a causeway. The remaining four large islands all show evidence for settlement in prehistory, and many were occupied up to the nineteenth century; Mingulay was the last to be abandoned in 1912.

Vegetation

One of the striking features of the current landscape of the Western Isles is the absence of trees. Many people find this aspect of the landscape a problem, those from the south in particular have an attachment to trees that makes their absence deeply disturbing and concerning. Descriptions of the islands by the arboreally complacent frequently employ terms such as 'barren' and 'inhospitable' to describe these landscapes. The treeless nature of the landscape is undoubtedly a characteristic that one has to get used to, but most people from the north will find this simply an exaggerated or extreme version of the landscapes that are commonplace in the majority of highland and upland Scotland. Most of the Pennine spine of England is similarly characterised by treeless moors that are comparable to the peat moors of northern Lewis, and many find the open vistas and distant views attractive rather than desolate.

One of the benefits of the peat landscapes is that they contain a comprehensive record of the environmental history of the islands. Peat preserves the pollen produced by flowering plants and therefore provides a historical record of the vegetation that covered this landscape since the end of the Ice Age. Pollen produced by flowers is carried in the wind into the landscape where it eventually falls to the ground. If the pollen grains fall on a part of the landscape where sediments are accumulating, such as a peat bog, then they will settle and be preserved by the wet conditions. As the deposits accumulate over time the earliest pollen preserving deposits will be covered by later pollen preserving deposits and these will accumulate to create a history of the vegetation at and around the location of the peat bog.

The pollen produced by flowering plants is species specific; every plant produces pollen that has a size and shape that is specific to that species, and which can be identified by these characteristics. However, pollen grains are tiny and require high-powered microscopes to enable identification to be made.

Identification also depends on the preservation of the skin of each pollen grain. Fortunately, the material that makes up the skin is very robust and can survive in many burial environments and is very well preserved in waterlogged deposits.

Palaeobotanists take vertical column samples through peat deposits that can be analysed to provide chronological histories of the vegetation in the location of the bog. The precise techniques used to extract and measure the pollen record from the bogs need not concern the readers of this book, but it is important to emphasise that there are methodological complexities that are challenging. Nevertheless, the overall patterns are now well documented as a lot of pollen analysis was undertaken on the islands by specialist palaeobotanists in the 1970s, 1980s and 1990s.

It is now clear that the islands underwent a gradual transition from Arctic tundra-type vegetation to woodland after the retreat of the final glaciers. The earliest vegetation appears to be heath and herb-rich grassland dominated by crowberry (*Empetrum nigrum*). As we move into the Holocene, willow and juniper shrubs appear on these herb-rich grasslands, and by roughly 8550 BC the landscape was increasingly dominated by birch and hazel woodland. Woodland was extensive throughout the islands, but it was not continuous and there are some pollen locations, such as Little Loch Roag, on Lewis where woodland seems to never have been established. As time progressed new species such as elm and oak became established though not in large numbers. This woodland remained largely undisturbed until about 6650 BC when there was a dramatic decline in the importance of trees in certain coastal areas that coincided, within a century, with the appearance of blanket peat as a significant component of these coastal landscapes. The precise cause of this decline is open to debate, but the scale of the decline makes it unlikely to be due to human activity as the number of Mesolithic hunter gatherers present in the landscape would have been relatively small.

A second major decline occurred between 3900 to 2400 BC but this seems to have been more gradual, starting and developing at different times across the islands. Eventually the whole island became relatively treeless, and the development of extensive blanket peat made it difficult for woodland to become reestablished. This second decline is likely to be the result of human activity though it is unlikely it represents a systematic desire to remove the woodland as there were always plenty of open areas that could be farmed. It seems more likely that the destruction of the woodland was the combined result of animal grazing, human exploitation and perhaps disease.

By the Late Iron Age, around 1500 years ago, it seems that very little woodland survived on the islands. There were likely to be patches of trees growing in the steep valleys and on inaccessible islands, locations that grazing animals could not reach, but elsewhere the evidence is that heather covered moorland was the dominant landscape character.

Animals

The early separation of the islands from mainland Scotland before the final glaciation of northern Britain has restricted the variety of land mammals present on the islands. All the land mammals would have been killed off by the final cold spell and any animals present today would either have had to make their own way there by swimming or flying, or were introduced by humans. The width of the Minch suggests that most of the land mammals present on the islands were introduced either deliberately or accidentally by people.[17]

Red deer are currently the largest wild animal on the island, and they are one of the few animals where it is a point of contention whether they were deliberately introduced or elected to swim the 25 km from northern Skye. These animals are good swimmers, and they have been observed swimming to Skye from the small island of Rhum. This is at least partly due to the very large numbers of deer on Rhum, and it is unclear whether similar population pressures would have existed on a large island like Skye, especially when predators such as wolves would have been present. The deliberate introduction of deer is believed to be a strategy employed by early hunter gatherers to stock the islands surrounding northern Scotland. If herds could be established, it would provide early colonists with a large mammal that could be hunted and would provide an important resource for food, antler and bone for tools, and skins for clothing. There is therefore an incentive for the early explorers to have brought captive deer to the islands and released them in the likelihood that they would create a breeding herd that could be hunted when it became time to colonise the islands. Hunter gatherers seem to have been moving around the islands of the western seaboard of Scotland from the middle of the seventh millennium BC and, though the evidence is poor from the Outer Hebrides, I see no reason not to assume that people were living on the islands from this period and that they introduced deer and possibly other large mammals such as wild boar at this time.

The colonisation of the islands by Neolithic farmers occurred sometime after 4000 BC. The rapid colonisation of Britain by groups of colonists from the immediately adjacent areas of Europe has now been well documented by DNA analysis of skeletal remains. Neolithic agriculturalists were probably on the islands sometime between 4000 and 3800 BC and they brought with them a package of animals and crops that formed the basis of the agricultural economy of the islands until the Viking conquest almost five thousand years later. The most important domestic animals were cattle and sheep. These were accompanied by pigs which were a numerically less important animal but one that was still present in significant numbers. Sheep tend to numerically dominate most animal bone assemblages from prehistoric settlements, but a few have cattle as the dominant species. Horse was probably introduced in the Bronze Age. By the Bronze Age, hulled six-rowed barley was the overwhelmingly dominant cereal crop, though small quantities of other crops are present in the archaeological record, including emmer wheat, oats and rye.

In contrast to mainland Britain, the islanders seem to have maintained an interest in hunting and consuming the meat of wild animals, and in certain areas of the islands red deer dominate the animal bone assemblages. The distribution of well-preserved animal bone assemblages across the islands is not even and so our understanding of the evidence may be biased, but it would appear that by the end of the first millennium BC communities living in the more agriculturally challenging rocky landscapes of Harris and south Lewis maintained large herds of red deer that were routinely hunted and provided the major protein component of the diet. In contrast among the landscapes of the Uists, where arable farming of cereals was important, red deer were present, but their exploitation was much less important and their contribution to the diet of the inhabitants was not critical. However, it seems likely that even in these more intensively farmed landscapes, deer were being actively managed. Deer are large grazing animals and, in an unenclosed landscape such as the Western Isles, they could potentially have a seriously damaging impact on any crops if they were allowed to roam free. Their survival on these islands must have been a deliberate decision by the islanders who realised that the resources they provided were sufficiently important to justify their continued presence. Deer provided not only meat and skins when hunted and killed, but every year they produced antlers which could be collected and brought back to the settlement to be made into important tools. Antler is a very important raw material as it formed the basis for a variety of tools and equipment throughout prehistory and into the Viking period.

A significant feature of the island economy in prehistory was the exploitation of the coastal zone and the sea. This was a feature which differentiated the islands from mainland Britain where wild animals, particularly those associated with the sea, appear to be largely avoided as a dietary supplement by most communities. On the mainland the arrival of agriculture coincided with a shift from a diet which was heavily focused on seafood to one where seafood played an inconsequential role at a nutritional level. On the islands, exploitation of the resources provided by the sea was more complicated; shellfish were collected in very large numbers and it is assumed this was as a food supplement; beached whales were processed and provided large bones that could be used to make tools and even architectural fittings; the bones of birds, particularly large seabirds, suggest they were hunted for their meat, feathers and bones.

The importance of fish in the Scottish islands is a topic of some complexity. A detailed analysis of aquatic biomarkers (microscopic chemical remains) in the fabric of the pottery recovered from settlements excavated on the islands suggested that fish eating effectively ended with the Neolithic colonisation of the islands. However, it is also clear that fish consumption gradually reemerged in later prehistory, around 3000 years ago, which contrasts with the mainland of Britain where it seems to have remained a taboo foodstuff until the Roman invasion in AD 43. Coastal fishing for saithe is well documented in the Late Bronze Age at Cladh Hallan on South Uist and became increasingly important in the Late Iron Age. At Bornais there is also evidence for the exploitation of salmon and/or trout though this may only have been for special meals. Saithe are an inshore fish and in the past large quantities were caught from the shore using both line and nets, so there is no need to assume that boats were used, and that people were venturing out to sea on regular fishing trips. Despite the evidence for fishing on the Scottish islands, analysis of human bones does not indicate that these made a major contribution to the diet of most people.[18]

The Western Isles are justifiably famous for providing the breeding grounds for many spectacular seabirds. The vertical cliffs that are a feature of St Kilda, Mingulay, Berneray and the Shiants provide ideal habitats for numerous species including gannets, fulmers, kittiwakes, guillemots and shags, but the absence of intensive agriculture and dense human occupation also encourages burrowing birds such as puffins, manx shearwaters and petrels. The machair plain and lochs of the Uists are the home for mute swans and large flocks of greylag geese, and the coastline and inland lochs provide an ideal habitat for many species of ducks and other wildfowl. It is not therefore surprising that there is a long history of the exploitation of wild birds which is famously still practised today. The men of Ness in the Butt of Lewis make an annual pilgrimage to the small and difficult to access island of Sula Sgeir where they cull immature gannets.

The exploitation of birds is clearly visible in the bone assemblages from prehistoric settlements on the machair.[19] The assemblages are very variable and indicate the exploitation of a wide variety of species that occupy habitats ranging from moorlands to lochs and the machair to the coast, and include birds that spend most of the time at sea. There is evidence for the preferential taking of seabirds like puffins and gannets which would have required trips to remote islands, but these trips could have been very productive if they coincided with the breeding season when large numbers of birds congregate and are easily available to hunters. Birds were undoubtedly a valuable resource for the islanders and, as well as providing meat to supplement the diet, could have contributed feathers which are a valuable resource that could be used in a variety of ways. Collecting eggs would also have been an important subsistence activity and may have been a routine day to day practice for any individual moving around the landscape in the spring. However, large collections could have been recovered from trips to the seabird colonies early in the spring when agricultural resources may have been at their lowest.

Conclusion

The main goal of this introductory chapter has been to outline the structure and objectives for the book. It will focus on the recent excavations at Bornais and Cille Pheadair on the island of South Uist and use these excavations to explore the nature of the Viking colonisation of the islands, the subsequent occupation of the islands by people of Scandinavian descent, and how these people eventually become the Scottish Gaels who formed the Clan societies of the recent historical past. The evidence from South Uist is given context by an exploration of the archaeological evidence for the Western Isles which, though imperfect and limited in many respects, still includes discoveries of international significance that provide detailed insights into the character of these societies. This introduction ends with a general exploration of the character of the islands which highlights some of the distinctive features of the landscape, the vegetational history and the natural resources. All of these resources provided an important backdrop to the Viking occupation of the islands and were exploited and nurtured by the inhabitants of the islands to make their occupation productive. At the beginning of this introduction, I described one of the more interesting finds from Bornais – two fragments of green stone. This stone, whilst attractive, is not the most obviously important find from the site. Nevertheless, the journey from Greece to the Outer Hebrides illustrates how the islands were part of the wider world and how archaeology has the ability to tell stories that illuminate our understanding of the past in many surprising ways.

Notes

1. The importance of green porphyry in Scotland was first documented by Cormack 1989, 43–47 and recent work on the Scottish finds has been undertaken by Chris Lowe in Owen and Lowe 1999.
2. See Tesch 2016.
3. The excavations at Bornais have been published in four large volumes, which provide many of the details which are summarised in this book. The full references for these publications are Sharples 2005; 2012; 2020; 2021. The excavations at Cille Pheadair are fully published in Parker Pearson *et al.* 2018.
4. The most important publications on the excavations at the Udal are Crawford 1975; 1981; 1986; 1988; Crawford and Switsur 1977; Selkirk 1996.
5. The use of the terms Viking and Norse will be discussed later in this chapter.
6. These excavations are reported on in Cowie and MacLeod Rivet 2015.
7. The precious metal hoards are described and discussed by Graham-Campbell 1995. The excavation of the burials at Cnip were reported in Welander *et al.* 1987 and Dunwell *et al.* 1995 and the analysis of the isotopes by Montgomery *et al.* 2003; 2014.
8. The most comprehensive account of the buildings of the Western Isles is in the Royal Commission Inventory of 1928 (RCAHMS 1928). The chronology of almost all the Medieval buildings on the western seaboard of Scotland is challenging, and has been much debated in recent years, but a recent programme of radiocarbon dating linked to an analysis of the lime mortar used to construct these buildings promises to be revelatory (Thacker 2016).
9. Broderick 1988
10. Paulson and Edwards 1981.
11. An audit in 2019 counted 15 monographs, 3 popular books, 78 academic papers, 38 interim reports and 40 doctoral and master's theses – more have been published since this audit was undertaken. The most relevant monographs are listed in endnote 3 but the remaining books are Branigan 2005; 2010; Branigan and Foster 1995; 2000; Gilbertson *et al.* 1997; Parker Pearson (ed.) 2012; Parker Pearson and Sharples 1999; Parker Pearson and Zvelebil 2014; Parker Pearson *et al.* 2004; 2021.
12. Mike Parker Pearson switched his attention to the Late Bronze Age settlement at Cladh Hallan.
13. Peter Marshall together with Chris Bronk Ramsey and Gordon Cook produced detailed reports on the radiocarbon chronology of the settlement at Bornais in Sharples 2012 and 2020 and for Cille Pheadair in Parker Pearson *et al.* 2018.
14. The natural history of the Western Isles is extensively studied, and several well written books are available on the subjects outlined in the text. The most recent synthetic account is by Stewart Angus in Angus 1997; 2001, but the best single volume work is the Boyd and Boyd 1990 volume in the Collins New Naturalist series.

15 The only recent scholar to argue for a survival of pre-Norse place names was Cox, whose study of the place names of the Carloway region in west Lewis argued for a significant survival of pre-Norse elements in the place names. His argument was not widely accepted, and Kruse produced a convincing argument that the linguistic features Cox identified as pre-Norse were simply regional variations of Old Norse that had been brought over by colonisers from different areas of Norway. The relevant publications are Cox 2002 and Kruse 2005. Broderick 2013, Clancy 2018 and Jennings and Kruse 2009 provide a recent review of the origins of the island names.

16 The machair plain of the Western Isles has been extensively studied by the leading researcher on this important landform, William Ritchie, and he has published a large number of papers exploring the development of the landscape, including Ritchie 1966; 1967; 1979; and Ritchie *et al.* 2001.

17 An overview of the introduction of plants and animals to the Western Isles is provided by Smith and Mulville 2004. Jacqui Mulville has also provided detailed examinations of the exploitation of cetaceans in Mulville 2002, and red deer in Mulville 2010; 2016.

18 Cultural attitudes to the consumption of fish have been the subject of considerable debate since the steep decline in fish consumption at the beginning of the Neolithic was first noted by Mike Richards in Richards and Mellars 1998, and the importance of fish to the Norse colonists of Britain was established by James Barrett in Barrett 1997. In recent years the overall significance of fish consumption in the diet of the Atlantic islands was explored by Lucy Cramp who examined organic residues from cooking in the pottery found in the region. This has provided valuable information not just on fish consumption but also the importance of milk, see Cramp *et al.* 2014; 2015. Claire Ingrem analysed the fish bone recovered from the excavations at Bornais and Cille Pheadair and her reports are published in the respective site monographs, particularly Sharples 2012 and 2021 and Parker Pearson *et al.* 2018.

19 Julia Best has undertaken an extensive analysis of the bird bone assemblages recovered from the recent archaeological investigations in Best 2014; Best and Mulville 2016.

CHAPTER TWO

Before the Vikings

Introduction – a bone die

In the summer of 1999, during the excavation of the floor of a house on mound 1 at Bornais, Cardiff student Jennie Preston came across a distinctive gaming piece that archaeologists refer to as a parallelopiped bone die (Fig. 2.1). These are four-sided bone dice made from an animal long bone, in this case probably the shaft of a sheep metapodial (the lower part of the leg), which has been carefully smoothed to create a roughly square cross section.

Dice similar to this example have been found throughout the Atlantic islands of Scotland, and I discovered a collection of five pieces in my excavations at Scalloway on Shetland which date to the fifth century, and a group of six dice of similar date was found at Dun Cueir on Barra.[1] A date in the middle of the first millennium AD was confirmed for the Bornais die by the radiocarbon dates from the house floor levels. The date is important as dice first appear in southern England and on the Continent in the centuries before the Roman conquest, but no early dice are known from Scotland.

Parallelopiped dice were originally thought to have been rolled like modern dice and to be associated with the introduction of games in the elite cultures developed by contact with the Romans in the early part of the first

FIGURE 2.1. The parallelopiped die from Bornais mound 1.

millennium AD, but this now seems a bit simplistic. The Bornais die is a very curved bone which would not roll evenly and there are other uneven dice that would have similar problems. An alternative possibility is that the dice were tossed into the air.

The numbers on the Bornais die are indicated by arrangements of ring and dot motifs inscribed into the surface of the bone and on this example the sequence is 1, 4, 6 and 3, which is an unusual arrangement. Numbers 1 and 3 have been incised carefully in the middle of the bone but the larger numbers appear to have been more difficult to inscribe, and the design splits the numbers into two groups placed at either end of the bone. In the process of creating the larger ring and dot motifs several false starts and mistakes were made (Fig. 2.1).

My diary entry for 10th of July 1999 records that we found this die in a 'charcoal layer and the bones in this layer are burnt black but this (bone) isn't. It was discovered with its end upwards (in a vertical position) and this suggests that it was pushed into the charcoal layer from above'. These observations are important as they provide a clue as to why the die was deposited. It was a particular act which had meaning and this in turn helps us to understand the role of these dice within this society. We will come back to this later in this chapter.

At the end of the 1999 season, when the excavation of mound 1 was completed, it was clear that the die was located near the centre of a circular house that had burnt down and then been rebuilt as a roughly rectangular or trapezoidal structure. At the end of its occupation in the fifth century the stone walls of this house were systematically dismantled, and the stones removed, probably to build another house within the settlement complex (Fig. 2.2). The destruction of the house has made it difficult to fully understand, but its dismantling appears to have been undertaken in a systematic fashion that preserved certain

FIGURE 2.2. Exposing the remains of a Late Iron Age wheelhouse on Bornais mound 1.

key elements of the building. The most important elements of the building to survive were the hearths, the floor, and the entrance thresholds, but with only small sections of the enclosing house wall. These elements appear to have had a symbolic significance to the occupants. Enough survived to indicate the shape of the original structure and there was also some unparalleled evidence for how the building was roofed.

The wheelhouse

The house identified on Bornais mound 1 was a circular building known as a wheelhouse (Fig. 2.3).[2] These are relatively well-known structures in the Western Isles[3] and are characterised by having a circular internal area with a periphery that is divided by short stone walls, or piers, that project from the internal wall face.[4] On the machair plain of South Uist these wheelhouses were built in a large pit or quarry dug into the sand dunes, with the roof emerging from the surface of the dunes. The circular internal wall of the wheelhouse backed on to the edge of the pit/quarry, and where gaps existed organic-rich middens were

FIGURE 2.3. A simplified plan of the wheelhouse on Bornais mound 1. The east side is fairly well documented in the archaeological record, but the west side is largely conjectural with only the worn sill stones of the entrance to provide a clue to the location of the west wall.

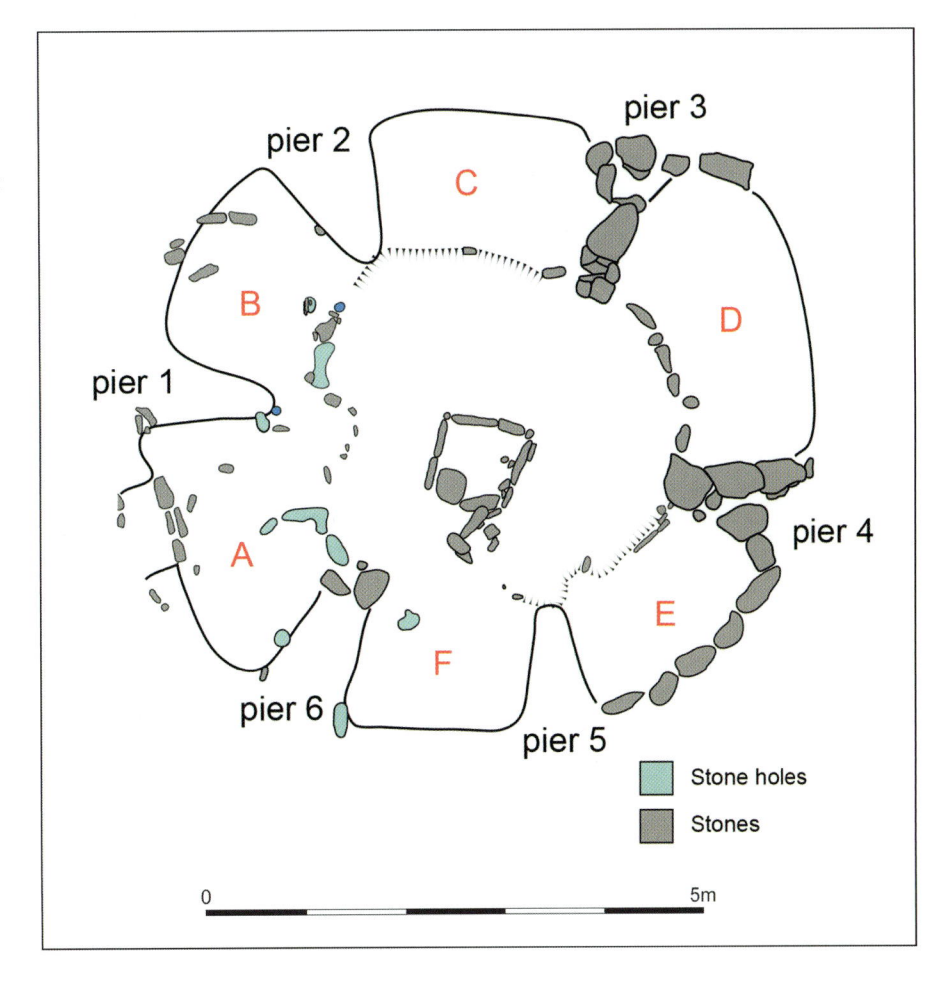

packed in behind the wall to give it added stability. Wheelhouses were also built on the upland moors, where more conventional double-walled structures were constructed.

The most convincing interpretation of the Bornais wheelhouse is that the peripheral area was separated into six rooms defined by projecting piers. Only two of these piers survived and these lay directly opposite a west-facing doorway defined by four vertically set stones that acted as the entrance threshold; the upper surface of the stones was polished smooth from foot traffic in and out of the house. An open central area was defined by a kerb of small upright stones and a slight drop in the floor level. Slightly to the south of the centre of the house was the hearth. This was a trapezoidal stone box that projected above the floor and had a slab interior with a kerb of small vertical slabs around three sides. A thin layer of peat ash covered the interior of the hearth and spilled out of its open south end to spread over the southern half of the house. Adjacent to the open end of the hearth were a couple of large upright slabs which appeared to be the remains of a stone box, possibly used for storing food, or perhaps as a slow cooker.

Radiocarbon dates indicate the wheelhouse was built in the first half of the fifth century. There is very little evidence for the accumulation of debris on the floor of the house during its occupation and very few finds were recovered from the ash layers near the hearth. It is possible that large parts of the floor were covered with skins which would have been an easy way of keeping the floor clean and also restricting erosion of the windblown sand on which the house was built. Our understanding of the wheelhouse was considerably enhanced by a fire that ended the life of this building. This occurred at the end of the fifth century when the wheelhouse had been occupied for between 40 and 110 years. There is no evidence for how the fire started, it could have been accidental or deliberate, but it caused the roof to collapse into the building (Fig. 2.4). The remains of the

FIGURE 2.4. Excavating the burnt roof timbers of the wheelhouse on Bornais mound 1.

FIGURE 2.5. An experimental reconstruction of a small wheelhouse at Old Scatness, Shetland. The photograph shows the entrance to two of the cells with their corbelled stone vaults and the timber roof that covers the central part of the house.

roof were preserved underneath the floor of the rebuilt house which means we not only have evidence for the nature of the roof but also the objects that were in the original house when the fire occurred. The collection of objects recovered suggests the house had not been systematically cleared prior to the fire but the absence of any accidental fatalities, animal or human, suggests it was not a catastrophically sudden event.

The Bornais wheelhouse is probably the best evidence we have for understanding the organic components of the roof of a wheelhouse. The accepted reconstruction of a wheelhouse is that the area around the periphery was divided into rooms roofed with individual corbelled vaults of stone (Fig. 2.5). Examples of this type of roof survive *in situ* at the wheelhouse of Cnip in the Isle of Lewis and at the settlement of Jarlshof on Shetland. There was no evidence that the central area of any wheelhouse was ever corbelled, or was an open court exposed to the elements. Neither of these ideas seems very likely and the consensus is that a pitched timber and thatch roof was used to cover the central area. This was confirmed by the excavation at Bornais, where the timbers of the burnt roof structure were found in a thick charcoal-rich soil. The roof appeared to comprise a criss-cross grid of squared timbers of spruce/larch, which supported a layer of turf. The turf may have been the basal foundation for a straw or reed thatch but if this was the case then the thatch burned away and left no preserved remains.

The timbers used in the roof were an important and difficult to access resource as the natural woodlands of the Uists were largely cleared of trees by the beginning of the first millennium BC, and the landscape looked similar to the treeless landscape we see today. The inhabitants had to rely on driftwood collected from the beach to roof the structure. We know this because the conifer species used in the roof, spruce or larch, are not native to Britain, but instead grew in North America. They were brought to Britain by ocean currents that traverse the North Atlantic, bringing warm water from the Caribbean up to the Scottish isles via the east coast of North America. The identification of these trees as driftwood is confirmed by the presence of bore holes from shipworms (Teredinidae) in the wood and the shells of these boring molluscs were recovered by an extensive sieving programme.

The preservation of the timbers in their carbonised form is unusual and indicates that the fire that destroyed the wheelhouse was not an uncontrolled blazing inferno. The amount of charred plant remains, and the lack of ash in the surrounding layer, indicate that the temperature reached by the fire was relatively low and the quantity of charred timbers indicates a lack of oxygen and a long slow burn. Detailed analysis of the soils surrounding the timbers suggests that turf covered the roof and as the fire caught hold the roof quickly collapsed, and the burning timbers were sealed by the turf. This oxygen-deprived fire allowed the carbonisation process to occur.

The turves used to create the roof were not from the machair landscape that surrounds the settlement. The mineral grains present contrast with the calcareous shell grains that constitute the machair sands and suggest the turf came from inland areas beyond the reach of the windblown sand that covers the coastal plain. These turves would have been better for building purposes, as the turf on the machair is not well developed and has a very limited soil component that would not have maintained any coherence when it dried out. The organic rich turves from the peaty inland areas would also have provided fuel for the fire that destroyed the wheelhouse.

The stone used to construct the walls of the wheelhouse was transported to this location as the machair naturally contains no stone. The easiest suitable building stone would have been blocks eroded by the sea at the point of Rubha Ardvule some 1.6 km to the southwest. There are certainly large quantities of stones on the beaches around the coast of this promontory today. The amount of stone required to build a wheelhouse would have been substantial as the internal walls would have been roughly two metres high, and the corbelled vaults that formed that part of the roof would have required large, structurally sound rectangular blocks or slabs. The decision to build these sophisticated wheelhouses on the machair plain was made with an awareness that they would require a considerable investment of skilled labour.

The occupation of the wheelhouse

Contained within the thick charcoal layer that surrounded the carbonised roof timbers was a collection of objects that provide an impression of how this building was used. One of the most distinctive discoveries was a large bar-shaped object with a sharpened cutting edge at one end. This was made from a whale bone, probably a jawbone, as this is denser than most whale bone and therefore makes a more effective tool. It was found wedged between two of the carbonised timbers of the wheelhouse roof, and one must assume that it was placed there when the wheelhouse was constructed and remained there throughout the occupation of the wheelhouse (Fig. 2.6). This blade could have been used to cut through the root mats of the turves used in the roof and would have been a handy tool to have when trimming and tidying the turves as they were laid on the timbers of the roof. There is no evidence that this tool was ever hafted, and it seems comfortable in the hand.

The most common objects recovered from the charcoal layer were stone tools made from water rounded cobbles that could have been sourced on the coast, particularly around Rubha Ardvule. There were 52 definite and another 11 possible cobble tools from the floor of this wheelhouse, which is an unusually large collection. They had a very distinct distribution in approximately seven clusters located close to the walls and piers around the periphery of the wheelhouse (Fig. 2.7); there was one cluster in the centre just beside the southeast corner of the hearth and a general scatter in the northwest segment. The distribution of these tools suggests they were kept in organic containers, woven bags perhaps, that were hanging from the walls and roof of the wheelhouse. Mixed in with these stone tools were animal bones that were probably also contained in the bags. These may have been raw materials that were to be transformed into bone tools.

Unfortunately, cobble tools are not the most informative objects to be recovered from the Late Iron Age. The assemblage can be split into several types that exhibit different forms of wear, indicating that some were used for fine and coarse grinding, whereas others were used for more robust hammering activities, but otherwise their purpose is unknown. These tools are very common discoveries on settlement sites of this date on the Atlantic coast of Scotland and they were clearly an important tool in any domestic household. However, the large number of these tools in the Bornais wheelhouse is unusual and suggests the house was used for storing unused or only partially made and used tools.

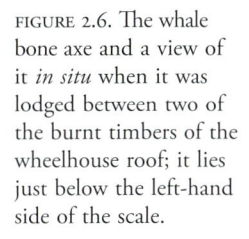

FIGURE 2.6. The whale bone axe and a view of it *in situ* when it was lodged between two of the burnt timbers of the wheelhouse roof; it lies just below the left-hand side of the scale.

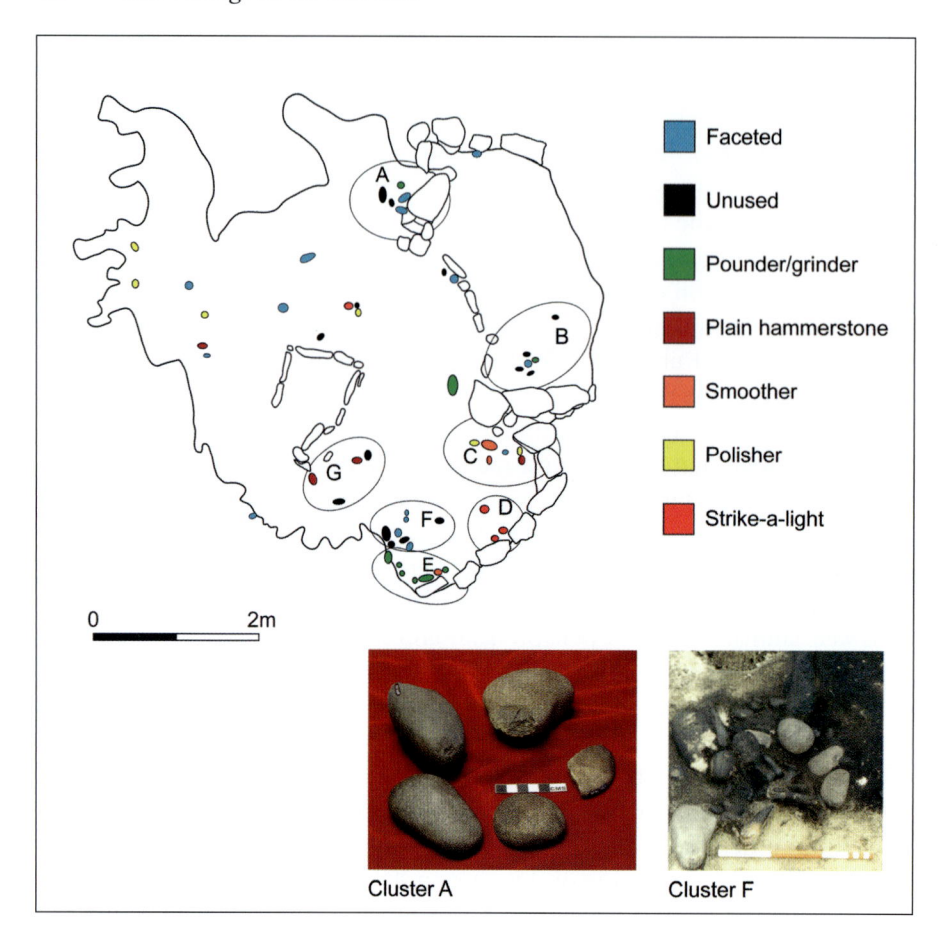

FIGURE 2.7. The distribution of stone cobble tools on the floor of the wheelhouse with insets showing the stone tools that comprised cluster A and cluster F during excavation. The clusters adjacent to the wall of the house also included bones which are clearly visible in the photo of cluster F.

Scattered across the interior of the wheelhouse and contained within the charcoal layer was an assemblage of bone and antler tools that were burnt black by the fire that destroyed the wheelhouse (Fig. 2.8). Most were handles of some sort but there was a small bone pin, and an iron pin (or bradle) mounted in an antler handle. The most interesting, though badly damaged, object in this layer was a comb made from a flat piece of antler which had a strip of iron cut with short stubby teeth inserted in one end. The surface of the antler was decorated by very finely incised lines that did not make an obvious coherent design, though it included grids and swirls that overlaid each other. There are no obvious parallels for this object. There were other bone combs dated to this period, and we will discuss these later, but none of them resemble this comb. The use of an inserted iron strip and the finely inscribed decoration are unique traits and suggest this was an important object (Fig. 2.9).

A considerable effort went into the recovery of the smallest fragments of debris from the deposits inside the wheelhouse, and all the other houses dug as part of this research project. The destruction layer produced a range of material including eggshell, crab shell, limpets, winkles, and animal and fish bone that

FIGURE 2.8. An outline of the floor layer from the original and the rebuilt wheelhouse showing the distribution of the objects found. The objects on the top are all burnt, whereas those on the bottom are unburnt.

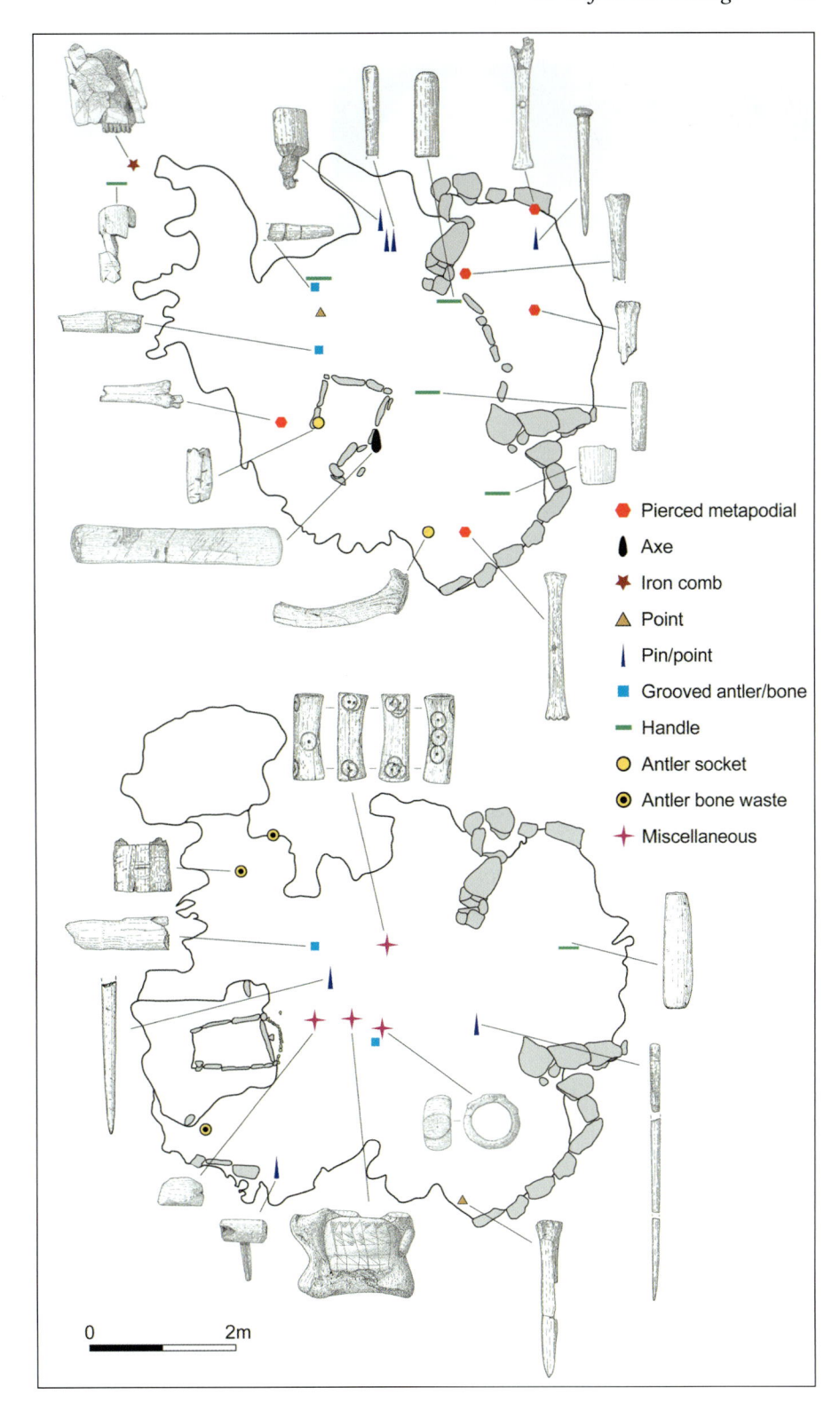

2. Before the Vikings 43

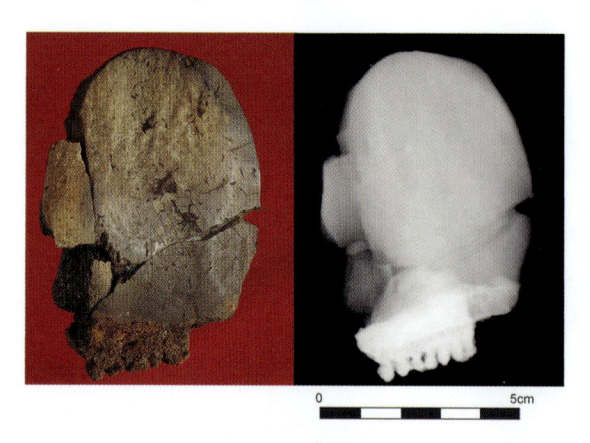

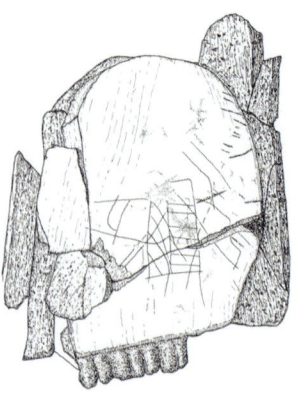

FIGURE 2.9. An unusual iron and antler comb showing the incised decoration on one side. This object was heavily burnt and fragmented, and was associated with the primary occupation of the wheelhouse.

suggest people did some cooking and eating in this wheelhouse, but the quantities are low and don't suggest the house was intensively occupied immediately prior to the fire. The absence of evidence for human activity is emphasised by a discovery at the back of the wheelhouse, immediately to the north of pier four, of a compressed layer of coprolite. This is a polite term archaeologists use to describe ancient shit. It coincides with a concentration of small fragments of bone that suggest a dog was tethered at this location in the period immediately prior to the destruction of the wheelhouse. Thankfully, the dog was not in residence when the house burnt down and dog bones are surprisingly rare in the animal bone assemblage; only one identifiable bone was found in the deposits belonging to this house, though the coprolite evidence suggests that dogs were living in the settlement.

Taken together, the evidence suggests that this wheelhouse was a relatively empty structure used to store stone tools and guarded by a dog immediately prior to its destruction by fire in the middle of the first millennium AD. It seems likely that the Bornais wheelhouse was a component of a much larger settlement, possibly a spare room attached to a larger wheelhouse that lay to the north; the charcoal layer continues in this direction but was not explored by the excavations.

Wheelhouses in the Western Isles

Wheelhouses are a thoroughly explored monument type in the Atlantic islands of Scotland and 29 examples have been excavated on the Uists. Many of these excavations have been very limited in scope and have revealed little other than confirming the presence of a circular house with distinctive internal piers (Fig. 2.10). However, in recent years there have been a few extensive and detailed excavations that have revealed the spatial and chronological complexity of these monuments.

The most extensive excavation of a wheelhouse complex that has taken place to date was at the Udal in North Uist. This complex and long-lived machair settlement[5] contained three wheelhouses and other structures. Unfortunately,

FIGURE 2.10. Plans of a selection of excavated wheelhouses from the Western Isles. A) Cnip, B) A'Cheardach Bheag, C) Allt Chrisal, D) A'Cheardach Mhor, E) Sollas.

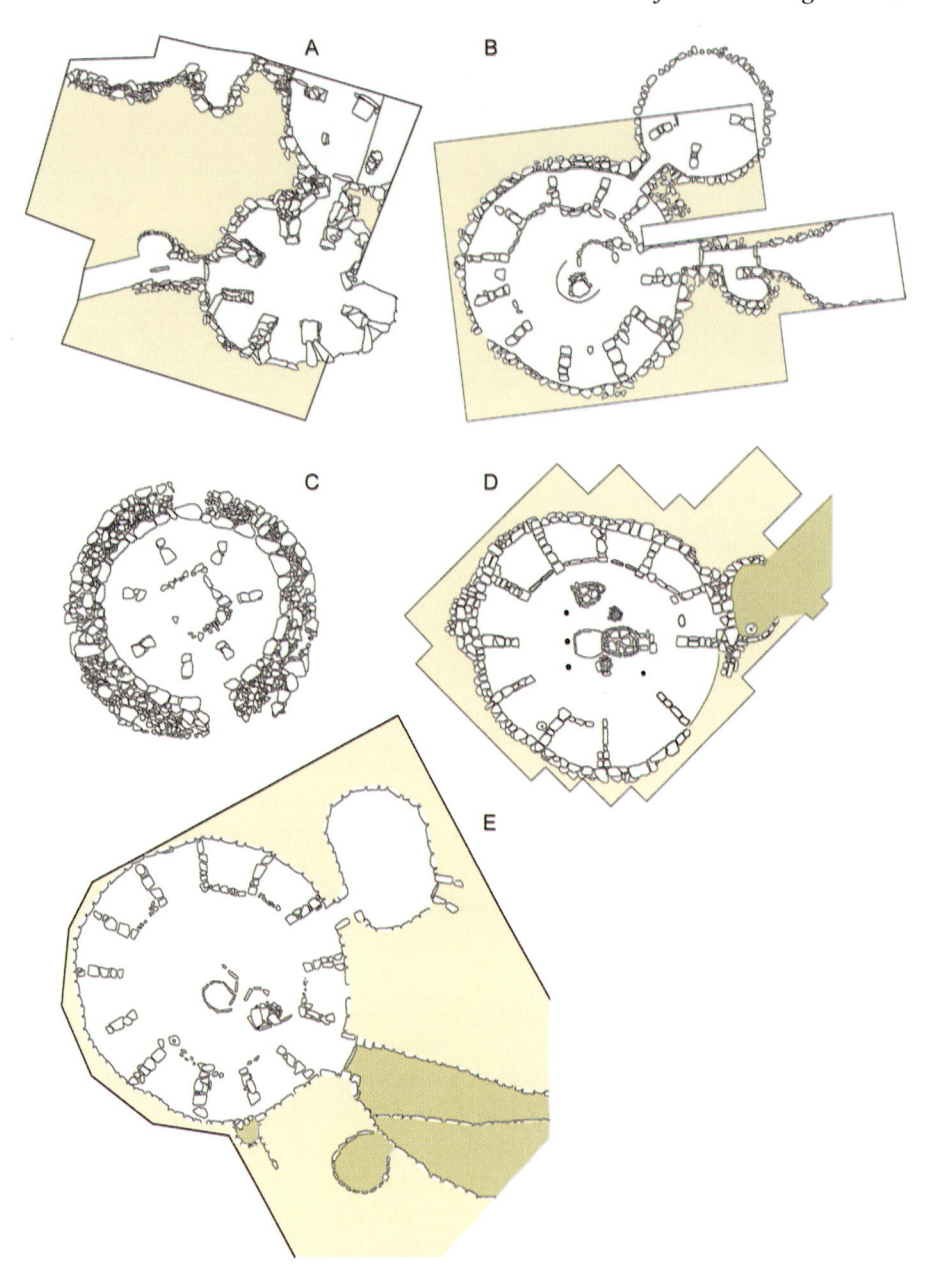

these excavations have never been fully analysed and published, so we know very little about what was found. Nevertheless, the wheelhouses were substantial structures; two were 10.8 m in diameter and one was 7.6 m in diameter. This makes them amongst the largest wheelhouses recently excavated; only a partially excavated structure in the Allasdale dunes on Barra appears to be significantly larger at 12.1 m. The size of the Udal wheelhouses and the presence of three apparently contemporary buildings suggests that this was a large settlement which may have housed at least three, probably related, families.

FIGURE 2.11. A view of the excavation of the wheelhouse at A'Cheardach Bheag in 1956. © Courtesy of HES. Papers of Dr Horace Fairhurst, archaeologist, Glasgow, Scotland.

In general, the extent of wheelhouse settlements on the machair is variable and it is often quite difficult to estimate how many individual wheelhouses are present and whether they were all contemporary and in use at the same time. There are examples of relatively isolated individual wheelhouses and A'Cheardach Mhor on South Uist is a good example of this (Fig. 2.11), but other wheelhouses can be deceptive. Kilpheder, also on South Uist, was an exceptionally large and impressive individual wheelhouse which was excavated by Tom Lethbridge in the early 1950s.[6] The wheelhouse was cleared out and left open as a visitor attraction, but the walls have gradually collapsed, and the interior filled with rubble and windblown sand. Kilpheder appeared to be an isolated building but, during its excavation, Lethbridge observed parch-marks in the surrounding grass that indicated the presence of another two buildings, and their existence was confirmed by a geophysical survey in recent years. It is therefore a much larger building complex and must have been an important settlement in this part of the island.

Excavations at the wheelhouse of Cnip on the Isle of Lewis also indicate that these structures have a complex history.[7] At this site, the excavations revealed the presence of two adjacent wheelhouses, though the limited excavation area and the degree of coastal erosion means the full extent of the settlement could not be established. One of the wheelhouses was unfinished and had been abandoned when the walls were only partially built and not all the piers had been completed. There was no hearth, and no floor deposits were identified as the house was never occupied. The structure was filled in and replaced by a small chamber accessed from the adjacent wheelhouse.

2. *Before the Vikings*   47

The area around the settlement of Bornais provides some idea of the density of these settlements at the beginning of the first millennium AD in the islands.[8] The machair plain in this area provided a relatively flat, easily cultivated landscape which was occupied at the end of the third millennium BC by farmers using distinctive Beaker pottery. Their settlements and fields appear to have been abandoned due to the instability of the windblown sand and it was not until the beginning of the first millennium BC that we see the reoccupation of this sandy plain, with the permanent settlements that formed the basis for the later wheelhouse settlements.

These settlements often survive as prominent mounds protruding from the surface of the machair and, where the brown occupation rich sand is disturbed by rabbits, clusters of bones, shells and ceramics are found. In the area to the north of Bornais these settlement mounds appear to be spaced roughly every kilometre but in the area to the south the settlement mounds are more frequent

FIGURE 2.12. A plan of the settlement mounds adjacent to the broch at Dun Vulan highlighting in red those with definite Middle Iron Age occupation.

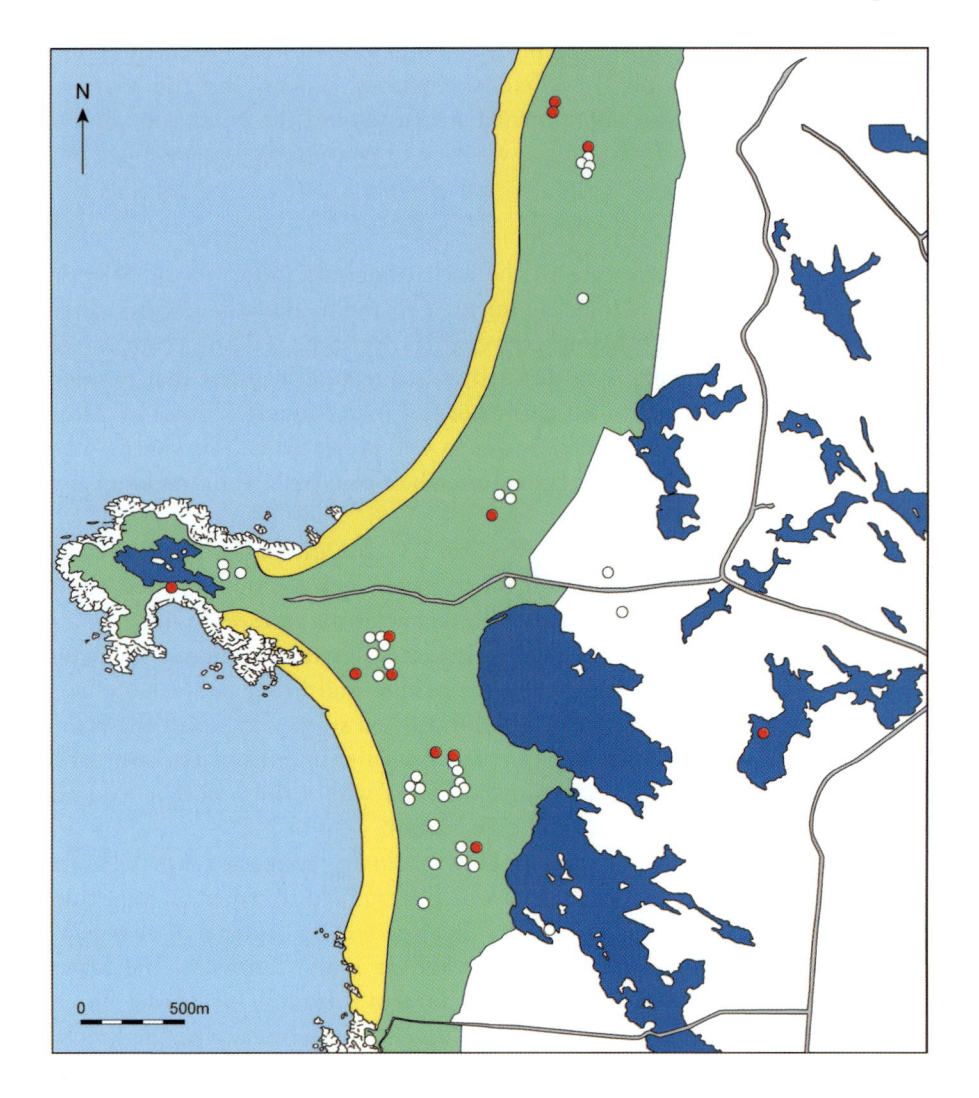

and occur every 5–600 m (Fig. 2.12). This suggests that there are at least forty wheelhouses on the machair plain of South Uist and possibly as many as fifty to sixty on the island as a whole.

Wheelhouses are also known to be present on the adjacent moorland areas of the Outer Hebrides and examples of these were amongst the first wheelhouses to be excavated. Some of the excavated examples are in very isolated locations. Allasdale on Barra is on the terraced slopes of Corra Bheinn and lies some 1.8 km from the occupied coastal plain. Allt Chrisal, also on Barra, lies in the remote and exposed southeast corner of the island and, though it is on the coast, the surrounding area of potential agricultural land is very limited. The valley it lies in managed to support a single croft in the recent past.

Wheelhouses are the standard house form on the Western Isles in the first centuries of the first millennium AD. Exactly when they emerged as the default house is a topic of interest, but it is not an issue that concerns this book. Of greater significance is when this architectural form stopped being constructed and this is considered below. Contemporary with the construction of wheelhouses are completely different structures, brochs, and the relationship between these overtly monumental structures and the concealed, almost subterranean wheelhouses is an issue we need to consider before we move on.

FIGURE 2.13. (*opposite*) A general view of the broch at Carloway, Isle of Lewis.

Brochs

Brochs are a distinctive feature of the archaeological landscapes of Atlantic Scotland, and they survived to be commented on and used by the Vikings. They are monumental circular buildings; the circular dry-stone walls of a broch were very carefully constructed, with distinctive architectural features that enabled the creation of walls that reached heights of 12.9 m at Mousa in Shetland. Most of the brochs in the Western Isles are not so well preserved and survive as large piles of rubble with only the occasional stretch of well-built wall providing any indication of their original form.[9]

The best-preserved broch in the Western Isles is Dun Carloway on the Isle of Lewis, where a large section of the broch stands up to 6.7 m high (Fig. 2.13). This broch provides a good example of the characteristic features of these buildings. The broch tower was formed by a circular wall with an external diameter of 14.3 m and an internal diameter of 7.4 m, the wall being between 3.0 and 3.6 m thick. At the base this wall was solid coursed stone with small chambers or cells created within it that were entered from the interior of the structure. Many brochs had a base that contained a gallery within the wall that reduced the amount of stone needed for the construction.

Above the basal level the wall at Dun Carloway split into two separate sections with an inner and outer face which were held together by long thin slabs that formed the floors of galleries that encircle the inner wall at regular intervals. Three galleries survive in the wall at Dun Carloway. The lower of these galleries enabled the occupants to move around inside the broch wall, and gaps in the inner wall provided access to the interior of the broch. There were no gaps in the outer wall that provided access to the external

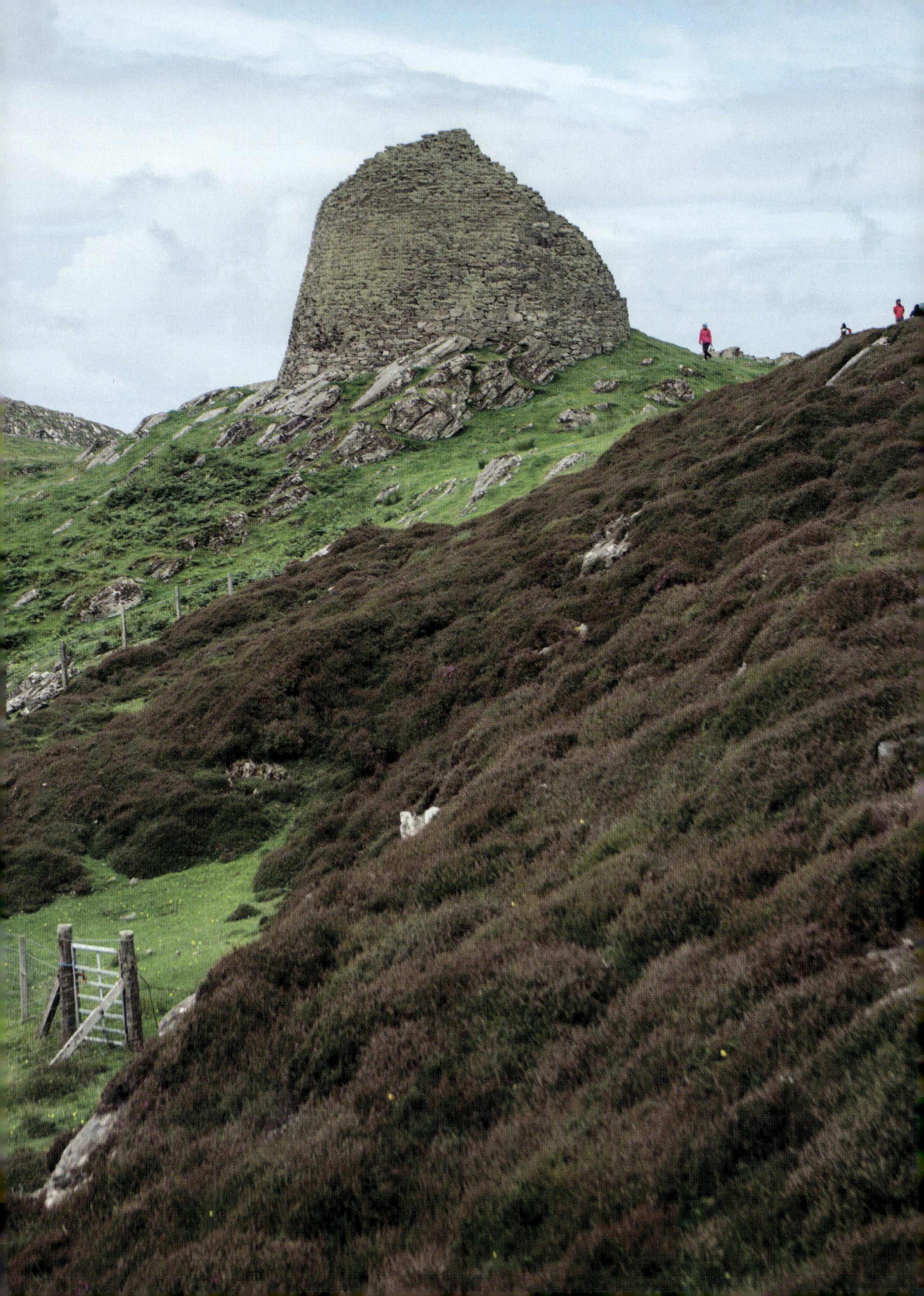

FIGURE 2.14. The remnants of the staircase of the broch at Dun Vulan, South Uist. These were truncated by the sea, and the passage into the interior of the broch is filled with earth and occupation debris.

world. As the construction got higher, the inner and outer walls came together and the gallery space was reduced, making it difficult if not impossible to move around within the wall at these higher levels. The lower galleries were accessed by a staircase that ran up through the broch wall from a chamber at the base of the wall that was located directly opposite the west facing entrance of the broch (Fig. 2.14).

The staircase provided access to the interior of the broch, approximately 2.1 m above ground level, where a wooden floor would have covered the central court of the broch and probably provided the main living room for the inhabitants. The timbers of this floor rested on a ledge, known as a scarcement, that was built into the inner wall face of the broch. The broch at Mousa in Shetland has an extra, much higher scarcement ledge which suggests multiple floors existed in some brochs. The nature of the roof is problematic as the wall heads have not survived even at Mousa. It seems very unlikely that the staircases of brochs such as Carloway continued very high up the wall. The purpose of the stairs was not to provide access to the wall head for use as a defensive platform from which attackers could be repelled.

The brochs of Uist are found on the west coast but unlike the wheelhouses they were not built on the machair plain that formed the principal agricultural lands of the island. They were located on the adjacent inland areas known as the blacklands, which are relatively low-lying and generally very wet, with numerous large and small lochs and extensive areas of peat. Most brochs were located within the lochs on both natural and artificial islands. They were often surrounded by water, with only a narrow, carefully constructed causeway connecting them to the dry lands nearby (Fig. 2.15). This distinctive island location is a characteristic feature of the brochs in the Western Isles and sets them apart from the other Iron Age settlements on the islands.

FIGURE 2.15. An aerial view of the broch of Dun Torcuil, North Uist, showing its location and the stone causeway leading out to the artificial island on which it was built. © Historic Environment Scotland.

To visit the occupants of a broch the individuals living in a wheelhouse such as Bornais would have had to walk through the fields of barley that surrounded their settlement and continue across the grasslands and wildflower meadows of the machair plain, where the community's cattle and sheep were grazing. There was then an abrupt transition as they came to the blacklands that were dominated by heather and a very different range of flowers; much of this transition area was taken up by large lochs. The topography of the blacklands is much more undulating, and rocky outcrops, peat bogs and lochs are common, though there are areas of flat land suitable for cultivation when drained, and this is where the current population of the island live. The route through these lochs and bogs would have been relatively restricted and most likely required the visitor to stick to a prescribed path that would eventually end at a causeway leading out into a loch. This would have been the only way to access the broch and exposed the visitor to scrutiny by its inhabitants. Crossing the water may have also had a religious significance and there is evidence from other areas of Scotland that water had an important role in defining religious places.

Access to the living space within the broch extended the journey. First, you would have to crouch low to enter the only portal in the imposing broch façade; this was effectively a tunnel that led to a door which had to be opened to let you through. The tunnel then continued past the entrance to a chamber known as the guard chamber, though what it was for is difficult to assess: perhaps you left your dirty shoes and outer garments, your dog or your weapons here. You then entered the broch's central space at the ground floor level. This area was used for storing grain and stalling animals. To gain access to the main living space, you normally had to turn left and walk around the broch wall to another doorway that led to a small chamber built into the wall which provided access to the staircase leading up through the wall and eventually out into the main living space. This was an impressive timber-floored room, with the broch tower rising around you up to a smoke-shrouded roof.

This journey was deliberately made protracted and difficult, and emphasised the separation between the normal domestic farmers living in the wheelhouses and the important families living in the brochs. The inhabitants of the brochs were community leaders, though the number of brochs and wheelhouses suggests they were not large communities (Fig. 2.16). In South Uist I would suggest there were 11 or 12 broch communities each consisting of at least five to six households. One of these households lived in a broch and this monumental structure symbolised the independence and importance of the community. The population of South Uist could have been as many as 700 people in the first two centuries of the first millennium AD.

Reconstruction and abandonment

Before we continue to interrogate the history of the wheelhouse at Bornais, we should return to consider the significance of the bone die we described at the beginning of this chapter. Why was this die not burnt like most of the other bones found in this layer? How did it get to be standing vertically within the charcoal layer? The obvious answer to these questions is that the die only entered the ash layer after the fire was over and the ash was no longer hot, and the vertical position suggests it was pushed into the layer from above.

There were a number of other unburnt objects scattered across the top of this layer and one of these stands out as exceptional; an unburnt cattle astragalus bone. Incised on the flat surface of this bone was a grid, five squares by six squares. Most of the grid squares were divided in two by a diagonal line and on one side of this line the square was filled with fine incised lines. These two objects, the die and astragalus, were found roughly in the centre of the burnt-down wheelhouse approximately a metre apart, but the likelihood of a link between these objects was enhanced by the discovery of another parallelopiped die and decorated astragalus in an archaeological trench to the west which explored layers of rubbish associated with the use of the wheelhouse (Fig. 2.17).

Normally when we find a die the assumption is that it was a gaming piece, but it is also possible these objects had a role in ritual practices, and I would argue that the presence of the objects in this location is an indication that

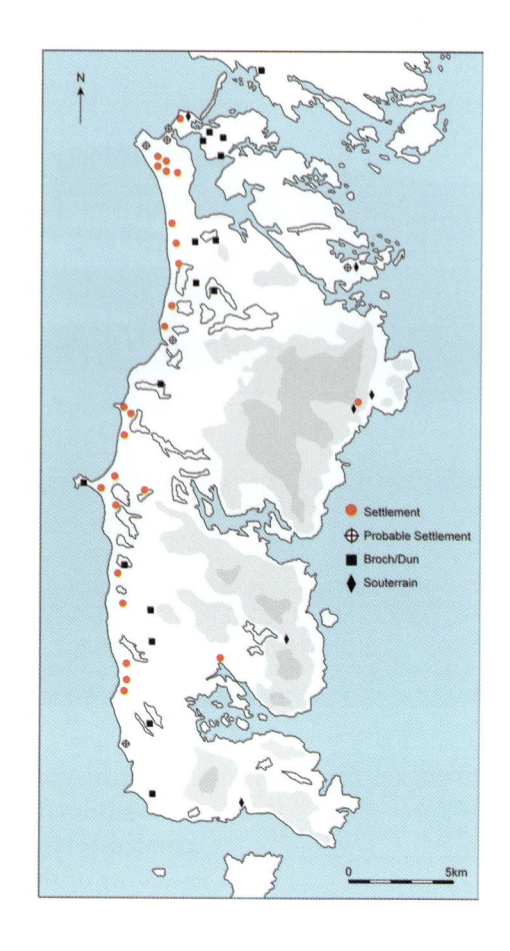

FIGURE 2.16. The distribution of Middle Iron Age settlements on South Uist.

FIGURE 2.17. The parallelopiped die and decorated astragalus found on mound 1, Bornais.

they were being used for divination. The burning down of the wheelhouse was clearly a traumatic event in the history of the settlement, no matter whether it was due to deliberate destruction by an enemy, or to an accident caused by domestic stupidity. It may have been necessary to consult the spirits, gods or ancestors for their advice on whether the wheelhouse should be rebuilt, or the settlement moved to another area nearby. In this case the decision was made using the die and astragalus in some form of ritual, and it was decided to rebuild the wheelhouse and place the ritual objects in the floor of the new house.

The rebuilding may have provided some continuity with the original wheelhouse, but it also seems to have involved a significant reconfiguration of the original house. It is difficult to be certain of the shape of the new house as it was systematically demolished when the settlement was finally abandoned. The east side of the original wheelhouse seems to have survived relatively intact and to have been used without much modification, but the west side was considerably altered, the projecting piers were demolished, and the entrance moved to face south. The new entrance threshold slabs were again deliberately left behind when the house was systematically demolished, suggesting they were one of the most significant features of the house. A best guess at the shape of the rebuilt house is that it had an internal area that was roughly trapezoidal and therefore it was no longer a wheelhouse (Fig. 2.18).

The principal feature in the interior of the new house was a hearth whose form seems to have replicated the plan of the house. The structure comprised a roughly trapezoidal box defined by thin upright stones on three sides and with

FIGURE 2.18. A view of the remains of the rebuilt wheelhouse on mound 1, Bornais.

FIGURE 2.19. A plan and photograph of the hearth in the rebuilt wheelhouse, showing the arrangement of cattle metapodials at the east end.

an open west end (Figs 2.19, 2.20). Unlike the hearth in the original wheelhouse, it had no internal slab base for the fire. Instead, the 'box' was allowed to fill up with ash from the peat fires that were lit here. The significance of the east end of the hearth was emphasised by an arc of upright cattle metapodials[10] that projected from two stone beach cobbles placed at the northeast and southeast

FIGURE 2.20. Excavating the hearth metapodials and adjacent floor layers. The hearth metapodials are pushed into the orange sand which represents the burnt down roof.

corners of the hearth box. On the north and south sides of the hearth further lines of cattle metapodials and some other bones were embedded in the floor, though not quite as regularly as the arc of metapodials at the east end. The arc of metapodials seems to deliberately mimic the curved east wall of the house, the only surviving structural element of the original wheelhouse.

The cattle metapodials are likely to have had a deep symbolic significance to the occupants that we can never really understand, but at a very basic level these bones indicated the importance of cattle to the agricultural economy (Fig. 2.21). Cattle are likely to have been the most prestigious of the domestic

FIGURE 2.21. Cleaning the central hearth in the rebuilt wheelhouse on Bornais mound 1.

animals owned by the occupants as they were the largest animal on the islands and carried the greatest amount of meat; they also provided milk and could be bled and were used for traction. In many societies the number of cattle owned was an indication of an individual's status.

The metapodials used to decorate this hearth came from at least seven animals and possibly as many as 12. Roughly 2,800 kg of meat could have been recovered by slaughtering seven cattle and this would be excessive even for a major feast. It is unlikely that all of these animals were slaughtered in one go and evidence for erosion and weathering of the bones suggests that some of the metapodials had been lying around for a long time before they were used in the hearth arrangement. Cattle metapodials are one of the most useful bones in the cattle skeleton as they are large, dense, long bones that are ideal for making bone points and handles. It is likely they were routinely collected and kept as a valuable raw material that would come in useful one day. Again, their use as a decorative element to the hearth is significant and might have been an attempt to emphasise the status of the household occupying the rebuilt house.

A careful analysis of the bones also highlights patterns that are significant though very subtle and probably not immediately obvious to visitors sitting in what would have been the gloomy interior of the house. The arc of bones at the end of the hearth was split; on the north side the bones were almost exclusively metacarpals (bones of the front leg), whereas on the south side they were almost exclusively metatarsals (bones of the back leg). The patterns were disrupted by one metatarsal on the metacarpal side and one metacarpal on the metatarsal side; both were positioned close to the end of the arc. Only the proximal ends of these bones were used in the eastern arc as the bones were snapped in half. This makes it more difficult to differentiate between front and back legs and it would have been almost impossible for a visitor sitting around the hearth in the Bornais house to appreciate the very distinctive arrangement of these bones. It seems this was a hidden pattern that meant something to the person who created the hearth, but exactly what that symbolism was we will never know.

Other hearths with animal surrounds are known in the Western Isles. The wheelhouse of A'Cheardach Bheag at the north end of South Uist had an arc of red deer mandibles (lower jaw bones) that were arranged around a roughly circular setting of stones that marked the primary hearth. Again, there seems to be a deliberate attempt to obscure the significance of the bones, as the jaw bones were placed in the floor with the teeth facing downwards and only the smooth undersurface of the bone was exposed. In the low gloomy light of the interior of the house it would be difficult to appreciate that this kerb was not just a collection of rounded pebbles. At Dun Bharabhat on Lewis a monumental roundhouse had a hearth defined by a setting of small upright slabs that was further embellished by a double line of animal teeth. A similar deposit of ox teeth was noted around the hearth in the wheelhouse at A'Cheardach Mhor on South Uist.

The hearth was a symbolically very important feature of the roundhouses in the Iron Age of Atlantic Scotland. It was almost always a significant structure in this society and formed the focus for social activity in a region with long dark winters where shelter from the elements was always an important concern. The critical significance of the hearth in these regions contrasts with the relatively insignificant hearths one finds in the Iron Age in southern England. These were seldom impressive constructions, and, in many buildings, they were completely absent. In Atlantic Scotland the hearth acted as a focal point of the house and the area around the hearth was conceived as quite different to the peripheral areas adjacent to the house wall. The central space was an open space designed for social activities that would have occurred in the light provided by the fire. The periphery, in contrast, was partitioned by piers projecting from the wall into rooms where individual privacy was possible. These spaces would have been relatively dark and possibly concealed by hanging fabrics or skins; they provided a place to sleep and to store materials.

The division of activity in the interior of the house into a centre and periphery may have provided a much broader conceptual cosmology that helped the occupants to understand and classify the social landscape they occupied. Each household believed themselves to be at the centre of their world, surrounded by a periphery that comprised other households. Together they created a community of closely connected families. It was a community that was relatively small scale, comprising perhaps six to 12 households that was coordinated, organised and arguably led by the household that occupied the broch. The broch symbolised the strength of the community, and its longevity as a structure provided a tangible link with the ancestors who had occupied this land for many generations in the past.

The presence of a well-defined floor and the recovery of a reasonable collection of bone and carbonised plant remains from the Bornais house suggests this structure was permanently occupied and was not an ancillary structure or spare room. It would be odd if it had not been occupied, as the amount of effort that went into rebuilding the house, creating a compact new floor on top of the burnt-down roof and constructing a fancy hearth, was substantial. It would almost certainly have been easier to build a new house at a new location than rebuild this ruin. There must have been a strong social imperative to continue living at this location and it seems unlikely it was solely based on the toss of a die.

The finds from the rebuilt house were concentrated at its centre and included bone pins, a bone bead and an antler finger-ring (Fig. 2.8). There was a scatter of isolated objects in the peripheral areas of the floor which included bone points, handles and waste material; there were no concentrations of stone tools in this floor layer. This distribution does not clearly identify any significant concentrations that indicate activity areas, but there is nevertheless a clear distinction between the decorative objects in the central public space behind the hearth and the more obviously prosaic and functional tools which were found in the private spaces of the periphery.

An antler finger-ring is an unusual find as very few obvious comparisons for this type of object are known in Atlantic Scotland. Andrea Smith, an expert in artefacts of this period, suggested that this segment of antler had been deliberately shaped into a large square bezel with shoulders on either side to resemble a distinctive Roman ring known as the 'Brancaster' type. This is found in the fourth to fifth century in Roman Britain and suggests that the inhabitants of Bornais had contacts beyond the islands and were aware of changes in dress and ornamentation that were taking place on the mainland.

Roman material culture is rare in the Western Isles, and it appears that though dress items, particularly brooches (Fig. 2.22), were circulating in the islands, they were not common. Only isolated finds have ever been found and there is no sign of concentrations to suggest that certain families had preferential access, as there was in southern Scotland. It is noticeable that the elaborate Roman brooches that have been found come from wheelhouses, such as Cill Donnain and Kilpheder, rather than brochs, which might indicate that the established island elites were opposed to contact with the empire.

FIGURE 2.22. A Roman brooch from the wheelhouse at Kilpheder (Cille Pheadair), South Uist. © National Museums Scotland.

The wider significance of these contacts with the outside world is an important question that we will consider later in this chapter.

A crisis

Sometime around the end of the sixth century or the beginning of the seventh century the inhabitants of the buildings on mound 1 decided they had to abandon the home they had occupied for somewhere between two and three hundred years. They moved 100 m to the north, to build a new settlement in the sand dunes at the location I refer to as mound 2 (Fig. 1.8).

The abandonment and destruction of the house on mound 1 was a carefully structured series of activities that marked a significant moment in the history of the settlement at Bornais. The first act was to cover the hearth and its associated bones with a discrete layer of relatively sterile sand that was intended to protect these fragile remains from disturbance during the dismantling of the house walls. The almost total removal of the stone walls of this structure must have been a very messy activity and it is difficult to imagine the hearth would have survived if it had been exposed.

Dismantling the structure probably began with the removal of the timber and turf roof over the central area. The timbers would have been carefully curated and reused in later structures. The removal of the walls and any surviving corbelled roofs would have almost immediately resulted in the collapse of the surrounding sand as the house was essentially built in a large sand pit. This might have motivated the work crew to leave the lower courses of the wall, but the walls were almost completely removed, with only a short stretch of the basal course surviving around the east side of the house. The presence of this stretch may be fortuitous, but it is clear that certain parts of the house were deliberately left undisturbed; the hearth was the most obvious element, but the stones of the entrance thresholds for both phases also survived when the walls had been completely removed on either side. This suggests that the surviving basal course of the wall had some social or ritual significance.

The removal of the stones had both practical and symbolic significance. The house was a source of good building materials which could be reused in any new structures, such as those that were being built on mound 2. The house stones were easily accessible and a lot closer than the primary source of building stone on the Ardvule peninsula. Their removal from mound 1 emphasised that this mound had been abandoned and yet it enabled a connection to be made between the houses by using recycled material with ancestral memories. Perhaps the hearth and the threshold stones embodied the original house and its occupants, whereas the walls could be envisaged as offspring that had moved on to a new life.

The abandoned house would have left a large unstable hole in the old settlement mound that would have filled both with sand collapsing from the exposed sides of the building pit and with windblown sand (Fig. 2.23). The presence of charcoal and artefact-rich layers just above the house floor suggests deposition was taking place immediately after the house was dismantled. The pottery assemblage from these layers was generally similar to that recovered from the house floor and there was a range of working debris, including simple tools

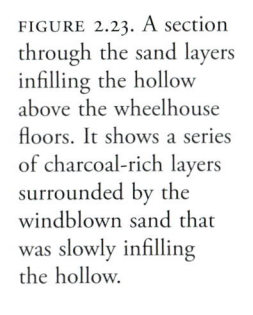

FIGURE 2.23. A section through the sand layers infilling the hollow above the wheelhouse floors. It shows a series of charcoal-rich layers surrounded by the windblown sand that was slowly infilling the hollow.

FIGURE 2.24. Weaving combs and weaving tablets from the charcoal layers filling the abandoned house. Note the wear marks around the holes at the corners of the weaving tablets.

and a few personal items. However, these layers also produced an exceptional collection of tools associated with textile production.

Four 'weaving' combs, three complete and one fragmentary, were found (Fig. 2.24), as well as three weaving tablets and a complete bone needle. Weaving combs, though iconic Atlantic Iron Age objects, are not very common discoveries in the Western Isles. Weaving tablets are even less frequent discoveries and very few are known from Atlantic Iron Age sites. The rarity, the undamaged nature of these objects and their presence in this destruction layer suggests their deposition was a deliberate act designed in part to mark the end of the house. These objects were clearly related to textile-working, and it raises the question of why this activity was associated with this house. Was the family that occupied the house known for their skilled production of high-quality textiles? There was very little evidence for textile production during the use of the house, but this is not a decisive argument: there would be no reason for material culture related to the use of a house to survive in a house that was routinely cleaned.

It is important to compare the sequence at Bornais with other wheelhouses, particularly those well-excavated examples that have provided good evidence for the end of wheelhouse use (Fig. 2.25). At A'Cheardach Mhor the fill of the wheelhouse was curiously devoid of stones or of any evidence for the natural decay of the building. If one accepts the evidence from the well-preserved wheelhouses at Cnip and Jarlshof, then the walls of this structure were originally

FIGURE 2.25. Drawn sections through the abandoned deposits in the wheelhouses at Kilpheder (Cille Pheadair), A'Cheardach Bheag and A'Chearadach Mhor (from top to bottom).

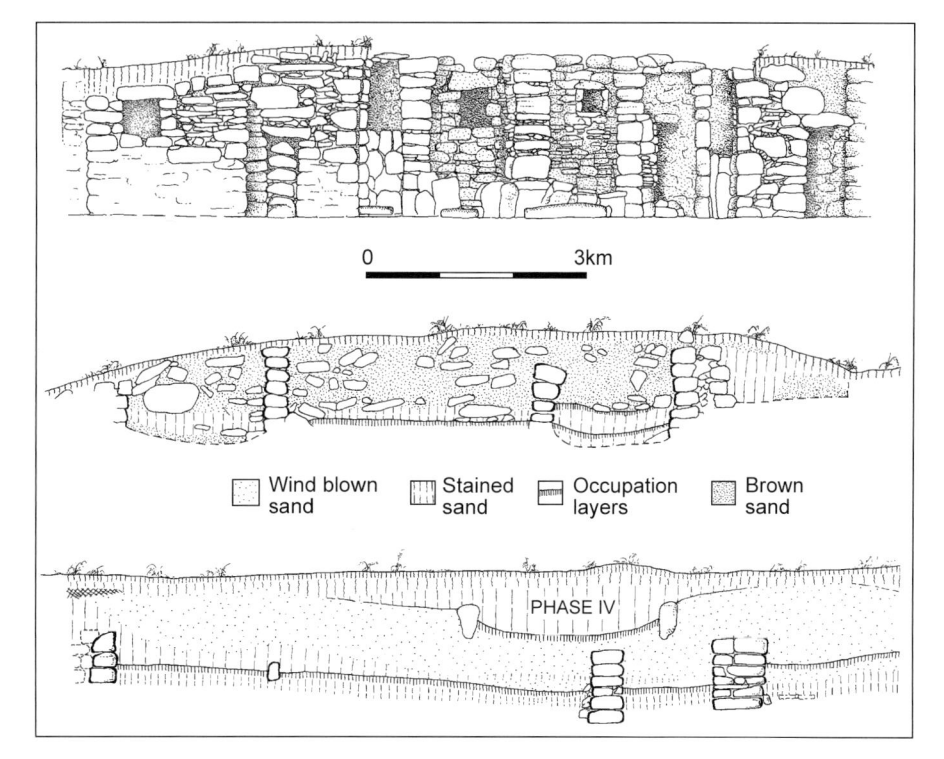

several metres high, and the peripheral compartments should have had corbelled vaults. These structural features do not survive; the building appears to have been deliberately dismantled and then allowed to fill up with windblown sand. The systematic nature of the stone removal suggests this was a specific event that marked the abandonment of the house and was not a long-drawn-out process of opportunistic robbing.

At A'Cheardach Bheag the evidence is quite different: a homogeneous brown sand infilled the structure and contained a large quantity of slabs. However, the drawings of the excavated houses indicate these stones were lying flat, which could not have occurred if the structure had collapsed after abandonment; in that scenario, the stones should have been pitched at an angle and leaning against the walls and piers. It seems likely, therefore, that the structure was dismantled and then deliberately filled in. At Sollas the evidence suggests a sequence very similar to A'Cheardach Mhor: the wheelhouse was systematically, but only partially dismantled, and allowed to fill with windblown sand. A similar situation was also noted by the author during the excavation of a wheelhouse in the Allasdale Dunes in Barra.

One of the few wheelhouses that does not appear to have been deliberately dismantled was the wheelhouse at Kilpheder. When first excavated, the walls of this structure survived to a height of over 2 m and showed clear evidence for the lower levels of the corbelled vaults. This structure was infilled with blown sand and showed no signs of any secondary occupation. Even at this site, however, there was no evidence in the fill for the upper levels of corbelling and these stones must have been deliberately removed.

Within one or two hundred years of their construction many of these wheelhouses had been systematically dismantled and abandoned. This can be clearly documented at Bornais and many other sites, and contrasts with the sequences of houses built one on top of another which is found in the later Norse phases at both Bornais and Cille Pheadair. Avoiding the sites of abandoned wheelhouses is surprising, as surveys of the Uist machair clearly demonstrate that settlement remains were still focused on certain specific locales on the machair plain throughout the first millennia BC and AD.

The reason for the abandonment of mound 1 is impossible for us to understand, but it seems unlikely to be for strictly economic reasons. The distance between the two Bornais mounds was not significant (100 m) and the topography of each location was identical. Moving from mound 1 brought no intrinsic agricultural advantages, the new settlement was not nearer to a freshwater resource or to the coast. The decision appears to have been cultural and, in some way, related to the beliefs of the settlement's occupants and may indicate a desire for a new beginning. More significantly it seems such beliefs were not restricted to the occupants of Bornais, as settlement abandonment and disruption seems to be widespread in this period. A major dislocation of the settlement record can be seen across the Western Isles in the middle of the first millennium AD and this could reflect cataclysmic climate changes that will be discussed later in this chapter.

Unfortunately, the complexity of the archaeology at Bornais meant that although we could identify the existence of a settlement on mound 2 dating to the seventh and eighth centuries, it was covered by the earliest Viking remains and we could never excavate a large enough area to fully understand the nature of this underlying early settlement. Fragments of structures were discovered underneath the Viking longhouses, and possible floor layers were identified, but these were only partial survivals, and much was destroyed by subsequent Viking activities.

The finds recovered from these seventh- and eighth-century deposits included some distinctive objects, most noticeably a bone comb and several bone pins (Fig. 2.26) whose shape and decoration indicate a date in the later part of the first millennium AD, before the Viking conquest of the island. The pottery was also characteristic of this period and demonstrated a decline in the quality of the ceramic traditions on the islands. The vessels tended to be large, slack-shouldered jars with rough unsmoothed surfaces; there was no decorative element, and the flaring rims were simple and unembellished.

The first millennium AD development in the settlement at Bornais was paralleled by the sequence at the Udal on North Uist. The extensive excavation of that settlement focused on two large settlement mounds, the north mound and the south mound. On the south mound the settlement sequence culminated in the construction of the complex wheelhouse settlement which we described earlier in this chapter. On the adjacent north mound, the settlement sequence started with a group of distinctive buildings described as 'simple oval-bodied buildings 5m by 4m with small satellite cells, slab lined hearths lying along the long axis, and a single internal revetted platform'[11] and culminated in 'figure-of-eight' houses or cellular houses, which date to the seventh or eighth century (Fig. 2.27). These cellular houses are typical of the architectural developments in the second half of the first millennium AD. Monumental roundhouses such

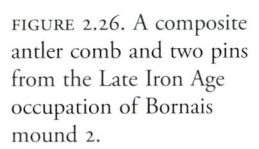

FIGURE 2.26. A composite antler comb and two pins from the Late Iron Age occupation of Bornais mound 2.

FIGURE 2.27. A view of a badly robbed Pictish house at the Udal, North Uist. © IAC, Udal Archives.

as wheelhouses and brochs stopped being constructed around the middle of the first millennium AD, and were replaced by smaller, less impressive structures that had more complex ground plans, with separate small rooms replacing the large open spaces of the earlier roundhouses.

The settlement at Bostaidh on the island of Great Bernera in Lewis is an important example of a Late Iron Age settlement from the period immediately preceding the Viking incursions. The site has a complex architectural history which is only imperfectly known as an unknown portion of the settlement was removed by the sea and much of it remains unexcavated.[12] Nevertheless, enough was excavated to reveal three largely complete cellular buildings, which the excavator refers to as 'ventral buildings'[13] as they have an axial symmetry which elsewhere has been used to argue for a slightly later date than the more irregular forms of cellular structure. The structures appear to be constructed in sequence and there was evidence for earlier structures and later structures immediately adjacent to the main area as well as modifications to the main structures. Despite this chronological development the material culture is homogeneous and suggests the settlement as exposed was short-lived. The ceramic assemblage is overwhelmingly of slack-shouldered or straight-sided, crudely made, undecorated jars that belong to the final phase of the Late Iron Age, and this date is supported by the presence of a substantial assemblage of double-sided composite antler combs. Both of these types of artefacts were recovered from the Late Iron Age deposits on Bornais mound 2.

The main house at Bostaidh (Fig. 2.28) gives a good indication of the character of the structures occupied by the inhabitants of the islands prior to the Viking settlement. It had two rooms oriented north to south, the south room

FIGURE 2.28. A plan of the Pictish house at Bostadh on Lewis. © Tim Neighbour.

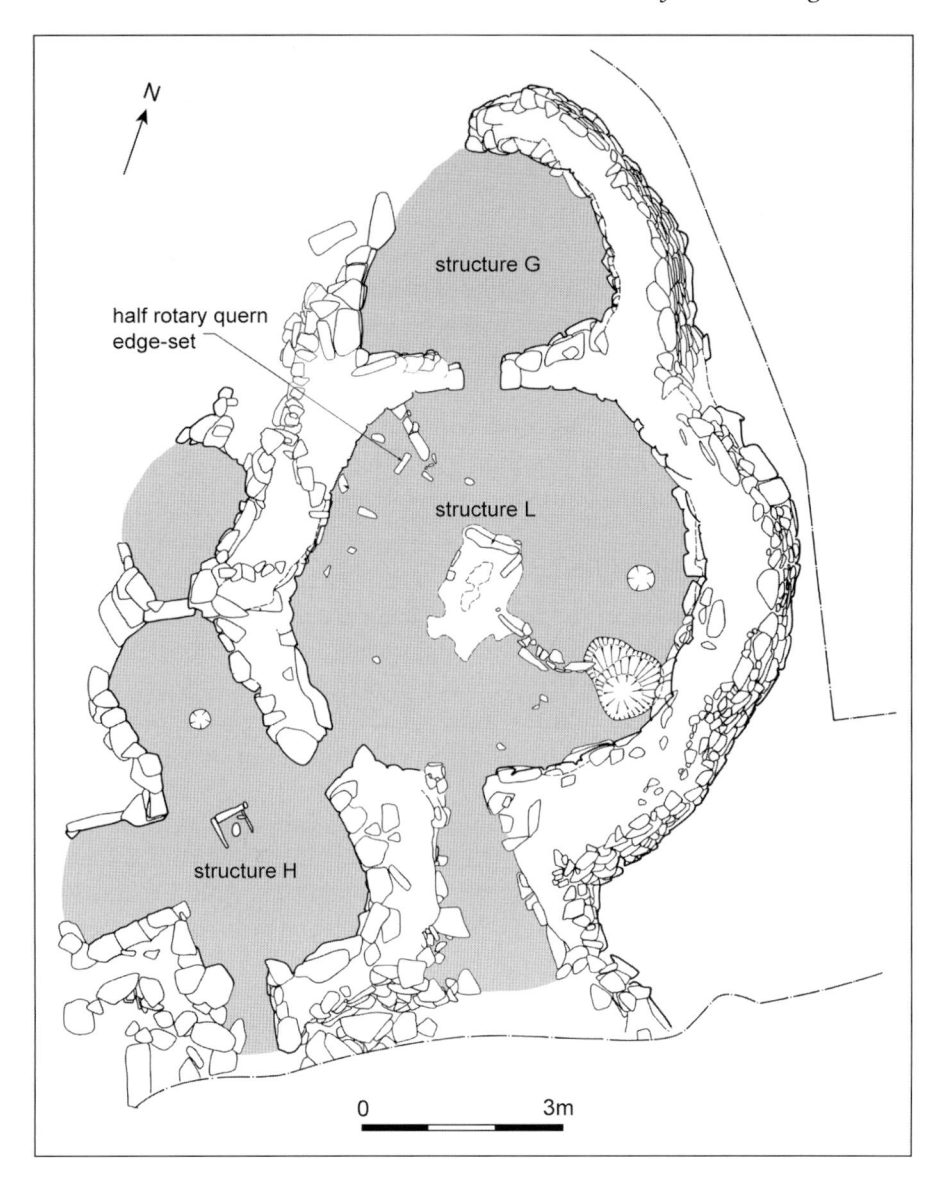

being 5.8 m in diameter and the north room 4 m by 3.1 m. There was a main south-facing entrance accessed by a short passage. A subsidiary entrance to the southwest provided access to a small ancillary room belonging to an earlier structure that was partially dismantled and rebuilt when the two-room main house was constructed. The hearth was in the main southern room and though another hearth existed in the ancillary room to the southwest, it is possible this was associated with the earlier building.

The Late Iron Age settlement at Bostaidh was reoccupied in the Norse period but there is no evidence for any continuity between the two periods as the Late Iron Age structures were sealed by over a metre of windblown sand.

The settlement is located in a narrow valley with only a limited area of flat land suitable for agriculture and occupation, so it is difficult to assess any deliberate continuity of occupation at this location where there was so little scope for relocation.

There is a consistent pattern across the islands that wheelhouses seldom show any evidence for secondary occupation in the second half of the first millennium AD and that later settlements, such as the Udal and Bostaidh, do not show evidence for significant earlier settlement activity at their locations. The only sites which exhibited continuous occupation across the sixth-century divide were brochs. The evidence from Dun Vulan on South Uist, Beirgh on Lewis and Dun Cueir on Barra demonstrated that these high-status residences generally had much longer, and more continuous periods of occupation that extended through the first millennium AD. They only really stopped being occupied with the Viking colonisation of the islands.

The appearance of 'individuals'

The significant disruption of the settlement sequence that we can demonstrate at Bornais and the Udal coincided with major changes in the material culture used by the inhabitants of the islands. Some of these changes suggest a gradual evolution of the indigenous cultures of the islands, but there were more abrupt changes that indicated the increasing importance of political developments on the Scottish mainland.

Combs changed from single-sided, high-backed combs such as those found at Dun Cueir and the Udal (Fig. 2.29) to simpler double-sided combs such as the example found at Bornais (Fig. 2.26). These composite combs become very important after the Viking conquest of the islands and will reappear several times in this book. The excavations at Bostaidh recovered an assemblage of six complete or near complete combs that represents one of the best collections of this date from the islands. With one exception these were double-sided combs with similarly spaced teeth on both sides, held in place by iron rivets. The sideplates were decorated with ring-and-dot motifs linked by saltire crosses. This unusually large assemblage of combs was associated with a substantial amount of antler waste which may suggest combs were being made at the settlement.

Bone pins were an important aspect of clothing in the early historic period and there was a change from very generic simple pins in the earlier part of the first millennium to more distinctive 'hipped' pins in the second half of the first millennium. The later pins were often small and included examples with elaborately decorated pinheads. At Bornais several distinctive pins were discovered, including a rare zoomorphic example with a simple dog's head carving (Fig. 2.26).

Decorative metal pins were popular in this period, and these were made in iron, copper alloy and silver. The status of the wearer was almost certainly determined by the use of more prestigious metal and the most elaborate decorative effects. One of the most distinctive types of pin present at this time

FIGURE 2.29. The fragmentary remains of an elaborate Late Iron Age comb from The Udal. © IAC, Udal Archives.

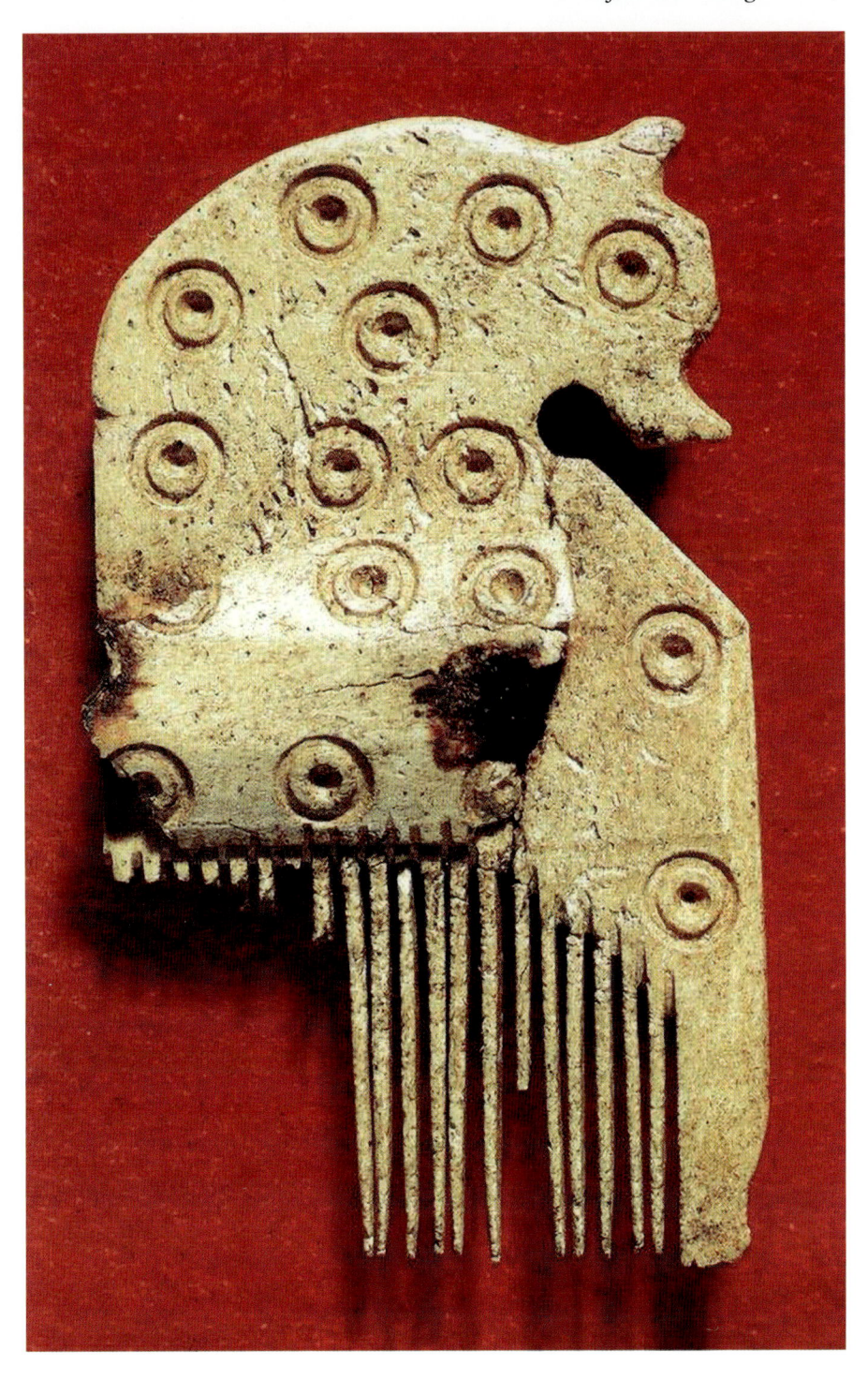

was the hand pin which has a decorative terminal in the form of a semi-circle with several small cylinders arranged along the straight edge. The semi-circle is thought to represent the palm of the hand and the cylinders the fingers. The presence of clay moulds for the casting of hand pins at the broch of Loch na Beirgh, Lewis and the settlement at Loch Olabhat in North Uist is interesting, as both sites are in relatively infertile agricultural landscapes (Fig. 2.30).[14] It seems that prestigious metalworking was being undertaken in relatively isolated locations and was not integrated in day-to-day practices. It is possible that these metalworking episodes represent short periods of activity by itinerant craftworkers moving around the islands.

Continuity across the middle of the first millennium AD was demonstrated by the development of the pottery. As already mentioned, the production of well-made ceramics in large quantities was a feature of the island communities of Atlantic Scotland and that distinguished them from their neighbours

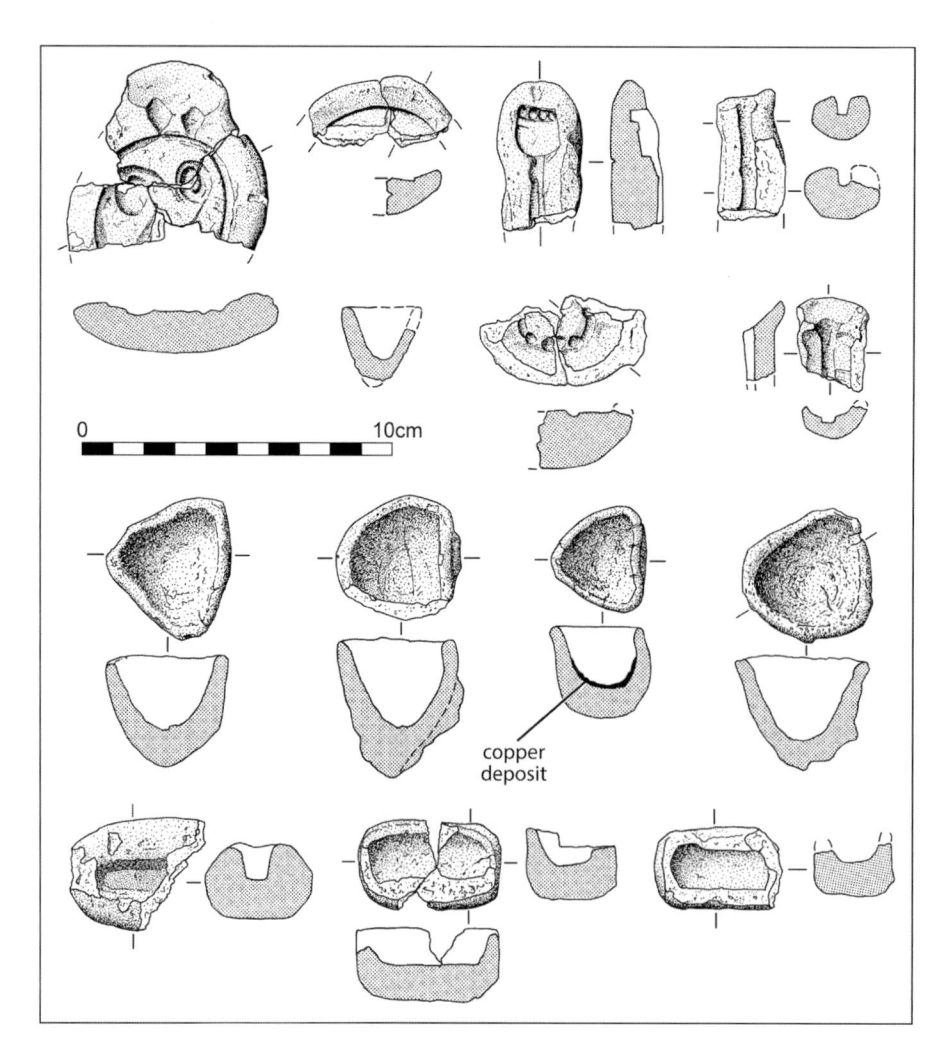

FIGURE 2.30. A selection of metalworking debris from a settlement at Loch Olibhat, including moulds for hand pins, brooches and decorated discs, crucibles and bar moulds. © Ian Armit.

FIGURE 2.31. A comparison of the large well-made vessel from the early first millennium wheelhouse on Bornais mound 1 with a smaller rather crudely made vessels found in the later first millennium deposits on Bornais mound 2.

in mainland Scotland. This pottery tradition continued throughout the first millennium AD. There was a pronounced deterioration in the quality of the ceramics produced at Bornais after the settlement had been relocated in the seventh and eighth centuries; the surface of the pots was no longer carefully smoothed, and given a uniform black colouring, the symbolically important wavy cordon was no longer applied and the distinctive jar shape with pronounced belly, neck and flaring rim was much less pronounced and eventually disappeared altogether (Fig. 2.31). These changes suggest a continuation of the pottery-making tradition, but possibly a gradual decline in the social significance of ceramics to convey important social statements about the producers and users of these objects.

These changes may seem to be inconsequential changes in fashion, but they probably indicate much more significant changes in power relations within the island communities. The decorative emphasis on the Middle Iron Age ceramics indicates the importance of communal food consumption, and probably drinking, at the central hearths in the large roundhouses of this period. The functional simplicity of the ceramics in the later Iron Age suggests this communal activity declined in social importance. Instead, the elaborate decoration of the human body became increasingly important. Hair had to be carefully combed, and clothes had to be decorated with elaborate and increasingly prestigious pins and brooches. These changes stress the increasing importance of the individual and suggest these individuals had the ability to acquire power and influence in these societies that was separate from the control of land and agriculture. We will return to the significance of these changes later in this chapter.

The 'Little Ice Age'

The disruption to the settlement record in the first millennium AD was not only a feature of the settlement sequence across the Western Isles, but has been recorded widely in both the historical and archaeological records of many societies throughout Europe at that time. The widespread nature of this disruption has encouraged scholars to suggest that the underlying cause of change was a powerful natural disaster, and in recent years a consensus has coalesced around the theory that a series of three significant volcanic eruptions in AD 536, AD 540 and AD 547 were the principal trigger for this change. The source of these eruptions is much disputed but North America seems to be the current favourite location. These were major volcanic eruptions which spread dust clouds around the globe, and they would undoubtedly have had a considerable effect on the weather as these dust clouds excluded and restricted the amount of sunlight. The cumulative effect of the three eruptions in close succession has been argued to have created a prolonged period of cold summers that lasted for over 100 years, until the middle of the seventh century. This is known variously as the 'Late Antique Little Ice Age', the 'early medieval climate anomaly' or the 'Dark Age climatic deterioration'.[15]

In northwest Europe the best evidence for the climatic effect of these volcanic eruptions are the tree ring records. Trees preserve a record of the climate at their location within the rings they form every year. If the conditions for growth have been good, then the rings will be wide; if the conditions have been more difficult, the rings will be narrow. Long-lived trees provide a history of the climate in their region which can span hundreds of years. Dendrochronological sequences extending back to the Neolithic have now been constructed for many areas in northwest Europe using long lived trees, large timbers in old buildings, timbers from archaeological sites and trees that have collapsed into bogs. The best-preserved record from northwest Europe is for Ireland and it is clear from the severely restricted growth of the tree-rings in the years AD 536 and AD 541 that there was a major climatic event in this period. The warming effect of the Atlantic currents may have meant it was not as cold as some continental areas, but it was very wet, and this would certainly have restricted the agricultural productivity of the region.

A complementary phenomenon that might have contributed to social and economic disruption in the middle of the first millennium AD was the spread of bubonic plague. Recent scientific advances in the study of DNA have included the discovery of *Yersina pestis* in Britain in the first millennium AD and this confirms the more ambiguous historical record that plague was present. The occurrence of a particularly virulent epidemic in the mid-sixth century is not very clear in the British historical records, though this may simply be because historical sources are not very extensive for this period. However, new genetic evidence from Anglo-Saxon cemeteries in the English Midlands makes it clear that the plague was present from the middle of the sixth century.[16] Its rapid spread throughout Europe may have been exacerbated by the climatic deterioration as people forced by bad weather to live indoors in close proximity to their animals would be increasingly likely to be infected by fleas carrying the disease.

The Picts

Another important change seen at this time was the political developments occurring in mainland Scotland. In the first half of the first millennium AD the loose confederations and regional groupings that characterised the political structures of northern Britain began to coalesce into more rigidly structured organisations that could be called tribes, and that would eventually become kingdoms. The initial driving force in these political developments was undoubtedly the appearance of the Romans. The violent intrusion of the military might of the Roman Empire forced the relatively fragmented societies of northern Britain to come together, initially probably under charismatic war leaders who had some success against the invaders. The Romans would have encouraged the development of these leaders by offering gifts, to buy peace and political influence in the region without the necessity for conquest and sustained military control. The Roman Imperial administration actively encouraged tribes to create leaders and central places as these were a lot easier to conquer, negotiate with or control than leaderless communities.

In the early centuries of the first millennium AD, Ptolemy's 'Geography' records the presence of up to 18 tribes in Scotland and provides the earliest names for the Hebrides (Dumna) and Skye (Scetis) that have been recorded.[17] The coherence and accuracy of the tribes located by Ptolemy is open to debate but there were undoubtedly regional variations in the nature of settlement that suggest significant regional distinctions existed within Scotland. These may have been used to create a sense of regional identity that was important to the local inhabitants, but it is debatable whether there were established leaders and preeminent central settlements that would have warranted the identification of tribes in the second century, when Ptolemy identified them. The detail provided by this early source disappears as we move into the later centuries of the Roman occupation of Britain, and it is in the third and fourth centuries that the more generic name 'Pict' started to be applied to the people of northern Scotland. At first this name was used by the Romans to refer to any barbarians living in northern Britain beyond Hadrian's Wall, and the term may have been derived from their habit of painting or possibly tattooing their bodies. These confederations provided a significant opponent to the Empire and several references suggest they were an effective military force that could make alliances and combine forces with their neighbours to put severe pressure on the Romanised settlements of northern England.

In the fifth and sixth centuries the name Pict appears to have shifted from a pejorative term used to describe the northern barbarians to a name proudly embraced by the indigenous inhabitants of northern Britain. This coincides with an increasing political centralisation of the region and the emergence of powerful kings in the sixth century. A notable individual was Bridei who lived next to the River Ness in the second half of the sixth century and who is mentioned in several of the Irish annals. Bridei had a significant role in Adomnan's life of St Columba, and this suggests the increasing importance of the northern Picts of Fortriu, the area around the Moray Firth. In the seventh century a dynasty developed in this region that dominated northern Britain, and records suggest an expansionist policy with attacks on Orkney and the Scots of Argyll. Eventually another individual, also named Bridei, became sufficiently powerful to defeat and kill Ecgfrith the king of the Northumbrians at the Battle of Nechtansmere in AD 685. This effectively ended the Anglo-Saxon invasion of the lands north of the Forth and marked the consolidation of the Kingdom of the Picts.

The historic record for the Picts is complemented by a similarly complex archaeological record, which though still imperfectly known, is beginning to emerge from the so-called 'Dark Ages'.[18] The most obvious evidence for the emergence of a very different cultural group, and one that spanned most of mainland Scotland north of the Forth Clyde isthmus, was the development of a very distinctive art style characterised by a range of unique symbols that were synonymous with the Picts.[19] These symbols are most commonly but not exclusively found on large memorial stones located in the landscapes of eastern Scotland. Their distribution extends north to the islands of Orkney and Shetland where stones and other aspects of material culture incised with Pictish symbols are relatively common discoveries. One of the most significant recent finds was an exquisite, incised bear that was carved on a slab which seems to have been an integral part of a late wheelhouse at Old Scatness in Shetland that was very similar in form to the wheelhouse at Bornais.

Pictish symbols are much less frequent discoveries in western Scotland. In Argyll, the territory of the Scots, an alternative tradition of carved crosses arose which derived from close connections between Argyll and Ireland and the importance of the Columban church in the conversion of the inhabitants of northern Britain. Nevertheless, there is a group of stones with Pictish symbols in Skye and a couple of outliers are present in the Outer Hebrides. On Pabbay, one of the smaller islands south of Barra, a large slab of local gneiss was found on a mound on the edge of a limited area of machair on the summit of which was a small chapel. Three motifs were carved into one face of the slab; the lowest was a flower symbol, just above that was a V-rod and crescent symbol and at the top of the stone was an incised Latin cross. The cross was more deeply incised than the Pictish symbols and its rather cramped position at the top of the stone has led to the suggestion that it was a later alteration to an original purely Pictish stone.

A second stone was found on the beach at Strome Shunamul near Benbecula airport. This is a polygonal slab of gneiss with two symbols incised on a flat face (Fig. 2.32). One symbol is a split rectangle with two symmetrical curves in one half; this was a fairly common symbol that is thought to represent a single-sided comb in a case. The other symbol is a circle containing three smaller circles joined by connecting lines which is slightly more unusual. These stones indicate that the islands had political connections with the Pictish kingdom to the east and there is no evidence of the elaborate high crosses that are associated with the Columban centres in Iona and Islay.

There were a number of simple crosses inscribed on stones in the Western Isles, but these are restricted to the southern isles, extending only as far north as the island of Taransay in Harris, though there is also a cluster on North Rona. There are no simple crosses in Lewis, which is surprising as there are concentrations of simple chapels on the coast of Lewis which were often associated with early Christianity. The chronology of both the simple cross incised slabs and the chapels are problematic and neither can be said to be accurately dated, so

FIGURE 2.32. The Pictish symbol stone from Benbecula in the National Museum Scotland. © National Museums Scotland.

it would be presumptive to assume they indicated the presence of a pre-Norse church in the islands.[20]

An exceptionally well-preserved eremitic monastery survives on North Rona, one of the smallest and most isolated islands in the Hebrides to have had a resident population (Fig. 2.33). The island is small (only 109 ha), and lies 71 km from the northern tip of Lewis. It is reputed to have been occupied by St Ronan but an alternative explanation for the name is that it derives from *hraun-øy*, the Old Norse for 'rough island'. On the southwest corner of this roughly triangular island, in an area with evidence for settlement remains and extensive cultivation ridges, is an oval enclosure containing an apparently early Christian oratory which was extended by the construction of a later twelfth-century chapel. The

FIGURE 2.33. An aerial view of the island of North Rona and a detail of the settlement complex which includes the Early Christian Oratory in the enclosure in the centre of the image. © Historic Environment Scotland.

oratory survives as a rectangular building 3.4 m by 2.2 m whose walls slope in gradually to form a triangular vaulted roof. A substantial collection of over 12 cross-inscribed slabs have been found in the surrounding enclosure, where they acted as grave markers in the recent past. This is a remarkable archaeological site which is unfortunately inaccessible to most visitors to the islands, but that is probably why it survives to the present day.

The presence of a substantive early Christian activity on the islands was also indicated by the occurrence of eight place names containing the element Papar. These include names such as Pabbay (four examples known) which means island of the priests and Payable (three examples known) which refers to settlements of the priests and Pabinish (one example known) the headland of the priests. The names are widely scattered along the Hebrides from the Bishop's Islands, south of Barra, to the Eye peninsula near Stornoway on Lewis. The place names suggest locations where the Vikings encountered priests and to some extent interacted with them. A recent survey of the significance of these names in the western and northern isles argued that they may represent locations of enhanced agricultural fertility where the Vikings could extract provisions for raiding parties heading south.[21] It is also noticeable that names of this type are restricted to the islands north of the Ardnamurchan peninsula and that this may indicate a specific association with a Pictish church that was clearly differentiated from the Columban church that dominated the landscape south of Ardnamurchan.

Understanding the significance of the sources is exacerbated because the historical record for the conversion of the islands is non-existent. Knowledge of the early Christian activity in the west is largely based on the *Chronicles of Iona* and the various sources associated with the life of Columba. If these sources are to be taken at face value, then there appears to have been very little definitive evidence for activity in the Outer Hebrides. However, this is a problematic observation as the Columban Church was very active in the Inner Hebrides with historical evidence for the establishment of a monastery by Donnain on Eigg, and good archaeological evidence for a monastery on Canna. A monastery was also established by Maelrubha on the Scottish mainland north of Skye at Applecross in AD 673 and if monks were progressing this far north, it is difficult to understand why they would avoid the Outer Hebrides. The most likely scenario is that the islands were firmly aligned with the Kingdom of the Picts in the seventh and eighth centuries and that the influence of the Church of Columba was deliberately blocked during this period due to its close association with the Scots. Their conversion was probably undertaken by different and more historically obscure figures.

A burial at Cille Pheadair

Another important feature of the archaeological record for the first millennium AD is the emergence of a formal burial style. Iron Age burials of the first millennium BC are unusually rare throughout Britain and, with the exception of an idiosyncratic group in East Yorkshire, cemeteries are generally unknown, with isolated burials as well as human body parts deposited in and around settlements. As we move through into the first millennium AD, however, things begin to change. In southern Pictland cemeteries become common and these are characterised by burials laid fully extended normally on their back, in graves defined by stone slabs, known as long-cist cemeteries.[22]

An example of a long-cist cemetery has been discovered at Galson on the north-west coast of Lewis. At least 14 burials have been recorded falling out of a sand dune that is being eroded by the sea.[23] These discoveries have been recovered over most of the second half of the twentieth century and are associated with evidence of a settlement probably of Middle Iron Age date though there is evidence for Norse activity somewhere close by. Three burials have been radiocarbon dated and indicate the cemetery belongs to the third and fourth centuries AD and pre-dates the Christian occupation of the islands. Inhumations eroding from the sand dunes around the coast are not unusual discoveries, but until radiocarbon dating becomes routine these will be difficult to date and understanding the context and significance of these isolated discoveries is problematic.

One of the most interesting discoveries was of a burial of a woman, between 35 and 45 years old, on the beach at Cille Pheadair, just to the south of the Norse settlement discussed later in this book. She was placed in a stone-lined grave under a square cairn, 2.5 m by 2.5 m, that was defined by short upright slabs laid on edge and probably with four tall corner stones, though all but one of these had been removed (Fig. 2.34). The body of the cairn was a single layer of carefully laid flat slabs that were rounded by water, and this was covered by a layer of beach pebbles. The grave was aligned roughly north to south, with the feet to the north, and ran almost diagonally across the interior of the square cairn. The body may have originally been laid out on her back with her hands crossed on her chest, but she had been disturbed sometime after her initial burial when her body was partially decayed. This disturbance involved moving her hands so that they lay down the side of her body, removing her sternum (breastbone) and twisting the upper half of the body so that she faced towards the west. To maintain this position one of the side slabs at the edge of grave was removed and placed behind her back. All of this took place before the burial was sealed by the overlying cairn, as there was no sign that the slabs of the cairn had ever been disturbed.[24]

FIGURE 2.34. John Raven excavating the Pictish burial surrounded by the kerb of the square cairn at Cille Pheadair. © Mike Parker Pearson.

Detailed analysis of the strontium and oxygen isotopes of her teeth suggests this woman was not a local islander. She appears to have been born and lived her early years some distance from the islands, either in eastern Scotland or somewhere further south, such as Ireland or England. She moved after she was about four years old and may then have lived much closer, possibly on Skye or the northern mainland, but her arrival in the Western Isles occurred relatively late in her life.

Two radiocarbon dates have been obtained from the burial. The first date of AD 640–780 (at 95% confidence) placed the burial in the period after the Bornais settlement had moved from mound 1 to mound 2, but this date was later than most of the dates that have been obtained from burials like this in other areas of Scotland, and a new date of AD 428–579 was obtained in recent years which seems to fit much better with the larger corpus of dates from these burials.

A very similar burial was found at Sandwick in Unst, Shetland. Two cairns were excavated on an eroding sandy beach, again close to a much later Norse settlement. The most interesting cairn was a parallelogram with sides 4.25 m long, defined by upright slabs and with erect monoliths in the corners and at the midpoints of the sides. Placed in a grave underneath the cairn was a woman, roughly 50 years old, who was laid on her side. The body was sealed by an alignment of seven large cover slabs which formed part of the overlying layer of water-worn blocks that formed the body of the cairn. The blocks were covered with a layer of small beach pebbles which included a large number of quartz pebbles. A radiocarbon date of AD 422–640 was obtained from the burial.

Comparable burials are known from mainland Scotland, and these are concentrated in the agriculturally rich areas of lowland Scotland, though they are known throughout most of the eastern counties. Cemeteries with cairns comparable to the Cille Pheadair cairn were found at Ackergill in Caithness, Garbeg near Loch Ness, and at Lundin Links in Fife. A more common occurrence in these lowlands are burials defined by a surrounding ditch which is all that remains of an earthen mound or barrow destroyed by centuries of agricultural activity. These enclosures can be either square or circular and they normally have a long, thin grave at the centre that suggests an extended inhumation, though due to the acidic soil conditions in most of Scotland, the preservation of human remains is rare, and often only the occasional tooth survives.

Most of the barrows and cairns that survive are small, and they occur in fairly tightly clustered cemeteries which differentiates them from Bronze Age barrow cemeteries. The barrows/cairns are often arranged in rows, and some are actually conjoined which suggests that kin relationships were important and were being marked out by this proximity. The largest concentrations of these barrow/cairn cemeteries are in North Fife and Angus and the Mearns. They are relatively common along the coast of the Moray Firth, and they extend as far as Caithness and the eastern glens of Inverness-shire. Only isolated examples are known from the western seaboard, but two examples have been identified on the Hebrides.

Small rectangular and circular cairn cemeteries dating to the Medieval period are known in other areas of Britain. Good examples have been excavated in Wales and Ireland and there are small groups in southwestern Scotland which seem quite separate from the distributions discussed above. A much earlier tradition with this type of burial is known in East Yorkshire, where many cemeteries of small square barrows, numbering in their hundreds, were created as a distinctive regional tradition in the middle of the pre-Roman Iron Age *c.* 300–200 BC. There seems to be no direct connection between these cemeteries and the much later cemeteries of northern Britain. Nevertheless, in both periods and regions the creation of these proscribed burial traditions was being used to make a statement about the identities of both the individuals buried and the communities they belonged to. The presence of a well-defined grave sealed by a mound surrounded by a boundary isolated and separated the individual from their community, clearly providing them with some independence and agency even in death. It suggests that some individuals were different and could claim a status and significance in these communities. They had the power to act in ways that other people didn't and deserved to be commemorated in death.

The construction of the cairn at Cille Pheadair may have been a recognition that the individual buried there was special. She came from the mainland, and perhaps this had provided her with a position in Hebridean society. She was possibly part of a deliberate attempt to control the islands by the developing Kingdom of the Picts: supporting a particular family in the isles by creating an alliance through marriage would be a common mechanism for achieving political influence. The cairn made these connections clearly visible to anyone who participated in the funeral and who visited the location in the years after its construction.

Conclusion

In this chapter I have attempted to provide the historical background to the Viking colonisation of the Western Isles. I explore the archaeological evidence for settlement at Bornais in the first millennium AD, which comprised an important fourth- to fifth-century house that was burnt down, reoccupied and then systematically dismantled and infilled prior to movement to a new location just 100 m to the north. The evidence from the original settlement is well preserved and makes a significant contribution to our understanding of the nature of settlement in the first half of the first millennium AD. This was a period when the islands appear to have been densely occupied and to have had vibrant and innovative cultural traditions that were regionally distinctive. Brochs and wheelhouses are amongst the most spectacular monumental buildings found in Europe and they represent an adaptation to the local environment which was innovative and informative. The ability of independent local communities is emphatically demonstrated by the construction of these buildings, and they were clearly designed to impress their neighbours and to deter any thoughts of aggressive acts.

This society was transformed in the middle of the first millennium AD, and it is clear that there was a climatic event of considerable significance in the middle of the sixth century which would have led to a period of severe weather that could well have significantly reduced the agricultural capacity of the land surrounding the settlements. Exactly how this affected the fragile machair landscapes where most of the settlement and agricultural land was located is unclear. An increase in the prevalence of storms and extreme gales may have destabilised the machair and encouraged large-scale erosion and redeposition of windblown sand. This may explain why settlements such as Bornais changed location at this time, and why most of the wheelhouses in the Western Isles have little evidence for continuous settlement across the first millennium AD.

This environmental catastrophe also seems to have impacted on the cultural independence of the islands. Monumental houses are not a feature of the latter half of the first millennium AD and the significant emphasis on regional and local identities seems to be subsumed by identities concerned with individual status and an association with the emerging Pictish state. This is most obviously demonstrated by the presence of Pictish symbol stones and high-status metalwork. The identification of sites belonging to this period is also much less common, and whilst this may be due to the reduced visibility of non-monumental buildings and the decline in quality of the local ceramics, it may reflect a decline in population levels. This might have been caused by the spread of the plague which seems to have followed the environmental catastrophe, and may have devastated populations already weakened by crop failures and long days and nights of rain-soaked gales.

If this interpretation is correct, then the Vikings would have arrived on islands that were relatively sparsely populated and were confronted by a society that had lost the strong regional bonds that could have pulled together an effective resistance to these outsiders. A society dominated by individuals who looked to the mainland state of Pictland for legitimacy could easily have its leaders removed and, once this had happened, resistance would be minimal, and one suspects ineffectual.

Notes

1. A full catalogue of the British dice was published by David Clarke in Clarke 1970, and this also explored the practicalities of using parallelopiped dice. Mark Hall has published numerous articles on the importance of gaming in early historic Scotland and the most relevant and comprehensive publication is Hall 2007.
2. The Bornais wheelhouse is described in detail in Sharples 2012, and this volume references many of the sites and finds mentioned in this chapter.
3. There are at least 29 partially excavated wheelhouses in the Uists, three on Barra and three so far identified on Lewis and Harris.
4. Wheelhouses can be divided into two types depending on whether the piers are neat rectangular blocks of masonry, which are separate from the surrounding internal wall, or triangular wedges of masonry that are bonded into this wall. These differences seem to be chronological, with the triangular bonded piers indicating the

house was constructed later, normally in the middle of the first millennium AD.
5   This site will be discussed in more detail in Chapter 3.
6   I am using the anglicised spelling of Cille Pheadair to refer to this wheelhouse as this was the spelling used by the excavator when he published his report, Lethbridge 1952.
7   The excavations at Cnip were carried out by Ian Armit and his publication of the work (Armit 2006) provides a consideration of the wheelhouse phenomenon.
8   The machair plain was surveyed by Mike Parker Pearson as part of the SEARCH project and the results discussed here are detailed in the *From Machair to Mountains* volume (Parker Pearson 2012).
9   The literature on brochs is rich, as these are iconic monuments that in many respects represent the ancient past in northern and western Scotland. The public encounter them as monuments packaged and presented by national, regional and local heritage bodies, but most of them survive as formless mounds. Archaeologists have been writing detailed accounts of these monuments since the eighteenth century and at the end of the nineteenth century and the beginning of the twentieth century, many brochs were excavated by well-to-do landowners intrigued by their presence. This archaeological interest in brochs has not resulted in a universally accepted understanding of their date, function or even appearance. Indeed, almost every aspect of brochs is regarded as controversial and worth arguing about. The literature on brochs is consequently vast, and I will not attempt to summarise it here. The views presented in this book could be challenged by my contemporaries, but I have defended them in several papers on the subject, which are referenced in Sharples 2012, and most recently I have argued for a holistic view of the broch in Sharples 2019. Alternative views can be found in Ian Armit's publications (Armit 1992; 1996; 1997; 2005). Important recent reports on broch excavations have been published by Dockrill on the broch and broch village at Old Scatness, Shetland (Dockrill *et al.* 2015) and by Cavers on Clachtoll in Sutherland (Cavers 2022).
10 These are the long bones of an animal's lower legs.
11 Crawford and Switsur 1977, 130.
12 The excavations at Bostaidh have not been published, but the excavator Tim Neighbour was kind enough to let me read a draft report which provides the basis for this description.
13 These are equivalent to the 'figure-of-eight' houses at the Udal.
14 The report on Eilean Olabhat is Armit *et al.* 2009 and on Loch na Beirgh is Harding and Gilmour 2000.
15 The significance of the changes in the middle of the first millennium AD have been widely discussed by many, and my understanding of the issue has been influenced by Comeau *et al.* 2023, Moreland 2019 and Coyle McClung and Plunkett 2020.
16 I must thank John Hines for an excellent lecture on this issue which I attended as I was writing this chapter.
17 See David Breeze in Smith and Banks 2002.
18 There has been a dramatic increase in archaeological interest in the first millennium AD of mainland Scotland, and a series of exciting new discoveries have been made that have transformed our understanding of the Picts and their neighbours. An excellent synthesis of the new discoveries is provided by Gordon Noble and Nicholas Evans (Noble and Evans 2022).
19 The most comprehensive and informative study of the art of the Picts was undertaken by George and Isobel Henderson (Henderson and Henderson 2004).

20 The Early Medieval crosses have recently been considered by Ian Fisher (Fisher 2001) and the chapels of Lewis by Rachel Barrowman (Barrowman 2023).
21 The most accessible information on this survey is the web page The Papar Project: Inception, parameters and Purpose. www.paparproject.org.uk – accessed 21/02/2025
22 These cemeteries are thoroughly explored in papers by Maldonado (Maldonado 2013) and in Mitchell *et al.* 2020.
23 Neighbour *et al.* 2000.
24 The details of the excavation and analysis of this burial are described in the report on the Cille Pheadair excavations (Parker Pearson *et al.* 2018).

CHAPTER THREE

The Viking colonisation of the Outer Hebrides

....

Introduction – the burial at Cnip

One of the most spectacular recent archaeological finds in the Outer Hebrides was a Viking burial at Cnip on Lewis. Skeletal remains were found eroding from a sand dune by holidaymakers in the summer of 1979. The remains were excavated by the finders under the supervision of the Procurator Fiscal almost immediately after its discovery, as at this time there were no professional archaeologists on the island. They did a good job recovering all the artefacts and bones and providing enough information to reconstruct how the body and the accompanying finds were laid out in the grave. The burial was of a 35–40-year-old woman laid on her back (with a slight twist to her shoulders) with her arms by her sides. Her head was towards the southwest and her feet to the northeast. She is estimated to have been 5'3" (1.6 m) tall.[1]

The burial is located on the Uig peninsula in west Lewis. This is a scenic peat and rock covered area of the island, isolated from the more densely occupied parts of north Lewis by mountains, moorlands and long sea lochs. The burial was found on the north-facing slopes of a headland that defines the south side of a beautiful sandy bay, close to a substantial Early Bronze Age cairn (Fig. 3.1). The adjacent machair plain provides an oasis of green in the otherwise heather-covered hills.

In the 1980s Edinburgh University began an archaeological field school in the Uig peninsula, and this resulted in the excavation of several important archaeological sites, largely of Middle Iron Age date. This archaeological presence meant that the eroding machair on the headland at Cnip could now be closely monitored, and additional Viking burials were discovered and excavated in 1991, 1992 and 1994. By the middle of 1990s seven burials had been recovered from what was clearly a Viking cemetery. To the woman's burial (A) could be added, a child (B), two men (C and D), another woman (E) and two infants (F and G).[2]

The original burial of a woman was accompanied by a variety of grave goods that make this particularly interesting for archaeologists. On her left side near her arm was a bone needle-case containing two iron needles, a short stubby-bladed knife with a wooden haft and a leather sheath, and a whetstone possibly used to sharpen the knife. On her right side was a large composite comb, broken at one end. Two elaborately decorated oval brooches were found on the upper part of her body (Fig. 3.2). These are very similar to each other, but they are not an

FIGURE 3.1. The Cnip peninsula on the west coast of Lewis; a Viking cemetery was found in the large erosion scar at the far end. © Crown Copyright: HES.

identical pair. Just above these brooches, in the neck area, was a group of 44 glass beads. These are vividly coloured yellow, blue, silver and gold, and most are segmented in shape but with five unsegmented beads present. Unfortunately, the record of the excavation is not sufficiently detailed to reconstruct how the beads were arranged. Positioned slightly lower on the chest was an iron sickle and a ring-headed pin. Below this lay a belt-buckle and strap-end decorated with prominent ornamental studs. An iron boat-rivet was also found in the grave and though its position was unclear, it may have represented a seafaring life that in other Viking graves was represented by an actual boat.

The objects found in this grave present a picture of the deceased that tell us a considerable amount about how this woman was perceived by her community. We always have to remember that these objects were placed in the grave by the mourners and therefore they may not be objects that belonged to the deceased. Nevertheless, several aspects of this person's identity were stressed more than

FIGURE 3.2. A pair of brooches and a necklace of glass beads from the Viking burial at Cnip on the Isle of Lewis. © National Museums Scotland.

others, giving us an insight into what was important to Viking society in this part of the North Atlantic. Arguably the most important aspect of identity conveyed at Cnip was the status and prestige of the individual placed in the grave. This woman was an important member of her community, and her wealth and status were emphasised by the placing in her grave of a range of items produced by skilled craftsmen, using exotic and valuable materials. Most men and women, including the three adult burials that were found close to this burial, were not accompanied by artefacts of this quality and significance. It is also clearly important that this individual was a woman, and her gender was indicated by the oval brooches and, though to a lesser extent, by the needle-case and needles. High-status Viking women had their own distinctive way of dressing, which was emphasised by these very distinctive, highly ornate and carefully crafted brooches.

The other main facet of her identity expressed in this grave was her ethnicity. The brooches not only indicate the gender of the deceased but her relationship to Scandinavia. The style and ornamentation of these brooches is distinctive and belongs to an art style that originated in Scandinavia in the first millennium AD. This form and the way the brooches were worn would have marked her out as someone whose dress was dictated by Scandinavian fashions. Most of the other objects in the grave were Scandinavian types and this was particularly true of the comb. However, one object challenged this Scandinavian identity: the ring-headed pin found on her chest. This pin could have been used to hold a cloak at the shoulder or it could have been associated with a shroud that covered the body and concealed it from the mourners around the grave. This pin was almost certainly made in Ireland and the style evolved in the first millennium AD from Roman prototypes. Ring-headed pins interested the Viking raiders, and numerous examples are found on the Atlantic seaboard of Scotland. They were taken from Ireland to Scotland, the Faroes, Iceland and back home to Scandinavia. It could be argued that this is just an example of the elaborate and valuable jewellery that was being looted by the Vikings and was in effect a symbol of their destructive tendencies in Ireland and western Britain, but it is also possible to argue that the inclusion of this object-type showed that Scandinavians were settling down in Ireland and wanted to express a hybrid Gaelic-Scandinavian identity by wearing distinctive non-Scandinavian jewellery. Perhaps this woman had Irish ancestry that was subsumed by marriage, forced or voluntary, to a Viking.

At the time this burial was excavated in the 1970s, considerations on the origins of the individual buried woman were idle speculations as there was no way of knowing where she had been born and had lived, but in the last decade new scientific techniques have been developed that provide ways of exploring these issues. Archaeologists can now find out much more about people's origins.[3] Detailed analysis of the strontium, oxygen and lead isotopes from three of the individuals excavated at Cnip shows that they were not brought up in the Western Isles. A combination of isotopic analyses suggests that the woman in burial (A) was brought up on the east coast of Britain, somewhere between southern Scotland and northern England. Her isotopic signature is very different from the patterns found in the male Viking burials from Westness in Orkney and Dublin in Ireland, which appear to indicate that these men had a Scandinavian homeland. Another woman from the cemetery at Cnip was brought up in a chalk landscape, so she may have come from either Wessex or Yorkshire.

A striking feature of the Viking burials in Britain whose isotopes have been analysed is that most of the men were brought up in Scandinavia, whereas the woman had much more diverse origins, indicating that they grew up in non-Scandinavian locations, probably in Britain and Ireland. As we have seen at Cnip, these non-Scandinavian women were dressed in distinctively Scandinavian clothes and with ornaments that originated largely in Scandinavia. How did these objects travel across the North Sea? Were they acquired by women who had been seized on raiding parties and brought back to Scandinavia to become wives? Or were the Viking raiders carrying heirlooms and wedding gifts with them when they set out on their adventures? These burials certainly indicate some of the complex issues of identity that arose during this period when people were moving around, crossing boundaries and mingling in ways that had not been seen for centuries. Individuals could be born and brought up in one culture and then suddenly be forced to adopt a new and completely different culture. We can only speculate on the agency involved in these transformations of identity, but the historical evidence suggests that a great deal of violence was involved. The next section will outline some of the key events in the historical records for the Viking and Early Norse period, which provide a context to explore the archaeological evidence from the islands.

The history

The beginning of the Viking period is marked by a series of events which are documented in several sources, including the *Anglo-Saxon Chronicle* and the *Annals of Ulster*, but there are no contemporary Scottish sources. These events include a landing in AD 789 at Portland on the south coast of England, which resulted in the death of a local official with the title of King's Reeve, who rather rashly tried to extract a landing fee from these new arrivals on the assumption that they were peaceful traders. There is a record of attacks on Lindisfarne in AD 793, on Skye and Iona in AD 795; the Hebrides were reportedly plundered

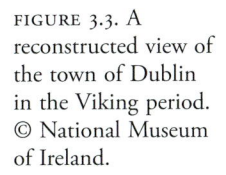

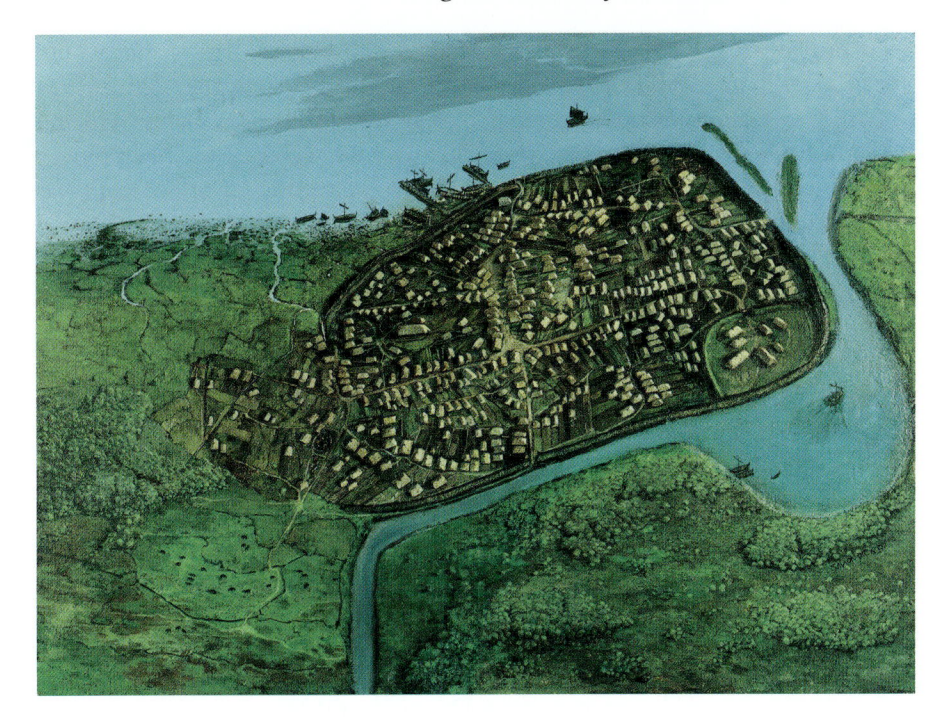

FIGURE 3.3. A reconstructed view of the town of Dublin in the Viking period. © National Museum of Ireland.

in AD 798. These early raiders are believed to have originated in Scandinavia, probably from Hordaland in Norway, but it is unclear if the raiders represent one sustained campaign which overwintered in western Britain or were a series of separate events. The Vikings continued to raid Ireland into the early ninth century before there was a relatively short lull, which may simply indicate that raiding was concentrated in areas not so well documented, such as the Western and Northern Isles of Scotland.[4]

In the 820s raiding in Ireland recommenced and it was now more sustained, involved more ships and occurred throughout the year. The Vikings seem to have operated from bases in Britain and the most likely location for these bases was the Western and Northern Isles of Scotland. These forward bases provided a safe place to retreat to when a raid had taken place, and a suitable location to secure the fleet over the winter months when storms could be extremely dangerous. Within a decade, camps for overwintering in Ireland were established and these included the *longphoirt* at Dublin in AD 838, which grew to become the most important town in Ireland. It was a craft and trading hub which had a political and social significance that encouraged the elites of the western seaboard to use it as a centre for their raiding and trading activities (Fig. 3.3). Residence in Dublin legitimated the power of the elite Viking leaders and provided a source of manpower for their battle fleets.

It is difficult to know what was happening in the Western Isles at this time. It seems likely that during the late eighth and early ninth century the islands were subject to frequent devastating attacks from Viking expeditions as their fleets progressed from the west coast of Norway to Ireland. The islands would not necessarily have been the primary target for these raids as they are unlikely to have been a source of wealth comparable to that which was available in the religious centres of Ireland and southwest Scotland. However, as the fleets moved from Scandinavia to Ireland, the journey down the west coast of Scotland was an opportunity to stock up on food and water. The islands, as relatively isolated and underpopulated outposts of Pictland, were unlikely to have the capacity to adequately defend themselves against these aggressive and highly mobile raiders.

The islands had one principal source of wealth that the Vikings desired: people (Fig. 3.4). The opportunity to capture and enslave the inhabitants of the Western Isles may well have been one of the principal attractions of the islands, particularly in the second half of the ninth century after the establishment of Dublin and other towns such as Waterford, Cork and Limerick. One of the principal economic activities in these towns was likely to have been the buying and selling of human beings.[5]

In AD 839 there was a great victory over King Eogánán of the Picts, and pressure from Viking raids was likely to have been one of the factors that eventually led to the merger of Picts and Scots under Cineád Mac Alpin, which occurred in the decade leading up to AD 850.[6] In the Irish Sea, after a period of conflict between competing Viking armies from Denmark and Norway, two Norwegian brothers of royal lineage, Olaf and Ivar, took control of Dublin in AD 853. They used it as a base from which to attack, defeat and subjugate, along with their allies the Scots, southern Pictland. In AD 870–871, they sacked Dumbarton and effectively destroyed the British kingdom of Strathclyde in southwest Scotland. Ivar died in AD 873 and on his death, Olaf was given the title of King of the

FIGURE 3.4. The Hostage Stone from Inchmarnock, Argyll. It is thought to depict a Viking with his captured slave. © National Museums Scotland.

Norwegian Vikings of the whole of Ireland and Britain. This suggests the King of Dublin controlled the Scottish Islands; Olaf died in AD 874.

Operating at roughly the same time as Olaf and Ivar was Ketil Fletnose, a figure who the Icelandic Sagas record had a major role in the early colonisation of the Hebrides, but whose historical reality is open to debate.[7] Thorstein the Red, son of Olaf and Ketil Fletnose's daughter, Aud the Deep-minded, took control of the Isles after Olaf's death and he campaigned with Sigurd the Mighty, Earl of Orkney in northern Scotland in the 870s and 880s, before being killed somewhere in the region. Viking control of Dublin was weakened at the end of the ninth century and in AD 902 the town was taken by the Irish and the Vikings were expelled.

In England a vast army of Vikings, known as the Great Host, arrived in Kent and East Anglia in AD 865. This army campaigned in eastern England throughout AD 866 and in AD 867 moved north and took control of York. The following year the Kings of Northumbria were killed, and this was the beginning of over a decade of warfare that culminated in the rise of Wessex, the last surviving Anglo-Saxon kingdom in England.

During the second half of the ninth century, adventurers from Scandinavia explored the northern latitudes of the North Atlantic and discovered Iceland, Greenland and North America. The traditional date for the discovery and settlement of Iceland is the 870s. The later historical records suggest that the initial colonisation included many Vikings from Scotland and Ireland, and among them were high-status individuals, such as Aud the Deep-minded, who were accompanied by Scots and Irish natives.

The Vikings did not return to Dublin until AD 917 when Ivar's grandsons Ragnall and Sigtrygg rose to prominence. York was taken by Ragnall in AD 918, and successive dynasties in Dublin spent most of the next four decades fighting to retain control of York. Amlaib Cuaran was the last King of both York and Dublin, in the middle of the tenth century (940s to 960s), and he was buried at Iona in AD 980.

In the latter half of the tenth century, texts began to record the emergence of individuals who claimed to be the rulers of the Scottish isles. Godfrey (Guðrøðr) Haroldsson was the first person to hold the title of *re Innse Gall* (King of the Islands of the Foreigners) and he may have ruled with his brother Maccus. They were closely related to the kings of Dublin and were actively campaigning in the Irish Sea in the 970s and 980s. Godfrey was eventually killed in Dál Riata[8] in AD 989 and his death coincided with the increased influence of the Earls of Orkney in the west. Earl Sigurd Hlodversson, 'the stout', took control of the Western Isles in the late tenth century. Sigurd was very active in the power politics of the Irish Sea, and was killed in Ireland participating in the Battle of Clontarf in 1014 alongside Hebridean warriors. His son Thorfinn succeeded to the Earldom of Orkney, though he apparently had to overcome opposition in the Western Isles. Thorfinn controlled the islands effectively throughout the middle of the eleventh century and warriors from the islands of Orkney and the Hebrides, together with Dublin, were part of a force led by Magnus Haraldsson

(son of Harold Hardrada) into England in 1058. This phase of Orcadian and Norwegian control was weakened by the death of the Earl of Orkney and many of his kinsmen in the battle of Stamford Bridge in 1066, when Harald Hardrada was defeated and killed by Harold Godwinson shortly before the latter was defeated at Hastings.

This summary of the historical evidence provides no more than a glimpse of what the sources can tell us, but the important point I want to make in this brief overview is that the sources are primarily concerned with individual people. It is the massive personalities that dominated events in northern Britain which attracted the writers of this period. Places are mentioned occasionally but even the establishment of important centres such as Dublin, which is of critical significance in the history of Medieval Ireland, is mentioned only in passing, and the Western Isles are hardly mentioned at all. There is very little in the texts that tells us about how these individuals lived and died, the houses they occupied, the boats they sailed, and the agricultural practices that were required to provide their everyday sustenance. To understand the totality of the Viking world, it is necessary to explore the archaeological evidence, and only once this is achieved can we talk with confidence about Viking society.

The archaeology

Unfortunately, the archaeological evidence for this phase of early Viking activity is also very limited. Finding evidence in the archaeological record for any particular historical event is always problematic. Archaeology can identify events, and I demonstrated in Chapter 2 that the destruction of the Late Iron Age wheelhouse on mound 1 was an event with some distinctive features of individual action that provide important insights into human behaviour. However, this act of destruction took place over three hundred years before the Vikings appeared, so they can't be blamed for this violent conflagration.

There are some remarkable discoveries in other areas of Britain which do evoke the violence and destruction that was part and parcel of the Viking assaults on these islands. In Dorset, close to where the slaughter of the King's Reeve occurred, the construction of a new road across the South Dorset Ridgeway led to the discovery of a pit containing the skeletons of 51 individuals (Fig. 3.5).[9] The remains were all of men with robust, well-developed physiques, and 70% appeared to be under the age of 25. All of these individuals had been decapitated and some had been subject to repeated violent assaults; after decapitation, the heads were piled in the southeast corner of the burial pit and the bodies placed at its centre. The stratigraphy and the disposition of the bodies suggest this was a single event that happened sometime between AD 970 and 1025.

The most obvious interpretation of this mass grave is that these are the remains of a Viking raiding party that was caught and executed. It is quite likely that they came from a ship with 25 pairs of oarsmen that had pulled up on the beach at Weymouth, a location clearly visible from the Ridgeway. The location of the burial pit was an historic execution spot on the parish boundary,

FIGURE 3.5. A view of the Viking burial pit on the South Dorset Ridgeway during excavation; a cluster of detached skulls lies in front of the two excavators.

and there is no need to assume the raiders were captured close to this location. Detailed analysis of the isotopes from the teeth of these individuals indicates they came from the coastal regions of northern Scandinavia, with one man coming from the Arctic. They do not seem to have been a homogeneous group from one region, but were probably recruited from across a relatively wide area of Scandinavia. The dietary evidence and the lead isotopes indicate that there were no individuals from Britain in the sampled group.

On the east side of northern Scotland, at the Pictish monastery of Portmahomack on the Tarbat peninsula, there is evidence for a devastating attack around AD 800. Workshops at the edge of the monastery were burnt down, cross-slabs of the most spectacular form were smashed and strewn across the monastic precinct, and monks were violently assaulted; some died, some were maimed for life (Fig. 3.6).[10] This seems to have been the result of a very violent attack by a Viking raiding party between AD 780 and AD 810. The site was at least partly reoccupied, and it became a metalworking centre of some importance in the ninth century AD, though it is doubtful that it ever regained the cultural significance of its eighth-century monastery with its spectacular stone crosses. The Firth lands surrounding Portmahomack later became a disputed borderland between the Vikings occupying Orkney and Caithness and the southern Picts, rather than the core of the northern heartlands of the Kingdom of the Picts that it had been before the Viking assault.

FIGURE 3.6. Two broken Pictish symbol stones from Portmahomack, Easter Ross. © National Museums Scotland.

These discoveries are a testimony to the potential archaeology has to shed light on this traumatic period of historical change. However, the evidence from the islands is still limited and requires more excavation and luck if we are to find further evidence of this quality. The most important evidence we have for the ninth-century period of raiding in the Western Isles comes from the discovery of a series of pagan Norse graves, such as the burial at Cnip discussed at the beginning of this chapter (Fig. 3.7). These burials are scattered along the west coast of Scotland, around the Irish Sea and into northern England. There is a cluster of graves in Orkney that extend into Shetland and to the Caithness mainland but examples from eastern Scotland are very rare, with only a single recent discovery from Dunbar in East Lothian to suggest any Viking presence there.[11]

In the Western Isles our records suggest at least 15 and possibly up to 24 burials have been discovered. Most of these discoveries were made a long time ago when the recovery of finds was unfortunately incomplete, and the burial locations were seldom accurately located in the landscape. Cnip is the only burial group that has been thoroughly excavated and analysed. Most of the other locations have produced isolated artefacts which may or may not have been associated with human remains. A feature of many of the burials' locations on the western seaboard is their association with rocky headlands adjacent to wide sandy bays, and this suggests that these burials were referencing the importance of seaborne communications in the early Viking occupation of the Isles.

These burials exhibit a range of material culture that was largely missing from the settlements of Bornais and Cille Pheadair. Large antler combs comparable to that from Cnip were not found in the early deposits at either site and nor were the elaborate zoomorphic pins of the type found in early settlements in the Northern Isles. The one settlement site which has produced objects that seem to fit into this period is the settlement of the Udal in North Uist, and it is important that we explore the evidence from that site in some detail despite the many problems associated with the excavation.

FIGURE 3.7. The distribution of Viking graves in Scotland and northern England.

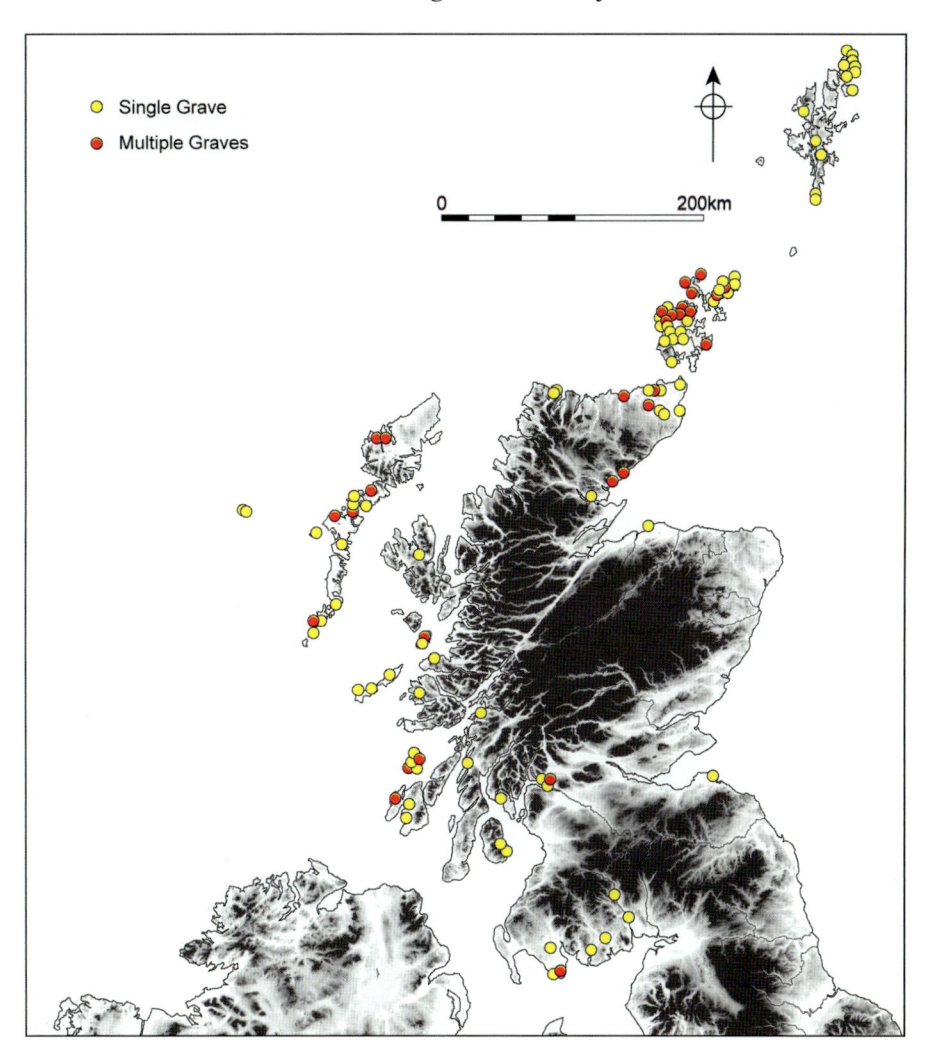

The Udal

The Udal is a very problematic site to understand, as we know so little about the settlement remains that were found during the excavations between 1963 and 1994. It has long been claimed that this is the key site for understanding the archaeology of the Western Isles, and yet relatively little is known about the results of the archaeological work as these excavations have never been written up and the director, Iain Crawford, has since passed away. The summary provided here is assembled from interim reports and a few synthetic papers that were published as the project evolved.[12] Detailed reports on the ceramics and the animal bone are available as these were published by independent specialists involved in the project. The excavations took place when very little was known about the archaeology of the Western Isles in the historic period and the results from the Udal were critically important for the characterisation by Alan Lane of a distinctive type of pottery used by the Norse settlers. It was this work that allowed Mike Parker Pearson to identify the ceramics recovered from plough furrows and rabbit scrapes at Bornais and from the coastal erosion at Cille Pheadair as Norse. The overall outline of the Udal's history is clear, but detailed description of the structures, stratigraphy and material culture is missing, and this inhibits any understanding of the site.

The sequence of occupation at the Udal spanned a long period and covered three very specific locations near the end of the Aird a'Mhorain peninsula close to a natural anchorage and beaching point (Fig. 3.8). The peninsula extends from the north coast of North Uist into the Sound of Harris, an important sailing route through the Outer Hebrides. Early prehistoric remains, a Neolithic settlement and an Early Bronze Age burial cairn, are located on the west coast of the peninsula and just inland from this are two large settlement mounds known as the South Mound and the North Mound. The South Mound was dominated by an extensive complex of well-preserved stone walled buildings which included the three classic wheelhouses of the Middle Iron Age discussed in Chapter 2. After the abandonment of the South Mound, the North Mound became the focus for settlement activity and the complete excavation of this mound revealed a sequence that started in the Late Iron Age, spanned the Viking conquest of the islands and continued up to the late seventeenth century.

FIGURE 3.8. The Aird a'Mhorain peninsula on the south side of the Sound of Harris. The Viking settlement of the Udal lies in the middle distance just inland of the small tidal islet. © Crown Copyright: HES.

3. *The Viking colonisation of the Outer Hebrides* 95

The earliest Viking occupation of the North Mound consisted of a group of short rectangular houses which Crawford dated to the middle of the ninth century. Three of these buildings were constructed inside Late Iron Age cellular buildings (see Chapter 2) and Crawford took this to indicate a sudden violent incursion into the region (Fig. 3.9). Associated with these early houses was a small stone-walled enclosure which is described as a 'fort'. This was short-lived, and the area became an 'industrial zone' with metalworking furnaces, grain-drying kilns and other ancillary buildings. In the succeeding phase there appeared to be numerous turf-built houses that were associated with rich occupation deposits containing large quantities of pottery and bone tools, including distinctive composite combs and pins. This occupation layer, radiocarbon-dated to the eleventh century, was sealed by a destruction layer linked to a raid by King Magnus Barelegs in 1098 (see Chapter 4).

People continued to live at the Udal throughout the later Norse period and the location was occupied relatively continuously up to the end of the seventeenth century or early in the eighteenth century, unusually late for a machair-located settlement. Some of the structures present in these later phases will be discussed in Chapters 4 and 5 and the end of settlement on the machair will be considered in Chapter 6.

An important feature of the settlement at the Udal is the suggestion, based largely on the material culture and a few radiocarbon dates, that its Viking occupation began relatively early, possibly in the ninth century and well before the settlement at Bornais (which will be discussed below). The character of

FIGURE 3.9. A schematic plan showing a sequence of houses at the Udal that begins with a jelly baby house of the eighth century, is followed by a Viking house of the ninth to tenth century, and sealed by a fourteenth-century house. © IAC, Udal Archives.

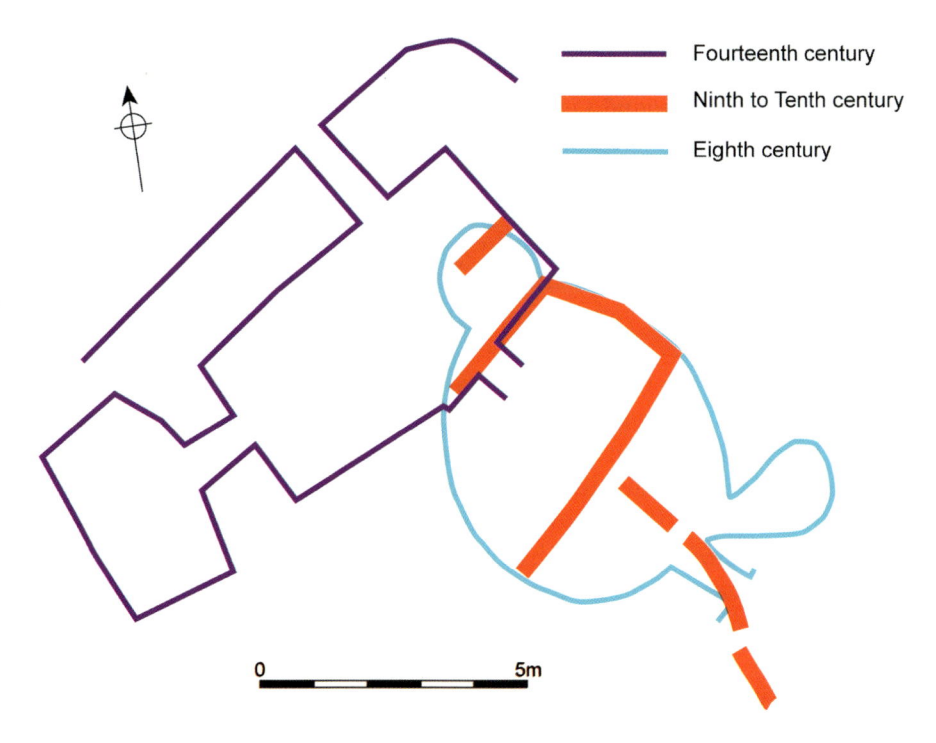

the Viking settlement at the Udal was also quite different to the settlements at Bornais and Cille Pheadair, as it comprised a collection of relatively small houses and an unusual stone walled enclosure. The location of the site is very distinctive as it sits on a promontory projecting into the strategically important Sound of Harris, with good anchorages and beaches available on the adjacent coastline. It is possible that this strategically placed early settlement was closely linked to the raiding activity down the western seaboard of Scotland and into the Irish Sea. Once the islands were largely stripped of their indigenous population the Udal seemed to have lost some of its importance and there is no evidence for the kind of large bow-walled longhouse that was characteristic of the high-status Viking settlements throughout the North Atlantic in the tenth and eleventh century.

Viking activity at Bornais

Evidence for ninth-century activity at Bornais and Cille Pheadair is limited. There does seem to have been some activity on mound 1 that belonged to this period, but the settlement seems to have only really got going early in the tenth century, when a large bow-walled longhouse was constructed on mound 2. The excavation of Bornais mound 1 focused on the wheelhouse that dates from the fifth to sixth centuries (discussed in Chapter 2). However, the original exploratory trench revealed a subterranean rectangular Norse longhouse, infilled with midden material, and a scatter of features that overlay the Late Iron Age deposits.[13] The Norse longhouse most likely dates from the twelfth to thirteenth centuries, but the scatter of features was radiocarbon dated to between AD 760–890. These are the only remains from Bornais that belong to the ninth century, the peak period of Viking raids in the western seaboard.

These features on mound 1 included several pits and a couple of hearths and are difficult to interpret. The best-preserved eastern hearth was associated with large quantities of 'clinker' that indicated sustained high temperatures in the hearth, hot enough to fuse the surrounding wind-blown sand. There was no clear indication as to why these hearths were used to achieve such high temperatures, but we have not found anything like these quantities of clinker on the domestic hearths of the Norse houses. The other pits had less distinctive fills but one produced a very large whale bone tool known as a 'scutcher' which was used to beat and comb the fibres of flax as part of the process that creates linen fabrics (Fig. 3.10). Other finds included fragments of a steatite vessel (a carved stone bowl), imported from Norway, and a distinctive fish bone assemblage, the significance of which is discussed below. Both these groups of material support the identification of Viking activity in the ninth century on this mound.

The area explored on mound 1 had been eroding badly prior to the excavation and several important finds were recovered lying on the surface which could not be definitively associated with either the Late Iron Age, the Viking or the later Norse activity. These included a small bone plaque with an ogham inscription and a silver coin that are worth detailed consideration.

FIGURE 3.10. A large whale bone object which can be interpreted as a 'scutcher' used to break up flax stalks as part of the process of making linen textiles. This was found in a small pit on Bornais, mound 1.

The ogham-inscribed plaque is a unique object that is unfortunately broken at either end (Fig. 3.11). It is a tapering rectangular plaque made from the rib of a cattle sized mammal that has been carefully smoothed on both sides. It is slightly burnt, possibly to deliberately create the red-grey colour that now characterises the bone. The text comprises five complete letters and the beginning of a sixth letter that is located at one of the fractured ends. The inscription stops short of the other end, which though broken, is probably close to its original end. Katherine Forsyth, an expert on ogham inscriptions, has suggested that the character of the text is distinctively Scottish and that it was probably a late inscription that could post-date the Norse conquest of the island.[14] Unfortunately, the brevity of the inscription and problems inherent in the translation of Scottish ogham means that the text cannot be interpreted with any confidence. The most convincing suggestion is that the inscription is a name and that it is inscribed on the plaque either for casting lots or as a label to be attached to some purchased commodity. Its presence suggests the community at Bornais had some degree of literacy.

FIGURE 3.11. The ogham inscribed plaque found on the surface of Bornais mound 1.

The coin is a silver penny of the Norwegian king Olaf Kyrre (Olaf the Peaceful; Fig. 3.12) who reigned from 1066 to 1093. It was probably associated with the occupation of the building to the north of the excavated area.[15]

The evidence for activity in the ninth century is difficult to understand. It suggests that an abandoned Late Iron Age settlement on mound 1 was occupied prior to the substantial reoccupation of mound 2. The scattered presence of hearths and pits may indicate just episodic visits, perhaps of raiding parties passing through on their way to Ireland. However, the hearths are substantial and well-made which suggests that these were used during more purposeful visits that had longer term aims. It is possible that more substantial early Viking settlement activity would be uncovered by further excavation.

FIGURE 3.12. A coin of the Norwegian king Olaf Kyrre (the Peaceful) from Bornais mound 1.

An Early Norse house on mound 2

The archaeological evidence from Bornais mound 2 is dominated by a sequence of three Norse longhouses in use from the tenth to the end of the thirteenth century (Fig. 3.13). The Early Norse longhouse, House 1, was a bow-walled longhouse roughly 23 m long, that was built in a large pit dug through occupation

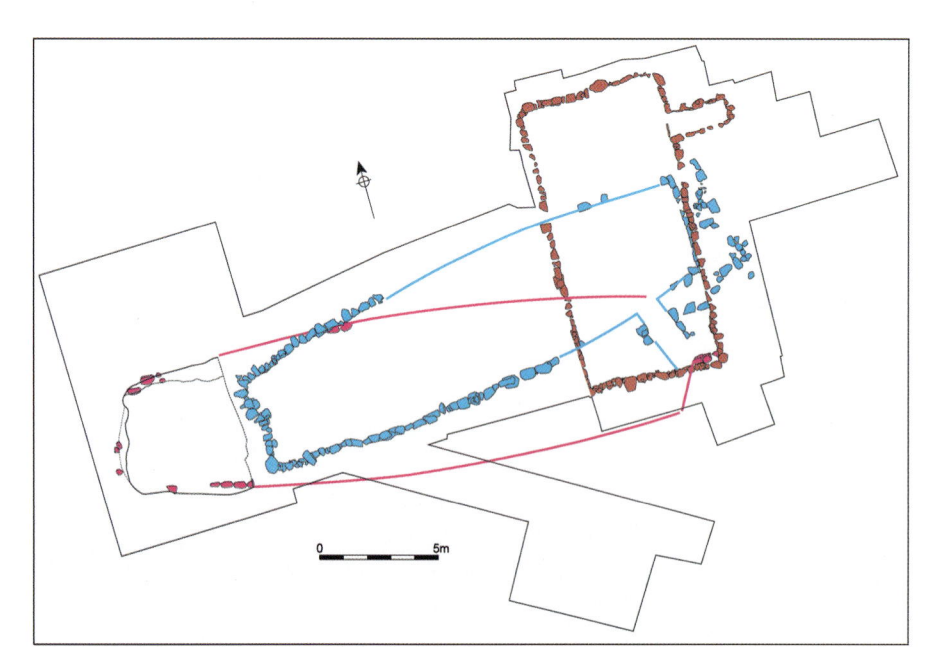

FIGURE 3.13. A plan of the three superimposed houses on Bornais mound 2.

FIGURE 3.14. The west end of House 1 on Bornais, mound 2. The two upper photos show the house floor before and after it was excavated. The drawings below these show the extent of the floor layer, the structural features below this, and then the pits which were dug as a foundational act.

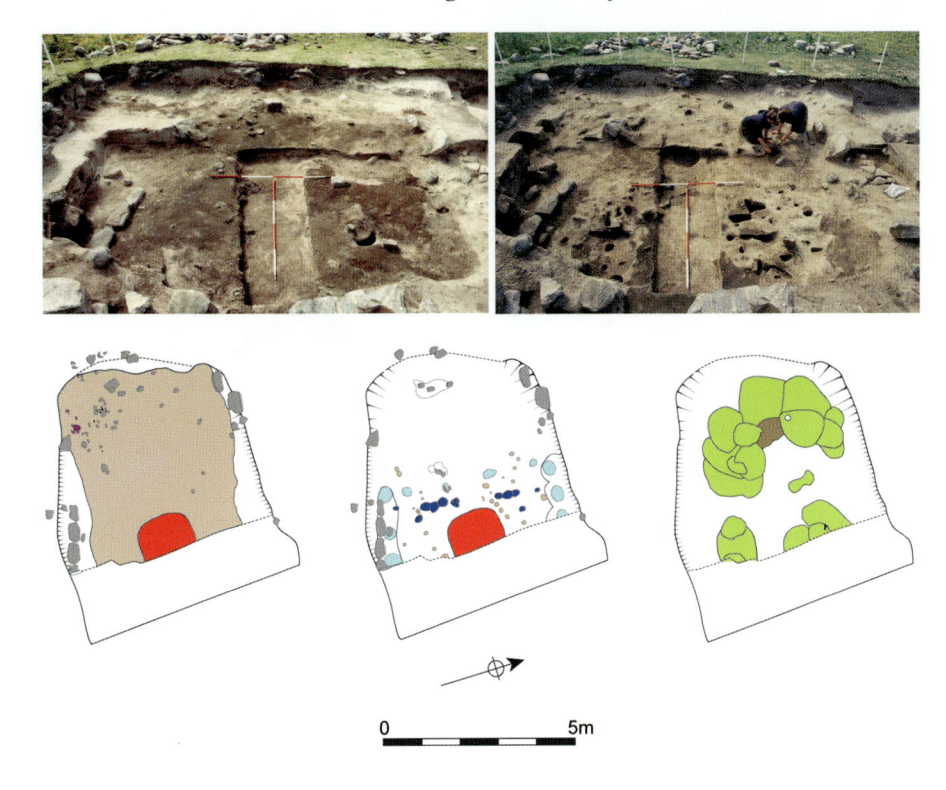

deposits and buildings dating from the seventh- and eighth-century settlement.[16] The primary purpose of this house-pit seems to have been to create a level floor for the construction of the longhouse and to provide stability and insulation for the house. The building of semi-subterranean longhouses was not common in Scandinavia, but it was well suited to the machair plains of the Western Isles. Almost all the machair wheelhouses constructed in the Western Isles were built in large circular pits dug into the windblown sand deposits of the machair and this was the case with the wheelhouse on mound 1.

Another idiosyncratic feature of this Early Norse longhouse was the presence of a series of shallow pits or scoops dug into the level base of the large house-pit. Three concentrations of these shallow pits were exposed at the west end of the house in a limited area where we excavated below the floor deposits (Figs 3.14 and 3.15). Almost all of these pits were enigmatic features that appeared to have been dug into the underlying sand quickly and with little concern for their size and shape. They were then almost immediately backfilled with the sand that had been excavated in their creation. Most of these pits did not contain any finds or unusual fill layers that could help clarify what purpose they served. One pit was different and is worth describing in more detail. This pit (Fig. 3.16) was circular in plan (1 m diameter), had vertical sides and was deeper than most of the others (0.61 m). The lower fill was a homogeneous grey-brown sand but 20 cm from the top was a layer of stones and bones that were deliberately placed in the pit. These included a fragment of sheep skull with its horn core,

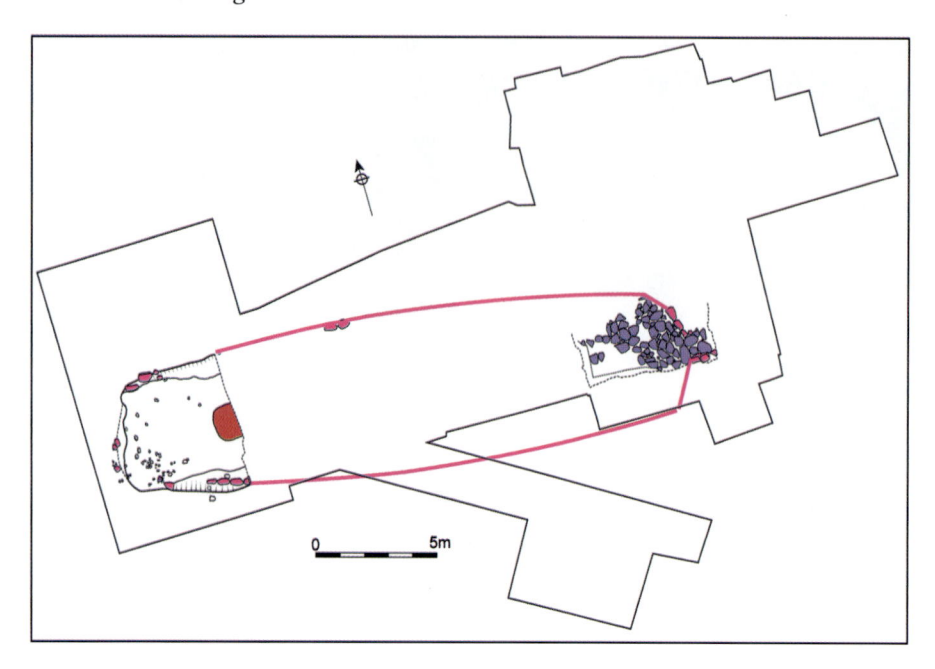

FIGURE 3.15. An overall plan of Bornais House 1, showing the excavated areas at the two gable ends.

FIGURE 3.16. A photo of a collection of finds exposed in the fill of a pit in House 1. The finds included a horn core, a cattle metapodial and a whale bone chopping board.

a whale bone chopping board, a spindle whorl and a steatite bead (both made from a reused vessel sherd), a small iron ring probably from a ring-headed pin, and a small assemblage of potsherds. There were some other objects, including fragments of a composite comb, that were probably redeposited from the earlier phase of Late Iron Age occupation.

Exactly why these pits were dug was difficult to explain but there were parallels for this kind of activity in the Iron Age settlements of the Western Isles. The wheelhouse at Sollas in North Uist had a series of pits and shallow scoops excavated underneath the floor and some of these contained special, placed deposits.[17] The various objects found in the circular pit in Early Norse house were not special or unusual, but they were not casually placed in this pit as rubbish. This was a formal deposit, a ritual act, which must have meant something to the people building the house. The absence of objects in the other pits and scoops is perplexing. It may be that the items placed in these pits were of organic materials and have vanished due to decay, but it might also be that the act of digging the pits was the most important aspect of the ritual. The tradition of pit-digging, like the semi subterranean character of the longhouse, is not observed in Scandinavian settlements and may point to the survival of a native labour force on the islands.

The excavation of the Early Norse longhouse floor revealed evidence for multiple lines of posts which must have been part of the structure of the house. The most substantial posts formed two lines adjacent to the edges of the house-pit and were major structural timbers to support the roof of the house. Only three posts in each line were identified, the row of posts did not reach the west end of the house but continued to the east into the unexcavated area. If these timbers supported the roof, then it suggests this was a hipped roof that was pitched downwards to the west from this point. A large number of smaller post holes were visible in the interior of the house, and they suggest that at least two lines of smaller posts formed a wall cutting across the house to separate the west end of the house from a large central room. The number of post holes suggests that the house had a relatively long life since the interior divisions must have been modified several times.

A small area of the east end of the Early Norse longhouse was also explored and had some quite different structural features. The inner edge of the house pit had a stone revetment wall, and the gable wall was broken by a paved entrance passage flanked by revetment walls. The floor of the house at the west end was at least partially paved, which suggests this part of the house was used to stall animals.

Our understanding of the use of the Early Norse longhouse comes from our work on the small area of the house floor that was excavated at the west end because the paved area at the east end was kept clean. Most of the floor survived as a thin layer of brown sand but in the centre of the house, at the eastern edge of the excavated area, an accumulation of peat ash indicated the location of the hearth in the central room. Many artefacts were found on the floor, including iron nails, holdfasts and roves, several bone points, a whetstone, a needle, a lead cross, and clusters of pottery and steatite vessel fragments.

The small lead cross is a very distinctive object which has parallels in north Wales and Cumbria (Fig. 3.17). It may indicate the Christian beliefs of the occupants of the Early Norse longhouse, but this cannot be said with absolute certainty as the form of the cross is not unambiguously Christian. The pottery and steatite came from discrete clusters in the southwest corner of the house. Both these assemblages comprised a small number of sherds that largely came from single bowls (Fig. 3.18). The main steatite vessel was a large hemispherical bowl (diameter 280 mm; depth 90 mm). This was a Norwegian vessel and had been well used before deposition. A repair hole reveals that it had cracked and was being held together presumably by a strap of hide. Amongst the other steatite vessel fragments from the house floor were pieces from sub-rectangular vessels that were produced in Shetland. The presence of steatite in this early house indicates the availability of commodities from the homelands and the Northern Isles but this trade in steatite vessels disappeared in the twelfth century when Irish Sea connections undermined relations with the north.[18]

FIGURE 3.17. The lead cross from the floor of Bornais House 1.

Adjacent to the steatite bowl we found a large tub-shaped pot (diameter 367 mm; depth 220 mm). This had a slightly thickened rim whose upper surface was decorated with incised diagonal lines. The vessel was made using a coarsely tempered clay and was unusually thick where the base met the walls. The presence of this pot on the floor of the Early Norse longhouse was important as it indicated the development of a Hebridean Viking pottery tradition almost immediately after the colonisation of the islands.[19] Vikings did not have a strong tradition of pottery production elsewhere in the North Atlantic and, where pottery making was established, it tended to be a later development. The early development of Norse ceramics in the Western Isles therefore has implications for our understanding of the nature of the colonisation process. It suggests potters of non-Scandinavian origin were living at Bornais when the Norse settlement was originally established, as it was very unlikely that Scandinavian potters existed at this date.

FIGURE 3.18. Examples of the large ceramic and steatite vessels from the floor of Bornais, House 1.

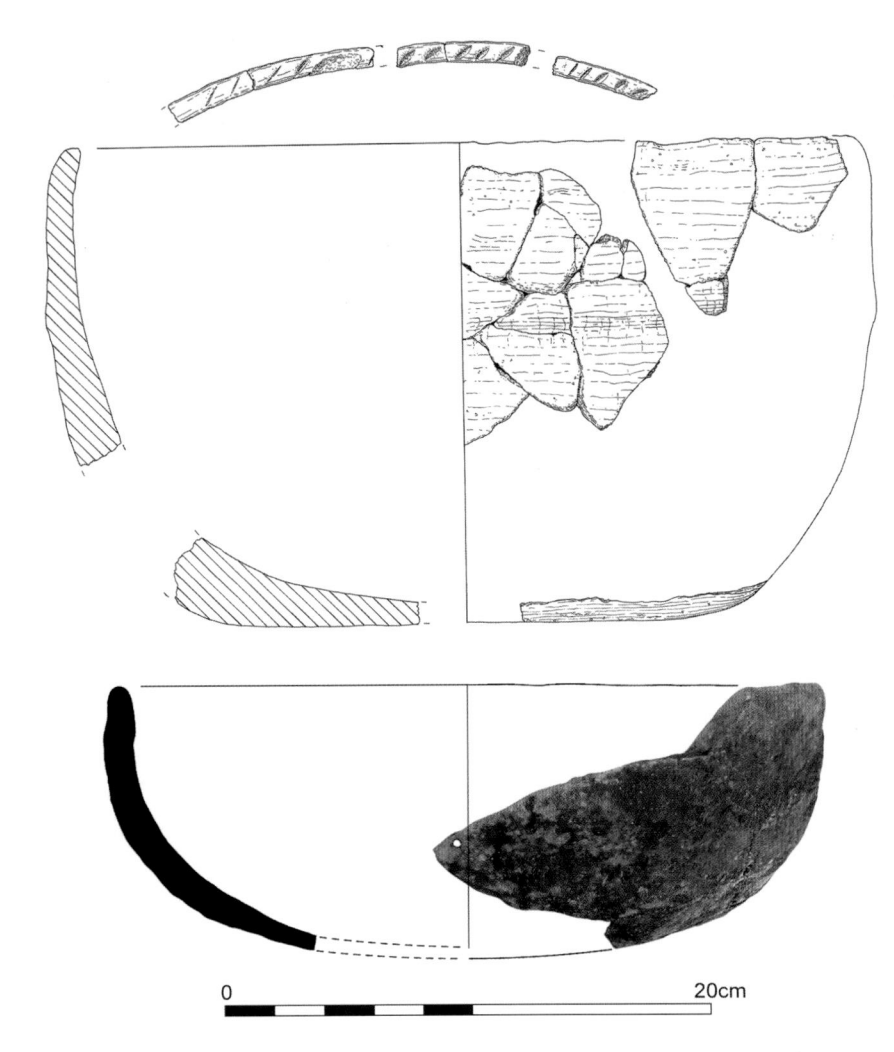

The Atlantic islands of Scotland have a long and sophisticated pottery tradition that extends continuously back to the Neolithic occupation of the island. In contrast, most of the adjacent areas of mainland Scotland including Argyll, were essentially aceramic in the period immediately prior to the Viking colonisation.[20] Perhaps, the continued use of pottery on Viking settlements is evidence for the survival of some of the indigenous inhabitants of the islands. However, the simple tub-shaped forms used by the Norse settlers were quite different to the shouldered jars that characterised the ceramics of the seventh- and eighth-century inhabitants of Bornais. The Norse occupants of Bornais also constructed their pots in a quite different fashion: the Late Iron Age vessels were made using a slab-built, tongue-and-groove construction method which contrasts with the angled coil or slab techniques of the Norse ceramics. The stylistic and technological changes that differentiate the Late Iron Age and

Viking pottery traditions are important and show that this was not a simple and untroubled progression. Pottery production is often a gender-specific task and these traditions were most likely maintained by women. It is possible that local women were enslaved by the incoming Vikings but, as the burials from Cnip indicate, it is also possible that women from other regions on the western seaboard were captured and brought to the islands.

The chronology of the Early Norse longhouse was secured by a large number of stratigraphically related radiocarbon dates that span the occupation of the building. They have been carefully modelled to produce a statistically reliable chronology for the occupation. The earliest activity associated with the Early Norse longhouse, the digging of the underlying pits, occurred between AD 850 and 945, the floor of the house accumulated between AD 920 and 980 and the house was abandoned between AD 1030 and 1075. In summary, the Early Norse longhouse was constructed at the beginning of the tenth century AD, was occupied for between 85 and 180 years, and abandoned in the middle of the eleventh century AD.

The west end of the Early Norse longhouse was sealed by a thick layer of sand deliberately dumped rather than accumulating as a result of natural processes, such as wind deposition. The large post holes that defined the house walls were filled with this sand, which suggests the posts were probably removed prior to the deposition of the sand. A stone wall that acted as an internal revetment to the house was removed at this time. All this activity suggests the house was deliberately dismantled and filled in before the construction of a new house and it seems unlikely that there was a lengthy period of time between the dismantling of the Early Norse longhouse and the construction of the succeeding Middle Norse longhouse.

The deposits in the sand infilling the Early Norse longhouse contained the largest collection of artefacts from this early phase of activity on mound 2 and many of these are unusual or complete objects, suggesting these were deliberately placed deposits similar to those found in the pit underneath the house floor. The objects included several complete bone pins, including one with a distinctive spiral decoration inscribed at the end (Fig. 3.19), a couple of comb fragments, two glass beads and one stone bead, several bone points and five spindle whorls.

One of the most unusual discoveries was a large iron object, pointed at one end, with a long rectangular shank split to create two points (though one is broken off) at the other end. This has been interpreted as a possible candlestick and it was clearly an important object as it is the largest iron object from the settlement (Fig. 3.20). Other iron objects from these fills include a ferrule, a horse bit and a point or awl. None of these objects were common refuse and it seems likely that they were deliberately placed as some form of offering.

The presence of large numbers of iron objects, mostly nails of various forms, clearly differentiated the Viking occupation deposits from those of the Late Iron Age where there were very few finds of iron. Iron nails were an essential

FIGURE 3.19. Two pins including a pig fibula pin with an incised spiral decoration which came from the sand deposits infilling Bornais, House 1.

requirement for Viking ships and accompanied the development of a major iron industry in Scandinavia. These ship nails were collected and recycled throughout the Viking diaspora. Natural iron can be sourced in many of the Atlantic islands, and, in Iceland, iron production was an important local industry in the Viking period. There is as yet little evidence for iron production in the Western Isles in the Norse period but exploitation of the sources on mainland Scotland may have been stimulated by the increasing interest in and utilisation of iron by the Norse incomers.

Agricultural activity at mound 2A

The excavation of Bornais mound 2A was designed to complement the excavations of mound 2. The geophysical survey suggested mound 2A was relatively small and not the site of a substantial house. It would therefore enable comparisons to be made between high- and low-status areas of the settlement. Furthermore, the focus of the excavation largely avoided the houses at the centre of this mound and was designed to remove the surrounding middens and explore the early deposits from the initial occupation of the mound. It was possible to recover a substantial assemblage of finds and environmental material from the Early Norse occupation of mound 2A, which has provided us with critical information on the agricultural regime of the tenth and early eleventh centuries.[21]

The earliest evidence for human activity at the location comprised ardmarks cut into the wind-blown sand (Fig. 3.21). Ardmarks are produced when a simple plough, known as an ard, cuts through a soil layer and drags the dark coloured soil down into the underlying undisturbed substrate, which on Bornais mound 2A was yellow windblown sand. A more complicated plough turns the soil over but there is no evidence that this happened at Bornais, so it is unlikely ploughs were being used. At Bornais the cultivation soil was enriched by deposits of rubbish from the adjacent settlement, so the ardmarks appeared as long streaks of dark brown sand, with occasional streaks of red where peat ash from the hearths was dumped, surrounded by the underlying yellow windblown sand. The ardmarks were oriented east–west but a later series of marks, only identifiable in a few areas, was oriented north–south and indicated a later phase of cultivation.

Embedded in the upper layers of the cultivated soil were a couple of simple hearths which were surrounded by layers of ash (Fig. 3.22). There was no sign of any structures associated with these hearths and the presence of clinker, similar to that found associated with the hearths on mound 1, suggests they were open air hearths that achieved high temperatures. There was relatively little later activity in the area excavated, and a thick, light grey sand accumulated over the hearths and cultivation soil.

A sequence of 25 radiocarbon dates have been obtained from mound 2A, and the stratigraphic sequence enabled a Bayesian model for the chronology of this mound. The earliest activity in this location occurred sometime between AD 870 and 950, but the majority of the material in the cultivation soil was probably

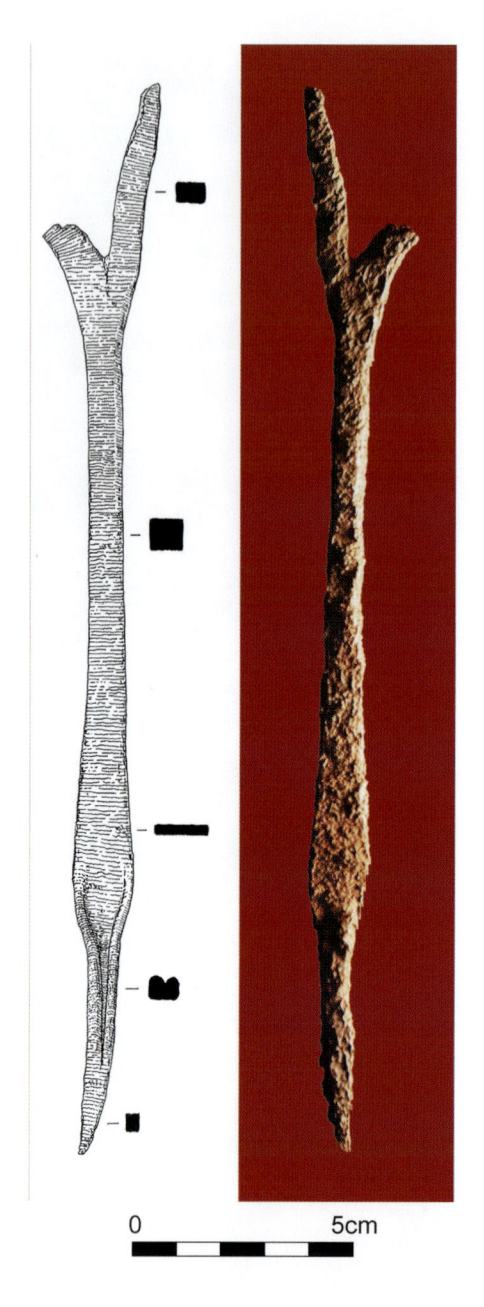

FIGURE 3.20. A possible iron candlestick from the sand deposits infilling Bornais, House 1.

FIGURE 3.21. The distinctive brown streaks indicating ard cultivation in the windblown sand at the base of Bornais, mound 2A.

deposited in the tenth century. The grey sand layers started to accumulate at the beginning of the eleventh century and this hiatus in the intensity of activity probably lasted until the middle of the eleventh century. The dates confirm that the material deposited in the cultivation soil on mound 2A, and the accumulation of the grey sand, are contemporary with the use of the Early Norse longhouse on mound 2.

The soil associated with the early phase of cultivation produced large quantities of artefacts (Fig. 3.23). These included a glass gaming-counter, a copper alloy ring from a ring-headed pin, tweezers, pins with perforated heads, and a pair of side-plates from an early comb. Several whetstones were recovered, and these included examples made from distinctive stone sources known as Eidsborg schist and purple phyllite which can only be found in Norway.[22] These must have been imported and appear to be a commodity, like steatite, that was regularly traded across the North Sea. One of the purple phyllite whetstones was a carefully made and delicate object, which had been perforated so it could be worn on a belt.

FIGURE 3.22. A cross section through a hearth built into the cultivation soil of Bornais, mound 2A.

FIGURE 3.23. A selection of finds from the cultivation soil on Bornais, mound 2A; including a glass gaming counter, two whetstones, a stone spindle whorl broken during production, the side plate of a composite comb, two bone pins, tweezers and the copper alloy ring from a ring headed pin.

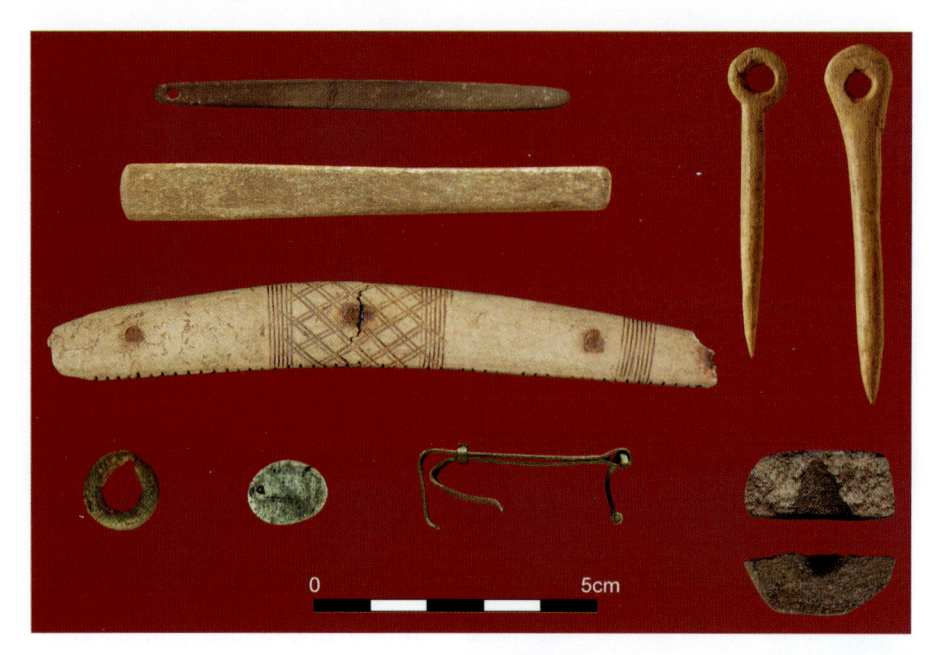

One characteristic of the assemblage from these deposits on mound 2A was the presence of debris from bone-working activities, including waste from the manufacture of bone pins. Other craft activities were indicated by the presence of distinctive textile production tools, including a pair of weaving tablets and a whale bone 'pin beater' used to beat down the threads in a loom. There was a small collection of needles and spindle whorls, and one of the whorls was in the process of being perforated when it split. It is also important to note the absence of loom weights in these deposits and from the settlement in all periods. These objects are relatively frequent discoveries in the Northern Isles and are evidence for warp-weighted looms in those islands.[23] Their absence at Bornais and Cille Pheadair suggests a different type of loom was used in the Western Isles; a two beamed vertical loom does not require weights. This slightly more advanced loom was not used in Scandinavia but had been introduced to Britain and adopted prior to the Viking colonisation. This may indicate the continuity of a technological innovation in the Western Isles due to the presence of indigenous women which was not possible in the Northern Isles. The finds from the cultivation soil suggest that this area of the site was closely associated with craft activities from the beginning of the Norse occupation.

Evidence from mound 2A suggests that in the early tenth century this area was on the periphery of the settlement. It was predominantly an intensively cultivated infield whose fertility and stability were enhanced by the deposition of large quantities of rubbish from the adjacent settlement. Towards the end of the tenth century this location started to be used for processing crops, and the hearths created may have been used for drying the grain grown in these fields. This was followed by a period in the eleventh century when very little was happening, and sand was allowed to accumulate in the abandoned fields. It was unlikely that the settlement was completely abandoned as rubbish was still occasionally dumped here, but activity was much less frequent than it used to be.

Cille Pheadair

The settlement at Cille Pheadair at the south end of South Uist was almost totally excavated by Mike Parker Pearson (Fig. 3.24).[24] It was a single small settlement mound that comprised a sequence of structures and middens very similar to the smaller mounds at Bornais, for example mound 2A. The settlement consisted of only a single house with associated ancillary buildings, but the house went through major structural modifications and complete rebuilding at least seven times over a period of between 160 and 220 years, from the middle of the tenth century to the beginning of the thirteenth century.

In the first phase a large rectangular enclosure, oriented north– south, was defined by a 1.5 to 2.0 m thick bank of sand that surrounded a complex of post holes and pits. Parker Pearson was reluctant to call this a house as the pits showed no evidence they contained posts, but a house seems the most likely interpretation to me. The internal area was roughly 17 m long and 5 m wide, though the west side was destroyed by coastal erosion before the excavation began. The entrance was on the east side, close to the southeast corner, and had a stone-revetted passage.

The pits dug within the interior of this house had sharp vertical edges and the fills were of relatively clean homogeneous sand which suggests they were filled soon after they were dug. The largest and most clearly defined pits

FIGURE 3.24. A view of the early house at Cille Pheadair during excavation. © Mike Parker Pearson.

formed two rows on the edge of the hollowed interior; one row had nine pits and the other six. The fills of most of the pits contained only a few finds but there were a couple with clusters of finds, particularly iron objects and nails, bone pins and a largely complete bone comb, which suggest these objects were carefully selected and placed in the pit for a reason. The post holes were also in two lines and indicated the presence of a three-aisled longhouse contained by the sand bank.

Modelling of the radiocarbon dates from this settlement indicated this early phase of activity dated to the late tenth or early eleventh centuries, slightly later than the Early Norse longhouse at Bornais.

Drimore and other excavations

A few other archaeological excavations in the Western Isles have recovered remains of Scandinavian settlements. On Lewis the excavations at Barvas and Bostaidh revealed the remains of Norse buildings and middens, and the evidence from these sites will be considered in later chapters. In South Uist a large house was discovered in the 1950s in the centre of the machair plain at Drimore towards the north end of the island.[25]

This house is described in the published report as a 'large bow-shaped hall', 14 m long and 5 m wide, with a large, roughly central, hearth and an entrance facing north close to the western gable end (Fig. 3.25). A large and distinctive antler comb suggests an early date in the later part of the tenth century for the use of this house. This date is supported by the recovery of steatite vessel sherds and a relatively small assemblage of pottery. No obvious Late Norse material was found, and it is important to note that the house was not covered by later middens or other structural remains; so it seems this settlement was relatively short lived.

The main problem with this excavation was the interpretation of the structural remains that defined the house. The house, as described by the excavator, was a rather odd collection of walls which do not inspire confidence in the interpretation of this building as a coherent single-phase house. The west wall was a curving orthostatic revetment wall, more reminiscent of Late Iron Age structures than Viking houses. The opposite east wall in contrast was the best bit of walling on the site but cut across the axis of the house at an acute angle and appeared to be a later construction, reducing the size of the original house. Neither of these gable end walls resembles the long side walls and these were also quite different to each other. It seems very unlikely that these structural remains were anything but the fortuitous arrangement of walls of several very different structures. However, the identification of a floor layer and the presence of the hearth at the centre of the complex of walls suggests a house did exist, though only further excavation can clarify exactly how the surrounding walls were connected to the house. Further excavation is still possible as the threat that led to the original excavation never materialised, and the site has remained undamaged since the excavations ended.

FIGURE 3.25. The excavation of a Viking longhouse at Drimore, South Uist. © Crown Copyright: HES.

Viking treasure

The Viking colonisation of the Western Isles marks a major shift in the power centres of Scotland. As discussed in the previous chapter, the increasing importance of the developing Pictish Kingdom coincided with a decline in the independence of the islands and was probably connected to a decline in population due to disease and malnutrition. As a result of these problems, the role of the individual and the use of precious materials and elaborate craftsmanship to distinguish high-status individuals became increasingly important throughout northern Britain. There is very little sign that the very high-status metalwork was available to people living in the Western Isles in the seventh and eighth centuries. The power centres of Late Iron Age Scotland were in the agricultural heartlands of the eastern lowlands, around the Moray Firth, and southern Scotland, particularly Angus and southern Perthshire. In these areas elaborate metalwork and richly ornamented stones provide archaeological testimony to the presence of important people; people who aspired to be kings and lords. The Viking colonisation of Scotland changed the nature of power relations and redistributed the people with power towards the north and west coasts.

FIGURE 3.26. The silver hoards from Dibidale and Stornoway Castle on the Isle of Lewis. © Museum nan Eilean.

The obvious signs of this wealth are the rich graves, such as Cnip, which was discussed at the beginning of this chapter. These graves contained objects which clearly indicated the status of the deceased and of the mourners attending the funeral, demonstrating the presence of high-status individuals on the islands. In the middle of the tenth century, another manifestation of wealth was circulating on the western fringes of northern Britain; collections of precious metalwork buried in isolated locations that are known as hoards. Four hoards are known from the Outer Hebrides and historical records suggest at least one other hoard may have been found and then lost. The surviving hoards come from Oronsay on North Uist and Stornoway Castle, Dibidale Moss and Barvas, all of which are on Lewis.[26]

The hoard from Dibidale Moss on the west coast of Lewis was found in a peat cutting in 1938. It comprised three complete silver arm-rings and two plain band finger-rings (Fig. 3.26). The arm-rings are in excellent condition and do not seem to have been circulating for long before they were buried in the ground. These arm-rings are also known as 'ring money' as they are believed to have been more important as a means of circulating precious metal than as a personal ornament. They were created by melting down silver coins and ornaments such as brooches and pins looted during raids. The molten silver was poured into bar moulds to make ingots that were then hammered into the shape of bracelets. They were probably originally produced in Ireland, but the largest collections of these objects come from Scotland. Very few ever made it back to Scandinavia.

The hoard from Stornoway Castle came from the gardens at the back of the 'castle' and was found in 1988. It consists of 57 pieces of hack silver and two Normandy deniers (coins) dating from the late tenth to early eleventh century. The hack silver was largely cut sections of silver ring money but there was also a fragment of a penannular brooch pin and a decorated, flat-sectioned arm-ring. Some of these fragments were contained in a cattle horn core and appeared to have been wrapped in a piece of linen cloth.

These hoards can be dated to the late tenth or, more likely, the early eleventh century, and were contemporary with the use of the Early Norse longhouse on

FIGURE 3.27. The hoard of gold rings from Oronsay. © National Museums Scotland.

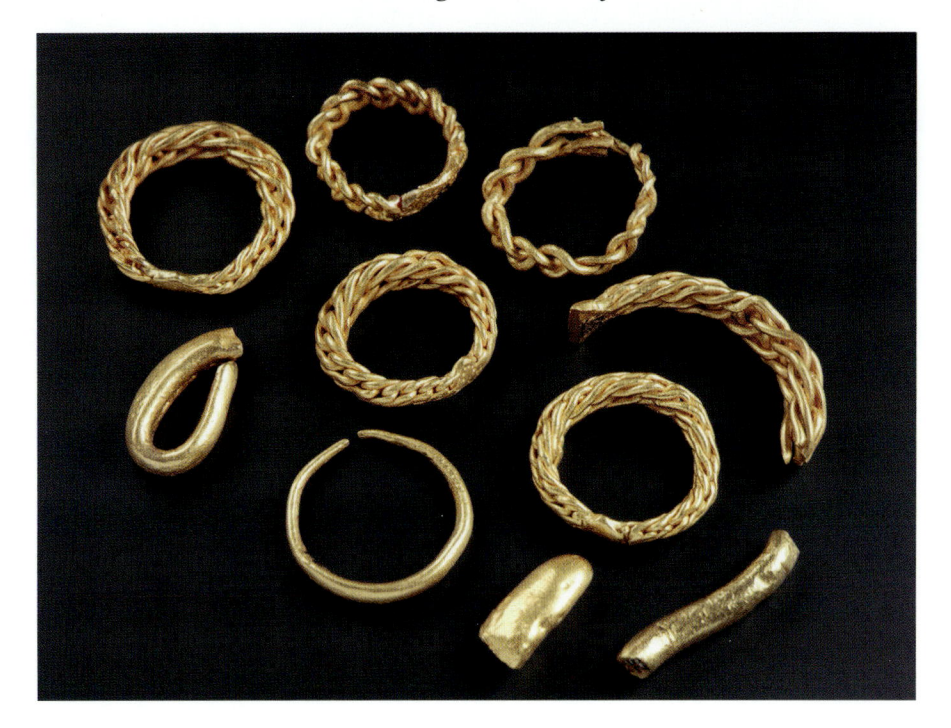

mound 2 at Bornais. They belonged to the second phase of Viking hoards in Scotland. The first phase, which occurred in the first half of the tenth century, was not well represented in northern Scotland but there is a hoard from Skye, the Storr Rock hoard, which was found on the coast just below this famous landmark. This is a chronological and geographical outlier of a group of hoards that were concentrated around the Irish Sea and across southern Scotland. It comprised 23 pieces of silver bullion and 111 coins. The coins included 19 dirhams from central Asia, 32 coins of Edward the Elder and 57 coins of Athelstan. The Storr Rock hoard was probably deposited between AD 935 and 940. There was then a 40-year gap before the second phase of hoards was deposited. This second phase is well represented in the Scottish islands, and Orkney has produced two very substantial silver hoards belonging to this period of deposition; the Skaill Hoard and the Burray Hoard.

A fourth hoard of precious metal from the Hebrides is of gold rather than silver. It comprised six and a half gold rings, three small fragments of gold ingots and a rod. Five and a half are plaited rings, one is plain, and they are all in good condition (Fig. 3.27). These were found in the 1860s though the location is not accurately known. A local landowner and well-respected antiquarian, Erskine Beveridge, reported that they came from the island of Oronsay on the north coast of North Uist and this seems to be confirmed by local memories. Dating these rings is difficult; they could be contemporary with the other hoards, but they could have been deposited as late as the twelfth century, though by this time the tradition of hoarding precious metal seems to have died out.

These hoards indicate the creation of a bullion economy, based around the circulation of precious metal, in this case silver, the value of which was assessed by weight and the quality (purity) of the metal. This type of economy arose in southern Scotland in the ninth century, possibly as a result of the presence of the Great Host in Northumbria in the 860s. However, it was not until the silver hoards of Storr Rock, Skye and Skaill on Orkney were deposited in the middle of the tenth century that this metals-based economy can be fully documented in northern Scotland, and it was only in the early eleventh century that bullion hoards appeared in the Outer Hebrides.

A small number of unstratified and later finds from Bornais and Cille Pheadair reveal that the occupants of these sites used bullion as part of their trading relations. These finds included small, standardised weights from both sites, and the hinge fitting of a balance arm and a piece of hack silver from Bornais. A small number of Anglo Saxon and Scandinavian coins were excavated at these settlements, indicating that the islanders were also involved in monetary exchanges. The historical record tells us that textiles (wadmill) were another commodity used in exchange relationships. The islanders clearly had a complex and diverse economy which was flexible and took advantage of a variety of valuables that were being exchanged across the North Atlantic colonies.

The Cille Bharra cross slab

The deposition of metalwork hoards may indicate the beliefs of the islanders, as one of the interpretations of these discoveries is that they are dedicated to the gods in payment for success in ventures such as raids in Ireland. However, the most obvious evidence for the beliefs of the islanders is the evidence for their conversion to Christianity. We have already mentioned the presence of a small lead cross from the floor of the Early Norse longhouse at Bornais, but the most striking evidence for the importance of Christianity was the discovery on Barra of a slab of local stone, carved on one side with an elaborately decorated cross and on the other with a runic inscription running vertically down the length of the stone (Fig. 3.28).[27]

The stone was discovered by Alexander Carmichael, a famous Gaelic scholar and author of *Carmina Gadelica*, in 1865 and was eventually shipped to what is now the National Museum Scotland in 1880. The slab was found in the graveyard of the parish church, which lies at the north end of Barra and is dedicated to St Barr.[28] There are three buildings in the churchyard. One of these dates back to the medieval period and was probably originally constructed in the twelfth century, but the others are more recent burial chapels. There are three decorated grave slabs of fifteenth- to sixteenth-century date which probably indicate the importance of the church to the MacNeill's of Barra. There are currently no remains that date to the late tenth century when the cross slab was carved, so it is possible that it was originally erected elsewhere and then moved to Cill Bharra when it became the religious centre for the island.

The stone would have stood erect and is currently 1.37 m tall, though it would have been slightly taller as the top has been damaged. The cross is defined by

FIGURE 3.28. The Viking gravestone from Cille Bharra. © Society of Antiquaries of Scotland.

two incised lines with four circular cup marks at the junction of the arms and the shaft, the cross is decorated with a neatly executed pleated interlace and the background has been decorated with s-scrolls and rectangular key patterns. The base of the slab is undecorated and may have been below ground level when it was erected. The runic inscription, on the other side, comprises three lines of text. The first two lines have been translated as:

> After Thorgerth, Steiner's daughter
> this cross was raised

The third line is unreadable due to erosion. The cross is compared to the large corpus of decorative stones found in the Isle of Man but in a recent authoritative examination of the decorative stones from the West Highlands, Ian Fisher suggests there were closer connections to the decorated stones from Govan in Glasgow and other isolated examples in Argyll. The best parallels for the inscription are in Scandinavia. The local source of the stone certainly suggests that it was carved on the island, and it seems therefore that there were Scandinavians living on the island who were aware of the stylistic fashions that were current in the region and in their homeland and who could competently carve these decorative motifs on the local stone.

This cross was almost certainly sponsored by Thorgerth to commemorate the death of his daughter and testifies to the importance of Christianity on the island in the second half of the tenth century.

The agricultural economy

Crops

The excavation of the soil horizon at the base of Bornais mound 2A provided an invaluable insight into the agricultural economy of the early Viking colonies in the Western Isles, as the fertility of these agricultural fields was enhanced by the dumping of large amounts of household waste including the ashes of household fires, major quantities of plant remains, the butchered remains of livestock and the residues of other foodstuffs.

The machair plain of South Uist is well suited to the production of cereals and even today the machair is ploughed and barley and oats are cultivated (Fig. 3.29). Historically the Uists were one of the most productive Hebridean islands, comparable only to Islay and Tiree on the western seaboard of Scotland in a landscape otherwise dominated by rock and bog. The historical record is supported by the results of our excavations and our programme of extensive flotation which was designed to recover as much evidence as possible for the agricultural economy of the settlements.[29]

The establishment of the Viking settlement at Bornais marked a significant change in the agricultural exploitation of the machair plain. In the preceding phase of the Late Iron Age, the inhabitants were almost exclusively focused on barley as the principal cereal crop and, though other crops such as oats and flax were known and present as small quantities of seeds, they do not seem to have played a major role in the agricultural economy. This changed dramatically when the Vikings established their settlement. The production of oats, rye and flax substantially increased, and they clearly became agriculturally important crops.[30]

A significant feature of the Viking deposits was the increased density of carbonised remains and cultivars present in the soil samples recovered. The density of cereal grains per litre of soil was calculated for every sample and an average worked out for each period and area. The average density for the Late Iron Age deposits on mound 2 was well below one cereal grain per litre of soil whereas for the floor of Early Norse longhouse the average density was over seven cereal grains per litre of soil, and in the cultivation soil on mound 2A, it was over 23 grains per litre of soil. Clearly there was a significant change

FIGURE 3.29. Barley cultivated and stacked to dry on the machair plain of South Uist.

in agricultural practice after the Viking colonisation of the islands. The most obvious conclusion is that the Vikings were growing a lot more cereals on the machair plain and perhaps the introduction of new crops gave them the ability to cultivate areas that had previously been regarded as unsuitable. Oats and flax will grow on very light sandy soils with only limited fertility. Rye, in contrast, could be grown on the acidic soils of the blacklands which lie adjacent to the machair and are only a short walk away.

The prominence of certain plants varied from mound to mound, and for the Viking period we can usefully compare samples taken from the floor of the Early Norse longhouse on mound 2 with samples from the cultivation soils on mound 2A (Fig. 3.30). The house samples were dominated by barley, though oats were clearly an important crop, and rye was also becoming significant. In contrast the mound 2A assemblages were dominated by oats, with barley a secondary though still very significant crop, and rye and flax were both present in substantial quantities.

There may be other reasons for the increased densities of carbonised plant remains on the site and one is likely to be a change in the way the crop was being processed. This was certainly a factor in explaining the differences in the assemblages from the house floor and the cultivation soil. The assemblage from the Early Norse longhouse floor is likely to represent crops brought into the house only in the final stages of processing before being turned into food. The assemblages from the cultivation soil, in contrast, were likely to derive from crops in the initial stages of processing, and the hearths in this area might have been designed to dry crops as part of this initial processing.

The importance of barley inside the Early Norse longhouse may therefore indicate it retained its significance as a foodstuff for human consumption, whereas the presence of oats in the cultivation soil may indicate this was used as a fodder crop to feed the settlement's animals in the winter when grazing was very poor.

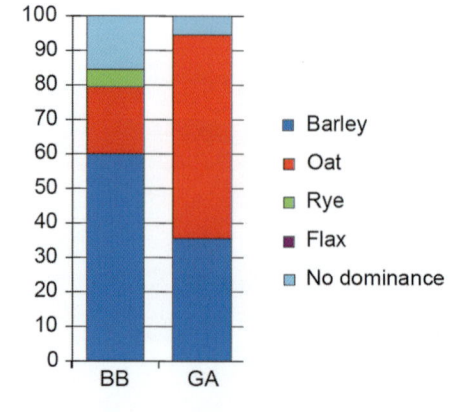

The increased quantities of grain in the archaeological record could therefore be partially explained by the development of grain-drying as an essential part of crop-processing in the Viking period. This would explain the very high densities of carbonised plant remains on mound 2A, but it seems likely that the overall increase in the densities of crop remains on the settlement reveals an intensification of cereal agriculture with the Viking colonisation. This was a significant change in the exploitation of the machair plain which may have been encouraged by the benign climate of this period, but in the long term it had negative consequences for this fragile landscape.

FIGURE 3.30. A diagram showing the variation in the different crops recovered from the early Norse deposits on mound 2 (BB) and mound 2A (GA) at Bornais.

Fish

It has long been recognised that the exploitation of the sea was transformed by the arrival of the Vikings. A detailed analysis of the dietary isotopes of carbon and nitrogen of the burials from a long-lived cemetery at Newark in Orkney demonstrated that fish only become an important part of the diet after the Viking conquest of the islands. A comprehensive analysis of the lipids in pottery confirmed that fish were absent from the prehistoric assemblages and only showed a significant presence after the Viking conquest.31

This has been argued to indicate that the prehistoric inhabitants of Britain had a religious taboo against eating fish that began with the introduction of agriculture in the Neolithic. It may not have been a complete or exclusive prohibition as there is some evidence that fish might have been consumed on special occasions, perhaps at times of famine or in relation to specific ceremonies. The reason for this taboo may have been related to the disposal of the dead. There is good evidence that large numbers of dead people were being disposed of in British rivers, together with large quantities of elaborate metalwork. This seems to be a distinctive religious tradition that created a problematic association of fish with the dead. It is possible that fish were believed to be part of the process of moving an individual from the realm of the living to the realm of the dead. This taboo appears to have declined in the Roman period in southern Britain as the archaeological record and the historical sources show the Romans were happy to eat fish. In the north these Roman influences were less significant and though fish-eating was beginning to appear by the middle of the first millennium, it was the arrival of the Vikings that transformed the fish-eating habits of the north British dramatically.

In the Late Iron Age deposits on Bornais mound 1 and mound 2 fish bones were present in only very limited quantities and the species present were dominated by saithe and salmonids (trout and/or salmon) which could have been easily caught from the shore or in inland rivers and lochs. In contrast, large quantities of fish bone were recovered and identified from all the Norse deposits at Bornais and Cille Pheadair, and they were also present in the assemblages from the Udal and Bostadh.[32] The assemblages from all these settlements were dominated by herring. This change in the species caught pre- and post-colonisation happened immediately and was so dramatic that it can be used to identify the presence of Norse deposits during an excavation.

The assemblages of herring bones were dominated by vertebrae, especially those from the abdominal region, whilst very few bones from the herring heads were recovered (Fig. 3.31). As both floors and midden areas were examined by the excavations, it seems likely that herring were being brought to the site already decapitated and presumably gutted. This indicates that processing the fish occurred at specialist sites on the shore or elsewhere on the island. The size of the fish suggests the fishermen were catching herring that were coming to the end of their third year and that these were probably from shoals in the spawning grounds around the coast and in the Minch. It is unlikely that voyages to the fishing banks of the Continental Shelf would have been necessary since historical records document large shoals of herring in inshore waters.

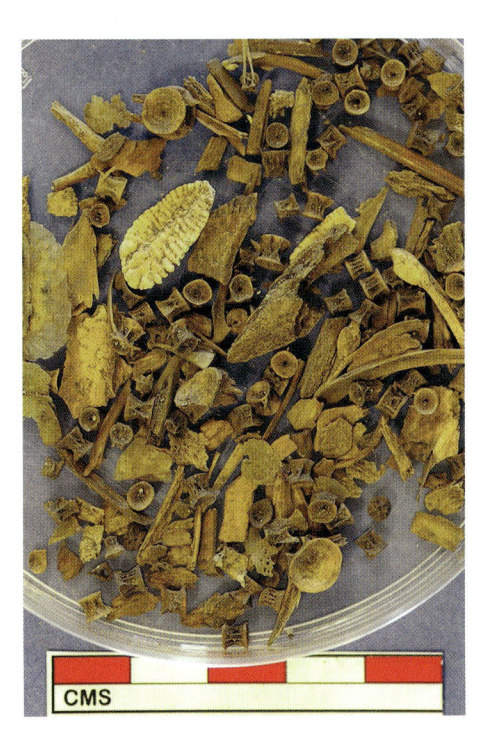

FIGURE 3.31. A photo of the fish bones recovered from careful sieving and sorting of one of the soil samples from Bornais. The large white bone is a Saithe otolith, but the other bones are mostly from herring.

The inhabitants of Bornais were also eating other fish, but these were processed quite differently. Saithe arrived on site as whole fish and were eaten fresh. Cod, hake and ling were present in small quantities but, in contrast to the herring, were represented by heads and their lower bellies. The prime meat fillets from the body and tail of these large white fish were missing and it seems likely these were air-dried and exported away from the islands. The same pattern was also noted at Cille Pheadair. These fish generally live in offshore waters; however, they are also known to prey on herring and are routinely found in amongst large herring shoals where they can easily be caught using baited lines.

The development of herring fishing in the Western Isles contrasts with the fishing practices of the Northern Isles, where large white fish such as cod and hake dominated the Viking and Norse assemblages. It is important to emphasise that the variation in fishing strategies between the Northern and Western Isles demonstrated the economic flexibility of the Viking settlers. They adapted very quickly to local conditions and the availability of different resources and species. They were not simply applying economic practices that had been developed in the Viking homelands.

The presence of processed fish indicated that the settlement at Bornais was a 'consumption' rather than a 'processing site', but the very large numbers of herring do suggest a surplus was available that could be traded. Herring is an oily fish and historically long-distance transportation as a commodity has required that the fish be pickled in brine or smoked. This contrasts with the white fish that dominated the assemblages from the Northern Isles, which could have been preserved by salting and air-drying. However, the fact that the herring from Bornais were decapitated may show that the fish were air-dried in a manner similar to the white fish of the Northern Isles, and similar practices have been recorded in Iceland. However, it is still difficult to understand how these fish could have been preserved for long-distance trade.

Animal bones

Our excavations at Bornais produced very large assemblages of animal bones and the Early Norse phase was well represented by an assemblage of over 4,200 identifiable bones from the cultivation soil on mound 2A, and an assemblage of just over 600 identifiable bones from the Early Norse longhouse on mound 2. The assemblage from mound 2A was the largest for any period of activity at Bornais. There were 746 identified bones from the Early Norse phases at Cille Pheadair.[33]

The distribution of the main domestic species during the life of the settlement is summarised in Fig. 3.32. Sheep[34] were the numerically dominant domesticate but cattle were only slightly less numerous. In the Early Norse period sheep appear to have been kept for meat production as large numbers were killed in the second year of life. Lambing did not appear to have taken place on the site. Older animals were rare and there did not appear to have been enough mature animals to make up a viable herd, which suggests that this assemblage was only revealing part of the pastoral economy. The age distribution of the cattle shows that small numbers were slaughtered in their first 18 months. There were reasonable numbers of young adults and about one-third were old animals. This herd profile suggests a focus on meat production and the use of older animals for traction (ploughing?) and milk production.

A feature of the assemblage was the presence of a significant quantity of pig bones in the Early Norse phases. In the cultivation soil, pig comprised over

FIGURE 3.32. The relative percentages of cattle, sheep, pig and red deer bones from Bornais, mound 2 and 2A, showing the changes through time.

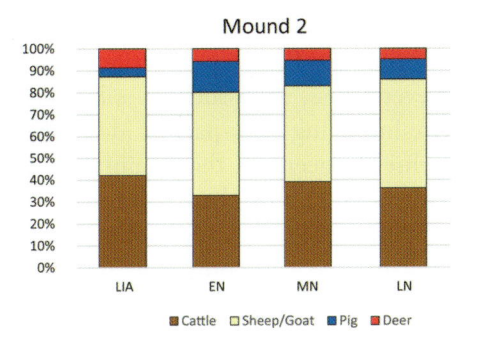

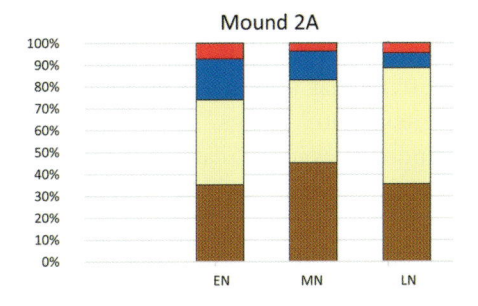

20% of the assemblage and in the floor of the Early Norse longhouse it comprised 14% of the assemblage. This contrasts markedly with the Late Iron Age deposits on mound 2, where pig was less than 10%, and also with the Late Iron Age assemblage from mound 1. On mounds 2 and 2A, the proportion of pig declined steadily after the Early Norse maxima until it was between 6% and 8% of the assemblage in the thirteenth and fourteenth centuries, a figure comparable to the pre-Norse occupation.

Recent work on animal bones from the Faroe Islands and Iceland highlight the importance of pigs in the early Viking settlements. It has been argued that keeping pigs was an environmental adaptation – 'Pigs are particularly well suited to feeding on the root systems of Arctic birch and willow, and …. may have acted as major agents of environmental change'.[35] However, this explanation for the large numbers of pigs isn't convincing, as there is no evidence that the Faroe Islands had any forest prior to the Norse colonisation, and the Hebrides were completely deforested by this time. Indeed, introducing pigs onto the fragile machair soils of the west coast of South Uist was a very dangerous decision, as their digging proclivities would have broken up the protective turf cover and encouraged windblown deflation. The introduction of pigs is therefore likely to indicate social pressures. Pigs are an easy way to produce meat. They require little in the way of complex management and can be fed on a variety of waste materials. Pigs were routinely used as a resource for feasting throughout prehistory and were well suited to a society where communal consumption and conspicuous waste was an important social strategy for achieving status. Other archaeologists have argued on the basis of the Orcadian evidence that pigs were indeed associated with feasting, and this interpretation was supported by the large numbers present on high status sites, such as Orphir in Orkney.[36]

Conclusion

In this chapter I have assessed the archaeological evidence for the Viking colonisation of the Western Isles. Scholarly opinion since the nineteenth century has been remarkably inconsistent about how violent and comprehensive this was. Capt W.F.L. Thomas, an important antiquarian, undertook one of the earliest studies of the Gaelic place names of the islands and was emphatic in his conclusion that the vast majority of these names had Norse origins and that they indicated the wholesale replacement of the Pictish population of the island by incomers from Scandinavia.[37] Nevertheless, the issue was still being debated in the 1980s and many people were indulging their pacifist ideals and arguing that the Viking takeover was an elite replacement that maintained a substantial proportion of the local population. The schizophrenia involved in these arguments is embodied in the publications of Ian Crawford, who argued in 1975 for a relatively limited incursion but by 1981 had completely changed his mind and was convinced there was a major colonisation of the islands, which were effectively cleared by Viking raiding parties. I myself have undergone something of transformation. In a paper on our initial exploration of the Viking settlements I suggested, with Mike Parker Pearson, that there were strong elements of continuity in the settlement pattern that indicated the survival of indigenous elements in the culture of the Hebridean Vikings.[38] However, after the completion of the excavation and the post-excavation analysis of the material recovered from Bornais, it is clear that a major change in the population has to have occurred.

The Viking incursions at the end of the ninth century seem to have been massive and immensely destructive, leading to the systematic abandonment of many settlements. An influx of settlers from Scandinavia brought with them the material culture of their homelands, including distinctive combs, pins and brooches, and objects such as steatite bowls and hones made from stone from Norwegian quarries. They had access to considerable quantities of iron which was used to make simple tools and fittings, and the presence of large numbers of iron objects clearly differentiates Viking settlements from Pictish settlements. The Scandinavian settlers built houses that replicated in shape and form the houses they had lived in in their homelands, and their way of life in these long bow-walled houses was based on communal feasting around a large central hearth. Choice cuts of meat were important to these societies and the increased importance of pigs in the bone assemblages indicates a preference for an animal closely associated with feasting and not well suited to the fragile machair environment of the Western Isles.

The most significant transformation in the diet and agricultural economy at this time concerns the crops grown on the machair. The arable economy of the Norse settlers was much more diverse than the barley monoculture of the Iron Age occupants of the islands. The cultivation of oats, rye and flax transformed the settlement landscape and indicates an innovative approach to the island's resources that was designed not only to maximise the availability of basic staple foods but also to introduce new crops that exploited the full potential of the landscape. The cultivation of flax is likely to be closely related to the production of linen textiles, and textiles were a staple commodity in the trading networks of the North Atlantic. The diversity of the arable economy seems to have been an innovation that did not reflect the situation in the Viking homelands and represents a need to maximise production to support a population that spent a lot of time raiding and trading around the North Atlantic. The Vikings were able to take advantage of a climatic optimum, which allowed them to exploit areas of the landscape that had hitherto been marginal due to the inclement weather conditions in the middle of the first millennium AD.

This adaptability is also evident in their approach to the surrounding seas. The Hebrideans, like the Scandinavians elsewhere in the North Atlantic, were catching and consuming large numbers of fish but, in contrast to the Orcadians and Shetlanders, they did not focus their attention on the large white fish such as cod and hake. Instead, they caught the locally abundant herring which historically were known to have shoaled in vast numbers in the waters surrounding the islands. The importance of fish in the diet of the inhabitants of Bornais is another feature which emphatically demonstrates that there was a major change in the population as, prior to the Viking period, fish formed only a minor component of the diet.

The overwhelming evidence therefore suggests that the population of the islands was largely replaced by Scandinavian settlers in the late ninth century and early tenth century, as part of a general colonisation that spread throughout the North Atlantic at this time. However, there are certain oddities in the archaeological evidence which might suggest that this picture is a little simplistic. The presence of ceramics alongside the steatite vessels in the floor of the Early Norse longhouse (House 1) at Bornais is a peculiarity, as most Viking settlements in the North Atlantic are aceramic, relying on steatite vessels imported from the homelands or made from other sources in the North Atlantic. This continuity of ceramic tradition could indicate the presence of female potters who survived the invasion and were taken as slaves or as wives by the incoming Scandinavian settlers. Their pottery skills were appreciated and provided an alternative source of vessels which reduced the need to import steatite from Shetland and Scandinavia.

All the indications are that there was a massive influx of foreign settlers. Most of the men came from Scandinavia but the women may have had more diverse origins and included individuals from all over the islands of Britain and Ireland. Some of the local inhabitants may have survived, and the majority of the survivors were probably female. All of these people adopted a lifestyle that was recognisably Scandinavian in many of its characteristics, but included features that derived from other societies encountered by the raiders and new features which evolved on the islands as a response to the local environment.

Notes

1 A full account of the burial at Cnip was published by Welander *et al.* 1987.
2 The additional burials were published by Dunwell *et al.* 1995.
3 The analysis of the Cnip burials is a good example of how scientific techniques have developed over time. The initial results of the isotopic analysis (Montgomery *et al.* 2003) suggested a very different origin than the later results (Montgomery *et al.* 2014) which were able to use a variety of different isotopes.

4   There has been a considerable interest in the history of the Viking period in the British Isles, and numerous well-written and researched accounts of this period are now available. The author found the following immensely valuable sources: Crawford 1987; Etchingham 2001; Forte *et al.* 2005; Woolf 2007; Jennings and Kruse 2009. Detailed references to the points made in this brief introduction can also be found in the section *Key Historical Events* in Chapter 11 of Sharples 2020.
5   See Wyatt 2009 for a detailed account of the importance of slavery in these Medieval societies.
6   The details of this merger are very obscure, and the historical sources are poor, but the lists of both Scottish and Pictish kings both appear to stop at AD 850.
7   The role of King Harald Fairhair in the establishment of the Earldom of Orkney is also problematic (Crawford 1987, 55), but his principal significance is in uniting the various regions of Norway into a single kingdom at the end of the ninth century.
8   This refers to the territory of the Scots and includes the counties of Argyll in Scotland and Antrim in Northern Ireland.
9   The burial pit at Weymouth is published in Loe *et al.* 2014.
10 The detailed report on the excavations is available in Carver *et al.* 2016, but a synthetic summary was published at the same time, Carver 2016.
11 There is an extremely useful summary of the Viking graves from Scotland in Graham-Campbell and Batey 1998.
12 The following references provide the most useful information on the excavations at the Udal: Crawford 1975; 1981; 1986; 1988; Crawford and Switsur 1977.
13 The excavation of Bornais mound 1 is described in Sharples 2012.
14 Katherine Forsyth provides an abbreviated discussion of this inscription in Sharples 2021, but a more detailed account is provided in Forsyth 2007.
15 The significance of this coin is discussed by Gareth Williams in Sharples 2012, 259–260 but a fuller discussion of the importance of all the coins from Bornais is presented by Williams in Sharples 2021, 106–107.
16 The house is fully described in Sharples 2020, chapter 2.
17 The excavations are described and discussed in Campbell 1991.
18 A detailed discussion of the importance of steatite use in the North Atlantic is provided by Hansen and Storemyr 2017.
19 See Lane 1990 and 2005 for a discussion of the significance of the identification of a distinctive Norse pottery tradition in the islands.
20 The most recent summary of the Hebridean pottery traditions was by Campbell 2002.
21 The excavation of the cultivation soil at Bornais mound 2A is described in Sharples 2020, chapter 3.
22 See Baug *et al.* 2019 for a recent discussion of the source of these stone types, and the significance of the development of these as traded commodities.
23 See Cartwright in Sharples 2021, 205.
24 They are fully published in Parker Pearson *et al.* 2018.
25 The excavations are detailed in MacLaren 1974.
26 The contents of the hoards, and the circumstances of their discovery are described in James Graham-Campbell's monograph on Scottish Viking hoards (Graham-Campbell 1995).
27 See Fisher 2001, 107 for a full description of the stone and its context.
28 It is generally assumed that St Barr was Finbar, not the more famous sixth-century Saint Finbar of Cork, but a less well-known Gaelic Scot who was Columba's teacher. See https://uistsaints.co.uk for a detailed discussion, accessed 24/02/2025.

29 We have so far washed 9,580 litres of soils and extracted the carbonised remains of over 131 thousand identified plant remains from Bornais.
30 A detailed report on the archaeobotanical remains recovered from the excavations at Bornais is provided by Summers and Bond in Sharples 2021 and from Cille Pheadair by Smith and College in Parker Pearson *et al.* 2018.
31 The original isotopic analysis of the burials from Deerness was published in Barrett *et al* 2001 and Barrett and Richards 2004, and the recent work on pottery isotopes was undertaken by Cramp *et al.* 2014 and 2015.
32 The fish bones from Bornais and Cille Pheadair were examined and discussed by Claire Ingrem and the reports are included in Sharples 2005; 2012; 2021; and Parker Pearson *et al.* 2018.
33 The animal bone assemblages from mounds 2 and 2A at Bornais were analysed by Claire Ingrem and Adrianne Powell and the reports are included in Sharples 2021. The bones from Cille Pheadair were analysed by Jacqui Mulville and Adrianne Powell and are reported on in Parker Pearson *et al.* 2018.
34 More precisely sheep and goat, as it is difficult to differentiate between the two species using only bones.
35 Vesteinsson *et al.* 2002, 110. See Church *et al.* 2005 for a similar pattern from the Faroes.
36 See Mainland and Batey 2019.
37 See Thomas 1876.
38 See Sharples and Parker Pearson 1999.

CHAPTER FOUR

The Kingdom of Man and the Isles

Introduction – a find of Ringerike art

On the 20th July 2000, we discovered one of the most important artefacts to be found at Bornais. This was not a treasure of precious metal, but a hollow cylinder of antler on which a skilled craftsperson had incised a distinctive mythical beast (Fig. 4.1). The broken fragments of the cylinder were found scattered in a layer of dark brown sand that covered the floor of a Middle Norse longhouse (House 2) at Bornais, close to the north wall of the house. All but two small fragments were recovered, and it seems likely that the piece was intact when it was deposited but broke after the abandonment of the house.

The cylinder is 76 mm long and has a flattened oval cross-section that narrows towards the top (Fig. 4.2). Adjacent to the bottom edge are three small holes, which suggest the cylinder was attached to some form of organic container. One interpretation of this object is that it was the mouthpiece for a leather drinking-flask. Whatever its precise use, the object had had a long life as one side was heavily worn and polished, probably from continuously being rubbed, which would have happened if it was attached to a belt and frequently worn or carried by its owner. This worn surface was less elaborately decorated than the outer side, but traces of an eroded knotwork pattern is still just visible.

FIGURE 4.1. A photograph of the antler cylinder decorated with a Ringerike beast from the floor of Bornais, House 2.

The animal in the main design has some classic decorative features, notably straight tails, 'horns' with abruptly curled tips, and a spiral hip joint, that identify it as a piece of Ringerike art (Fig. 4.2). The Ringerike style is one of six distinct styles recognised by archaeologists who study Viking art.[1] In chronological order these styles are: Oseberg, Borre, Jellinge, Mammen, Ringerike and Urnes. They span the period from AD 775 to AD 1125 with the Ringerike style current between AD 990 and AD 1050.

FIGURE 4.2. A drawing of the antler cylinder decorated with a Ringerike beast from the floor of Bornais, House 2.

Animals were a central feature of Viking art and the figure on the Bornais cylinder is comparable to other 'Great Beasts' which became the central motif of the later styles from Mammen to Urnes (Fig. 4.3). The Bornais design is stylistically similar to animals found on memorial stones in southern Sweden, notably the Ringerike stones at Storra Ek and Norra Åsarp in Västergötland, but it is also similar in layout to the Tullstorp stone in Skåne which has been attributed to the earlier 'Mammen Style'. These designs were carved onto monumental stones so were considerably larger than the Bornais figure, but the 'Great Beast' also appeared on smaller objects including weathervanes, such as that from Heggen Church, Modum, Norway, and ornaments, such as a brooch from Espinge, Skåne, Sweden. All of these renditions suggest a fairly savage animal, such as a lion, was being depicted and they contrast with the animal on the Bornais cylinder, whose depiction suggests this artist had a much more delicate animal in mind, perhaps a stag, when he incised this design.

FIGURE 4.3. Great beasts in Viking art. Bornais is 2 and it is compared to the much larger images on the memorial stones of 1. Tullstorp, Skåne, Sweden; 3 Stora Ek, and 4. Norra Åsarp, Västergötland, Sweden.

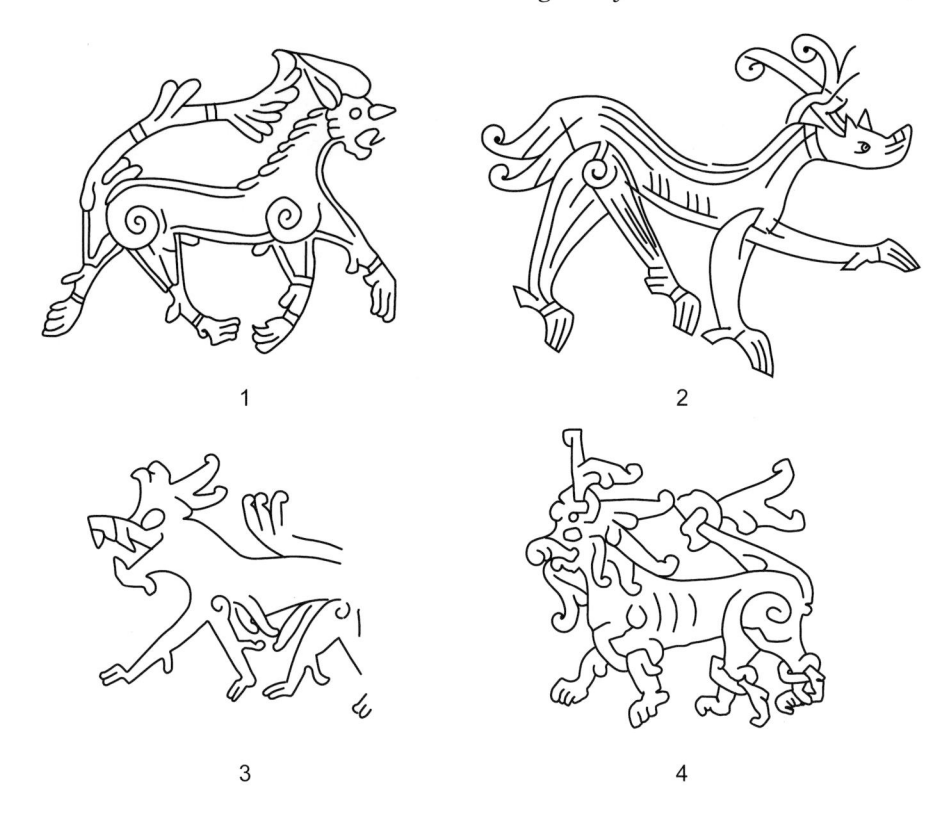

Ringerike style artworks spread throughout Europe. An important centre of production was established in London when Cnut, King of Denmark, became King of England. The best example from this workshop is the end-slab of a stone coffin found in the churchyard of St Paul's in London which has a classic depiction of a 'Great Beast' that was probably produced by an artist trained in Scandinavia. Another workshop was established in the Viking town at Dublin, possibly due to disruption of the London workshop on the death of King Cnut in AD 1035, and this produced a distinctively regional style of Ringerike art throughout the eleventh and early twelfth centuries.

Examples of Ringerike art are not common in Scotland and the Bornais cylinder is probably the best example we have. The simple style of the art on this cylinder, with an absence of motifs filling in the blank spaces surrounding the beast, suggests this was a relatively early piece of Ringerike art. It is very different from the later styles that developed in Dublin and London, and it seems likely that it was imported from a workshop in Scandinavia where it was made early in the eleventh century. It was deposited on the floor of the Middle Norse longhouse probably early in the twelfth century which implies it was in use for around 100 years; the wear on the object shows it was in use for a lengthy period of time, which would agree with the chronology proposed. A pinhead from Cille Pheadair decorated with a very simple Ringerike knotwork design shows that other objects were circulating in the Western Isles and demonstrated an awareness of the fashions within the Scandinavian homelands (Fig. 4.4).

The cylinder is just one of a large number of objects that were found on the floor of the Middle Norse longhouse at Bornais and this house and the finds in it will be the focus of this chapter. The Ringerike cylinder was undoubtedly a special object as it had been decorated in a very distinctive fashion. The beast depicted must have conveyed a meaning not only to the owner of the drinking flask to which it was attached but also to companions who watched him use it. Exactly what this meaning was is unclear, but it suggests mythical tales of gods and monsters. The Ringerike style would have been relatively old and possibly unfashionable by the time the cylinder was deposited on the floor of the house, and so may have been cherished more as a symbol of a distant homeland than as a contemporary piece. It had certainly travelled some distance from its place of manufacture, in both space and time. There are other objects from the same house floor which underwent similar journeys and had long and eventful lives, such as the green porphyry described in Chapter 1. However, before I describe and discuss these significant archaeological discoveries, I must outline some of the historical background that provides a context for our stories.

FIGURE 4.4. The broken head of a bone pin from Cille Pheadair decorated with a Ringerike knot.

The history

1066 was an important year in the history of Britain and Ireland. For many, the Battle of Hastings stands out as the most significant event but for the people of the north and west of Britain the preceding battle at Stamford Bridge, just south of York, was even more important. At Stamford Bridge the newly crowned English king, Harold Godwinson, defeated an invading Norwegian army led by their king, Harold Hardrada, who claimed to be the rightful heir to the throne of England. This battle arguably marked the end of the Viking Age in Britain as it represented the last significant invasion of England by a Scandinavian army and with this Anglo-Saxon victory, many important Norse leaders from northern and western Britain were killed. One of the survivors of Stamford Bridge, Gofraid Crobán, took refuge in the west and eventually established himself as King of Man and the Isles in 1079. He had an unusually long life during which he competed with various Irish kings to control the town of Dublin and actively supported the north Welsh kings in their resistance to Anglo-Norman incursions. It is possible he had a power base in the Scottish isles and his death from the plague on Islay in 1095 may reflect the importance of this island and the southern Hebrides at this time. He was an important figure in Manx mythology and in the following centuries the Kings of Man and the Isles all claimed to be descended from his lineage.

Gofraid Crobán's death was followed by an important intervention by the Norwegian king, Magnus Óláfsson berfœttr (Barelegs). He launched the first of two expeditions to the west in 1098 to assert Norwegian authority over the isles, and to make himself overlord of the Viking enclaves in Ireland, if not the whole of Ireland itself. His passage through the Hebrides appears to have been devastating and it was recorded that:

> in Uist the king deep crimson made
> the lightning of his glancing blade;
> the peasant lost both land and life
> who dared to bide the Norseman's strife[2]

Magnus Óláfsson captured Gofraid Crobán's son Lǫgmaðr in the northern Hebrides and in a later Icelandic source, the *Morkinskinna*, he is referred to as 'the prince of Uist'[3] which inferred that he was a resident in the islands. During this raid King Magnus may have met the king of the Scots and agreed respective areas of influence in the west. Scotland was to have control of the mainland and the Norwegians the islands and Kintyre. The historian Alex Woolf has questioned the veracity of this famous meeting, particularly as the wrong king of Scotland was mentioned in the historical record, and he suggests it might have been a much more local division of the Clyde estuary that was referenced. King Magnus was forced to return to Ireland in 1102 to sort out a dispute and, although the main problem was apparently resolved by a marriage, the trip ended in disaster when he was ambushed and killed in eastern Ulster.

There followed a period of over 150 years when the Norwegian kings appear to have had little interest in their territories in the west, and the Kingdom of Man and the Isles was allowed to develop its own political structure. Arrangements for taxation would have been adopted and modified over the period, legal representations would have been arranged, and appropriate representatives sent to an assembly at Tynwald in the Isle of Man from all the major islands in the Kingdom.

A major political development in the middle of the twelfth century was the appearance of Somerled, a Norse-Gaelic lord of considerable significance. His origins are unclear,[4] but he must have belonged to a family of some status that owned land in Ireland and Argyll as he was able to link himself to the kings of Man and the Isles by marrying the daughter of Ólafr Guðrøðarson, Gofraid Crobán's son and heir. His historical significance was enhanced by the significance of his descendants who formed the Lordship of the Isles that controlled Argyll, the Inner Hebrides, and eventually the Outer Hebrides up until the end of the fifteenth century. The Battle of Epiphany in 1156, between Somerled and Guðrøðr Ólafsson of Man, was an important event in the rise of Somerled and, from this point, he controlled at least some of the southern islands of the Inner and Outer Hebrides. Exactly which islands were controlled by Somerled is in dispute, and how much control over the islands was re-established by Guðrøðr on Somerled's death in 1164 is also unknown. However, by 1210 the Uists, Benbecula and Barra may have been part of the territory of Angus, a son of Somerled, and these islands were subsequently incorporated into the Lordship of Garmoran with the small isles (Rhum, Muck, Eigg and Canna) and Ardnamurchan, Knoydart and Moidart on the mainland, under the sons of Ruari; the MacRuaidhrís.

Archaeology and the Kingdom of Man

The archaeological record for this period on the Outer Hebrides is substantial and a detailed survey of the machair plain of South Uist has revealed 24 Norse settlements, all relatively untouched by modern development (Fig. 4.5).[5] These settlements survive as substantial mounds which have produced, from exposed and eroding deposits, distinctive ceramics that belonged to this period. Alan Lane defined the form of these vessels when he worked on the ceramic assemblage from the Udal in North Uist, and his identification of a very distinctive, flat baking plate known as platter has made it possible to identify settlements even when they have only produced small sherds of these ceramic plates.[6] There are therefore a large number of settlement mounds which would, if carefully excavated, provide more important evidence for the economy and social life of the islands in the Norse period.

The consolidation of political power by the Kings of Man and the Isles at Tynwald in the Isle of Man suggests that this was the period when the administrative structures of the Medieval state were imposed on the islands.[7] This included the Church, whose organisation was strongly associated with the development of state power. By the thirteenth century many of the religious centres on the islands were established, or re-established; the parish structure was formalised under the leadership of the Bishop of Sodor and individual churches established to ensure that everyone had access to the correct Christian message.[8] Taxes would have been an important mechanism for the administrative control of the Kingdom and would have been based on the ownership of land. The islands were divided into units known as ouncelands or *tir unga*,

FIGURE 4.5. A map of South Uist showing the location of settlement mounds producing Norse ceramics, the possible early church sites, fortifications and administrative boundaries (based on information in Raven 2005).

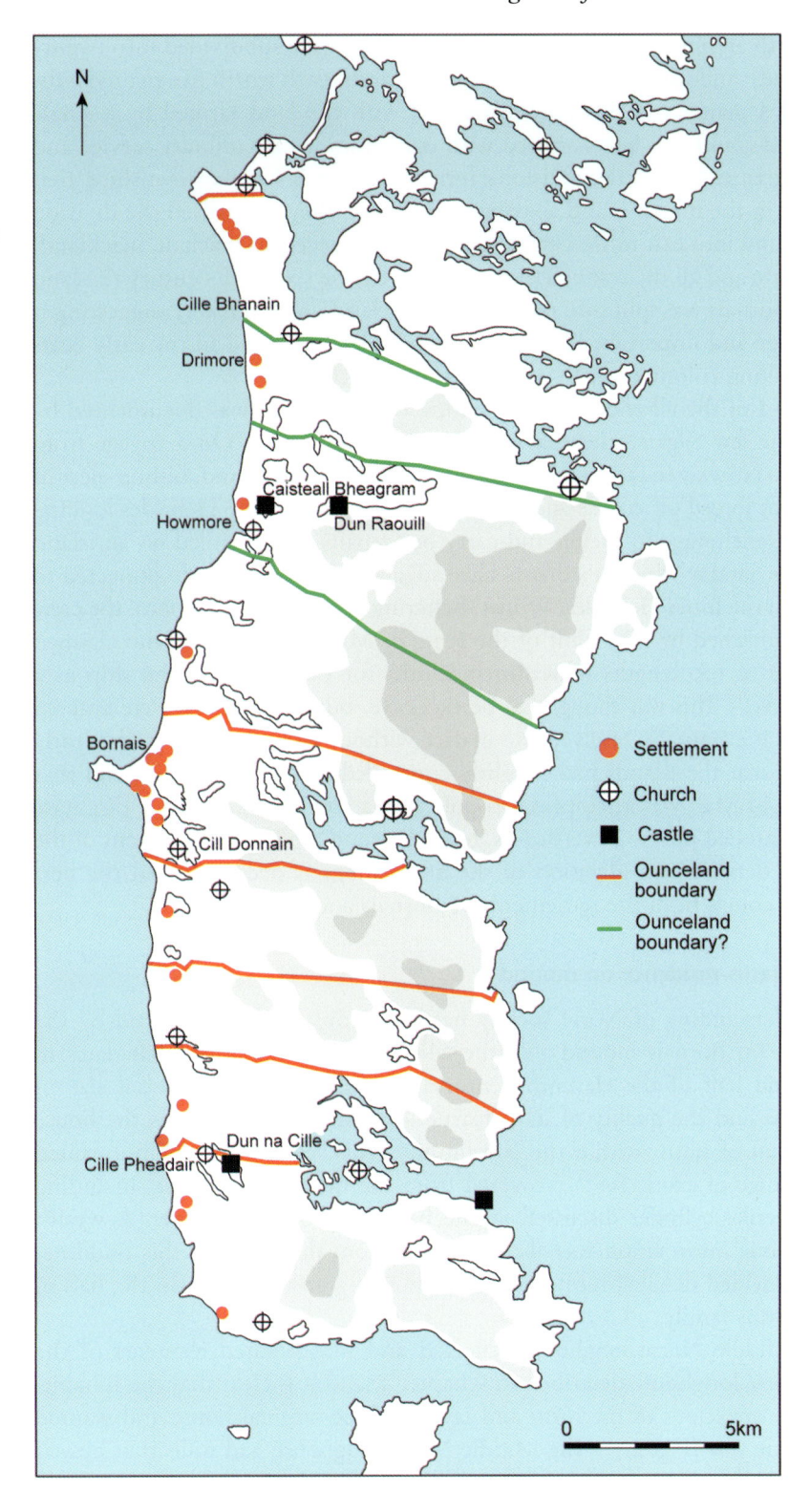

each worth an ounce of silver. In most cases these were subdivided into twenty pennylands, and further divided into quarterlands, each worth five pennylands. A tax of a penny was probably associated with the land farmed by a single house and could also be associated with contributions for military service and other activities. These tax divisions formed the basis for the townships that emerged in the fifteenth and sixteenth centuries. They formalised the division of the island into east to west strips that provided access to machair, blackland, hill pasture and all the resources in-between. By the sixteenth century the land around Bornais was split into two seven pennyland units, possibly suggesting it was a large and important land unit which had been settled in the early years of the Viking colonisation.[9]

An idea of the all-encompassing nature of governance was documented by one of the few Saga stories that mentioned the Hebrides. On a voyage from Iceland to Norway in 1207 a merchant ship carrying Gudmound, bishop-elect of Holar, was forced off-course and ended up sailing around the Hebrides looking for a safe anchorage to shelter and carry out repairs. They landed on an island known as Sanday which historians have suggested was the island connected to Canna, in the Inner Hebrides. Whilst sheltering in the natural harbour, the crew were approached by the bailiff of the King of Man and the Isles who claimed land-dues of 100 lengths of wadmell (cloth) for each man on the ship as a harbour fee.[10] This was thought to be excessive, but negotiations were entered into which eventually resolved the matter without violence. This story clearly indicates that the islands had a tightly controlled system of taxation and that the King of Man was attempting to police what at first seems like a disparate and unbounded polity. Nevertheless, to understand the Norse settlement of the islands a detailed consideration of the archaeology is necessary, and the best evidence comes from the settlements at Bornais and Cille Pheadair.

A high-status residence on mound 2

Our understanding of Norse society has been considerably enhanced by the discovery on Bornais mound 2 of the Middle Norse longhouse that dates to the second half of the eleventh century (Fig. 4.6).[11] The substantial size of this house and the quality of its construction indicated that it was the house of a person of status within the community. This status is also demonstrated by the range of exotic finds recovered from the floor of the house, including the Ringerike cylinder discussed at the beginning of this chapter. A wealth of economic information was also recovered from the floors of this building, which provided detailed information about eating and drinking in the hall of a high-status family.

The Middle Norse longhouse reflected and incorporated elements of the Early Norse longhouse described in Chapter 3, and it is clear that the inhabitants were conscious of the form and layout of the original house and wanted to replicate this (Fig. 4.7). The Middle Norse longhouse had walls that bowed in the middle reaching a maximum width of 5.8 m but narrowing to 4 m at

FIGURE 4.6. A photograph of House 2 from the east during excavation.

each end and it was just under 20 m in length, which was roughly three metres shorter than the Early Norse longhouse. It had a distinctive three-aisled organisation of the interior, and the entrance was located at the east end of the south wall. The orientation of the Middle Norse longhouse was roughly east to west, but it was slightly different to the orientation of the Early Norse longhouse: this must have been a deliberate act as it would have been easier to build the later house inside the footprint of the larger, earlier house.

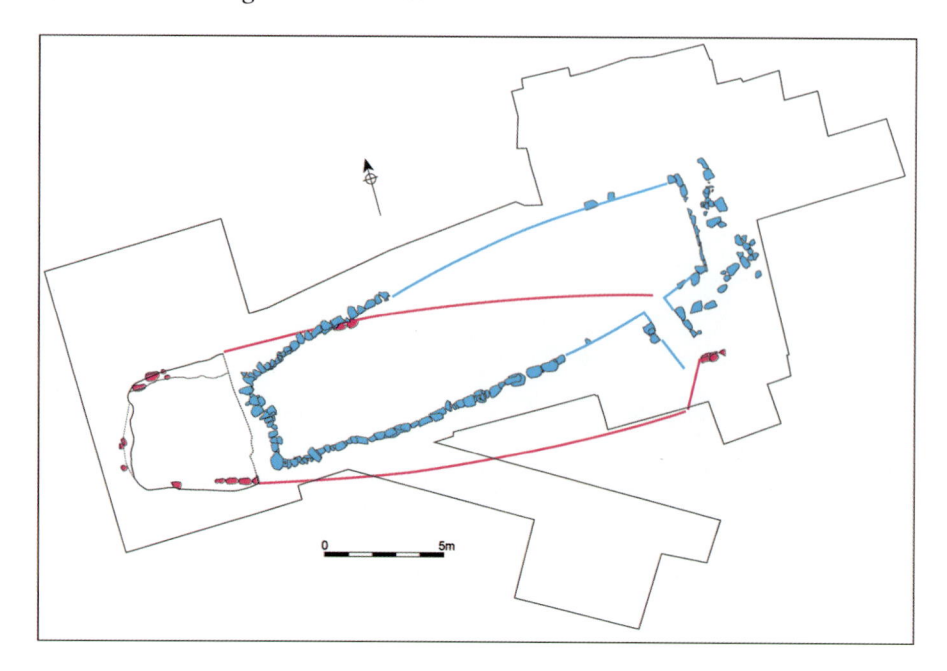

FIGURE 4.7. A plan of House 2 showing its relationship with the underlying House 1. Note the reuse of the northeast gable wall of House 1 as an entrance passage wall in House 2.

There were certain points where elements of the Early Norse longhouse were incorporated into the structure of the Middle Norse longhouse. The most obvious example of this reuse was where a fragment of the gable end wall of the Early Norse longhouse was used to form the east wall of the entrance passage to the Middle Norse longhouse, and the paving stones that formed the floor of the Early Norse longhouse acted as the floor of the entrance passage to the Middle Norse longhouse (Fig. 4.8). These connections could be dismissed as coincidences caused by the repeated construction of houses in the same spot over the centuries, but there was more to it than this. In all the house sequences excavated at Bornais and Cille Pheadair, there were numerous instances where later houses were carefully positioned to overlap with earlier structural features so that these elements could be incorporated into the later house. Quite often this was the only fragment of the earlier house walling that survived. These relationships may have provided opportunities for the occupants of the later house to recite genealogical histories that linked the different generations of families that occupied this settlement mound. The knowledge of the past was embedded and fixed by the architecture, and this legitimised the continued occupancy of the house.

Each house seems to have lasted for at least two or three generations and the knowledge of these architectural links must have been passed on from one generation to the next. These links tended to be quite subtle, and their significance might not have been obvious to anyone who was not around when the original house was dismantled and the new one built. They could have been genealogical secrets whose significance was understood only by elders who passed on the

FIGURE 4.8. The excavation of the entrance to House 2 showing the large whale bone rib that lay in the infilling sand.

knowledge and the stories to a select few. Alternatively, perhaps they were well known and formed the focal point of tales regularly told around the hearth.

An obvious difference between the two houses on mound 2 was the stone wall that acted as an internal revetment wall to the pit in which the Middle Norse longhouse was built. This was a substantial wall which survived to a height of over a metre and was built using good-quality medium-to-large slabs (Fig. 4.9). These were squared stones, oriented and positioned in the wall to provide a relatively smooth vertical internal wall face. The quality of the walling contrasted with that used in contemporary structures built on mound 1 and mound 2A, which had much more ramshackle walls that used all sorts of irregular stones, including rounded cobbles straight from the beach.

The presence of this substantial wall draws attention to the absence of a stone wall around the Early Norse longhouse. A few stones around the edge of the house floor seem to have been aligned and suggest the presence of a wall but if this was the case, and not simply the foundation for a timber structure, then the wall must have been completely removed when the house was dismantled. During our work at Bornais, it seemed at first unlikely that this wall could have been completely removed, but large sections of the wall around the eastern half of the Middle Norse longhouse were also removed leaving nothing behind, so the inhabitants were capable of removing an entire wall and carting all the stones away. It also has to be remembered that there are no stone outcrops on the machair plain, so constant cannibalisation of existing

FIGURE 4.9. A view of the internal wall on the north side of House 2.

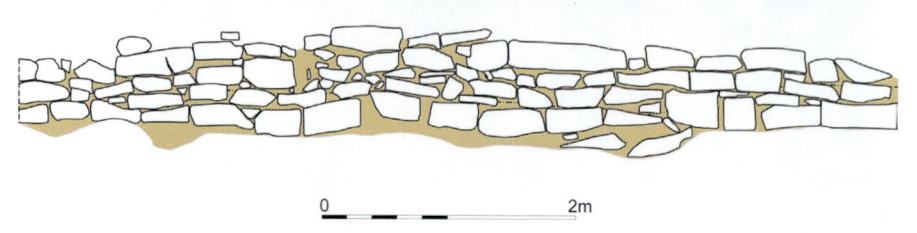

structures was the simplest solution to the resource requirements of any new building. It was therefore quite likely that the Middle Norse longhouse was built by robbing-out the stones used in Early Norse longhouse. Furthermore, the quality of the stonework used suggests that it might have originally come from Middle Iron Age structures, such as the wheelhouse on mound 1, as these required good-quality building stone for their structural integrity. The Middle Iron Age was probably the period when these stones were first brought onto the machair from the adjacent rock outcrops on the shore.

The act of demolition and reconstruction had both a rational and a symbolic significance. Using the good-quality building stone already present on the mound was obviously an expedient solution when building a new house but the acts of selection, removal and re-building also created a specific relationship between the different generations of people involved. It was not always the case that pre-existing structures were thoroughly and systematically destroyed for their resources. Some of the houses at Bornais retain walls standing to their original height but with other sections completely removed. These patterns suggest that complex relationships of respect were in play.

The occupation

Inside the Middle Norse longhouse, the layers of sand and occupation debris associated with the construction, occupation and abandonment of the house were well preserved and provided a lot of information about the activities that took place inside the house.

As with the Early Norse longhouse, one of the distinctive characteristics of the Middle Norse longhouse was the presence of a number of infilled pits underneath the floor which appear to have been dug during the house's construction. The most significant of these was a large rectangular pit, which lay on

FIGURE 4.10. The pit below the floor of House 2 containing Cardiff University student Katherine Adams.

the central axis of the house directly below the hearth in the main living area. When the house was occupied, this hearth was the focal point of social life, and it must be significant that the pit was dug at this point. The dimensions of the pit were those required to fit an extended burial of an average-sized individual, but no one was found in it (Fig. 4.10). Other pits were found underlying the axis of the house and a pair of rectangular pits lay in the eastern half of the house and preceded the accumulation of the central hearth deposits (Fig. 4.11). None contained any obviously special deposits or human remains, so it was impossible to be certain about their function. Nevertheless, it was significant that they were present, and they indicated a tradition of pit-digging as a foundational act in the creation of houses that was long-lived in the Western Isles.

The deposits that accumulated on the house floor clearly divided the house into three zones running lengthways down the house; a central zone covered with peat ash, and two peripheral zones adjacent to the two side walls (Fig. 4.12). These three-aisled zonal patterns occurred in most of the Norse longhouses known from the North Atlantic region. Three-aisled longhouses have recently been identified in excavations in Orkney at Quoygrew, Birsay and Skaill, and they were particularly well defined on these islands because of the use of the local flagstones to define the edge of the different aisles.[12] Furthermore, typical three-aisled houses were recognisable in Iceland, and well-excavated

140 *The Vikings in the Hebrides*

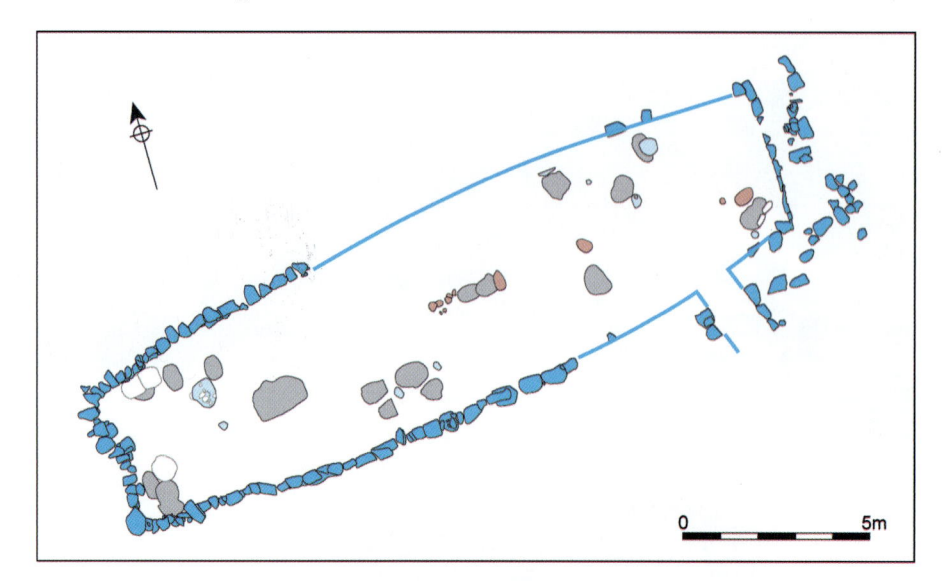

FIGURE 4.11. A plan of House 2 showing the pits that lay below the house floor.

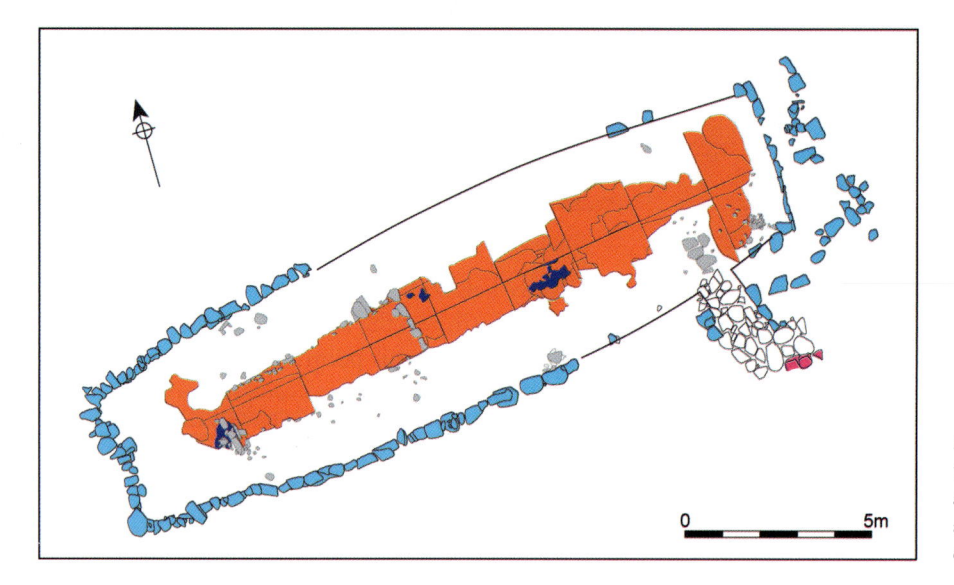

FIGURE 4.12. A plan of the interior of House 2 showing the extent of the ash layers that define the central aisle.

and recorded examples at Aðalstræti in Reykjavik and Granastaðir in northern Iceland provided good evidence that was directly comparable to the Middle Norse longhouse at Bornais (Fig. 4.13).[13] Usually, this organisational structure was related to two lines of posts running down the centre of the house which supported the roof. These posts were not clearly visible at Bornais, and it was possible that the inhabitants were forced by a shortage of timber to devise another way of roofing the house that did not require large timber uprights.

The central aisle was the main axis for movement up and down the building and we think that the side aisles were benched areas for sitting and sleeping. The occupation surfaces of the side aisles were brown sand layers with occasional

4. *The Kingdom of Man and the Isles*   141

FIGURE 4.13. Simplified plans of Viking longhouses from the North Atlantic: A) Bornais House 1; B) Bornais House 2; C) Cille Pheadair; D) Snjáleifartóttir, Iceland; E) Niðri á Toft, Faroes; F) Granastaðir 9, Iceland; G) Oma, Norway; H) Aðalstræti, Iceland; I) Hofstaðir, Iceland.

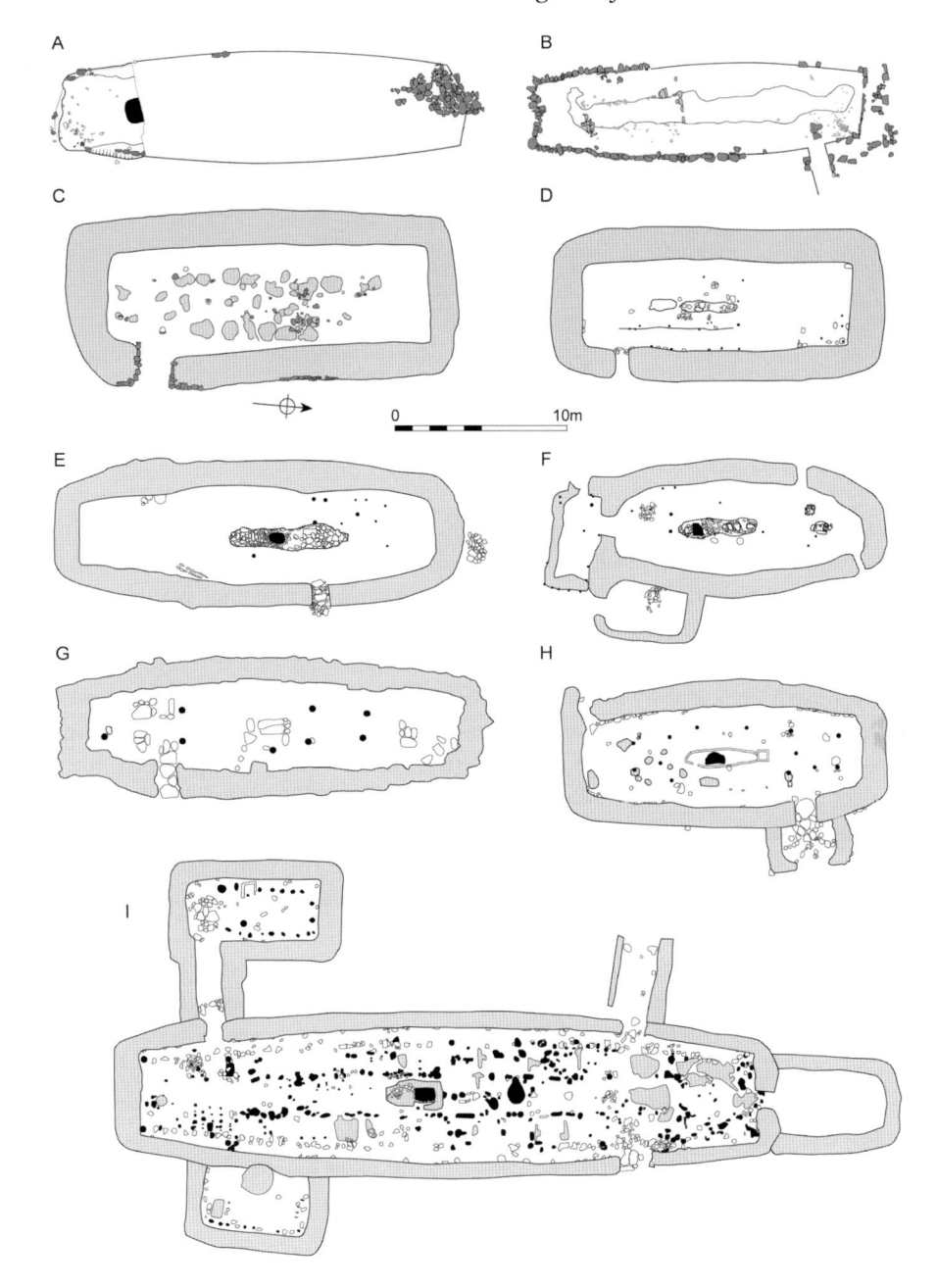

patches of brightly coloured ash. The central aisle was covered in colourful ash layers produced by the peat fires that provided heat for the inhabitants and where cooking was undertaken (Fig. 4.14). Detailed soil analysis of this central zone revealed that the deposits in this area comprised numerous micro-lenses of ash that varied significantly in colour and composition. The colours varied from dark brown to orangey red, indicating the varying quantities of iron in the peat

FIGURE 4.14. A section through the ash layers that define the central aisle of Bornais House 2.

or turf that was burnt on the fire, and reflected how hot and oxidising the fire was. Ash from the main cooking hearth and subsidiary warming fires was spread out across this central area to create a hard-wearing surface that would not be churned up by the regular foot traffic of people moving up and down the house.

An area 5.6 m long, in the centre of the western half of the house, was the main hearth area; slabs were laid at either end, and short upright stones were placed along the edge of the central aisle in this area. However, this hearth was ill-defined compared to other Norse houses. The hearths in the Norse longhouses at Granastaðir and Aðalstræti in Iceland, and Niðri á Toft in the Faroes were relatively central features that had well-defined kerbs and at least partially paved interiors. The hearth in the house at Drimore on South Uist, discussed in Chapter 3, was also a well-defined paved area towards the rear of the house, away from the entrance.

One reason for the ill-defined nature of these hearths was that the peat fires created by the inhabitants of the Middle Norse longhouse were treated differently to hearths used for burning timber used in the houses in Iceland. Peat fires were relatively easy to control and maintain, burning more slowly than firewood, and it was possible that hearths were created at irregular intervals all along the central aisle in the Middle Norse longhouse as and when they were needed. The evidence for these peat fires would have been easy to eradicate by raking and trampling.

A profusion of objects

Excavation of the floor deposits in the Middle Norse longhouse was one of the most exciting undertakings of the excavations at Bornais and almost every day interesting objects were being discovered. The assemblage was impressive both in the quantity and range of objects found, and although there were not many spectacularly prestigious metal artefacts, such as those examined in the previous chapter, there were objects present that were treasured by the inhabitants of the house and by the archaeologists that found them.[14]

FIGURE 4.15. A selection of unusual finds from the floor of House 2 including a decorative fragment of amber cross, a fragment of an early Norse comb, a lead pendant, two clipped silver coins, a folded section of gold strip, a fragment of green porphyry, and a blue glass bead.

Valuable items included fragments of a gold strip, a piece of green porphyry from Greece, part of an amber cross, two cut silver coins, a lead amulet, glass beads and the Ringerike cylinder (Figs 4.1 and 4.15). The gold strip was probably scrap awaiting transformation, but it could also be regarded as bullion with a certain value dictated by its weight. Coincidentally a much larger section of the same gold strip was found at Cille Pheadair. The green porphyry was an exotic Mediterranean import, discussed in detail in the introduction to Chapter 1, and was likely to have been a Christian relic. The fragment of an amber cross may have originally been embedded in the cover of a sacred manuscript. The coins were a cut farthing of Æthelræd II (AD 978–1016) and a fragment of a coin of Olaf Kyrre, king of Norway (AD 1067–93). The Ringerike cylinder, discussed in detail at the beginning of this chapter, was a relic or heirloom imported from the Scandinavian homelands.

The assemblage of combs and pins from the Middle Norse longhouse (66 comb fragments, 48 pins), was one of the largest assemblages from Britain. The pins were mostly simple bone pins with expanded or nail heads, but there were also examples with elaborate ornamental heads i.e. rectangular, beehive- and mace-headed pins which were seldom found in other areas of the settlement (Fig. 4.16). There were eight copper-alloy stick pins which were a typical Irish Sea type found in large quantities in the urban centres of Dublin and Waterford and at the religious centre of Whithorn in Galloway (Fig. 4.17).

In contrast to the pins, which were largely complete, the combs were in very poor condition at the time of deposition, and many were in the process of being dismantled. The only complete comb (Fig. 4.18) was quite old when it was deposited and was probably of a type that was going out of fashion. More typical of the late eleventh century were the combs in Fig. 4.19. These were a distinctive Irish Sea type which again was widely distributed around the western seaboard of Scotland. The comb in Fig. 4.20 was of a type that was becoming more common and would dominate in the twelfth century. This example was slightly unusual and exemplified the transformation these combs seem to have undergone at the settlement. This

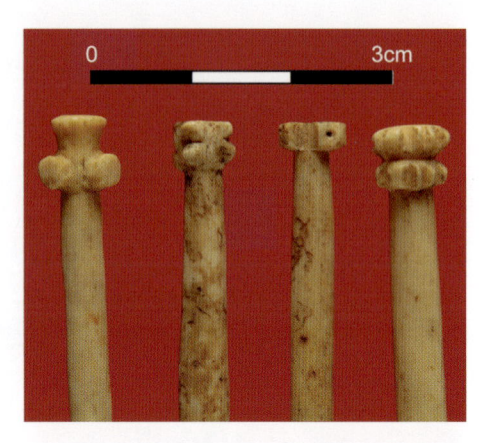

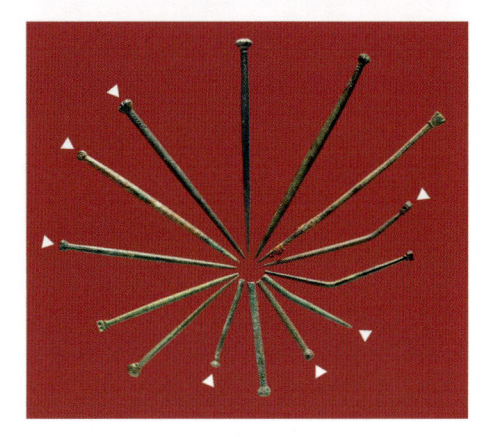

FIGURE 4.16. Four of the more elaborately carved bone pinheads from the House 2 floor.

FIGURE 4.17. The copper alloy stick pins from Bornais; those from the floor of House 2 have a triangle next to the pinhead.

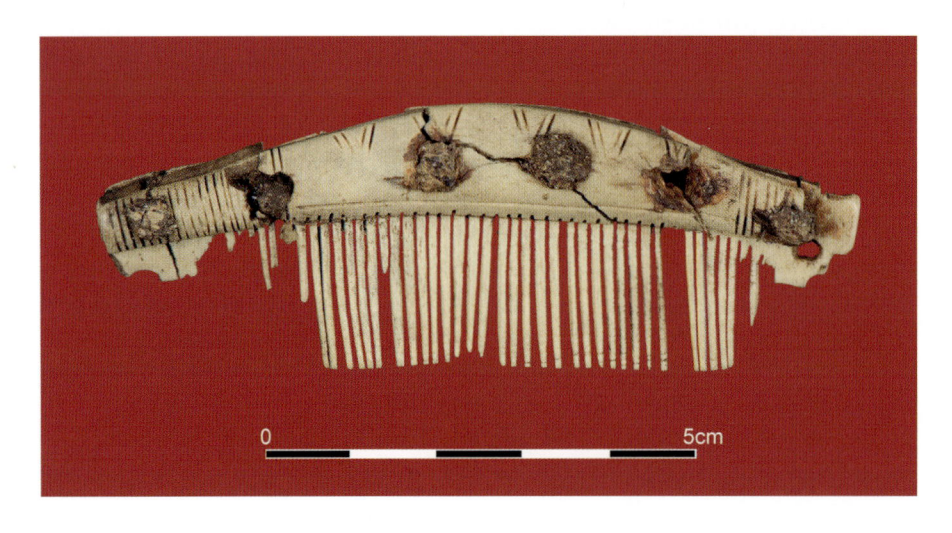

FIGURE 4.18. An Early Norse comb from the floor of House 2.

FIGURE 4.19. Two Middle Norse combs from the floor of House 2.

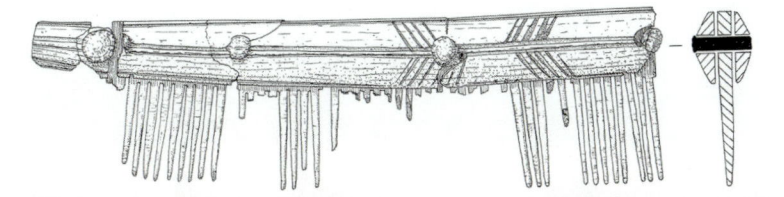

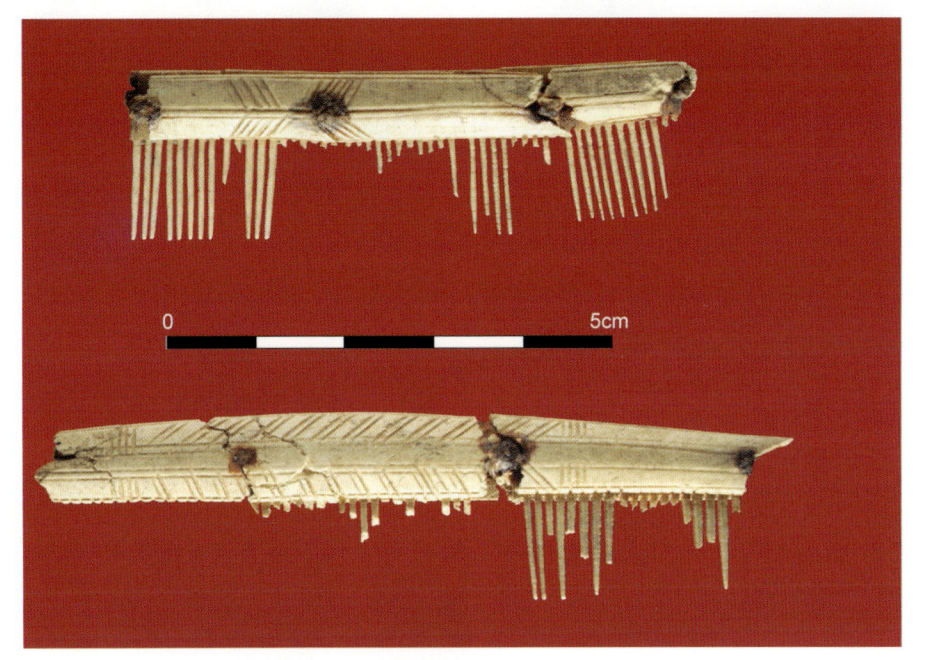

comb type was normally quite a long and thin comb, but the Bornais example had been cut down and the tooth plates from one half of the comb had been removed to enable this section to act as a handle; an extra rivet was put in to maintain the rigidity of this part of the object.

Other comb fragments seem to have been transformed into ornaments. The comb fragment in Fig. 4.15 was one end of a very large early Viking comb, with a decorative panel of interlace ornament running down its centre. This was almost certainly brought to Britain from Scandinavia during the early colonisation phase in the ninth century and it was the type of comb found in graves such as at Cnip (see Chapter 3); it must have been over 100 years old when it was deposited. This fragment was broken where the side-plate approached the

FIGURE 4.20. A comb from the floor of House 2.

FIGURE 4.21. Two decorated antler tines.

terminal of the comb, but the other end had been carefully trimmed to create a curving edge, forming an attractive triangular pendant. Unfortunately, the broken end means we will never know if it was perforated for suspension.

A distinctive category of finds was a group of socketed antler tines which were found almost exclusively in these house floors. There were five of one type where the interior of the tine had been completely hollowed out and a single example of another larger type, which has a shallow V-shaped socket with a perforation or rivet hole on the inside of the curve (Fig. 4.21). Similar elaborately decorated tines are known from other Norse settlements including Jarlshof, Waterford and York, but archaeologists have not previously recognised their distinctive form, and they have been rather superficially interpreted as handles. They don't make very sensible or functional handles, as they were fragile objects and the large tine with the shallow socket would have been particularly difficult to use for any activity that applied pressure to a tool inserted into the socket.

In the final publication of Bornais, I suggested that these objects were associated with the feasting and drinking that we might expect in a great hall, and they could be either handles for horn spoons or the decorative finials of drinking horns. A possible parallel were the ceremonial spoons that were used by the First Nations of the northwest coast of North America, particularly the

FIGURE 4.22. The drinking horn held by a queen in the Lewis chess set. © National Museums Scotland.

Haida and the Tlingit, at the end of the nineteenth century. These spoons were elaborately decorated with the stylised animals that were central to the art of that region, representing mythical beings who played an important role in all aspects of social life. The spoons were used for the consumption of special foodstuffs at ceremonial feasts and, as the spoons effectively represented or embodied the ancestors, this was the means by which these ancestors participated in the feast.

Another possibility was that decorative finials were attached to the bottom of drinking horns. Drinking horns were an important feature of medieval feasting cultures and would have been relatively common on settlements with high-status individuals. These individuals had to entertain and socialise to maintain their position in society. Unfortunately, the organic nature of horn means that it could not survive in aerobic and acidic environments and no trace of it will ever be found in the shell sands of Bornais. There are artistic depictions of horns and two of the queens in the famous chess set from Uig in Lewis (see Chapter 5) were holding drinking horns (Fig. 4.22).

The floor of the Middle Norse longhouse also produced a large collection of tools which illustrate the kinds of objects available to the people who lived at Bornais. The most basic tools that the inhabitants possessed were knives and whetstones. There were nine iron knives from the floor deposits, most of them complete. Fig. 4.23 shows drawings of seven of the better-preserved knives; there is little consistency in the size and shape of these knives. 6359 is a short stubby knife with a blade length of only 40 mm, whereas 6030 was a long knife with a blade length of 76 mm. The knives were all of 'whittle tang' form, which means they were forged with an integrated tang onto which a handle was fitted. The length of the tang varied considerably, and several knives had preserved mineralised remains of wooden handles (Fig. 4.24). There was also good evidence for the making of antler handles at Bornais in the Late Norse period, but these were not designed to accommodate the long tangs of these knives. The presence of wooden handles suggests that the knives were imported as finished artefacts, since good quality wood was not easily available on the islands and locally made knives would have had bone or antler handles.

The iron used for the knife blades was of the highest quality but would have required constant sharpening with whetstones, and it was not surprising that there was one whetstone for every knife in the house. Whetstones had a cultural significance that exceeded their functional utility: they were one of the few tools from the site that were imported from Scandinavia. The

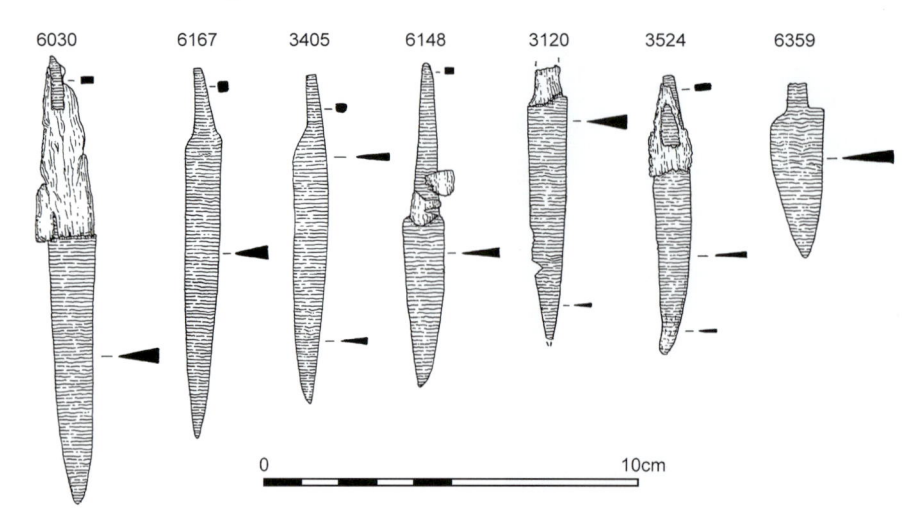

FIGURE 4.23. A selection of iron knives from House 2.

FIGURE 4.24. A photograph of an iron knife (6030) before cleaning and conservation showing the vestigial remains of the wooden handle on the left side.

assemblage from the house floor included three examples of Eidsborg schist from quarries in the Telemark region and three of purple phyllite from the Trondelag region, both in Norway (Fig. 4.25).[15] These were some of the few objects from this period that revealed definite contact between Bornais and Scandinavia; the Ringerike cylinder and the large comb pendant indicate connections, but these were likely to have been from some time prior to their deposition. The whetstones may show that people were still moving relatively freely between the Western Isles and Norway, but it is also possible that these were heirlooms or curated objects, brought over in the early part of the colonisation period when such travel was still routine. Most of the whetstones showed evidence for heavy use and several were mere fragments of what was originally a much larger object.

Textile production and maintenance seem to have been important as 17 or 18 spindle whorls and nine needles were found on the floor. Spindle whorls were weights that were attached to the end of a long spindle to help maintain the spin that transformed the mass of woollen fibres into yarn or thread, which then wound around the spindle above the whorl (Fig. 4.26). The whorls we found on the house floor were made from a variety of materials including bone (eight), ceramic (three), stone (two) and lead (three). The range of weights

FIGURE 4.25. Two broken whetstones from the floor of House 2. These were imported from Norway; that on the right is of Eidsborg schist and that on the left purple phyllite.

FIGURE 4.26. A selection of the complete spindle whorls recovered from all the occupation periods at Bornais.

of these whorls suggests they could have been used to make different quality yarns. Spindle whorls were relatively common discoveries throughout the region occupied by the Vikings but the emphasis on bone whorls in the Western Isles was noticeable, and differentiates them from the Northern Isles where stone whorls were more common. The collection of lead whorls from the Middle Norse longhouse was unusual and perhaps another indication of the high status of the inhabitants in this building.

The needles were of either bone (six) or copper alloy (three) and, again, they would have allowed for a variety of threads to be used (Fig. 4.27). Some were very crude and may have been for mending fishing nets. Two needle-cases were also found; these were long segments of sheep metapodials that had been hollowed out and showed evidence of repeated use and high polish (Fig. 4.28). They were often found in graves accompanying burials such as the woman at Cnip (see Chapter 3), where the needle-case contained two iron needles.

The only weights found in the Middle Norse longhouse were quite large and heavy and are likely to have been fishing or thatch weights rather than loom weights. The general absence of loom weights from Bornais suggests that the inhabitants used two beam vertical looms to weave cloth. These were very different to the warp-weighted looms used in the Northern Isles, as the latter required large weights which were a common find on settlements such as Jarlshof and Norwick on Shetland. Warp-weighted looms were a Scandinavian type and their absence in the Western Isles suggests that the incoming Scandinavian settlers adopted the indigenous two-beam vertical loom, which had been in use since the Late Iron Age. This suggests the continued presence of indigenous craftswomen or the importation of craftswomen from areas to the south who were skilled in the use of these more advanced looms.

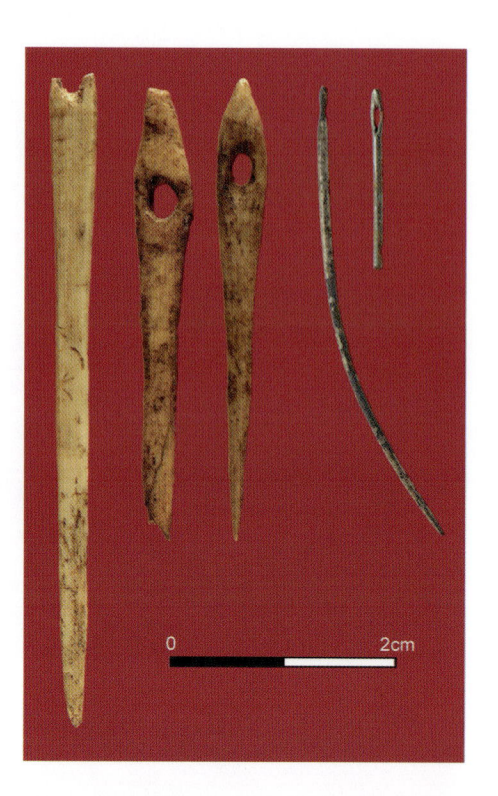

FIGURE 4.27. A selection of bone and copper alloy needles from Bornais House 2.

FIGURE 4.28. Two bone needle cases from the floor of Bornais House 2

Much of the metalwork present in the Middle Norse longhouse consisted of broken and relatively useless fragments of iron, lead and copper alloy that were deliberately collected to be recycled. The large quantity of iron scattered across the floor included many boat rivets and fragments of iron sheet, possibly the

FIGURE 4.29. A flexible iron cauldron handle from the floor of Bornais House 2

remains of large cauldrons that had been deliberately dismantled; two complete cauldron handles were also found (Fig. 4.29). Iron was an important resource, but it does not appear to have been produced on the islands in the twelfth and thirteenth centuries. It is therefore likely that most of the simple tools required for everyday tasks were made from imported iron which was then recycled (Fig. 4.30). Iron was produced in very large quantities in Scandinavia, and iron rivets were an essential prerequisite for the production of the Viking ships that made the colonisation of the North Atlantic possible. It was estimated that a 30 m longship similar to Skuldelev 2 (a well-preserved longship in Denmark) would have required just under 8,000 rivets for its construction. Recycling was probably the principal source of iron for settlers in many of the Scottish island groups, though bog ore would have been readily available from local sources.

A very large assemblage of pottery was recovered from the floor of the Middle Norse longhouse; this came from vessels smashed more or less *in situ* at the west end of the hearth. The complete profiles of several vessels could be reconstructed, and these are illustrated in Fig. 4.31. These were simple vessels which varied considerably in size from small cups to large tub-shaped containers. They were very simply made and as the photos (Fig. 4.32) demonstrate, they were not designed to look pretty. Many of them showed evidence for direct contact with the fire and their exteriors were often encrusted with soot and cooking residues. Biomolecular analysis of the interior of the potsherds recovered traces of fatty acids, a mix of dairy, ruminant and non-ruminant adipose fats and marine products. These results indicated that the pots were almost all multi-purpose vessels used for cooking a mixture of meat and vegetables with fish. They were locally produced and often broken and discarded soon after manufacture.

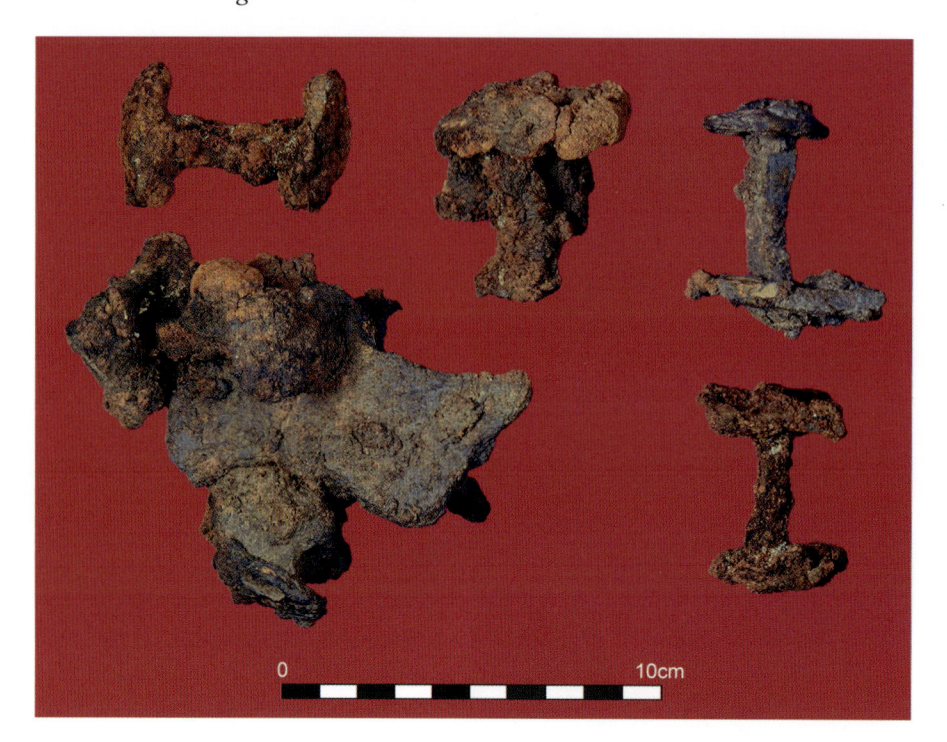

FIGURE 4.30. A bag of iron scrap, largely holdfasts but including a broken axe.

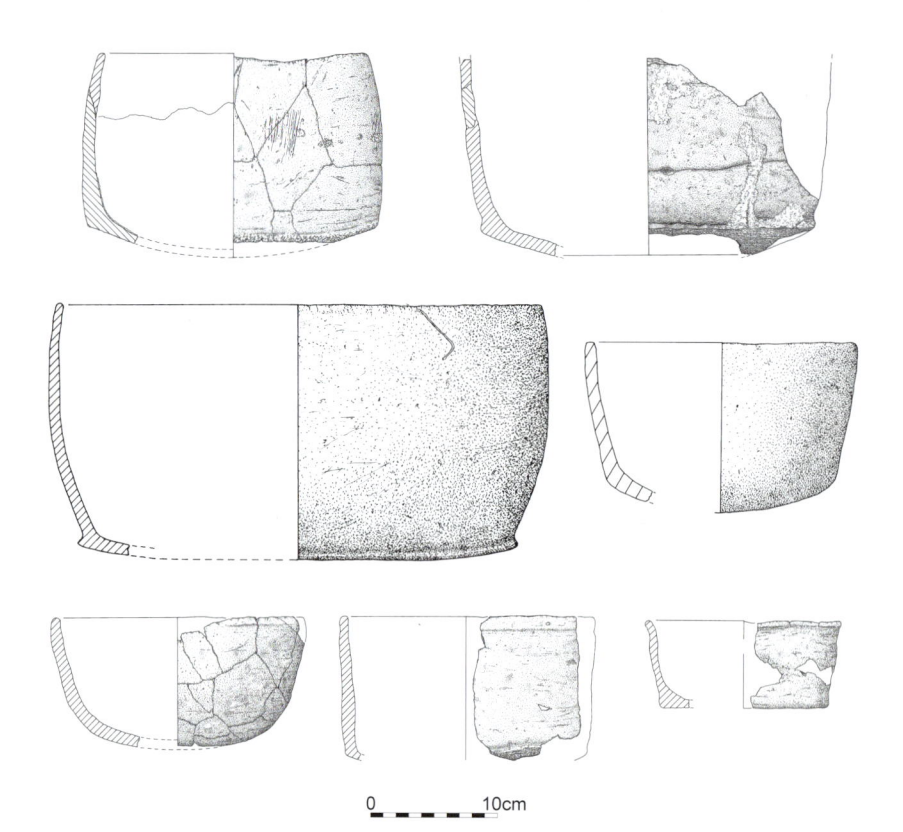

FIGURE 4.31. A drawing of some of the almost complete pots from the floor of Bornais House 2.

FIGURE 4.32. A photo of one of the well-preserved pots from House 2 showing the soot-blackened surface that indicates repeated use for cooking on the hearth.

FIGURE 4.33. The fragmentary remains of a pot imported from the southwest of England.

There was nothing exceptional about the vessels used by the inhabitants of Bornais except for the presence of one imported pot, which originated from the area around the River Severn in southwest England. This was a relatively simple cooking pot with a flat base, a curved belly and an upright collar below a slightly thickened rim (Fig. 4.33). It was not glazed or decorated in any way. Similar vessels were in use in the medieval towns of Bristol, Hereford and Cardiff during the late eleventh century, and fragments of these vessel types have also been found in late eleventh-century deposits in Dublin. A single imported vessel was also identified in the pottery assemblage from Cille Pheadair: an elaborately decorated tripod pitcher of Minty-type ware probably from north Wiltshire in England. These vessels would almost certainly have been brought to South Uist from Dublin. Although the possibility cannot be ruled out that the occasional vessel travelled direct from Bristol to the isles, it seems more likely that the two pots testify to the thriving trade between Ireland and the Hebrides.

A peculiarity of the assemblage from the Middle Norse longhouse was the relatively small quantities of platter present. Platters were circular ceramic discs, about 7 mm thick on average, with diameters that ranged from 340 mm to 510 mm. The basal surface was covered with extensive grass/chaff marks whereas the upper surface was covered with fingertip impressions and often stabbed with a small, rounded tool that could perforate through to the base. Platters were ceramic versions of the steatite baking plates found in Shetland and Norway. They represented a new form of ceramic invented specifically to bake flatbreads, brought to the islands from the Scandinavian homelands. Experiments at Cardiff University have replicated the production of the platters and successfully used them to bake flatbreads (Fig. 4.34).[16] The clay discs were probably simply air-dried and then partially fired during the cooking process. The absence of sooting, or any fatty residues or lipids in the fragments of platter recovered from Bornais, makes it very unlikely they were used for cooking fatty foods.

Compared to the contemporary deposits on other parts of the settlement, the amount of platter ware in the Middle Norse longhouse was very low, forming only 3% (103 sherds) of the assemblage from the house. The sherds were also concentrated in the east end of the house, the opposite end from where most of the large tub-shaped vessels were found. This may indicate that flatbreads were not cooked inside the house but were being cooked nearby and then brought into the house.

FIGURE 4.34. A modern replica of a Norse platter that was used to bake a flatbread.

Eating plants and animals

During excavation, the floor of the Middle Norse longhouse was divided into one metre squares and the finds from each square were recovered separately and their location recorded. The floor deposits were bagged up square by square and taken away to be carefully sieved to recover the smallest of finds.[17] This process was designed to capture carbonised plant remains, such as cereal grains, which were seldom larger than a few millimetres (Fig. 4.35). The carbonised grains recovered by this process provided the only evidence for the crops grown and consumed by the inhabitants of the settlement, and detailed examination of the larger residues collected in the sieve also identified small, fragmented materials that would not have been collected if we had dug the floor in a conventional manner. The residues from this house floor included large quantities of fish bones, bird bones, small rodent bones, fragments of egg, crab and urchin shells, which were analysed alongside the fragments of mammal bones and seashells recovered by normal excavation techniques.

The intensive use of sieving and flotation at Bornais achieved near-total recovery of all the material left on the floor of the house. This provided not only the information required to reconstruct the agricultural economy of the settlement, but also gave us a picture of how the house was used and the different types of activities that occurred inside and outside a high-status Norse longhouse. The differences between the occupation layers inside the house and the deposits from the external midden seem to have been minimal. Only a couple of material categories showed significant differences; for example, eggshell was normally found in much higher densities in the internal occupation deposits, whereas slag was rare in these internal deposits.

It was noticeable that the ash layers of the central aisle of the Middle Norse longhouse produced fewer large finds than the floor layers in the side aisles, which was a consistent pattern throughout all the houses. Analysis of the micro-residues shows the ash layers of the central aisle had high densities of burnt bone and burnt organic material (B.O.M.), as would be expected from an area where fires were being lit. This area also had higher densities of crab and eggshell, which suggests the inhabitants were eating crab and eggs around the fire and throwing the waste directly into the ashes. Mammal and fish bones in contrast were concentrated in the floor layers in the side aisles (Fig. 4.36).

The animal bones recovered from the floor were mainly the remains of young cattle, which would have been a prime source of meat. Bones of pig, deer and fish were also found on the floor and were concentrated in the western half of the house. These show that people ate a varied selection of meats; beef, pork

FIGURE 4.35. Flotation of the various soil samples recovered from the excavations was a messy process which took place in one of the local farmyards. The process was essential for recovering representative collections of carbonised grains and the small bones that documented the importance of fishing. It also produced a large assemblage of eggshell, pictured on the right, which would otherwise not have been recovered.

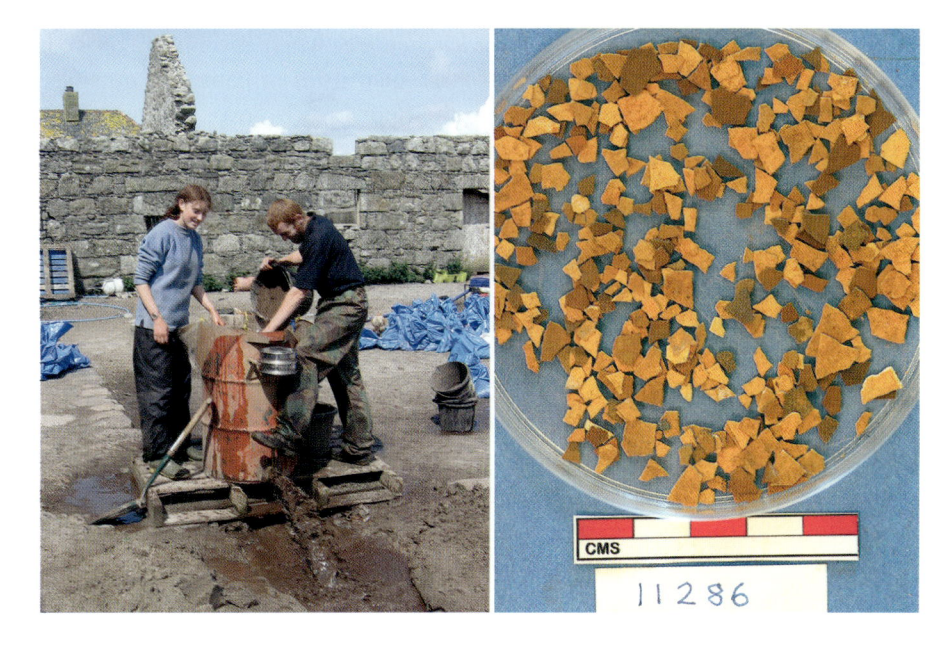

FIGURE 4.36. A comparison of the density of different categories of material in the peripheral floor layers, the central, ash-covered, aisle and the pit fills of House 2.

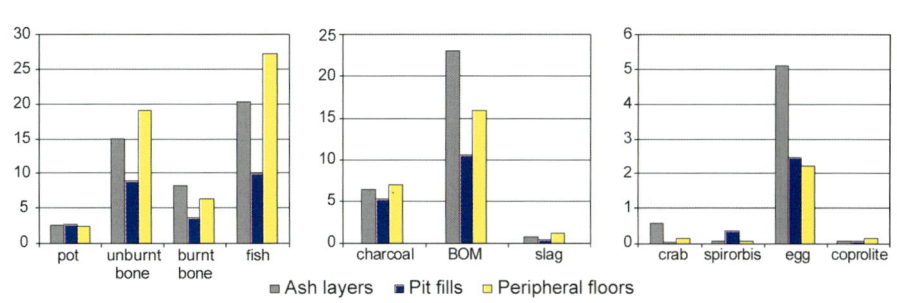

and venison, and support the idea that a high-status family lived in the Middle Norse longhouse. Barley dominated the assemblage of burnt cereal grains and though the densities of oats and rye were less than in the earlier house floor, such grains were still present in large quantities. Areas with very large concentrations of flax seeds were present, and this crop was at its most ubiquitous in these floor layers. There were also very large concentrations of goosefoot (Chenopodiaceae) and dock (*Rumex*) seeds in the hearth deposits which might be waste material from cleaning harvested cereal crops, but could also indicate that these plants were deliberately collected to be used by the inhabitants of the house.

Living in the house

There were significant variations in the deposition of material along the length of the Middle Norse longhouse, and these variations could be used to provide an interpretation of how the house was lived in during its occupation. Essentially the house was divided into four spaces running across the three aisles: the west end furthest from the door, the west central area, the east central area and the east end.

The west end can be interpreted as the kitchen area where meals were cooked. It was characterised by the presence of large quantities of complete pots (see Fig. 4.31) that were found smashed over the floor in this area. There was also a concentration of small vertical-sided pits that were created early in the life of the house and stayed in use throughout its occupation. Pits similar to these have been found in other longhouses and may indicate the location of barrels and other containers for water and other liquids.

The eastern edge of the spreads of pottery and the pits coincided with the beginning of the ash layers that defined the central hearth area (Fig. 4.12). The thick ash deposits that extended up the middle of the house in this section were partially defined by a kerb of small stones that suggested there was a formally defined hearth in the western half of the central aisle of the house. Most of the objects discussed in the previous section – bone pins and antler combs, iron knives and stone whetstones, needles and spindle whorls, bone and antler waste, iron structural fittings and sheet fragments, plus many other exotic and interesting objects – were found on either side of this hearth in the west half of the house (Fig. 4.37).

The objects were found in clusters, which suggests that certain people had their own particular seating areas within the house. Clusters 1 and 2 lay to the north of the hearth and were well defined with lots of finds. Clusters 3, 4 and 5 lay to the south and had fewer finds; cluster 5 in particular was not well defined.

The distribution of the various categories of artefacts provided some information on the status and gender of the individuals occupying these particular locations. It seems likely that the north half of the house was where the high-status members of the household were located, as the area contained important objects such as: the fragment of green porphyry, the Ringerike cylinder, and several

FIGURE 4.37. The overall distribution of small finds found on the floor of House 2 showing three concentrations of finds.

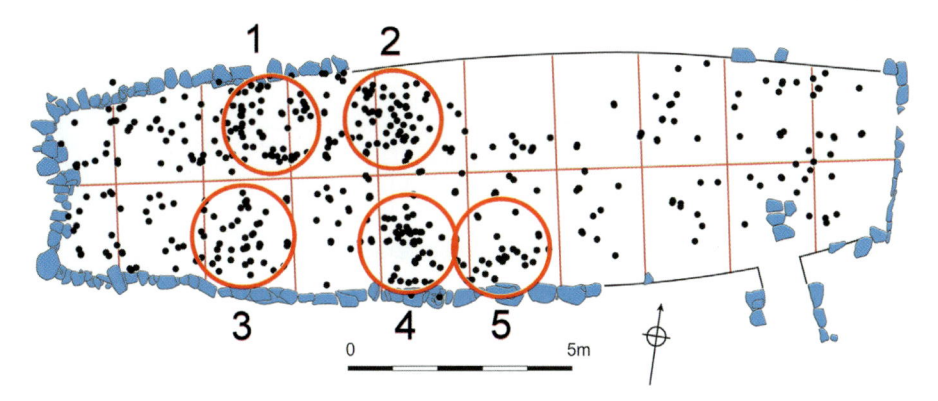

of the decorated tines. The latter two objects probably indicated conspicuous high-status drinking was taking place at these locations.

The distribution of iron fittings whilst generally widely scattered included concentrations of nails, staples and fittings at location 1 and 2, and these might have indicated the presence of furniture, such as chairs, at this location (Fig. 4.38). There were some references in the historical literature in Scandinavia that suggest position 1 would be appropriate as the location for the head of the household.

The possible gender of these individuals may be indicated by the distribution of textile related equipment, as this task was closely associated with women in Norse societies (Fig. 4.38). If this is accepted, then locations 2 and 4 were occupied by woman as this was where the textile equipment was concentrated. Interestingly there seems to have been a significant difference between the textile working on the north and south side of the hearth. Needles were almost only found on the south side whereas spindle whorls were found on both sides but with more on the north side.

Many of the other object share no clear relationship with gender or status but do suggest a connection with individuals. The knives and whetstones for example are clearly related to the four main clusters, and in clusters 2, 3 and 4 there were two pairs of knives and whetstones (Fig. 4.38). Other craft activities, such as the manufacture of bone and antler tools, were undertaken on an *ad hoc* basis in the house but the evidence for specific workshop areas is ambiguous. Fragments of bone shaped and ready to be made into objects were widely distributed across the floor of the house but there were concentrations of prepared antler in clusters 2, 3 and 4.

Pins and combs were the most numerous personal items on the floor, but their distributions were not so obviously clustered with the tools. There was a concentration of complete bone pins in cluster 1 which also contained two copper alloy pins. Cluster 5 was also essentially defined by a group of five complete bone pins and a broken one.

158　*The Vikings in the Hebrides*

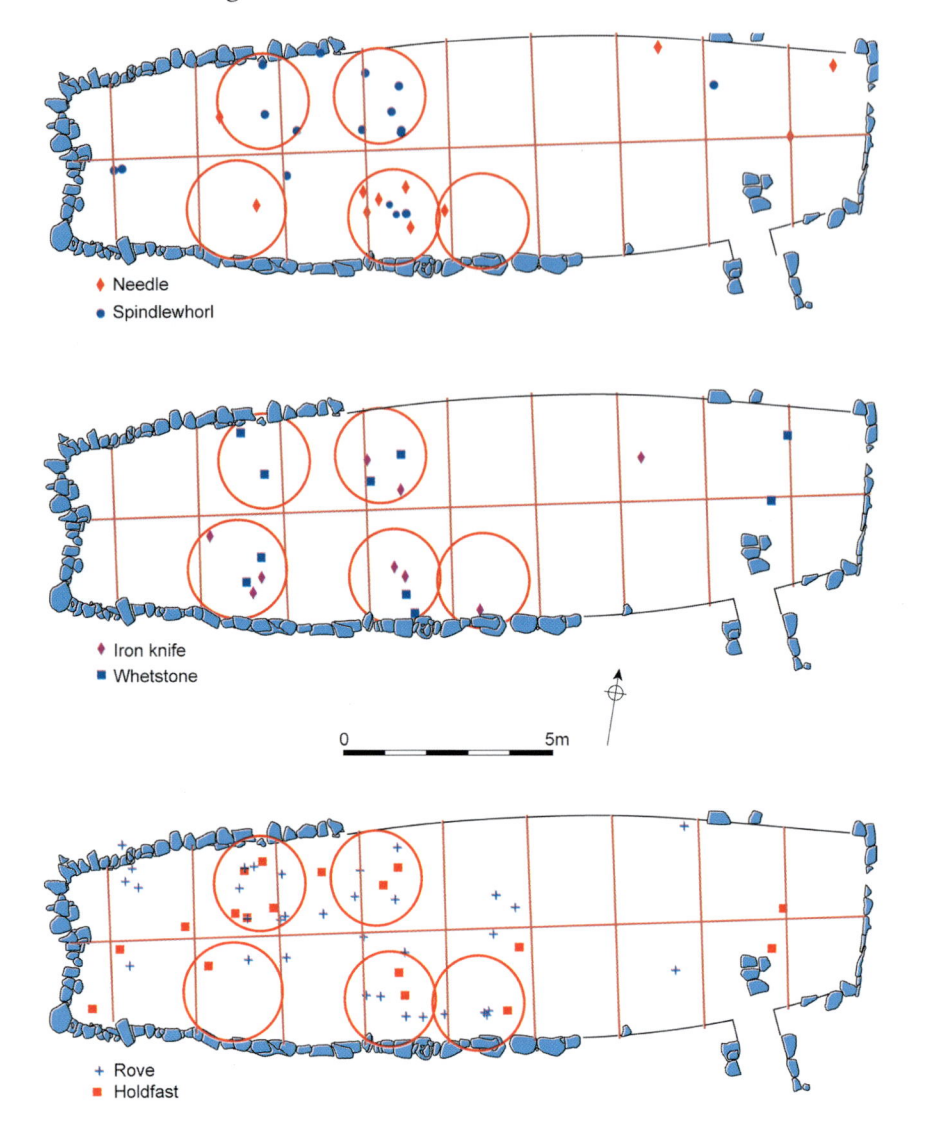

FIGURE 4.38. The distribution of needles and spindle whorls, knives and whetstones and roves and holdfasts on the floor of House 2.

These clusters of objects suggest that individuals were repeatedly and habitually occupying particular locations in the Middle Norse longhouse. It could be argued that the male head of the household regularly occupied a position on the northwest corner of the hearth area and to his left was a high-status woman, arguably his wife. Directly opposite on the south side of the house were a less important man and woman and to the right of this woman there may have been an individual of lesser status whose gender is unknown. The character of the assemblage deposited by these individuals indicated a range of activities taking place in the house:

- the use and maintenance of iron knives;
- spinning and sewing, but not weaving;

- the care and maintenance of the body;
- drinking and the consumption of food;
- the systematic dismantling and reworking of antler combs;
- the breaking-up of sheet iron vessel(s), and possibly lead and copper-alloy objects.

As one moved east towards the front door of the house, the quantities of material recovered from the floor declined sharply. There were very few tools, ornaments and fittings from the eastern half of the house; the only finds recovered here were antler/bone waste, flint, and iron fragments, and these were found in smaller quantities than in the western half of the house. Similarly, the quantities of animal bone and pottery also declined sharply in this area and the density of carbonised plant remains was low. However, at the extreme east end of the house, there was a significant concentration of pottery in the southeast corner, which included a substantial proportion of the platter assemblage from this house. There was a dump of animal and fish bone in the northeast corner.

In summary, the Middle Norse longhouse can essentially be divided into four spaces (Fig. 4.39):

- the west end was a cooking area.
- the west-central area was the principal social space, where most of the indoor activities of the inhabitants took place.
- the eastern half, where distinct activity areas were difficult to identify, might have been used for storage or sleeping.
- the east end was an area where very few personal items were present, but food refuse was allowed to accumulate.

The radiocarbon dates suggest that the occupation of this Middle Norse longhouse might have lasted only a couple of generations, probably for only 50 years. This is perhaps a bit surprising given the quantity of material recovered

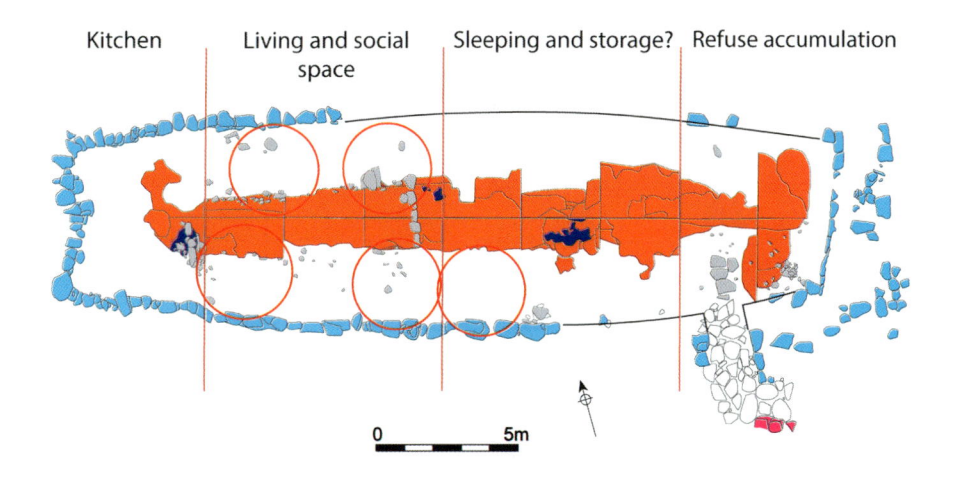

FIGURE 4.39. A possible division of Bornais House 2 into four spaces, probably rooms divided by internal walls, showing the position of the five finds clusters in relation to hearth layers.

from the house, but there was no evidence that the floor was ever entirely replaced, unlike the floors belonging to the Late Norse longhouse (House 3; see Chapter 5). Instead, the floor seems to have been patched up and renovated on a piecemeal basis during its occupation.

Norse houses in the North Atlantic

The patterns exposed at Bornais seem to be directly comparable to those uncovered in other well-excavated bow-walled longhouses in the North Atlantic region. One of the best-preserved houses, Oma in southwest Norway, was examined by Norwegian archaeologist Bjørn Myhre, and he suggested the interior of the house was divided into a large central living room with a hearth, flanked by two gable-end rooms. At Granastaðir, in Iceland, the main house was divided into essentially three areas: room I in the north gable end was a kitchen and work area, with a possible religious role; room II–III was a large living room for work, leisure, recreation and consumption, possibly with a vestibule where the main west-facing entrance was located; and room IV in the south gable end was a storage space or drying room (Fig. 4.40).[18] This house had an additional annexe attached to its south end, which contained a kitchen, and subsidiary task-specific rooms were added to the house at a later date.

The excavator of Granastaðir suggested a gender division of the main living room, with women on the west side near the main door and men on the east side, though the evidence for this was minimal. He then hypothesised a division of the living space connected to a series of binary oppositions and argued that the organisation and categorisation of space inside the house could be used as a metaphor for the categorisation of the surrounding landscape. For example, the opposition between private indoors and public outdoors was mirrored inside the

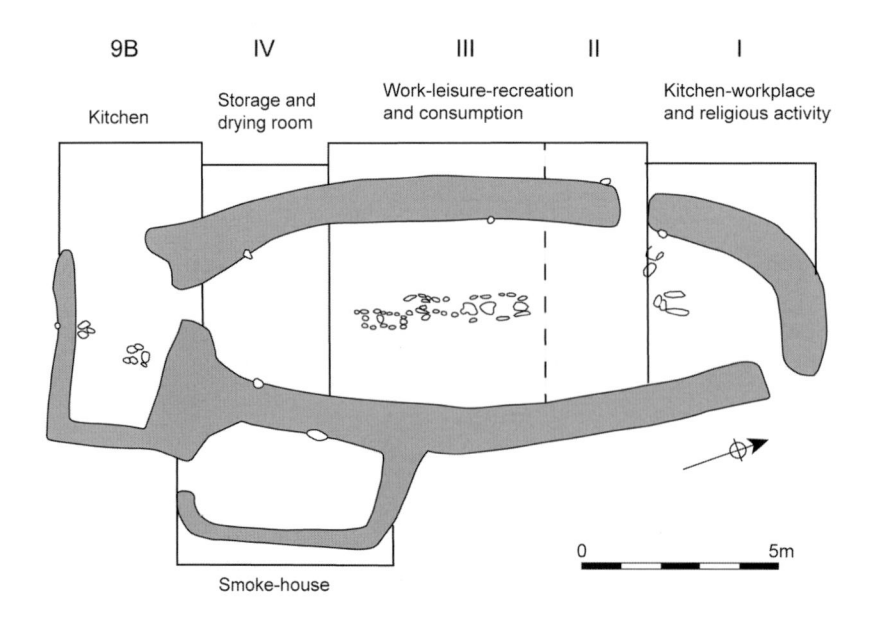

FIGURE 4.40. The spatial organisation of the house at Granastaðir in northern Iceland as suggested by the excavator Einarsson.

house in the division between a room for public entertaining and socialising, and peripheral rooms that were for more private activities.

The most thorough recent examination of an Icelandic house has been undertaken by Karen Milek.[19] Her detailed examination of a house excavated at Aðalstræti in Reykjavik, was based on geochemical sampling, soil micromorphological examination and the analysis of finds distributions that were all directly comparable to the analysis undertaken at Bornais. However, comparisons were limited given the very different soil conditions. The most obvious problem was the poor preservation; no bone or antler artefacts were recovered at Aðalstræti and this must have resulted in the loss of a considerable number of important household artefacts.

The house at Aðalstræti had a symmetry that revolved around the central living room (Fig. 4.41). The house had two entrances. The north entrance was the principal public entrance and had a porch protecting visitors as they entered the house. The southern entrance was a subsidiary entrance, relatively narrow and with no sign of a porch. Each doorway opened into a vestibule that allowed access into transitional rooms at the opposite ends of the central corridor in which the hearth was located. Arranged around these transitional rooms were several small rooms. At the south end of the house these rooms seem to have been associated with textile production and contained a loom within the main living space and a room for washing and dyeing wool. At the north end there appeared to be a storage room, a toilet area and stalls for stabling a small number of animals. The central area had two large open spaces on either

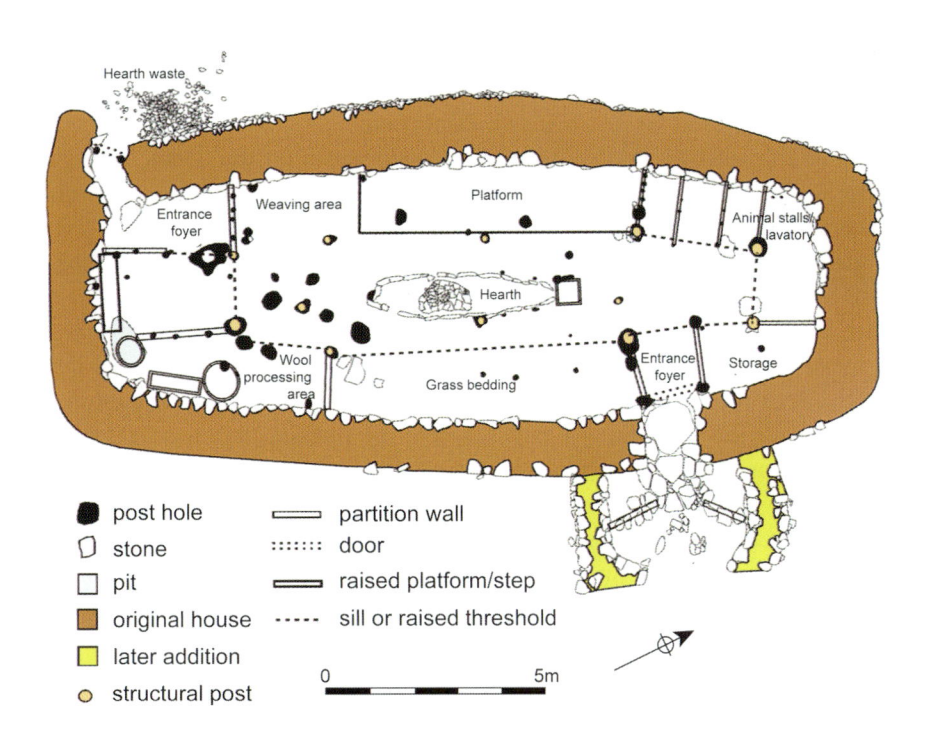

FIGURE 4.41. The spatial organisation of the house at Aðalstræti in Iceland as suggested by Milek. © Karen Milek.

side of the hearth; to the west was a raised platform, possibly with a timber floor and, to the east, a layer of 'grass bedding' covered a similar-sized space, though this was not raised. Milek argued that the raised platform meant that the occupants sitting on the west side had an elevated position above the rest of the household.

The house at Aðalstræti produced 46 objects but only one knife and one whetstone. Milek considered that most of the finds from the central area of the house at Aðalstræti were the result of accidental losses trampled into the floor layers. Larger finds were restricted to nails, probably from wood burnt in the fire, and isolated large objects lost near the walls of the internal partitions. The only exceptions were the loom weights in the southwest corner, which she thought indicated where textile-working had taken place.

The artefact assemblages from the Icelandic houses were significantly smaller than the large assemblage from the Middle Norse longhouse floor at Bornais. The largest assemblage of finds recovered from an Icelandic house came from a house at Suðurgata, close to Aðalstræti in Reykjavik. This produced 56 finds including 23 loom weights, seven spindle whorls and a weaving sword. This collection of objects suggests that the occupants specialised in textile production. The seven knives and eight whetstones from Suðurgata was comparable to the 10 knives and nine whetstones from Bornais.

The pattern of finds deposition in the Icelandic houses was therefore quite different to the pattern at Bornais. Nevertheless, there was some similarity in the overall allocation of space. The Middle Norse longhouse at Bornais could be divided into essentially four spaces. A large central room, split into two sections either side of the centre of the house, was flanked by two smaller rooms at each end, though the evidence for the structural walls separating these spaces was minimal. This seems to have been a much-repeated pattern found at Oma in Norway as well as at Granastaðir and Aðalstræti.

Significant differences are visible when one focuses on the detail. The space at the west end of the Bornais house was a kitchen and food preparation area. Although this was arguably paralleled by the kitchen in the southern annexe at Granastaðir, there was also a hearth at the north end of the Granastaðir house, close to the entrance. At Aðalstræti there was no evidence for cooking at the south end of the house; on the basis of the burnt bone distribution, this activity seems to have taken place in the eastern side aisle, at the north end of the hearth. Both the latter two positions were very public and provide a dramatic contrast with the situation at Bornais, where the cooking area was in the most inaccessible part of the house due to the absence of a second subsidiary entrance, which was a common feature in Icelandic houses.

This location of the kitchen possibly highlights a significant gender distinction. If cooking was a female activity, as recorded in the sagas, then Icelandic and Norwegian women had a much more public position than Hebridean woman for their activities in the house. This might indicate that women had a significantly reduced status in the Hebrides and that their presence in the

Hebridean house were either as slaves serving high-status Scandinavian women, or as low-status wives.

Norse houses in the Hebrides

A number of houses contemporary with the Middle Norse longhouse at Bornais are known from the Western Isles. These include a partially excavated house (House 6) on Bornais mound 1, House 12 on Bornais mound 2A, House 500 at Cille Pheadair and a house at the Udal on North Uist. All these houses were much smaller than the Middle Norse longhouse on Bornais mound 2, and do not exhibit the prominent bow-walled architecture that was so distinctive and also archaic by this time in the late eleventh century.

The only one of these houses to be completely excavated and published was Cille Pheadair House 500 (Fig. 4.42).[20] This north–south oriented house was constructed on top of an earlier smaller house which dated to the end of the eleventh or the beginning of the twelfth century and, though most of the structure of the earlier building was completely robbed out, sections of its enclosing wall were reused for this later house. The entrance was located at the south end of the east wall and included a paved passage 2.5 m long that was accessed through an elaborate forecourt. There was no sign of an external stone wall around the house, and it seems likely that it was surrounded by a turf bank.

The interior of the Cille Pheadair house was defined by an internal stone revetment which acted as the base for a timber wall. The wall enclosed an internal space that was divided into two rooms, a large living space, 10.3 m by 4.9 m, and a small subsidiary room, 2.8 m by 2.3 m, entered through a passage in the north gable end of the main room (Fig. 4.42). The small room to the north had less compacted floor layers and was probably used for storage.

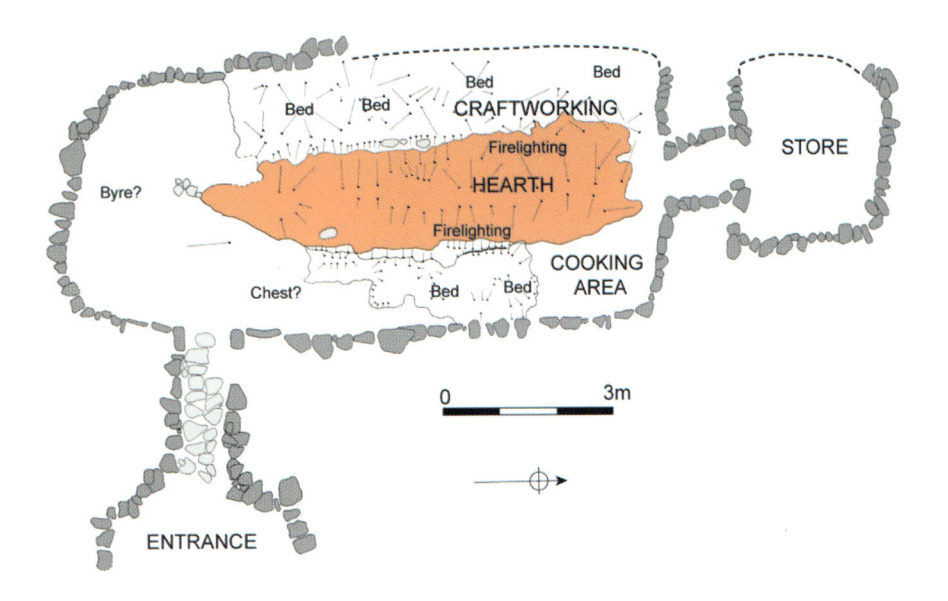

FIGURE 4.42. The occupation of House 500 at Cille Pheadair on South Uist. © Mike Parker Pearson.

164 *The Vikings in the Hebrides*

The main room was divided into three longitudinal strips that ran almost the full length of the house. The central strip was a mound created by multiple layers of peat ash where the fire had been. The edge of the hearth was a trampled, depressed area, showing where people had moved around this hearth. On either side of this central zone, loose sand appears to have been deposited to create raised platforms that were probably covered by a wooden floor or by some form of bedding material.

The finds assemblage from this house was substantial, much larger than from any other house at Cille Pheadair, and most of the finds came from floor layers associated with its occupation. Analysis of the finds distribution showed that the north end of the hearth and the northeast corner of the house was a cooking area, characterised by large amounts of pottery; craft-working debris was more common in the northwest corner. Several broken combs and bone stick pins were found on either side of the hearth in the centre of the house, and these distributions suggest personal spaces used for socialising and presumably sleeping. In contrast, bone tools tended to come from the south end of the house and suggest this was used for different tasks.

An interesting and important find was a small bone pendant cross which was recovered from the north end of the hearth (Fig. 4.43). This was unburnt, and like the bone die referred to in Chapter 2, it must have been pushed into the ash deposits of the hearth when these had cooled down, suggesting again that we were looking at a ritual act, possibly immediately preceding the abandonment of this phase of the house. Unlike the lead cross from the Early Norse longhouse at Bornais, there was no ambiguity about the Christian symbolism of this object and, as bone possessed no intrinsic value, it cannot be considered loot. It clearly refers to the religious sensibility of the inhabitants of the house.

FIGURE 4.43. The bone cross pendants from Cille Pheadair. The cross on the right came from the north end of the interior of House 500.

There was no evidence for a formal byre within the house. Although there would have been space for a docile animal in the south end, analysis of the soils showed none of the high phosphate levels here that would be expected if an animal had been kept indoors. The floor generally contained a high frequency of coprolites, which implied the presence of dogs, and there were also very large quantities of small mammal remains, thought to come largely from owl pellets deposited when the house was abandoned. Similar large numbers of small mammals were found in the Middle Norse longhouse floor layers at Bornais, but these were not common in-house floors in other periods at either Bornais or Cille Pheadair. This suggests that something unusual was happening to the rodent populations of the Uists in the twelfth century, though I am not sure what this could have been.

The other two houses at Bornais that were similar in date to House 500 at Cille Pheadair also had some similarities in their construction (House 6 on mound 1 and the House 12 on mound 2A). Both these houses were semi-subterranean and had internal revetment walls, just under a metre high. The mound 1 house (6) had a room attached to one end which was entered by a passage from the main room, but there was no sign of this in the mound 2A house (12). Both houses were constructed using less regular building stones and their position on smaller settlement mounds suggests they had a lesser status to the main house at Bornais. Neither house was fully excavated, and no contemporary floor levels were examined.

A house similar to the Cille Pheadair house was excavated at the Udal.[21] The structure had two rooms; a large room and a small room (Figs 3.9 and 4.44). The building was not subterranean but had a thick wall with external and internal stone revetments, and it resembles the Cille Pheadair house rather than the high-status Middle Norse longhouse on Bornais.

Small subsidiary rooms arranged on the same axis as the main room, such as those found at Cille Pheadair, Bornais mound 1 house (6) and the Udal, were not common in Medieval Scotland and this organisation of space was not paralleled in the Norse buildings of Orkney or Shetland. Instead in the Northern Isles the expansion of the house involved the addition of much more substantial linear extensions, and these were normally entered from outside rather than connected to the main area of domestic space. A good example was a house at Quoygrew on the island of Westray, Orkney.[22] These northern developments were not directly comparable to the subsidiary rooms found in the South Uist houses.

One aspect of these architectural changes that is worth noting was that they were organised in diverse ways in different regions of the North Atlantic diaspora. All the island groups exhibited the same trend away from large communal living spaces that resulted in farmhouses with numerous rooms or separate buildings with quite different functions: barns and byres, craft workshops and external kitchens. However, the arrangement and organisation of these rooms/buildings showed considerable regional diversity, which was clearly expressed in the Late Norse period.

FIGURE 4.44. A view of the fourteenth-century house at the Udal. © IAC, Udal Archives.

The agricultural economy

Our understanding of the agricultural economy of the islands was considerably enhanced by the excavation of Bornais mound 2A.[23] Around the middle of the eleventh century the use of this part of the settlement changed dramatically. Instead of being a relatively unimportant part of the infield that was regularly cultivated, it became the location of a subsidiary settlement mound. The excavated area contained a pair of kilns sitting on a platform, immediately to the north of the centre of the mound where a sequence of houses was constructed (Fig. 4.45). These were likely to have been grain-drying kilns used to dry the crops grown on the surrounding fields.

The technology of grain-drying seems to have evolved quite radically during the 500 years of the settlement's occupation. It was possible that the open hearths identified in the Early Norse deposits of mound 2A were involved in grain-drying, as these appear to have been isolated constructions built in the fields surrounding the settlement on mound 2. The Middle Norse kilns on mound 2A were clearly more sophisticated. These had dry-stone revetment walls that stood 0.6 m and 0.67 m high and were 1.85 m and 1.2 m long, with narrow entrances and an open top. The stones in the kiln walls were heavily burnt and the deposits within and around the kilns contained large quantities of clinker. We found some of this material in association (see Chapter 3) with

FIGURE 4.45. A plan of the Middle Norse kilns and platform on mound 2A with photographs of them during excavation.

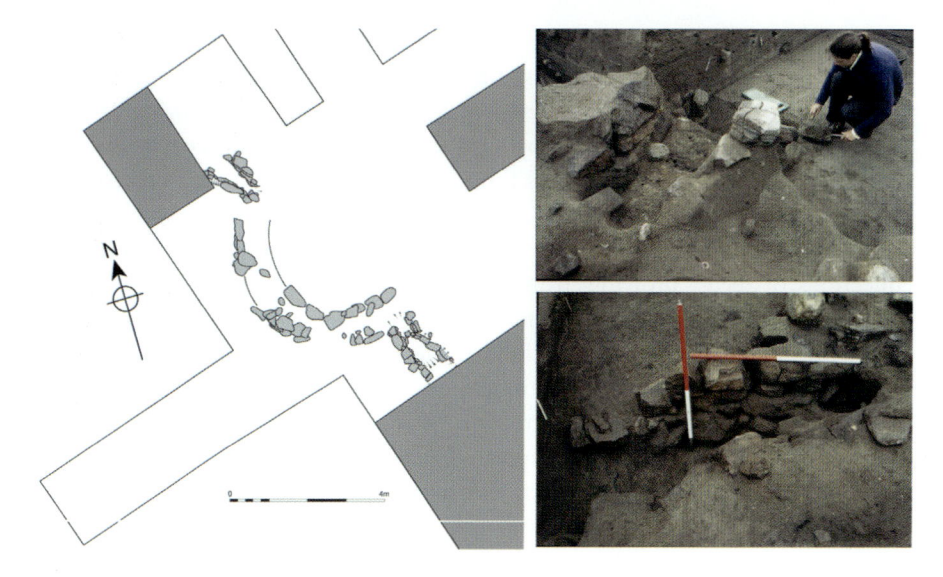

the earlier hearths, but much more was found with these kilns and the pieces were much larger, indicating sustained periods of high temperatures.

If these kilns are correctly interpreted as grain-drying kilns, then the high temperatures were a design fault. Drying grain needed sustained low temperatures. High temperatures were produced by fires burning too fast and out of control, probably as result of the islands' strong winds. It would have been important to maintain control of the fire in a kiln as large quantities of combustible materials were likely to be present in and around the kiln, and any spark or wayward flame could have resulted in a fire that would destroy the drying crop. The crops were amongst the most valuable products of the agricultural economy and any widespread destruction would have been a catastrophe.

Evidence for just such a disaster was found in the occupation deposits that accumulated around the kilns. During the excavations we noticed on a particularly windy day that the layer adjacent to the kilns contained vast numbers of carbonised grains. These were made visible because the wind was blowing away the fine machair sand but leaving the carbonised grains in place. Eventually all the individual grains stood on tiny little plinths of soil; these were only a couple of millimetres long, so they were not normally easy to spot, but in this case the creation of the plinths and the sheer number of grains made them very visible. Several samples were taken from this layer and after we had carefully washed and floated the samples, we calculated that the density of grains ranged from 90 to 2,111 grains per litre of soil. Therefore, tens of thousands of grains of oats were scattered over the middens on the east edge of this settlement mound.

This deposit must have represented a disastrous event for the farmers at Bornais, but it provided us with considerable information about the nature and organisation of arable farming. The most important characteristic of the grain deposit was that it was almost exclusively oat (with only small quantities of barley and rye). This confirmed the significance of this crop to the Scandinavian settlers of the islands and emphasised the importance of oats to the household that lived on mound 2A, already evident in the Early Norse deposits.

The dominance of a single crop also contrasted with the composition of most deposits of carbonised grains found on the settlement. Our soil samples generally produced assemblages that contained mixtures of all the main cereals and large quantities of weed and wild seeds. These deposits were cumulative collections of seeds, probably from accidental losses during the cleaning and processing of foodstuffs for the community, and some might have been collections of waste used as fuel to help light the hearths. The large deposit of cleaned oats on mound 2A was very different, and must have represented a crop cleaned, processed and stored, ready to be transformed into food.

The large burnt deposit also indicated that oats and presumably the other cereals were cultivated separately as distinctive crops. This may seem obvious but, in many regions, different crops may be grown together as they respond to different environmental conditions in quite different ways. Certain species might thrive in a dry summer with lots of sun whereas others might need extra moisture and thrive in a wet summer. If they were mixed together, then their success and failure balance each other out, ensuring at least some yield from the harvest at the end of the season. However, growing these crops separately allowed the Norse farmers to sow them in the most favourable areas of the landscape for optimal soil and drainage conditions.

The archaeology of mound 2A emphasised the importance of cereal cultivation in the economy of the settlement. It represented the addition of a specialist farm onto the original settlement that was based on mound 2. We did not excavate the centre of this mound, where the main residential buildings existed, but it is likely that the excavated kilns were part of a farm unit that was based on a household that was either related to the main family on mound 2, or was in service to this family.

Size and status

The settlement at Bornais was large. The geophysical survey suggests approximately 4,625 sq m was covered by the settlement in the Middle Norse period. A survey of the machair plain of South Uist by Mike Parker Pearson identified 24 mounds that had evidence for Norse settlement.[24] Most of these mounds were quite small, around 15 m in diameter. However, some of the mounds were larger: such as mound 99 on the Howmore/Dreumasdal boundary (60 m by 20 m), mound 191 in Baghasdail (50 m by 30 m) and mound 186 at Machair Mheadhanach (35 m diameter). None of these settlements came close in size to the main area occupied by Bornais (75 m by 100 m), excluding mound 1 which was over 50 m in diameter. The large settlement mounds were fairly evenly spaced, 7 km to 12 km apart, on the machair plain of the island, and there was no evidence at any other site for the clustering of settlement mounds seen at Bornais.

The excavation of Cille Pheadair revealed a settlement mound (roughly 40 m by 15 m) that was directly comparable to the smaller mounds, such as mound 2A, at Bornais. Both mounds were occupied by a single household, living in a house surrounded by ancillary buildings that provided additional space for a range of different activities. On mound 2A, the main domestic space was rebuilt at least four times, and at Cille Pheadair, six architectural phases were identified and completely excavated. It seems likely that the unexcavated mound 2B at Bornais was of a similar size and significance, and that mound 3 may have been two contiguous settlement mounds of this size. Bornais mounds 1 and 2 had a different character.

Mound 2 was a large settlement mound, and our excavation here indicated a sequence of large houses had formed the core of this mound. Although the excavated area was relatively restricted, and largely delimited by the Early, Middle and Late Norse longhouses (1, 2 and 3), additional structures were identified extending outside this area. Some of these were probably ancillary buildings, but others appear to have been substantial houses, either the dwellings of subsidiary households dependent on the main family, or possibly living quarters for slaves. Further excavation would be required to fully understand the nature of the activity on mound 2, but it was clearly more complex and extensive than the other mounds.

Mound 1 was a large settlement mound in a detached location, 50 m south of the main mound complex. The geophysical survey revealed an arrangement of four to five substantial buildings arranged in a square that defined an open space, roughly 20 m by 30 m, at the centre. Excavations confirmed the presence of one of these structures, and the material infilling this building clearly indicated that it predated the twelfth century. The rectangular arrangement of the structures was very distinctive and contrasted with the settlement patterns exposed on mounds 2, 2A and 3, where the centre of the mound was occupied by the principal house.

The evidence suggested that the normal pattern for Norse settlement on the island of South Uist comprised a single house associated with a limited number of ancillary buildings. A single household has been estimated to consist of between 10 and 20 people. Some settlements were larger, and this probably indicated that they were the homes of important people, who could be expected to have owned slaves and to have attracted dependants. At Bornais we think at least four households, including one of high status, occupied their own separate mounds (2, 2A, 2B and 3, in the northern part of the settlement), and that a further four or five houses were located on mound 1. A conservative estimate would be that the settlement had a potential population of between 90 and 140 people in the eleventh and twelfth centuries. Bornais was clearly exceptional in Hebridean terms, and it would also have been unusual anywhere in the Northern Isles, Iceland or the Faroes. Urban settlements existed in Scandinavia, Ireland and England at this time, but they did not resemble the settlement at Bornais, and it would be misleading to suggest that Bornais resembled a town.

The most important Norse settlement in Orkney was the Brough of Birsay, and this offers the closest comparison to Bornais.[25] The major focus for the Norse settlement at Birsay was site A, which was of a comparable size to Bornais mound 2. The presence of a Late Iron Age settlement at Birsay site A, directly preceding the Norse settlement, and the complexity of the settlement sequence, which probably included a large hall, was reminiscent of the sequence within Bornais mound 2. The area at Birsay referred to as Area III was similar to the areas covered by mounds 2A, 2B and 3. There were two major settlement sequences in Area III, site C and site D, which, if the environmental conditions had been similar to those at Bornais,[26] could well have become settlement mounds comparable to mounds 2A and 3. To the north and east, there was a scatter of small, isolated structures, some of which could have been houses, and this area was reminiscent of the scattered spread of isolated structures that occupied the areas between mounds 2A and 3. The major difference between the two sites was the church that formed a central focus for the Birsay settlement. There was no recognisable evidence for any ecclesiastical structure at Bornais.

The extensive size of the area of archaeological remains on the Brough of Birsay was exceptional (Fig. 4.46). Most Orcadian Norse settlements comprised single farmsteads, though these often achieved sizeable proportions. The evidence for rebuilt settlements larger than a single homestead is negligible. At Skaill in Deerness,[27] the excavations revealed a settlement that covered a large area, but this was not continuous. This settlement was probably a single farmstead occupied for several millennia, with repeated rebuilding which created a gradual spread over a large area. It was likely that larger, more complex high-status farms were present on Orkney, and the partially explored site at Tuckquoy on Westray[28] may have been a more extensive high-status settlement. Both Tuckquoy and Skaill were associated with important churches.

On Shetland there is little evidence for a major political centre and the settlements excavated at Sandwick, Underhoull, Belmont and Hamar on the northern island of Unst were those of individual farms scattered in the landscape. Some of these settlements, such as Belmont and Underhoull, had long sequences of occupation but others, such as Sandwick, were relatively short-lived. The largest and most famous settlement in Shetland is Jarlshof, which lies at the south end of the Shetland mainland. This was an unusually large farm, but it did not come close to emulating the size of settlements such as Birsay and Bornais. At its greatest extent it appears to have been occupied by at least three separate households: the nature of the settlement and the manner of its development suggest this was the farm of an important individual who was surrounded by an extended family. The importance of the settlement at Jarlshof and its occupants could have been related to its strategic position: it was the first landfall for people arriving on Shetland from Orkney, and it was one of the few areas of windblown sand on Shetland which made it ideally suited for arable agriculture. There were also rich fishing resources in the turbulent sea immediately to the south.

FIGURE 4.46. Comparative plans of the settlements at Finlaggan, Islay, Bornais, Birsay in Orkney, Jarlshof in Shetland and Ardtornish, Morvern.

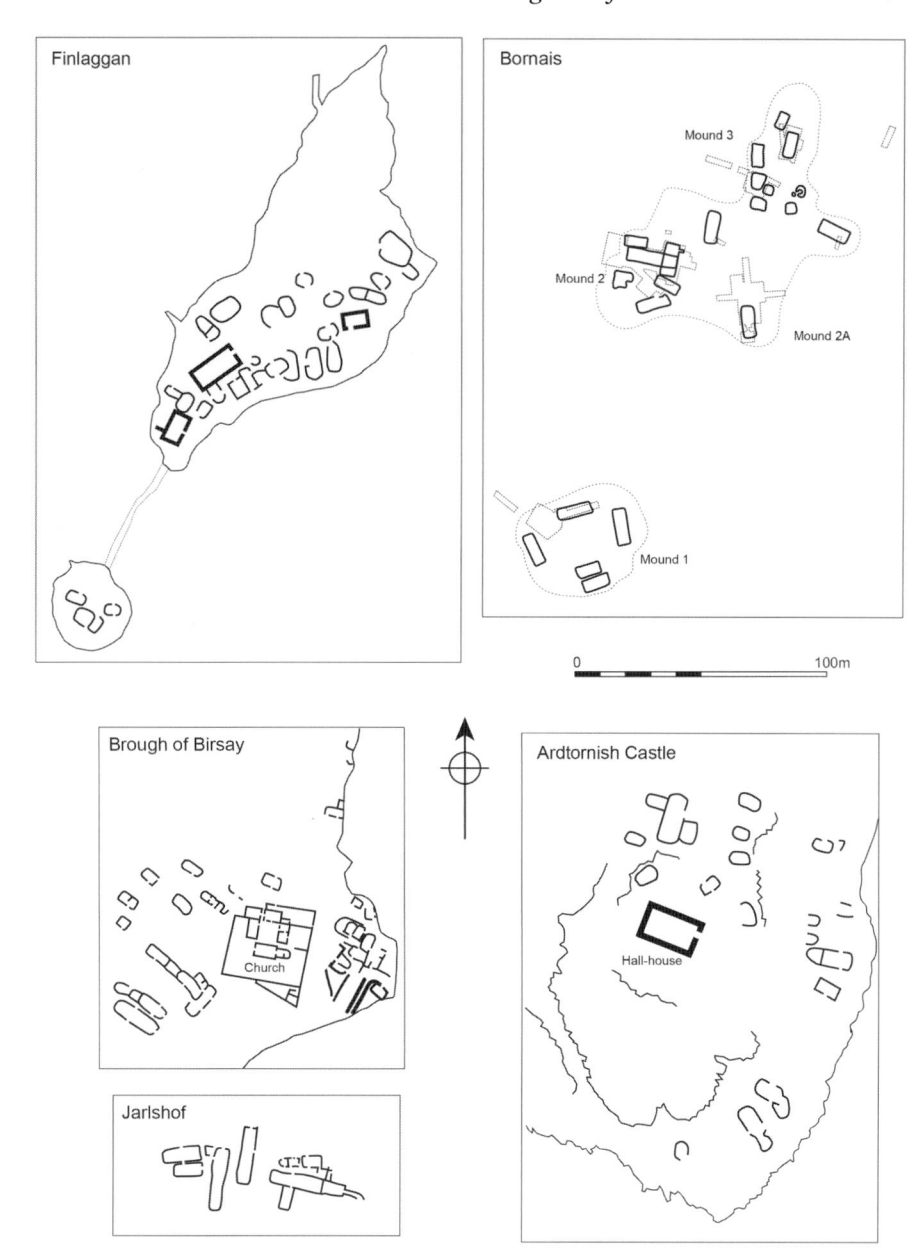

Comparable settlements are virtually unknown in the southern Hebrides, as very little excavation and field survey has taken place in this region. The most thoroughly explored settlement is Finlaggan on Islay which historical records indicated was an important residence of the Lords of the Isles.[29] The leaders of the Clan Donald were inaugurated at Finlaggan, and it was there that they met for the 'Council of the Isles'. The settlement covered two islands in a small loch in the interior of the island of Islay (Fig. 4.46 and 4.47). The principal island, Eilean Mòr, contained at least 20 ruinous buildings, including two large halls and a church, and this was connected by a causeway to Eilean na Comhairle, the Council Isle, where a further three structures were visible. Most of the buildings survived as earthwork enclosures but there were some upstanding mortared stone walls – and these included the church.

The occupied area on Eilean Mòr was roughly comparable to the main Bornais complex, and Eilean na Comhairle was comparable in its location to Bornais mound 1. However, the layout of the settlement was very different to that at Bornais, as the Finlaggan houses appear to have been much more densely packed together in an integrated settlement.

FIGURE 4.47. A view of Finlaggan, an important settlement on Islay that acted as one of the centres for the MacDonald Lords of the Isles. © Crown Copyright: HES.

Recent excavations by David Caldwell revealed that most of the visible buildings were relatively late in date, though not the hall and the church, which dated to the fourteenth century AD. There seems to have been a major phase of rebuilding in the fifteenth and sixteenth centuries and this obscured the Medieval settlement, which seems to have had a quite different configuration that is currently impossible to reconstruct.

The evidence from Orkney and Shetland suggests that Bornais was an unusually large Norse settlement in Scottish terms. The occupants would have consisted of a diverse group of several households, including families that probably had considerable status in the Norse diaspora of the Atlantic seaboard. The expansion of the settlement seems to have coincided with Gofraid Crobán's ascendancy and the establishment of his dynasty on the throne of Man. It was possible that the head of the family that occupied Bornais consolidated his position by participating in the campaigns that established Gofraid Crobán and that this resulted in the expansion of the settlement in the twelfth century. The architecture and material culture of the Bornais settlement do suggest that the occupants were significant actors in the political dramas of this period and would have had a role at the council of Tynwald in the Isle of Man. The historical records suggest that the islands sent 16 representatives to the parliament, and it was possible that one of these was the occupant of the Middle Norse longhouse on mound 2.[30] However, the importance of the main family at Bornais may have been relatively short lived as the longhouse was abandoned after only 50 years, and for between 110 and 170 years there was no obvious high-status building. The abandonment of the Middle Norse longhouse may have coincided with the expedition to the Hebrides by Magnus Barelegs in 1098, but we cannot be certain.

Church and Thing

The twelfth century was a period when the Christian Church in the West was systematically reorganised. The papacy effectively took over and imposed a consistent bureaucracy that enabled it to exert considerable control over the running and organisation of the spiritual life of the inhabitants of western Europe. The Western Isles were no exception to this. The islands became part of the diocese of Sodor set up by King Óláfr Guðrøðarson in 1134, and were deliberately organised to be contiguous with the territory of Man and the Isles.[31] The Bishop was elected by the monks of Furness Abbey and the diocese was administered from the Archdiocese of York. There clearly had been bishops in the kingdom since the time of Gofraid Crobán, if not before, although it is unclear what their jurisdiction was.

In 1153 the administration of the diocese was transferred to the newly established See of Nidaros (now Trondheim) in Norway, which retained spiritual but not secular authority during the transfer of secular power from Norway to Scotland in 1266. It retained nominal control until 1387, though there were disputes with the King of Scotland, most notably over who had the power to appoint the bishop. The documentary records for the first couple of centuries of the diocese are limited and the list of bishops is muddled and confusing, but they appear to have been peripatetic, moving around the isles between the major churches of the region.[32] The central cathedral of St German at Peel on the Isle of Man was constructed in the middle of the twelfth century but again the documentation is poor. For most of the early period the most important religious centre in the Hebrides was the monastery at Iona, though this was never an established cathedral.

Óláfr Guðrøðarson was also influential in introducing the new reformed orders of monasticism into the kingdom. He established Rushen Abbey on the Isle of Man in 1134 and was an influential patron of many of the new religious houses around the Irish Sea. These were most notably Furness Abbey in Cumbria and the priory at Whithorn in Galloway, which both had privileged access to land and resources in Man.[33] Somerled and his descendants also seemed to have acquired this enthusiasm for the new reformed orders of monasticism. Somerled's son Ranald founded the Benedictine Abbey and the Augustinian Nunnery at Iona, and Saddell Abbey, a Cistercian foundation in Kintyre, all at the end of the twelfth or early in the thirteenth century. A later and more unusual foundation was Ardchatten Priory on Loch Etive, established by Duncan MacDougal in 1230 or 1231. This was a priory of the Valliscaulian order which had foundations only in France and Scotland.

The development of a network of parishes was a critical administrative goal of the diocese of Sodor but it is unclear how long it took to establish a comprehensive system across the region. There are no Medieval records of when these parishes were established in the Western Isles, nor where the parish churches were located. Woolf identified 13 parishes in the Western Isles: Ness, Eye, Barvas and Uig in Lewis; Kilbride and Rodel in Harris; Sand, Kilmory and Carinish in North Uist; Benbecula; Howmore and Kilpheder (Cille Pheadair) in South Uist, and Barra.[34] Identifying the churches that acted as the centre of these parishes is difficult. Only a couple of buildings could be identified with some certainty to date to this period.

One of the most established and well documented parish churches is Howmore (Tobha Mòr) in South Uist. This comprised a complex of surviving buildings, most of which dated to the Late Medieval or post-Medieval period and will be discussed in later chapters. However, there was one substantial building, Teampull Mòr, which was almost certainly a parish church dating to the early thirteenth century. The church was substantial, roughly 20 m by 8 m, but most of the walls are now reduced to the level of the foundations, with only the east wall surviving to any height. This wall contained 'two narrow splayed windows with segmented heads and semi-circular rear-arches, below and to either side of which are a pair of aumbries (or wall-cupboards)'.[35] These would originally have been covered with dressed sandstone mouldings, fragments of which were systematically robbed from the structure. Detailed analysis of the lime mortar from the wall core identified chips of imported sandstone, that revealed that the stone mouldings were shaped on site at the same time as the mortar was being mixed.[36] The walls of the church were very well made and suggest a sophisticated structure built by experienced masons. Parallels for the structure exist in Argyll at Fincharn and suggest that the stimulus for the construction of this church, and arguably the establishment of the parish system, was the acquisition of the southern islands by the descendants of Somerled in the early thirteenth century.

Another possibly early thirteenth-century church was Teampull na Trionaid at Carinish, North Uist. The Book of Clanranald attributed its foundation to Bethag, prioress of the nunnery at Iona and daughter of Somerled, but other sources attributed it to Amie MacRuaidhrí and Amie certainly had an association with the church. It was believed to have been a nunnery and had a reputation as a seat of learning in the Medieval period, the Franciscan philosopher Duns Scotus is reputed to have been partially educated here. The building was substantially robbed of all its architectural elements in the recent past and this makes a chronological assessment difficult.

An important church, and one that was only rediscovered recently, lies in the township of Cille Donnain to the south of Bornais.[37] It lay on a promontory on the south side of Loch Chill Donnain and comprised a major stone-built bicameral church with a nave (8.5 m long by 4.4 m wide) and chancel (3.1 m long by 2.3 m wide), surrounded by a complex of buildings of uncertain function that included some relatively recent structures (Fig. 4.48). A nearby island in the loch with four buildings on it appears to have been part of the complex and was connected by a causeway to the mainland.

There are no historical records for the church at Cille Donnain, but a relatively early date in the twelfth century is suggested by the distinctive plan. Comparable churches with a separate nave and chancel were concentrated in the Earldom of Orkney. This design is not known on the Isle of Man and it

FIGURE 4.48. A plan of the church at Cill Donnain to the south of Bornais on South Uist. After Fleming and Woolf 1992.

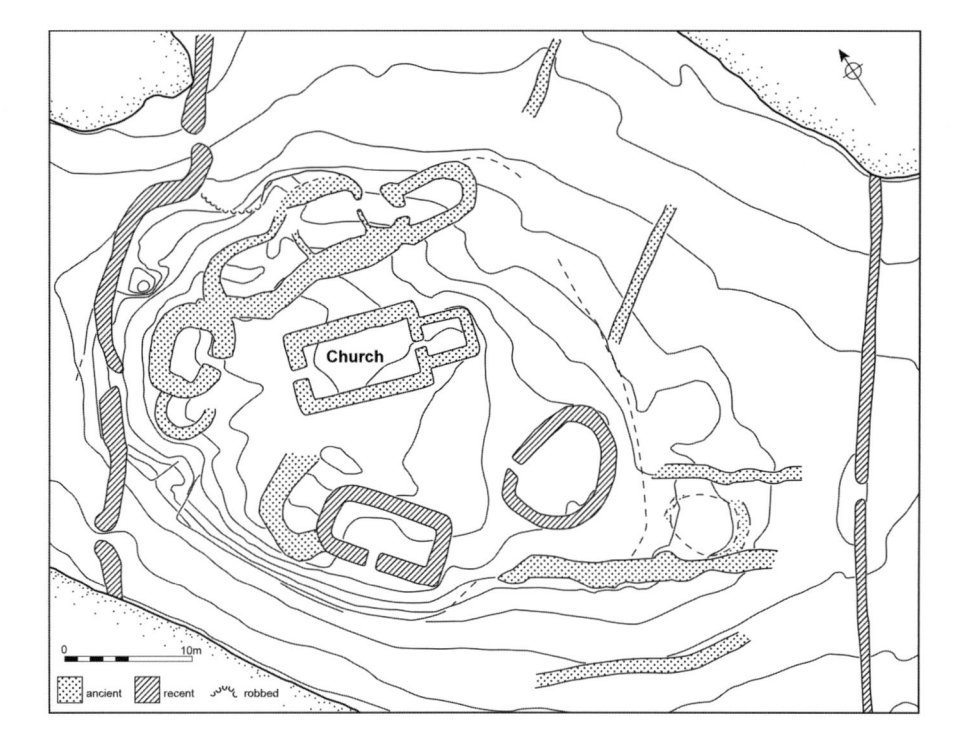

seems likely that Cille Donnain was constructed when the Outer Hebrides were closely linked with the Earldom of Orkney in the twelfth century. There was no evidence to suggest that this was a parish church and it was most likely a private chapel associated with a rich landowner.

Private chapels were well known in the Northern Isles and the historical and archaeological evidence from Orkney clearly demonstrates that the secular and sacred were inexorably linked. Orcadian parish churches '... are situated most often within 300 m of a settlement or within a settlement area'.[38] It was clear from the *Orkneyinga Saga* that, although the social behaviour of a high-status individual involved feasting and drinking, this did not interfere with regular attendance at church services, which could have taken place several times a day, making the proximity of a private chapel convenient.

It is surprising, therefore, that the church at Cille Donnain was not located close to a Norse settlement. The nearest known settlement is a large mound in the machair almost a kilometre to the northwest. There was no evidence for a church in the complex of buildings at Bornais, or anywhere nearby, and none of the potentially Medieval churches in the Western Isles appear to be closely associated with Norse settlements. This suggests that the Norse inhabitants of these islands had locational preferences for churches that privileged certain landscape characteristics over convenient access. The churches may have been located on pre-Norse religious sites and thus demonstrate a continuity of knowledge and Christian tradition across the conquest period.

A general preference for the creation of sacred space on islands, on promontories and in lochs in the Western Isles also demonstrated similarities with ancient prehistoric preferences which emphasised the significance of these locations. There were several church sites on the Uists that may have been built on islands, including Cille Bhànnain and Cille Pheadair; part of the complex of Cille Donnain was built on an island and the main church was on a promontory in the loch. It is also possible that the complex of buildings at Howmore was surrounded by water in the Medieval period.

One other major monument that should have existed in the Medieval landscape of the Western Isles was as an assembly site, a Thing or meeting-place for the wider community where decisions were made, and laws promulgated.[39] This had an important role for the settlement at Finlaggan on Islay, and Donald Monro, Dean of the Isles, recorded how the Lord of the Isles met with his councillors – who included MacLeans, MacLeods, MacNeills, McKinnons, the leaders of Clan Donald (MacDonald of Kintyre, MacDonald of Keppoch, MacIain of Ardnamurchan and Clan Ranald), the Bishop of the Isles and the Abbot of Iona – on Eilean na Comhairle (the Council Isle), to decide the laws of the Isles.

It has been suggested that the island adjacent to the church at Cille Donnain was a council island, as it had some similarities to the Council Isle at Finlaggan. I have also argued that mound 1 at Bornais was a possible candidate for a Thing mound. It was one of the most substantial and prominent mounds on the machair but was clearly separated from the main settlement area. This separation could have provided an element of neutrality, and its archaeological history—the Iron Age houses it contained—might have given ancestral significance to the decision-making processes that would be undertaken at a Thing.[40] The discovery of an ogham plaque (Fig. 3.11) on mound 1 may be relevant, as this could be Norse in date, and one of the possible explanations of this plaque was that it was a ballot token cast in legal proceedings. The arrangement of the structures on this mound, which created a rectangular quad with an open central area, was distinctive and suggests that the buildings may have had a special function.

There has been a considerable amount of recent research on Thing sites that has re-emphasised the importance of assembly in the Medieval period. Historical records testify to the significance and proliferation of councils in early Medieval Ireland and in Anglo-Saxon England. Most of the work on Things in Scotland has focused on the place-name evidence, which is problematic for the Western Isles where there has been significant linguistic change over the last millennium, particularly in the Uists.[41] Nevertheless, in Scotland it has been observed that assembly sites were associated with mounds, both man-made and natural, with examples including the mound at Dingwall in Sutherland; Doomster Hill at Govan, Strathclyde; and Tynwald on the Isle of Man. Shetland is relatively well documented, and it was clear that a network of local assembly sites existed that worked in tandem with the main site at Tingwall in central Mainland. The Tingwall Thing was located on an artificial island which had had a broch constructed on it in the Iron Age.

The evidence suggests that assembly sites were distributed throughout the islands of northern and western Scotland, and we should therefore expect at least one such site to be present in South Uist. Mound 1 at Bornais would have been an appropriate location, given the proximity of the exceptionally large settlement at Bornais, but the island location close to the church at Cille Donnain is another possibility. Churches would have been an important feature of the landscape of the Western Isles and there are important examples, such as Howmore, Cille Donnain and Teampull na Trionaid, that appear to have been contemporary with the Kingdom of Man and the Isles, and which have survived as archaeological monuments to the present day. Both monument types were essential to the governance of this unusually dispersed kingdom. The presence of one or more Things would provide a tentative glimpse of the bureaucracy of kingship in the Medieval period.

Conclusion

The evidence from the recent excavations at Bornais and Cille Pheadair have transformed our understanding of the eleventh and twelfth centuries in the Western Isles and have provided some of the best evidence archaeologists have for social and economic life in the Medieval societies of Scotland. The contrasts and similarities of the two settlements are important[42] and it is clear that the social status of the Bornais settlement and, in particular, the household occupying mound 2, was higher than the social status of the family living at Cille Pheadair. The distinctions between the two settlements should not be exaggerated, however, as they are complex, and both were wealthy and prosperous.

The most important distinction was the size and location of the two settlements. The central mound at Bornais was a much larger settlement mound than that at Cille Pheadair, and Bornais was established on an existing Pictish settlement, whereas Cille Pheadair was established on a previously unoccupied part of the machair plain. The continuity of place at Bornais was important for a number of reasons that were unconnected with the presence or absence of a remnant Pictish population. The mound itself provided an obvious focus in the landscape, elevating the houses from the underlying water table. The presence of occupation deposits provided consolidated sediments in which a house could be constructed. Resources such as stone could be reused and the land surrounding the mound was likely to have had enhanced fertility due to regular cultivation. The immediate landscape of the Bornais settlement would have been a much more attractive location for any Viking settlers than the sand dunes at Cille Pheadair, and it was not surprising that Bornais was occupied before Cille Pheadair and potentially by a more powerful family that could have kept hold of their acquisition of the land if challenged in the scramble that early colonisation was likely to have been.

The significance of this location was confirmed by the subsequent development of the area into one of the largest Scandinavian settlements known from Scotland. It was clearly occupied by a significant number of people and the only documented settlement in Scotland comparable in size was the settlement at Birsay in Orkney. Birsay was an important political centre for the Orkney islands and had a significant role in the historical narrative for the Earldom of Orkney, presented by the Orkneyinga Saga. It gives us a glimpse of the kind of activities that were taking place at Bornais, though there were clear differences between the two polities. The Outer Hebrides were just one part of the Kingdom of Man and the Isles, and it is unlikely they were ever the most important part. Political power was always centred on the Isle of Man, with Islay probably the most important of the Hebridean isles given its agricultural potential and size. Nevertheless, in occupying the largest settlement on the Uists, the occupants of Bornais were likely to have provided one of the delegates from the islands who attended the regular assemblies at Tynwald on the Isle of Man. The development of Bornais, a significant centre for the Uists, may have reflected its position in the islands. As discussed earlier, the settlement was strategically located to access sea lanes on both the west and east coasts of South Uist that linked Scandinavia and the Northern Isles to towns such as Waterford, Dublin and Cork in Ireland and Chester and Bristol in western England.

There is a possibility that the Bornais settlement had an important administrative role, and mound 1, a detached and separate mound south of the main settlement, may have had a specialist function, acting as a local assembly site or Thing. This could explain the unusual arrangement of buildings and the presence of an ogham-inscribed plaque on this mound. However, the one special building that we might have expected, a church, is not visible. Churches seem, at least in the southern part of the Hebrides, to have been located away from the settlements, and this contrasted with the situation on Orkney and Shetland where they were often associated with each other.

Religion was clearly important to the people occupying the main houses at both Cille Pheadair and Bornais. At Cille Pheadair a bone cross was found embedded in the floor of the house and at Bornais fragments of green porphyry acted as some form of Christian relic. Fragmentary relics appear to have played an important role in the life of the inhabitants and it is clear that many of the objects found on the floor of the Middle Norse longhouse at Bornais were relics from the previous century. This was certainly the case for the Ringerike cylinder and several of the comb fragments. These objects symbolised the heroic Viking past that originated in Scandinavia, and came across the North Sea to Scotland when raiding was a commonplace activity.

In some respects, the Middle Norse longhouse at Bornais was in itself a relic of earlier times: it replicated the structure of the Early Norse longhouse which was built during the initial colonisation of the islands. The organisation of the interior into three aisles with a central hearth area, and the presence of a cooking area at the end opposite the entrance, also recreated occupational patterns present in the early houses. Feasting, drinking, personal grooming, and conspicuous discard of prestige items were all behavioural traits that harked back to the unsustainable years of raiding in the ninth and early tenth centuries. The inhabitants of this house were effectively living in the past and were trying to maintain an independent Viking ideal in a period when kings and statecraft were becoming well established in the North Atlantic.

These archaic practices were abandoned during this period and houses roughly contemporary with the Middle Norse longhouse on mound 2 seem to have been developing a very different structure and organisation. The living space was shrinking and became less of an arena for display and socialising in large extended family groups. Instead, it was designed for small groups of immediate kin to consume their daily meals. It was also possible that separate private spaces were being created that could be secured and were off-limits to some members of the household. These private spaces may have been for storing valuables that belonged to individuals rather than the general household, or they could have been for sleeping, used as the private bedchambers of the masters of the house. Whatever the case, it was the beginning of a trend in the architecture of the Uists that split off activities that originally took place in the public space of the communal hall into separate rooms, and in the Late Norse period these rooms became separate buildings. The partitioning of these buildings embodied major changes in social relationships which will be explored in Chapter 5, but it is interesting to note that these changes seem to have been instigated in lower-status households at Cille Pheadair and Bornais mound 2A, rather than within the elite household on mound 2.

In terms of material culture and agricultural economy, there seems to be little to separate the two settlements. Both had access to important Scandinavian goods and had a wide range of pins and combs used to decorate and groom the body, and both had evidence for coin use and access to gold. One of the significant differences was the evidence for feasting and drinking. It may be significant that the floor of the Middle Norse longhouse at Bornais produced a number of antler tines which were shaped and decorated. These were either finials from drinking horns or spoons for specialist consumption practices. Either suggestion emphasises the importance of ceremonial feasting and drinking, and it is clear the longhouse was designed for just such events. These would have been the ideal opportunity not only to emphasise the importance of family and community, but also to highlight status distinctions within that community.

Notes

1. Viking Art is well covered by a number of books. The original scheme was laid out by Willson and Klindt Jensen 1966, and the most recent comprehensive survey is by Graham-Campbell 2020. Signe Fuglesang provided a comprehensive survey of the Ringerike style in Fuglesang 1980.
2. Sturluson 1964 quoted by Parker Pearson et al. 2018, 584.
3. McDonald 2019, 83–84.
4. Sellar 1966; Woolf 2005.
5. These mounds were identified by Mike Parker Pearson and are published in Parker Pearson 2012.

6 See Lane 1990 and 2005 for the initial definition of these ceramics and a later discussion of their significance.
7 The establishment and nature of the administrative organisation of the Kingdom of Man and the Isles is discussed in detail by John Raven (Raven 2005).
8 See Woolf 2015 for a discussion of the early history of the Diocese of Sodor.
9 This paragraph has greatly benefitted from the knowledge and help of John Raven.
10 Crawford 1987, 135.
11 The excavation of this house is fully documented in Sharples 2020, chapter 4.
12 The excavations at Quoygrew were published in Barrett 2012, the excavations at Birsay were published in Morris 2021 and the excavations at Skaill were published by Griffiths *et al.* 2019.
13 The excavations at Aðalstræti are documented in Milek 2006 and the excavations at Granastaðir are documented by Einarsson 1995.
14 The relation of these artefacts to the occupation of the house is discussed in Sharples 2020, but the wider significance of the objects is discussed in Sharples 2021.
15 The identification of the source of the purple phyllite occurred after the volume on the Bornais finds was published, and the significance of these quarries is discussed in Baug *et al.* 2019.
16 See Freer in Sharples 2021, 69 for a detailed discussion of her experiment in making platters and then using these for cooking.
17 This process is known as flotation and involved suspending the sampled soil on a mesh. Water was then passed through the soil, and the lighter organic materials floated away through a channel that led to another very fine sieve where only the lightest organic materials were captured. The washed soil sank through the mesh and left behind a residue that included larger stones and archaeological materials such as pottery, bone and shell.
18 The excavations were published in Einarsson 1995.
19 Milek 2006.
20 This is described in Parker Pearson *et al.* 2018.
21 See Crawford 1981.
22 See Barrett 2012.
23 See discussion of the crop remains by Summers and Bond in Sharples 2020, chapter 12, and in Sharples 2021, chapters 3 and 4.
24 The survey results are described and discussed in Parker Pearson 2012.
25 There has been a long programme of excavations and survey at the Brough of Birsay, and this has recently been comprehensively published by Chris Morris (Morris 2021).
26 Settlement mounds require the presence of blown sand which accumulates in the structures and in doing so preserves these structures and their accompanying deposits.
27 See Buteux 1997 for a detailed report on these excavations.
28 See Owen 2023 for an interim report on these excavations.
29 A series of detailed interim reports on these excavations is available on the internet (Caldwell 2010) and were used to produce this summary. The final publication should appear soon.
30 See Crawford 1987, 205 for a discussion of the administration of the Kingdom of Man.
31 Towards the end of the twelfth century the new diocese of Lismore was established to cover the Gaelic-speaking part of the west mainland of Scotland. The circumstances behind the establishment of the diocese are unclear, but it seems to be closely related to the growing importance of the descendants of Somerled, and in particular the

rising importance of the MacDougall lords who had a stronghold in the nearby castle of Dunstaffnage.
32 See Woolf 2003 for a detailed discussion of the list of bishops.
33 See McDonald 1997 and 2019.
34 Woolf 2003.
35 Fojut *et al.* 1994, 42.
36 A detailed analysis of the mortars was undertaken by Mark Thacker and is available along with an important discussion of the architectural developments in the region in his PhD thesis (Thacker 2016).
37 The church was discovered in the early years of the SEARCH project and a detailed report was promptly published (Fleming and Woolf 1992).
38 Gibbon 2006, 171.
39 A comprehensive recent discussion of the importance of these assembly sites is Semple *et al.* 2020.
40 The significance of mounds in the Scandinavian areas of the North Atlantic is examined by Harrison 2013.
41 See O'Grady 2008.
42 One of the original goals of the project was to excavate two contemporary settlements so that they could be compared and contrasted.

CHAPTER FIVE

Scots and Gaels

Introduction – the Lewis chessmen

One of the most important archaeological discoveries ever made in Britain occurred on the west coast of the Isle of Lewis, probably in the spring of 1831, though the circumstances of this discovery were shrouded in mystery. One of the accounts of the discovery was published in 1851 by Daniel Wilson, one of Scotland's pre-eminent antiquarians.

> In the spring of 1831, the inroads effected by the sea undermined and carried away a portion of a sandbank in the parish of Uig, Isle of Lewis, and uncovered a small subterranean stone building like an oven, at some depth below the surface. The exposure of this singular structure having excited the curiosity, or more probably the cupidity, of a peasant who chanced to be working in the neighbourhood, he preceded to break into it, when he was astonished to see what he concluded to be an assemblage of elves or gnomes upon whose mysteries he had unconsciously intruded. The superstitious Highlander flung down his spade, and fled home in dismay; but incited by the bolder curiosity of his wife he was at length induced to return to the spot and bring away with him the singular little ivory figures, which had not unnaturally appeared to him the pygmy sprites of Celtic folk-lore.[1]

This story may be fanciful, but it was generally agreed that a large quantity of finely carved chessmen was found by Malcolm MacLeod in the township of Uig sometime before the spring of 1831 (Fig. 5.1). The precise location was not recorded at the time of discovery and several possible find-spots are still open

FIGURE 5.1. A group shot of Lewis chessmen © National Museums Scotland.

despite detailed consideration of the various accounts of the discovery. The current consensus favours the sand dunes on the south side of the inlet known as Camus Uig and the condition of the pieces agrees with the story narrated above, that the pieces came from shell-sand deposits in an area of machair.[2]

The discovery was exceptional for a number of reasons, not least because the international significance of the objects was based not on the monetary value of the precious materials used to make the chessmen but on their artistic attributes. This is not a treasure comparable to the silver hoards of Stornoway Castle or Dibidale, which could be melted down and weighed to give a value. Rather, we have a much more tangible insight into the aesthetic sensibility and social mores of the period when these objects were carved by supremely gifted craftworkers.

The discovery at Uig comprised 93 pieces of carved ivory – 78 chessmen, 14 table men and a buckle. Most of the pieces have been carved from the tusks of walrus, but a small number have been carved from sperm whale teeth. Walrus ivory was an important commodity that was prized for its pristine whiteness and uniform texture and was used as a raw material for carving objects of the greatest significance throughout Europe. Ivory became popular and was used widely in the Roman period when elephant ivory was relatively easily accessible but, as elephant ivory became increasingly rare in northern Europe in the middle of the first millennium AD, walrus ivory from the far north became an increasingly significant material.[3]

Early supplies of walrus ivory came from hunters in the Barents Sea to the north of Scandinavia but, as the Vikings expanded across the North Atlantic, new sources became available. Greenland was an important source and large quantities of walrus ivory were exported from the Viking colonies on the island and provided the principal traded commodity for these colonies. This was exported essentially as a raw material to towns such as Trondheim and Bergen in Norway and then on to the great medieval towns of continental Europe. The current consensus is that the Lewis chessmen were carved in Trondheim, probably in the late twelfth or early thirteenth century, because a small number of comparable figures have been found there.

The carved figures are evocative and inspirational works of Romanesque art which have stimulated many artistic representations in a variety of media but perhaps most famously featuring as props in chess games in movies such as *Beckett*, *The Lion in Winter*, *The Seventh Seal* and most recently in *Harry Potter and the Philosopher's Stone*. The Lewis chessmen also inspired a much-loved television cartoon *Noggin the Nog*, which encouraged many young viewers to take an interest in Norse mythology and culture. The figures are undoubtedly expressive despite the relatively formulaic nature of the carvings, and they have distinctive accoutrements that represent the roles held by the pieces in the social hierarchy.

The kings sit on thrones, wear cloaks with decorated hems and have crowns (Fig. 5.2). They hold a sheathed sword on their knees and have long, braided hair and full beards (with one or two exceptions). The sides and backs of their chairs are elaborately decorated with scrolls of foliage, geometrical designs and

FIGURE 5.2. A photo of a bishop, a king, a queen and a warder from the Lewis chess set © National Museums Scotland.

mythical beasts. The queens are also seated on elaborately decorated thrones and wear crowns and long cloaks. Their cloaks open at the front to reveal undergarments of various complexity. Their hair is worn long in braids and is often covered by a veil. The right hand is upright, resting on the cheek and chin, and most of the queens have the left arm placed flat on their knees with the hand cradling the elbow of the right arm. However, two queens have a drinking horn in their right hand.

The bishops are a much more varied group (Fig. 5.2) and include both standing and seated figures (again on elaborately decorated chairs) who wear a variety of vestments normally covered by either a cloak or a chasuble and sometimes both.[4] They wear horned mitres with ribbons extending down their backs. The precise form of the mitres varies, and it has been argued that these are mostly twelfth-century forms, but they include some that may be early thirteenth century. All the bishops hold a crozier, and some hold a book, presumably a Bible, whereas others have their right hand raised in an act of blessing.

The knights are mounted on ponies which have well-defined stirrups and bridles. They carry a spear in the right hand and a shield covering a sheathed sword on the left-hand side. They wear a helmet, and a long cloak divided at the front and back; the helmets vary though they are relatively simple forms which are documented in images of the late twelfth and early thirteenth centuries. The warders are dressed similarly to the knights, with large cloaks and helmets. They carry their shields on their left shoulder or hold them covering their front (Fig. 5.2). The latter pose enables four examples to be carved biting the top of the shield, a pose that is associated with 'berserkers'. All the warders have unsheathed swords held upright in the right hand. The shields for the knights and the warders are variations on the kite shaped form that was popular in the late twelfth and thirteenth centuries. They are decorated with simple geometric motifs that appear to precede the complex heraldic patterns that were beginning to define genealogies in continental Europe at this time.

All the designs were unique, and their individuality is a significant feature of the pieces despite the argument that they belong to four to five chess sets. The assemblage also included a group of upright non-figurative pieces which were identified as pawns and 14 flat circular discs or table men which were used to play other games.

These carvings clearly demonstrated that the insignia of kingship were firmly established in the Scandinavian lands, and more importantly that the queen was recognised as a powerful person in her own right, expected to sit on a throne and wear a crown. The king had a sword, though sheathed, an acknowledgement of the implicit violence that supported his position. The knights and warders, in contrast, forcefully display their role in violent warfare by brandishing their swords and spears.[5]

For a long time, it was implied, if not explicitly argued, that the Lewis chessmen told us very little about life in the Western Isles as the pieces were clearly intrusive and probably ended up on the islands by accident as a result of the sinking of a merchant ship sailing around the islands on its way south to richer more civilised places. However, this was an unnecessarily derogatory interpretation. The chess set could have been owned by an important landowner resident on the islands., and there were suggestions in some of the stories surrounding the discovery that the pieces were in a building, perhaps the ruins of a settlement or even a religious establishment in the Uig area.

Games were recorded as an activity of the island elite in a poem to Aenghus Mor MacDomhnaill dated to around 1250; the poem refers to an inheritance from his father.[6]

> To you he left his position
> yours each breastplate, each treasure,
> his hats, his staves, his slender swords,
> yours, his brown ivory chessmen
>
> Yours, your father's hounds' slender chains,
> each treasure chest's in your share;
> all his houses and his tax,
> yours, Domhnall's horses and herds[7]

Clearly, the chessmen were an important symbol of wealth and power, and it was to be expected that an individual living in an important settlement, such as Bornais, would have access to a chess set to provide entertainment on a long winter's evening. The presence of the chessmen on Lewis also indicates that connections with Norway were still important in the thirteenth century and this is an issue of significance that will be returned to below.

The history

The purpose of this chapter is to examine the final phase of occupation at Bornais and to consider the Western Isles in the thirteenth and fourteenth centuries. I have labelled this period Late Norse, but it could be more accurately described as 'Scottish', because the key historical event that marked the period was the transfer of the Western Isles from the Kingdom of Norway to the Kingdom of Scotland by the Treaty of Perth in 1266.

The Treaty of Perth was clearly a very significant event that had major ramifications for the political, cultural, social and economic lives of the people living in the Western Isles but, as we have discussed in previous chapters, we should not get obsessed with the precise chronology of the Treaty. It is almost impossible to date the houses, structures and deposits exposed by archaeology with the precision required to align them with historical events, though we will have a go later in this chapter. It is unlikely that life in the Western Isles was instantaneously transformed by the signing of a treaty in distant Perth. This event must be seen as a subtle shift in emphasis from the hybrid Norse/Gaelic traditions of the Kingdom of Man and the Isles to the developing hybrid Gaelic/Norse traditions that had been evolving in the MacSorley (Clan Somhairle) chiefdoms of Argyll. In the twelfth century the King of Norway had only an intermittent interest in and little control over the lands at the edge of his domain. In the thirteenth century the Kingdom of Scotland was becoming an increasingly powerful and dynamic polity, expanding and exploring the disputed lands on its boundaries. 1266 was an event which concluded some changes that had already occurred, but it also instigated processes that were to develop over the succeeding centuries.

After the death of Somerled in 1164, Guðrøðr Óláfsson, the King of Man, seems to have re-established control over the Western Isles, but some of Somerled's children acquired control over certain areas of the western seaboard. Lewis and Harris remained within the Kingdom of Man and the Isles, but by 1210 the Uists, Benbecula and Barra may have been controlled by the sons of Ruaraidh, a descendent of Somerled. The MacRuaidhris, despite being the kin of Somerled, were strongly allied with the Norwegian kings and, in 1230, an appeal for support in a local dispute led to the dispatch of a large fleet by the King of Norway. This fleet was led by Uspak, another descendant of Somerled, but the expedition was not a success, Uspak was killed, and the fleet returned to Norway. However, Dugald MacRuaidhri maintained contact with Norway and was recorded as visiting Bergen in 1248, 1249 and 1253. In 1258 Dugald led a great raid to the west coast of Ireland.[8]

By the middle of the thirteenth century, the Norwegian King Haakon Haakonsson had consolidated his position in Norway, and he moved to re-affirm control over the islands in the west, which was being undermined by the Scots. Alexander II had tried to purchase the Hebrides but was rebuffed and this led to a military expedition in 1249 which ended with his death from fever on the island of Kerrera in Argyll. His son, Alexander III, was only seven years old at his father's death, but his stated ambition on ending his minority was to complete his father's project to take control of the western seaboard. His first act was to send diplomats to Norway to negotiate the purchase of the Western Isles, but Haakon rejected these overtures and instead led a substantial fleet to the west coast of Scotland in 1263. He was fully supported by his MacRuaidhri subjects, but not by the other descendants of Somerled; the MacDonalds were only reluctantly persuaded to join the fleet and the MacDougalls refused because they were closely allied with the Scots kings. Alexander deliberately avoided a naval engagement against the vastly superior fleet of Haakon and waited for harsh weather. After a brief skirmish at Largs in the beginning of October, Haakon withdrew and sailed back to overwinter in Orkney where he died from an unknown illness. Subsequent attacks on Haakon's supporters in the isles by allies of Alexander III led to the realisation by the Norwegian king, Magnus the Lawmender, that it was no longer possible to control the Western Isles, and negotiations were started that culminated in the Treaty of Perth and the purchase of the islands by Alexander III.

The death of Haakon and the purchase of the islands does not appear to have lessened the MacRuaidhri connections with Norway and, after Dugald's death in 1268, one of his sons lived on to become an earl in Norway. Nevertheless, despite these Norwegian connections the MacRuaidhri seem to have retained control of the Uists and Garmoran. They eventually emerged from the Scottish Wars of Independence in relatively good standing after a late switch to support Bruce. However, this was a somewhat pyrrhic victory as the head of the clan died fighting with Edward Bruce in Ireland in 1318. The real winners that arose from the Wars of Independence were the MacDonalds of Islay and, in 1346, John of Islay inherited the Lordship of Garmoran after his wife Amie MacRuaidhri became heir because of the murder of her brother.

There appears, therefore, to have been a relatively stable overlordship of the southern part of the Outer Hebrides by a hybrid Gaelic/Norse family, the MacRuaidhri, throughout the thirteenth and early fourteenth centuries. This family was happy to express fealty to both the Norwegian and Scottish kings, which was not unusual at this time. Whether the MacRuaidhri were principally Gaelic or Norse speakers is unknown. I suspect they moved easily between both languages as and when it suited them.

The archaeology

The archaeology of the thirteenth and fourteenth century is relatively well represented in the Western Isles. The settlements at both Bornais and Cille Pheadair were occupied and that at Bornais appears to have flourished during this period. The large hall was rebuilt with a new and distinctive floor plan. All the various mounds appear to have had contemporary houses, and although these are much smaller than the main hall on mound 2, they had distinctive floor plans which reflect changes in social relations. The excavations also revealed a variety of ancillary buildings on these peripheral mounds, which provide insights into

5. Scots and Gaels

craft production and agricultural activities. Bornais was the largest settlement on the island of South Uist throughout this period, and contrasts markedly with Cille Pheadair, which was a small farmstead abandoned by the middle of the thirteenth century.

The situation is less clear elsewhere on the islands. It seems likely that the authority of the Church was fully established and that the island was split into parishes with churches. The churches were likely to have been small stone-built structures and many of these can be identified in the islands today. However, in the absence of any distinctive architectural elements available to date these buildings, we are unable to definitively identify the Medieval churches of the Western Isles, with the exception of Howmore which will require consideration later in this chapter. A similar problem exists with the archaeology of elite secular buildings. The islands have a number of castles and substantial masonry structures which may date back to the thirteenth and fourteenth centuries, but at the moment it is impossible to conclusively date most of these structures, and this creates problems for our interpretation of this late Medieval society.

A Late Norse hall

The dominant structure at the settlement of Bornais in the Late Norse period was House 3 on mound 2, the third and final house built on this settlement mound (Fig. 5.3). This Late Norse house (3) was constructed in the middle of the thirteenth century, probably after the Treaty of Perth had been signed. This house was larger and more carefully built than the Late Norse houses on the other settlement mounds, revealing that mound 2 was still the favoured residence of the high-status family who controlled this unusually large settlement.[9]

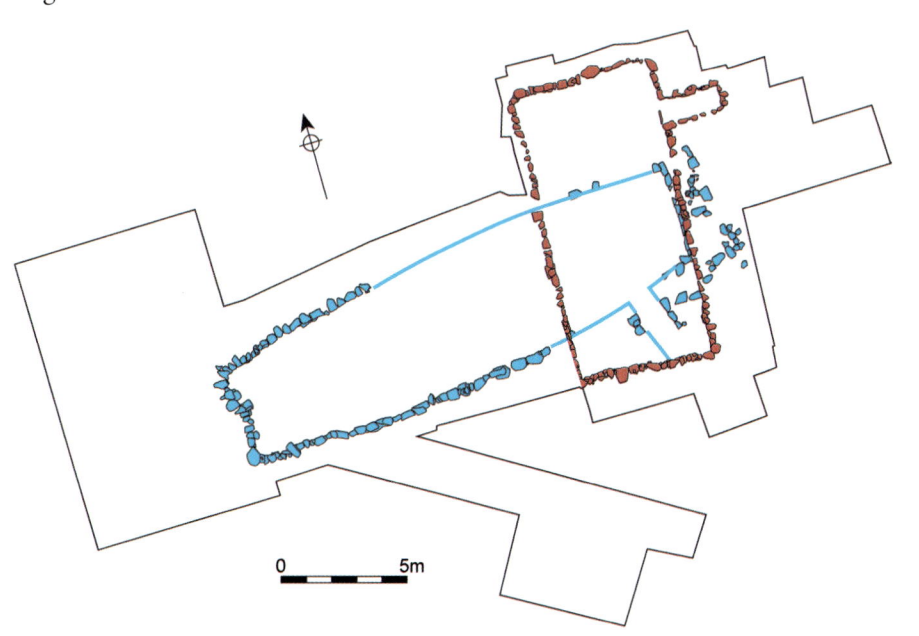

FIGURE 5.3. A simplified plan of Late Norse House 3 at Bornais, showing its relationship with the Middle Norse House 2.

FIGURE 5.4. A view of Bornais Late Norse House 3 from the north during the excavation of the floor.

Whereas the two earlier houses on mound 2 were bow walled longhouses that clearly signalled the Scandinavian allegiance of the occupants, the Late Norse house was a completely different shape. In plan, the Late Norse house had playing-card proportions, with very straight sided stone walls and sharp corners, and was oriented north–south. The internal space was 12 m long and 5.6 m wide and the defining inner revetment wall stood up to 0.6 m tall (Fig. 5.4). The south wall was the best-preserved and had up to five courses of stonework surviving. The east wall, in contrast, survived to no more than one course high. The stone revetment wall was probably built with a turf backing just over a metre thick, and a single course of an external stone kerb was identified on the west side of the house. The absence of collapse from the internal revetment inside the house and its relatively even height around most of its circuit suggests this wall had survived to its original height and that it acted as the base for a timber frame that supported the roof timbers. Wood panels may have been attached to the main timber supports and these would have covered and concealed the turf wall. The width of the internal space suggests the need for roof supports, which were almost certainly placed on flat stone pads found on the floor. The interior was a wider, more open space than that of the earlier bow-walled houses.

A single entrance was located at the north end of the east wall, and this comprised a stone revetted passage, 2.6 m long and 1 m wide (Fig. 5.5). To enter the Late Norse house, a visitor was required to step down into the passage, and at its end to step over two prominent upright sill stones, 0.25 m high. Presumably a timber door closed the outside entrance to the passage, and perhaps a heavy

FIGURE 5.5. The east facing entrance passage to the Late Norse House 3.

cloth curtain hung above the inner sill stones to keep the heat in and the wind out. The use of upright stones to define the boundary between the interior and exterior world was not found within the earlier Scandinavian longhouses. This distinction between interior and exterior was becoming more socially significant. The asymmetrical location of the entrance, in contrast, maintained traditions that were established by the Scandinavians and were brought to the islands with the bow-walled longhouse style.

The occupation of the Late Norse house (3) was intense, and resulted in the accumulation of a complex sequence of floor layers, hearths, pits and post holes which took a long time to excavate and produced a lot of detailed technical information which is not easy to summarise (Fig. 5.6). The house had a complex life which involved an initial aborted phase of construction on a slightly different alignment, after which three major periods of reflooring were observed. There was a constant renewal of the hearths which were gradually relocated over the life of the house. This all took place over a short period of between 30 and 60 years in the second half of the thirteenth century. This represented two or three generations of inhabitants, and it may be that the episodes of reflooring marked the transfer of control between generations within the family.

An important feature of the initial activity in the interior of the house was the digging of pits and post holes that preceded the occupation, and may have been associated with the creation of the house. The most prominent features were a cluster of at least three shallow pits in the centre of the house (Fig. 5.7).

FIGURE 5.6. Excavating floor layers and pits in Late Norse House 3.

FIGURE 5.7. The foundation pits at the centre of Late Norse House 3.

These were very shallow scoops, unlike the deep pits that lay below the Early and Middle Norse longhouses. Two of them were scoops less than 10 cm deep, and the deepest was just under 30 cm. A distinctive feature of the fill of the pits were layers of charcoal, which lined the bottoms of two and covered the top of the third pit. These dumps of material had been burnt somewhere else and then brought to the house and deliberately and carefully placed in the shallow

FIGURE 5.8. A charcoal rich layer at the base of one of the foundation pits of Late Norse House 3.

pits. Similar charcoal-rich fills were noted in pits dug to mark later refurbishments of the house (Fig. 5.8).

The floor layers were dark brown charcoal-rich sand that covered most of the internal area of the Late Norse house (Fig. 5.9). The floors contained coloured ash which defined discrete hearth areas along the central axis of the house. This was a notable change from the way the earlier longhouses were organised; with three longitudinal zones running the length of the houses, the central one being the peat ash layers of the hearth. In the Late Norse house, the main hearth in the primary floor was in the southern half of the house and comprised a sequence of peat ash deposits created by separate burning events. Each event occurred on the same spot but used slightly different fuels, leaving different coloured ash. The final deposit in the hearth was a layer of winkle shells that had been burnt a distinctive blue colour and were spread across a large area of the surrounding floor.

Winkle shells were found in large quantities across this primary floor layer but the concentration over the hearth was unusually dense, and essentially comprised a layer of shells and nothing else. The next most common find from

FIGURE 5.9. Three plans of the floor layers in Late Norse House 3 showing the pits and peat ash layers. The earliest floor is on the left the latest on the right.

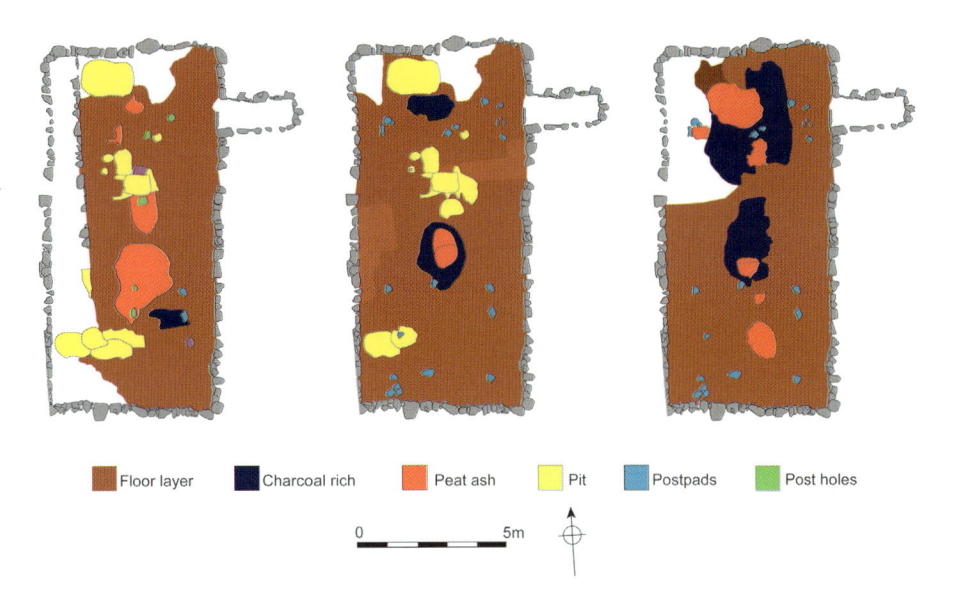

194   *The Vikings in the Hebrides*

the Late Norse house floor was fish bone, and this was concentrated in the northern half of the house, opposite the entrance. Fragments of mammal bone were also present in reasonable quantities and, again, the densities were higher at the north end of the house.

The higher densities of food refuse in the northern half of the house contrast with the distribution of artefacts which, though limited in number, were concentrated in and around the southern hearth (Fig. 5.10). Many of these objects were small and broken and they could have been accidental losses in the floor layers. However, there were some important complete tools, including two iron knives, an iron awl with a mineralised wooden handle, a bone point, an antler socket, and a whale bone comb. The latter was crudely made and clearly was

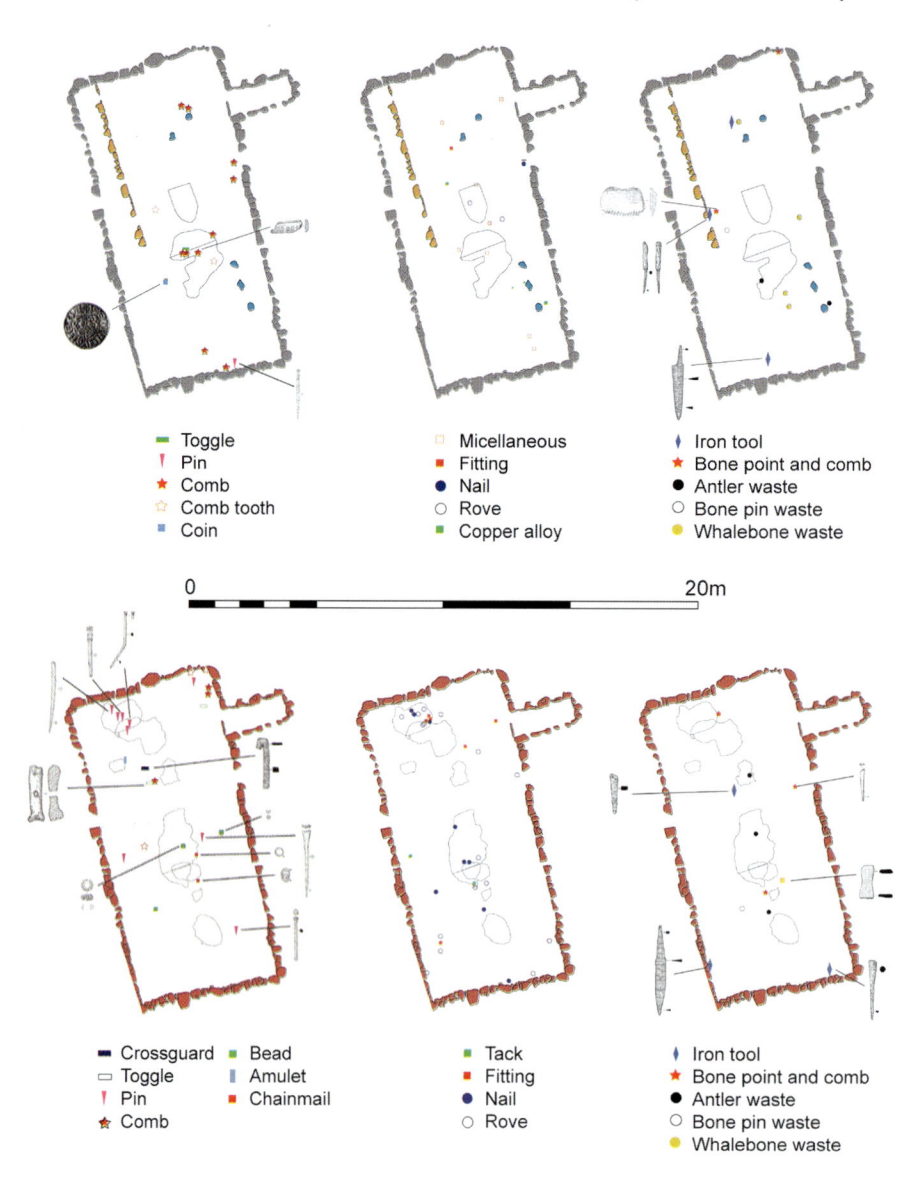

FIGURE 5.10. The distribution of the artefacts found in the early and late floors of Late Norse House 3.

FIGURE 5.11. A whale bone comb from the floor of Late Norse House 3.

originally a much a larger piece that had been chopped down to its current size (Fig. 5.11). The badly worn teeth show it was heavily used, probably in the manufacture of textiles. There were several composite hair-comb fragments, three glass beads and a complete pin, but only the latter was likely large enough to suggest it was deliberately discarded rather than accidentally lost. The most valuable object from the floor was a Continental imitation of a 'long cross' penny dating to AD 1248–1270.

The coin from the Late Norse house was one of three thirteenth-century coins from Bornais (Fig. 5.12). A silver short cross penny of either John (AD 1199–1216) or Henry III (AD 1216–1272) was found in the midden layers to the east of the Late Norse house, and a silver long cross penny of Henry III came from activity adjacent to one of the Late Norse houses on mound 2A.[10] Cille Pheadair produced a cut, short cross halfpenny of John, dating to AD 1204–1210, from the floor of a small shed built within the final house. This upsurge in coin use in the Western Isles coincided with the transfer of sovereignty to Scotland in the middle of the thirteenth century. It is interesting that all the coins belonging to this period were English since both the Scots and the Norwegians were producing their own coins at this time. England had become an important economic influence in the Kingdom of Man and the Isles at this time, and the political threat this implies may have been one of the reasons behind the Scottish takeover of the islands. The connections between Man and the islands may have been related to the recruitment of mercenaries from the islands to enforce English political power in the Irish Sea province.

FIGURE 5.12. A continental imitation of a long cross penny made between 1248 and 1270. Found on the floor of Late Norse House 3.

The primary floor layer of the Late Norse house on mound 2 was sealed by a secondary floor which completely covered the interior of the house with a relatively thick layer of mottled dark and light brown sand. The main hearth was a neat oval of ash located in the centre of the house (Figs 5.9 and 5.13). Immediately to the north of this was a cluster of small pits, and in the south-west corner of the house was another cluster of pits, some with distinctive charcoal layers (Fig. 5.9). However, the most substantial pit cutting through these floor deposits was a steep-sided, rectangular pit adjacent to the north wall of the house. There was no clear and obvious function for this or any of the other pits.

The most frequent finds in this floor layer were, again, winkle shells, and these were all that was present over much of the floor (Fig. 5.14). It is difficult to understand what advantage a floor of winkles would provide but it was definitely a deliberate creation. Fish bones were common in the floor layers, but they were not as common as they were in the primary occupation deposits, and mammal bone fragments were recovered in greater densities. The fish bone was concentrated in the northern half of the building, though this was not as pronounced a distribution as it was in the primary floor, and there was

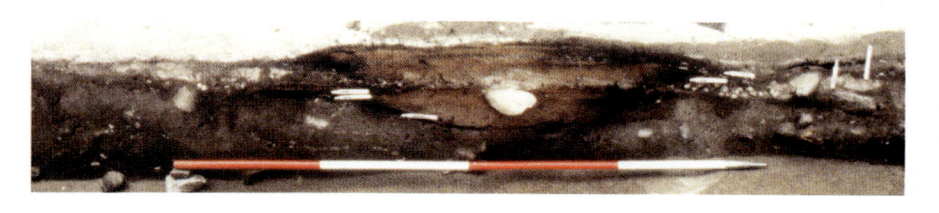

FIGURE 5.13. A close up of a section through the ash layers of the central hearth in Late Norse House 3.

FIGURE 5.14. The distribution of mammal bones, fish bones and winkle shells showing the density for every half metre square of the floor layers excavated.

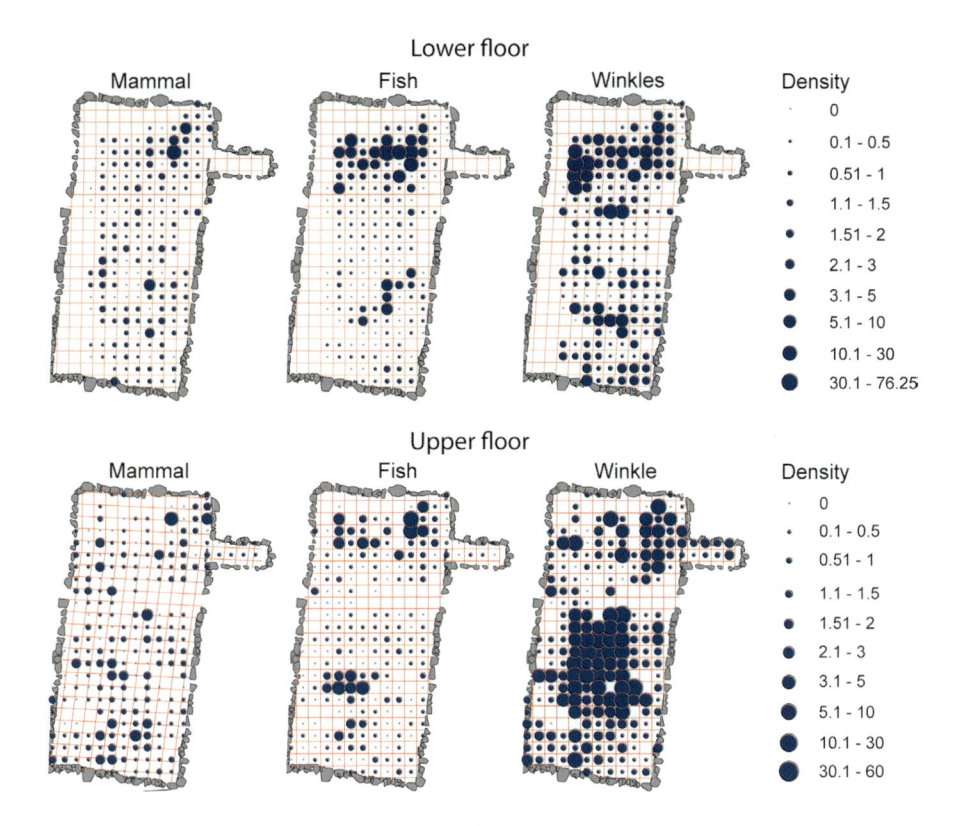

a subsidiary concentration in the south. The mammal bone was more evenly distributed but included a dispersed assemblage of bones in the northeast and at the south end.

There were again only a limited number of finds in this secondary floor layer. In contrast to the primary floor of the Late Norse house, the finds were dispersed throughout the house, both north and south, and there was a concentration of ornaments and fittings in the upper fills of the large pit against the north wall (Fig. 5.10). Objects from the secondary floor included three bone points, an iron knife, a whetstone and a fragment of a spindle whorl. Another iron object could have been a punch, or a bodkin-type arrowhead, and there was a possible sword guard and several small, interconnected iron rings which may come from a suit of chain mail. The chain mail was one of the few indications that warfare was important to the lives of the occupants. There were more ornaments in this layer than in the primary floor of the house, and this included three metal and five bone pins, two glass beads and six comb fragments. There was also a reasonable selection of metal fittings such as roves and holdfasts, which were noticeably rare in the primary floor.

The assemblage of pottery from the Late Norse house also revealed significant changes were taking place in the food culture of the inhabitants. The use of the large ceramic discs known as platters declined significantly during the life of the house; fragments of these distinctive ceramics were found in the primary floors, but they were almost completely absent in the secondary floor. Perhaps the people who lived at Bornais were shedding obviously Scandinavian habits, such as the eating of flatbreads. At roughly the same time, or possibly slightly earlier, there were subtle changes in the shape of basic cooking vessels.[11] These acquired a distinctive everted rim, and the quality of the vessels improved. They became thinner and had a harder surface finish. It is unlikely that the everted rim reflected changes in culinary practice; their purpose may have been more cultural. Everted rims were a significant feature of the Iron Age ceramics of the islands and their re-appearance may indicate there was a memory of this style that was being deliberately revived as the cultural agenda shifted towards the Gaelic traditions of the Lords of the Isles.

The final occupation layer in the Late Norse house shows us that the focus of activity had shifted to the northern half of the house. At this time, the house was almost completely refloored, but the floor layers were thicker at the north end where a new hearth was established directly in front of the entrance. The original hearth in the southern half of the building continued to be used and to accumulate peat ash during this phase of refurbishment, though it was of much reduced significance. The contents of the refurbished floor were very similar to the material from the previous floor, with only a slight increase in the density of mammal bone present.

The Late Norse house on mound 2 was abandoned by the beginning of the fourteenth century. It was probably deliberately dismantled at the end of its life, as the large amounts of timber used for the roof and walls would have been an important resource that would not have been wasted by the occupants and their descendants. A thick layer of soil developed on top of the original floor layers, probably due to erosion of the surrounding turf walls, and the structure was briefly used to pen animals.[12] This period of abandonment was brought to an end by the construction of an ancillary structure in the southern end of the house which will be discussed in Chapter 6.

'Peasant' houses

The Late Norse house on Bornais mound 2 was a large building, and the size may indicate it had a special role, either as a meeting place or as the residence of a high-status family. This house was constructed around the time the islands were formally annexed by the Scottish kings, and it is possible that this new Scottish style of building was imposed on the island. However, this would be a very simplistic reading of both the archaeology and the history, and we need to be more considered in our analysis of this building before we leap to any conclusions. The contemporary housing inhabited by the bulk of the population may have been smaller in size but, in many ways, these buildings were similar in style to the Late Norse house on mound 2, and indicate how the main feature of these houses evolved in the Uists.

FIGURE 5.15. Simplified plans of the late Norse houses at Cille Pheadair and Bornais mound 3.

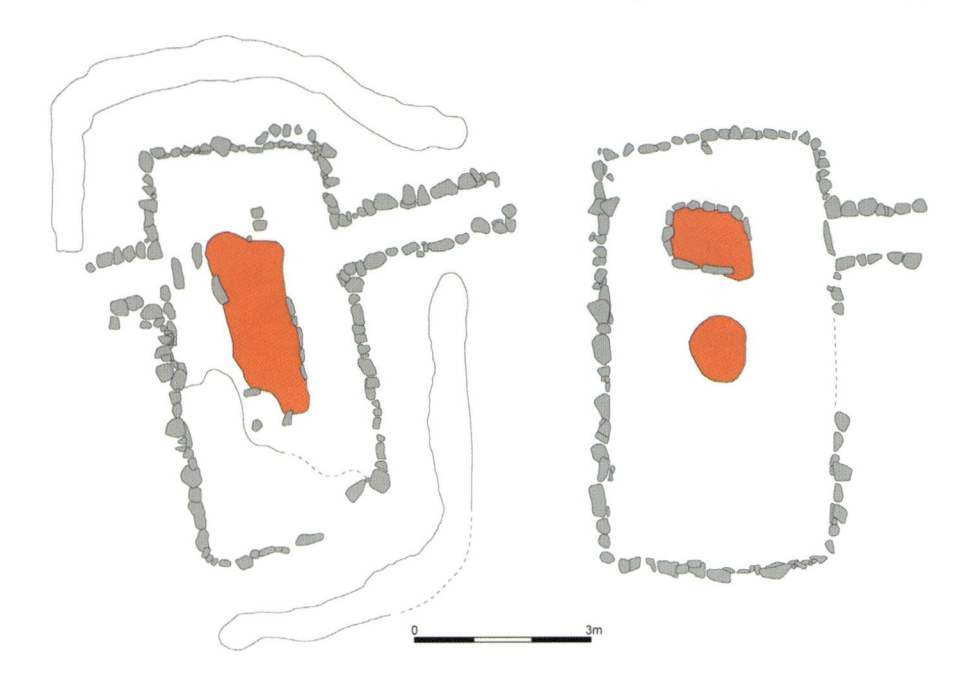

Other well-preserved examples of Late Norse houses were exposed on mound 3 at Bornais and in the final phases of the occupation at Cille Pheadair (Fig. 5.15).[13] The house on mound 3, Bornais House 5, was built at the end of the fourteenth century when the Late Norse house on mound 2 had fallen into disrepair. The final house at Cille Pheadair (House 009) was built in the late twelfth century, between 1155 and 1185, about half a century before the construction of the Late Norse house on mound 2. These houses were the last to be built on their respective settlement mounds, and a similar Late Norse house was identified on Bornais mound 2A, though this was not as well preserved.[14]

Bornais House 5 on mound 3 was defined by a stone revetment wall that demarcated an interior space 4.0 m wide and 7.2 m long (Fig. 5.16). This revetment wall was not substantial, comprising only two to three courses of small- to medium-sized waterworn boulders in a wall that stood 0.25 m high. It was oriented north–south and there was a single west-facing entrance passage, 1.7 m long, at the north end of the east wall. The interior of the house was separated from the passage by a threshold slab and the floor level

FIGURE 5.16. A view of the late Norse house on mound 3, Bornais with Beinn Mhor in the background.

FIGURE 5.17. A view of the excavation of the Late Norse house on Bornais mound 3 with the hearth in the foreground.

was lower than the passage floor. Directly opposite the entrance, on the central axis of the house, was a roughly rectangular hearth defined by a kerb of small upright stones (Fig. 5.17). This was filled with peat ash surrounded by charcoal flecked sand layers. Three floor layers were identified, the lowest did not seem to cover the entire floor but excluded large areas at the south end of the house, which may have been covered by furniture.

A reconstruction of House 5 on mound 3 (Fig. 5.18) depicts the house as a turf-walled structure with an internal timber frame that supported the roof. The main structural timbers were embedded in a timber wall-plate that sat on

FIGURE 5.18. A reconstruction drawing of the Late Norse house on mound 3.

the stone revetment wall. These upright timbers supported timber beams at head height, into which the rafters of the roof were set. The rafters supported laths, then a base of turves on which the thatch was set. The thatch was likely to have been straw, as we know there were fields growing cereal crops around the settlement, but reeds would also have been suitable, and they could have been found in the lochs that lay to the east of the settlement. The thatch would have been secured using weighted ropes, as severe winds are a prevalent feature of the local climate.

The final house at Cille Pheadair (House 007) was also oriented north to south and the interior was 6.9 m long and 3.15 m wide, defined by an internal revetment wall comprising five courses of medium-sized water-worn cobbles (Figs 5.15 and 5.19). It had two entrances, an east facing entrance passage 2.9 m long and a west-facing entrance passage 1.45 m long, which were arranged opposite each other in the north half of the building. Both entrances had threshold slabs, and the east-facing entrance was blocked off during the life of the house. Running north to south down the centre of the house was a rectangular hearth 2.86 m long and 1.16 m wide, partially defined by upright stones. This hearth was deliberately constructed to favour the northern half of the house and was thickest and widest between the two doorways. A charcoal-rich floor layer was identified, and this was a thick layer in the northern half of the house, but an imperceptible presence in the southern half. Externally, the house was partially defined by a small ditch or gully. Its absence on the southwest side was where a path led from the west doorway to a small outhouse.

There were some clear similarities and differences between these two houses at Bornais and Cille Pheadair (Fig. 5.15). Both were small, rectangular buildings with turf walls and inner stone revetments that acted as supports for a timber superstructure. The house at Cille Pheadair was slightly subterranean, whereas House 5 on mound 3 at Bornais was built on the ground surface. This rise to the surface appears to have been a general trend, as the sequence of structures exposed on mound 2A consistently become more deeply embedded in the mound with time. Houses of the eleventh century at both Cille Pheadair and Bornais were essentially subterranean, whereas houses built in the fourteenth century were constructed on the ground surface.

FIGURE 5.19. The Late Norse house at Cille Pheadair during the excavation. © Mike Parker Pearson.

A significant difference between these two small houses was the shape and size of the hearth. At Cille Pheadair the size of the hearth was substantial, and it was likely that this was a loosely defined location in which fires were lit where and when they were required. The resultant ash was spread out to create a compact surface that could be walked over. This was similar to the hearths of the Middle Norse houses at both Cille Pheadair and Bornais. However, the hearth in Bornais House 5 was quite different. It was a small well-defined structure, permanently located at the north end of the house, directly in front of the doorway (Fig. 5.17). There seems to have been a gradual evolution from the amorphous spreads of the Early and Middle Norse longhouses to a fixed position at the north end of the house near the doorway. At the time of the construction of the large Late Norse house on mound 2, a long hearth running down the centre of the house was no longer desired. Instead, there were discrete hearth areas placed on the central axis. Eventually the northern hearth area became the dominant location in this high-status house. This location opposite the entrance was the only location suitable for a hearth at the end of the fourteenth century when Bornais House 5 was constructed, and its position became permanent and defined by the construction of a kerb of stones.

These changes in the form and location of the hearth must be considered important as the hearth was the principal feature of the house, and had great social and symbolic significance. It provided the heat and light that allowed the house to be occupied, it enabled the cooking of food, and it allowed water to be boiled for washing and drinking. As the focus for these activities, the hearth also provided the location for social activities such as eating meals, talking, telling tales of great events, and composing and reciting poems in praise of great people. It was the place where visitors would be met and provided with hospitality. The house was the only enclosed, roofed, warm space in these communities, and in an exposed landscape with severe winters, such as the Western Isles, social interaction was largely an indoor activity.

The position of the hearth in front of the entrance to the house emphasised its significance to anyone entering the house, and empowered the person sitting at the hearth facing the doorway. It seems likely that individuals most closely associated with the hearth were the female heads of the household as they were responsible for providing the meals, one of the most important responsibilities of the household. Other female craft activities such as weaving and spinning may also have been undertaken close to the hearth, as they too required warmth and light.

The repositioning of the hearth during the thirteenth and fourteenth centuries suggests that women played an increasingly significant role in the house. In the eleventh and twelfth centuries the principal cooking areas associated with the long hearths in the Middle Norse longhouse on Bornais mound 2 and Cille Pheadair House 500 were deeply embedded in the interior of the house, as far from the entrance as possible. The repositioning of the hearth at the doorway in the thirteenth century therefore represents a major change in the social status of women in these communities.

The change in location of the hearth may have been associated with other significant changes in the use and architecture of the house. These small late

FIGURE 5.20. A schematic plan of the last two houses at Cille Pheadair showing their relationship and the contemporary ancillary buildings to the southwest.

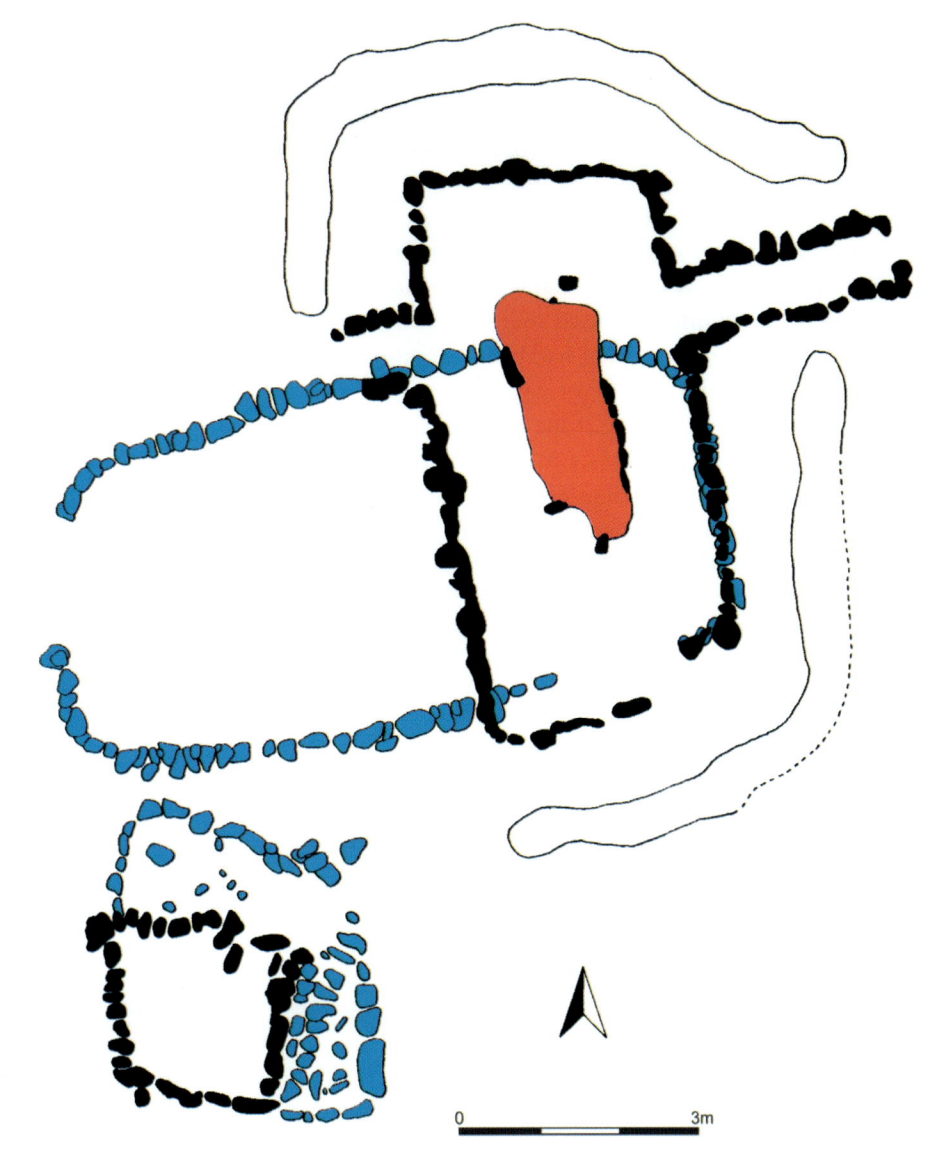

houses were almost invariably associated with separate outhouses which, in the Western Isles, were completely detached and separated from the main residences (Fig. 5.20). In other regions of the North Atlantic, these ancillary buildings were often attached to the main house, forming separate rooms in large, agglomerated structures. In Orkney and Caithness, these additional structures had a linear arrangement which created the distinctive longhouses of these regions. In Iceland, a much more complex arrangement of rooms was seen in the passage houses of the region.

A comb-maker's workshop

These ancillary buildings indicated the removal of certain activities from the main domestic arena, and if the gendered interpretation of domestic space is accepted, these would have been activities associated with male members of the household. At Bornais we excavated a couple of outhouses where specialised activities seem to have taken place. These include a comb-maker's workshop on mound 2A, and a crop-processing building on mound 3.

The workshop was located at the north end of mound 2A, immediately to the north of the domestic houses that were found on this mound. It was a very poorly preserved structure that had been damaged by the construction of a later house, but it was probably never very substantial in the first place (Fig. 5.21). A couple of partially surviving stone foundation walls defined the east and west sides of a building, roughly 5.5 m by 4.4 m, which was probably essentially a timber shed. We identified several floor layers, which appeared to have been deliberately created from compacted peat ash spread from a hearth. The hearth was probably located in a pit adjacent to two large stones in the centre of the northern part of the building.

Large quantities of antler were found in the floor layers, and most of it seems to have come from the production of composite combs, though other objects including antler handles and ivory gaming pieces were also being produced. The larger of the two stones next to the hearth pit was at the centre of a spread of antler waste, and may well have acted as a seat. The process of making an antler comb was straightforward, but it nevertheless required the care and attention to detail that only a skilled craftsman with considerable experience was likely to have had.

FIGURE 5.21. Cardiff students excavating the floors of the ancillary building on Bornais mound 2A.

FIGURE 5.22. A diagram showing the different stages of antler working that are required to produce a composite comb.

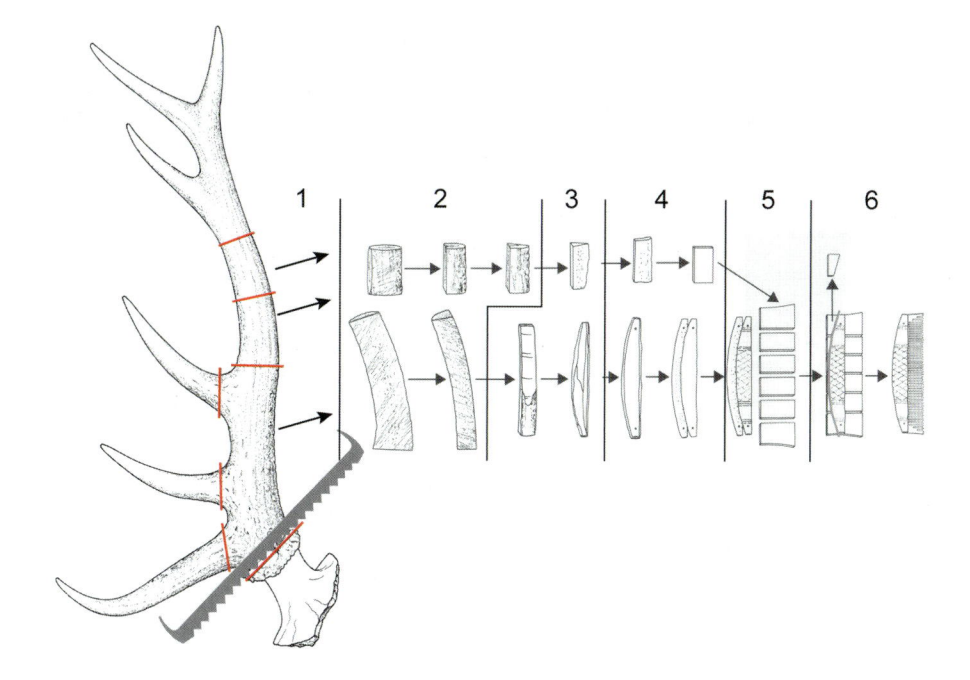

There were essentially six stages in the production process (Fig. 5.22).[15] The first stage involved dividing the raw antler into sections that could be used for making the different component parts of a composite comb; the side plates and tooth plates. The craftworker required straight sections of the compact outer tissue of the antler, so areas like the pointed and often twisted tines and the burr at the base were removed at the start of the process. These pieces were not used for combs, but they were not wasted as they could be used for other purposes. The remaining antler beam was sawn into sections whose size indicated the type and size of the comb to be produced.

The beam sections were then split into segments (Fig. 5.23). The easiest way of doing this was to make at least four cuts through the compact outer tissue of the antler, until the soft inner cancellous tissue was reached. The beam was then split by hammering a wedge into the cancellous tissue; a discarded tine tip would have made an ideal wedge. This created four triangular segments of antler.

The next stage was the removal of the inner cancellous tissue and the rough outer surface of the antler. A chisel was used for the initial removal of this unwanted material, but once the dense tissue was exposed, the pieces had to be carefully smoothed and squared off (Fig. 5.23). This was achieved using metal files, but rough grinding stones and fine abrasive materials, such as dogfish skin, could also have been used. It might have been necessary to straighten some of the longer side plates at this point, which could be easily done using steam while manually straightening the individual plates.

Once the side plates were straightened and carefully shaped to the desired profile, they were ready for decoration. This could be done before or after the

FIGURE 5.23. Antler working debris from Bornais mound 2A. On the top, the sections of antler retain the rough outer surface, on the bottom the antler segments have been smoothed and are ready to be incorporated into a comb.

comb had been assembled. On the combs from Bornais, decoration largely comprised incised lines and ring-and-dot motifs, often used in combinations to create complex patterns. The incised lines were normally created with very fine saws, some with double blades less than 0.35 mm thick. The ring-and-dot motifs were produced using similarly specialised engraving tools. These tools could only have been made by specialist metalworkers, and such rare and no doubt precious possessions are seldom found by archaeologists.

The side, tooth and end plates were then assembled and rivetted together. Most of the combs recovered from Bornais have iron rivets, and these were placed at the edges of every alternate tooth plate, and the two end plates had rivets through the centre of the plates. The end plates were probably the first plates to be rivetted to the side plates and provided the overall form of the comb. The tooth plates were shaped, and the teeth were cut with fine saws. This occurred after the combs had been rivetted together, as the saws often run into and cut the side plates. The final act was to round off the tips of the comb teeth as this made the comb run smoothly through the hair.

All these stages, ranging from the initial segmentation of the antler through to the fine shaping of the tooth plate blanks and the riveting together of the tooth and side plates, occurred in this workshop. The primary debris of raw antler, beams and tines, was widely scattered across the floor of the workshop, but the secondary debris, the segments and blanks, was concentrated around the northeast corner, adjacent to the large stone which may have been the comb-maker's seat (Fig. 5.24). One of the concentrations of antler waste appeared to be half of a well-defined circular spread, probably a bag full of useful pieces of antler left lying on the floor. This collection of antler waste included 10 blanks in the process of being made into teeth and side plates. One of the tooth plates was carefully finished and almost ready to be inserted into a comb. Amongst the debris were two pieces of whale bone which had been carefully shaped into rectangular plates, and these were clearly intended to be part of a composite comb. The presence of this bag of useable material suggests that the antler working stopped abruptly. There were numerous blanks that had been carefully shaped for use, and yet this valuable material was discarded and ultimately buried.

Amongst the tooth plate blanks found in the workshop were three that were clearly for double-sided combs, as they had well-defined, flat, central areas that tapered towards the edges on either side. Side plate blanks were rare, but included a piece 190 mm long which would have been for a long, single-sided comb. Most of the remaining side plates seem to have been for shorter combs and the preferred type appears to have been a short, double-sided comb, similar to some examples that were found at the Udal (Fig. 5.25).[16]

The production of short double-sided combs in this workshop suggests the craftworker was influenced by Scandinavian comb fashions. A very distinctive composite comb was found in the midden layers on the east side of mound 2A (Fig. 5.26). This type of comb is referred to as a 'fish-tailed' comb because of the distinctive double-curved terminal plates at either end.[17] These combs had other distinctive features; they were relatively short, and one side had fine teeth and the other coarse teeth. They had multiple copper alloy rivets which were clearly designed for a decorative effect.[18] The comb plates were often decorated with

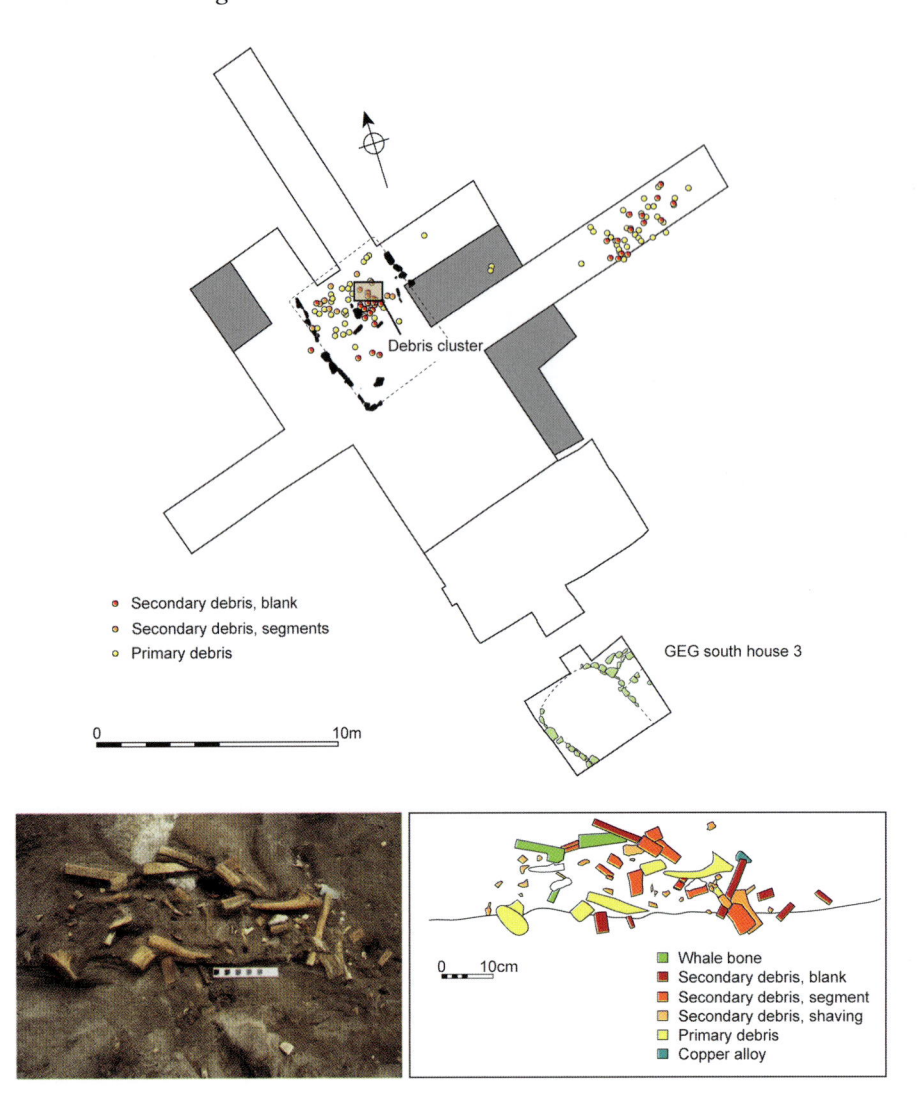

FIGURE 5.24. A plan of the area excavated on Bornais mound 2A showing the Late Norse structures and the distribution of comb making debris. The inset shows a cluster of debris that probably indicates a bag of material left behind when the workshop was abandoned.

ring-and-dot motifs and the example from mound 2A had three ring-and-dot motifs in the curved spaces created by the terminal plates.

This comb was not particularly well preserved, as all the fine teeth were missing and one of the curved ends had been broken, making its original length unknowable. Another slightly better-preserved example of this type of comb was discovered in mound 2 where it was found to the west of the large Late Norse house (Fig. 5.26). This comb did not have the ring-and-dot decoration of the previous example but both ends have survived, and the teeth were slightly better preserved. The comb had been heavily used; on the fine side, the teeth had been worn away at the centre. Even the more robust teeth on the coarse side had a distinctive grooved profile, caused by repeated combing of hair.

FIGURE 5.25. A selection of relatively complete composite combs from the Udal, North Uist. © IAC, Udal Archives.

These 'fish-tailed' combs have been found on several Norse settlements in Scotland, including Jarlshof in Shetland and Freswick in Caithness. However, the largest collections have been found in Norwegian towns such as Oslo, Bergen and Trondheim, where they were almost certainly being manufactured. They came in a number of variants that were exported throughout the North Atlantic, and were one of the last types of composite antler comb to be made in Scandinavia. They were produced in the mid-thirteenth century when most of Europe, including England, had replaced this type of comb with single piece combs made from horn or boxwood.

The presence of an antler-working craftworker on mound 2A was important. Making composite antler combs was an ancient and dying tradition that could have been undertaken by a craftworker trained in Scandinavia. The Bornais combs were copying Scandinavian prototypes and some of these imported combs were also being found on the site. These combs clearly reflect the continued movement of people between the Scottish islands and Scandinavia that is documented in the historical record. They suggest the islanders had a desire to maintain a shared sense of identity with the Scandinavian homelands.

As well as making combs, the craftworker was producing gaming pieces and had access to ivory, in the form of sperm whale teeth though not the top-quality walrus tusks. Sperm whale teeth were an important source of ivory and scientific analysis has shown that some of the Lewis chessmen were made from this material. Finds from the Bornais workshop included cubes ready to be made into dice, and simple playing pieces, that included upright forms that were either pawns from a chess set or pieces for the game of hnefatafl

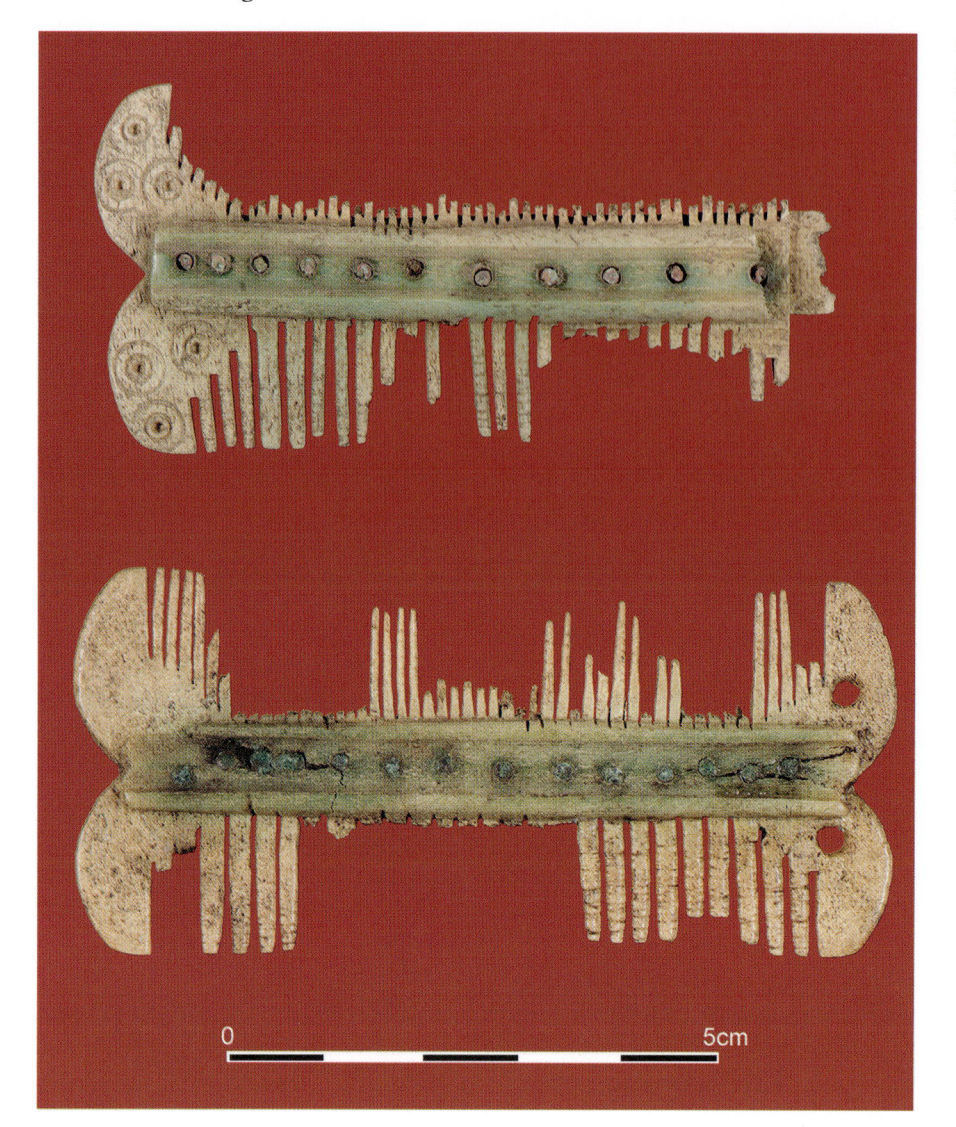

FIGURE 5.26. The two relatively complete 'fish-tailed' combs from Bornais, the comb on the bottom came from mound 2, that on the top from mound 2A.

(Fig. 5.27). The latter game has two armies of undifferentiated pieces, one army attacks and the other defends the king whose piece starts in the centre of the board and moves towards safety in one of the four corners. Some of the large playing pieces from Bornais could well have been king pieces for hnefatafl (Fig. 5.28).

The craftsmanship on display in the material from the Bornais workshop does not demonstrate any of the intricate carving skills that would have been required to create a chessman of the quality exhibited by the Lewis chessmen, so there is as yet no suggestion that these were produced on the islands. It may also be unlikely that there were enough elite families in the Western Isles to

FIGURE 5.27. A selection of gaming pieces from Bornais. Most of these are unfinished and come from the workshop on mound 2A.

FIGURE 5.28. Antler gaming pieces from Bornais.

maintain a workshop that could produce such exceptionally complex pieces. Nevertheless, the production of pieces for board games indicates that the island's elite were enjoying leisure activities that were commonplace throughout Medieval Europe.[19]

The Bornais workshop seems to have been a short-lived structure that went out of use abruptly. Perhaps demand was not sufficient to justify its long-term existence, even for the creation of relatively commonplace items, such as antler combs. It was likely that access to raw materials was critical, and the quality and quantity of antler on the island may have been problematic. There was no sign that contacts with Iceland or northern Norway were sufficient to guarantee a regular supply of ivory.

Red deer

The amount of red deer antler recovered from the comb-maker's workshop and other areas of the settlement emphasises the importance this animal had for the economy of the island. However, the presence of red deer on a small island such as South Uist was not something that should be taken for granted. There were clearly well-established herds of deer throughout the Outer Hebrides in prehistory, and the evidence indicates that humans carefully managed their relationships with these wild animals.[20] On any small island, unrestricted hunting of red deer would quickly lead to their extinction. Indeed, the Viking colonisation of the Orkneys seems to have coincided with the rapid decline and extinction of red deer in these northern islands.

The evidence from Bornais indicates that, during the Norse occupation of the settlement, red deer were being regularly hunted. In the Early Norse period adult deer were hunted and large numbers of unborn or new-born calves were killed. This is surprising because these fawns would not have provided a significant amount of meat, bone or antler that could be used as raw materials. It was possible that they were killed to obtain the distinctive spotted coats that newborn fawns have until they are about two months old. Another possibility is that, in this period, hunters were deliberately attempting to eradicate the deer population of the island by targeting the pregnant does. A sizeable deer population would have been a constant threat to the cereal crops grown around the settlement, as deer would descend from the nearby hills in the evening to graze on the lowlands before returning to the hills at sunrise.

This strategy of targeting neonatal animals increased during the Middle Norse occupation of Bornais, so it seems unlikely that this was an attempt to eradicate the population as it clearly failed. In the Late Norse period, the strategy shifted, and adult deer dominated the bone assemblage. This suggests the inhabitants had a more sensitive hunting strategy that was better designed to maintain a healthy deer herd. The presence of an antler craftworker at Bornais would have emphasised the importance of antler, which was collected after it had been shed by the deer on the hills of the east side of the island. It was brought back to the settlement to produce a range of important tools as well as the combs and gaming pieces discussed in the previous sections.

The red deer population of the Uists tend to be smaller than the red deer population of mainland Scotland, and this reflects evolutionary pressures on isolated island animal populations that act to reduce the size of large mammals. Measuring the antler at Bornais showed that these were at the smaller end of the range of antlers from medieval towns, and that southern workshops preferred to use much larger antlers. Comb-makers in particular favoured large antlers because flat, straight sections of antler were required for making the side plates of combs.

The local antler resource available to the craftworker at Bornais must have been limited, and the presence of whale bone may have been an experiment designed to assess how suitable that material was for comb-making. It seems that it was not ideal as very little whale bone was found in the workshop which in any case was abandoned after a relatively short period of time. The abandonment of the workshop was messy, as lots of useable material was left behind. The presence of a bag of prepared segments and blanks on the floor suggests this was an abrupt event which was not prepared or planned for. The absence of any of the iron tools, such as saws and chisels used to work the antler, was also significant. Perhaps these were personal items carefully curated by the craftworker and routinely carried by them rather than left in their workshop.

Kilns

A very different kind of outhouse was found dug into the wind-blown sand deposits accumulating at the edge of mound 3 at Bornais. This was sub-rectangular in plan, with internal stone revetment walls defining a space 3.8 m by 4.6 m; the east wall was the best preserved and had up to seven courses surviving to 1.0 m high (Fig. 5.29). An entrance passage, 1.6 m long and 0.6 m

FIGURE 5.29. A view of the grain-drying kiln on Bornais mound 3.

wide, was built on the west side of the building where the mound sloped down. Directly opposite this entrance, a recess was constructed in the wall head which was probably a ventilation hole that allowed a draft to pass across the building from the main entrance. This is known as a winnowing hole and is a feature observed in many traditional barns. It helps in the cleaning of crops indoors by creating a draft of air that passes through the building. Exiting through the south wall was the flue of a kiln. In its final form, this had a passage 2.65 m long with a small parching bowl at the south end. An accumulation of peat ash at the entrance to the kiln indicated the fire was lit at this point, inside the building. This kiln was built on top of an earlier kiln with a short passage between the fire and the bowl, and the two phases of construction are reflected in the two floor layers that cover the interior of the structure.

This building was a variant on the grain-drying kilns that were a common feature of the Atlantic islands of Scotland. They were still an important feature of the agricultural landscapes in the early twentieth century, and were recorded in some detail by ethnographers and by archaeologists interested in the crofting landscapes of the eighteenth and nineteenth centuries. The kilns varied from island group to island group, and these variations appear to have been similar to regional variations in other building styles that emerged at the end of the Medieval period.

In the Western Isles the eighteenth- and nineteenth-century kilns were normally completely contained within a rectangular building, which was split in two. One half was empty of any architectural features whilst the other half

FIGURE 5.30. Excavating a nineteenth-century kiln at Frobost, South Uist.

contained the kiln surrounded by an elevated platform (Fig. 5.30). The flue entered the kiln at ground level from the edge of the platform, and access to the parching bowl was from the surface of the platform. To operate the kiln, twigs were laid across the parching bowl, which was then covered with straw on which ears of barley were laid. The evolution or change that improved upon the design used for the Bornais kiln was for the parching bowl, located outside the building in the thirteenth and fourteenth century, to become incorporated within these much larger buildings. This must have occurred sometime in the sixteenth or seventeenth century.

The appearance of these specialised grain-drying kilns appears to have been an innovation that occurred sometime in the twelfth century. Two kilns were found on mound 2A that were earlier in date, but these were outdoor structures not contained within a building. The mound 2A kilns provide some evidence as to why they operated more effectively when contained within buildings. Both kilns were filled with layers of clinker formed by molten sand which had fused together to create glassy slags. This would have occurred if the hearth fires were operating at high temperatures, causing the surrounding sand to melt.

High temperatures would be achieved if a strong wind was coming in the right direction to create a powerful draught in the kiln. Strong winds are a routine feature of life on the islands, and they would make controlling an open-air kiln problematic. Kiln-drying does not require high temperatures but rather a low, steady heat; an uncontrolled fire could set the grain alight, and this appears to have happened on mound 2A where thousands of carbonised grains were found in layers adjacent to the kiln.

The ability to control the air flow to the fire and thus the heat passing through the kiln would have been one of the main benefits of the building on mound 3, but the extension of this structure to include the parching bowl would be a final improvement that did not occur until the sixteenth or seventeenth century, after Bornais had been abandoned.

Crops and the agricultural economy

The Viking conquest of the isles, as discussed in Chapter 3, resulted in an increase in the diversity of the crops grown on South Uist, and an increase in the importance of cereal agriculture in the economy of these farming communities (Fig. 5.31). Barley continued to be the staple foodstuff, but oats and rye now made a much more significant contribution to the diet. Flax was an increasingly important crop.

The assemblage of plant remains retrieved from the floors of House 5 and the kiln/barn on mound 3 at Bornais were very different and clarify the use of these structures. Both floors were extensively sampled for carbonised plant

FIGURE 5.31. Oat stooks on the machair plain of North Boisdale, South Uist.

remains; the floor in House 5 had grain densities comparable to other houses at Cille Pheadair and Bornais mound 2, but the floors of the kiln/barn had much higher densities, and there were even higher densities associated with the hearth at the mouth of the kiln. These grain densities confirmed our interpretation of this structure as a grain-drying kiln and it seems likely that waste from the processing of the crop (from winnowing, sieving and cleaning) was used as fuel for the hearth. The ash produced was then spread across the interior of the structure to make a compact floor surface.

Oats and barley were the dominant crops processed in the kiln/barn; in the primary floor barley was dominant but in the later floor oats were much more prevalent. Rye was also present in both floors. Flax seeds were completely absent, but the presence of flax waste indicated that this crop was cleaned in the structure. The grain assemblages from House 5 were, in contrast, dominated by barley, with oats very much the secondary crop. However, the most distinctive characteristic of the House 5 floor deposits was the large quantity of flax seeds present in the lower floor layer, with very high densities immediately south of the hearth. These clearly indicate flax-processing activities were associated with the people living in this house. Flax provides two major products: oil was produced from the seeds, and the stems of the plant were processed to produce linen.[21]

The increasing quantities of flax seeds in the Late Norse house floors could indicate an increase in the production and processing of flax or the close association of flax-processing with the dominant female members of the household. It was clear from the written sources that textile production was a gendered activity largely controlled by women in the Medieval period. The increasing occurrence of flax seeds in the houses may therefore indicate some aspects of flax preparation took place within the house. Unfortunately, very few artefacts were recovered from these late houses, so it was not possible to fully understand the nature of the activities and organisation of work undertaken inside.

The carbonised plant remains from Bornais mounds 2 and 2A indicated a considerable degree of homogeneity in the processing and consumption of plant remains on both these mounds. This suggests that the importance of crop processing had declined on mound 2A, possibly because the kiln on mound 3 had become the main grain drying structure for the settlement. If the link is accepted, then it suggests the settlement was an integrated farming community rather than a collection of autonomous farms. The increased density of crop remains in this phase suggests crop production was becoming increasingly important, and provided an incentive for the creation of the specialist crop drying structures on mound 3.

Animals and the agricultural economy

Sheep continued to dominate the animal bone assemblages during the Late Norse occupation, and hind limbs continued to be the favoured portion of meat. There was an unusually high concentration of cattle bones in the final occupation of last house on mound 2A (12) that suggests this structure was used for the primary butchery of cattle, perhaps after its use as a domestic house had come to an end. This was an unusual deposit as most bone waste came from mixed deposits with all species present. Pig continued to be consumed in small quantities and pig's head appears to be a favourite delicacy, frequently deposited in this period. There was a significant concentration deposited during the construction of the large Late Norse house on mound 2.

Fishing strategies remained unchanged in the Late Norse period, herring bones dominated the assemblage and large quantities of gadid heads were recovered. The densities of fish bones recovered indicated that fishing was becoming increasingly important, and there may be a slight increase in the diversity of species caught.[22] The highest densities on mound 2 came from the primary floor layer in the large Late Norse house on mound 2, and even higher densities were noted from the floors of the final house on mound 2A. There was a similar rise in the quantities of shellfish brought to the site, and very large quantities of winkle shells were recovered from the floors of the large Late Norse house on mound 2.

The consumption of eggs, in contrast, declined significantly in the Late Norse period. Only the earliest of the floors on the Late Norse house on mound 2 had large quantities of eggshell comparable to those found in the Middle Norse longhouse. This is a slightly odd pattern, as domestic fowl increased in significance in the bird bone assemblage from this period. Potentially, the decline in overall use represents a reduction in the use of the eggs of wild birds, and a more exclusive use of domestic fowl eggs. The bird bone assemblage indicated a decline in the importance of large gulls but there is a significant concentration of gannet and cormorant bones in the mound 2A midden layers.[23]

There is therefore nothing in the archaeological record to indicate any major changes in the agricultural economy relating to the Scottish takeover. If anything, the evidence suggests the gradual development of a regional economy and culture that evolved organically from the Scandinavian culture introduced in the ninth century. This regionality is something that can be seen across the Viking diasporas of the North Atlantic region and may be a response to reduced contact with the homeland in the twelfth century. A resurgence in Scandinavian influence in the thirteenth century may be indicated by the change in comb fashions, and this possible revival of contact with Scandinavia ultimately culminates in Haakon's disastrous trip to the islands in 1263.

Castle and church

Castles and churches are some of the most impressive and important buildings constructed in the Medieval period, and the Western Isles have a few iconic examples. These impressive buildings appear routinely on the covers of books and biscuit tins and Kisimul Castle (Fig. 5.32) on the Isle of Barra is one of the most photogenic castles in Scotland. It sits on an island in the middle of the harbour at Castlebay, and can be seen up close from the decks of ferries bringing most of the visitors to Barra. Unfortunately, the dating of this and other castles has proved to be problematic largely because of the limited historic records for the islands, but also because of the lack of distinctive architectural elements that provide any firm evidence for chronology.

Two different perspectives exist; one argues that the relatively simple nature of these castles, particularly enclosure castles such as Castle Tioram in Morvern, indicate an early date in the twelfth century. The other argument proposes a later chronology in the fourteenth and fifteenth centuries. It seems likely that the later chronology is correct, and few people now believe any of the castles in the Western Isles precede the fourteenth century. Most of the potentially early castles were located in Argyll, and were built as an extension of royal power by the Scots king and his proxies in the region. The Lords of the Isles then adopted and amended the concept of the castle to suit their need to dominate and control the population of the west. These indigenous castles are perhaps best exemplified by the castles of Aros and Ardtornish in the Sound of Mull, which were essentially large halls with massively thick, mortared-stone walls. Hall castles were very popular in Ireland and seem to have represented a continued commitment to the importance of communal feasting and drinking as a major part of the elite's relationship with their subjects.

Borve Castle (Caisteal Bhuirgh) on the island of Benbecula is the best example of this type of castle in the Western Isles. It is a rectangular hall-tower, 18.2 m by 10.1 m, with mortared walls 2.7 m thick, and after later modifications may have stood three stories high. Its current position on the machair plain of

FIGURE 5.32. A view of Kisimul Castle from the pier at Castlebay, Barra.

Benbecula is rather misleading, as there is cartographic and historical evidence that shows it was strategically located on the coast next to a sheltered natural harbour that provided access to the sea and the important fishing grounds that lay nearby. This landscape was completely reconfigured by the deposition of metres of blown sand which smoothed out the natural topography, concealed the coastline and buried much of the lower stories of the castle and an adjacent chapel. The clan histories ascribe the construction of the castle to Amie Mac-Ruaidhri and it is mentioned in the charters of John, Lord of the Isles, and in the second half of the fourteenth century by Fordun.[24]

The development of these hall-tower castles seems to have been a natural evolution of the Late Norse house as exemplified by the large Late Norse house 3 on Bornais mound 2. The internal area of the Bornais house is comparable to the internal area of Borve Castle, and only slightly smaller than Ardtornish and Aros. The abandonment of the Late Norse house on Bornais mound 2 in the early decades of the fourteenth century, and the construction of Borve in the middle of the fourteenth century, suggests that the elite were upgrading and monumentalising their residences in an effort to emulate the elites of mainland Scotland.

Borve may be the only castle to have been built in the fourteenth century, before the forfeiture of the Lords of the Isles, but there are distinctive local fortifications, which will be discussed in Chapter 6, that might date to this period. The only other substantial buildings with mortared walls that may have been built in this period are the churches, but it is unclear how many of the upstanding survivals date to this period. Most of the important locations such as Cille Bharra on Barra, Howmore on South Uist, Cairinis in North Uist and Aignish in Lewis have churches that are likely to have been established in the twelfth century. By at least the fourteenth century, the church buildings were increasingly significant architectural statements, although it is still difficult to provide a precise chronology for most of the surviving structures.

A good example of the problems that exist is the complex at Howmore in South Uist. This has been interpreted in a variety of mutually inconsistent ways in the last three decades. All scholars agree that Teampull Mor was built in the thirteenth century (see Chapter 4), but the date of the other major church building, Caibeal Dhiarmaid, is disputed. John Raven and Andrew Reynolds believe it predates Teampull Mor, whereas Mark Thacker has argued that it is a sixteenth-century construction associated with the development of the complex as a centre for Clan Ranald. The small chapel of Caibeal Chlann'ic Ailean (Clan Ranald's chapel) has been interpreted by Raven and Reynolds as an early structure repeatedly rebuilt, but by Thacker as at most a two-phase structure that originated as a bequest by Eoin Muirdearlaich in 1574. In this latter interpretation, the important dog-toothed mouldings in this chapel are interpreted as architectural elements removed from Teampull Mor in the sixteenth century. Hopefully this confusion can be sorted out by further architectural analysis of the upstanding masonry, and in particular by radiocarbon dating of charcoal contained in the mortar within the surviving masonry.

Conclusion

The Treaty of Perth in 1266 was probably not the dramatic change in the islands' story that one might think. The Norse society of the Outer Hebrides was already gradually evolving in its own idiosyncratic manner. The form of the domestic buildings was being transformed, and at the lower end of the social spectrum a simple form of short, rectangular house with associated outhouses was emerging, a building form that would serve the islanders of the Uists until the early twentieth century. The conspicuous consumption of material wealth, a feature of the deposits in the bow-walled longhouses in the twelfth century, was no longer regarded as appropriate by the inhabitants of the Late Norse house (House 3) on mound 2; perhaps there was less portable wealth available as raiding in Ireland and southern Scotland slowly declined. The agrarian economy seems to have been relatively settled, and the impression is of a varied diet amply provided with meat from cattle and sheep, fish in abundance, and a variety of cereal crops.

The distinctive shape and form of the Late Norse house on Bornais mound 2, once considered to be an alien imposition of an imposed Scottish aristocracy, now seems to have had a more local ancestry. The sequence at Cille Pheadair demonstrated gradual changes in the nature of the domestic architecture that occurred well before the mid-thirteenth century. The basic trajectory of this development was a gradual reduction in the size of the main building, and the creation of contemporary outhouses. The final building at Cille Pheadair was a rectangular house with the simple playing-card proportions, similar to those of the Late Norse house on Bornais mound 2, though on a smaller scale. This building unusually had two entrances, and the interior was dominated by a long hearth which spanned the length of the building. This house was built between 1160 and 1185, roughly 100 years before the Scottish takeover of the islands. It clearly demonstrates that some of the characteristic features of the late houses, in particular the rectangular shape and playing-card proportions, were present before the Scottish takeover. The final developments at Bornais appear to have occurred in the early fourteenth century, when the hearth became a contained and controlled feature located at the north end of the house opposite a single, east-facing entrance. This occurred after Cille Pheadair had been abandoned, but evolved during the life of the Late Norse house on Bornais mound 2 and was visible in House 5 on Bornais, mound 3.

Interpretation of these changes is still uncertain. The historical sources open up the possibility that Somerled already held control over the islands by the middle of the twelfth century, so it could be argued that Scottish influence on the architecture at Bornais occurred at this early date. However, this may be completely the wrong way to understand these changes. It is probably misleading to think of Somerled and his descendants as either Scottish or Norse, or to attribute the change in the architecture of the settlement to the cultural influence of one group in these hybrid cultures.

In my view, the architecture gradually evolved its own unique features to create a distinctive Hebridean vernacular, which owed its origin to the Norse longhouse and yet was very different in its final form. By the later fourteenth century, domestic architecture, as seen in the final house (House 5) built on mound 3, had achieved a form that was the template for the future. This was an 8 m long by 4 m wide rectangular house with playing-card proportions, turf walls, a short entrance passage and a small, kerbed hearth located directly inside the doorway. This new style of house was accompanied by outhouses that included grain-drying kilns with distinct regional characteristics. These buildings were not identical to the buildings of the nineteenth and early twentieth centuries, although there are many similarities in style, plan and layout.

In this chapter I have perhaps underplayed the architectural significance of the Late Norse house on Bornais mound 2 in relation to the events of 1266 a bit too much. The house itself may not represent a major cultural transformation imposed on an ancient, Scandinavian influenced landscape, but its construction was a significant event. There had been no high-status residence on mound 2 for roughly 150 years, and yet it was clearly understood that this was the appropriate location to build the new house. Its construction clearly conformed to previous traditions of succession by being crafted to create a physical overlap with the earlier high-status house; the side wall of the Late Norse house lay directly on top of the end of wall of the Middle Norse longhouse, and clearly created a physical link that emphasised a possible genealogical link with the previous inhabitants.

This event does seem to be closely related to the date of 1266, and it is possible that the circumstances around the Treaty of Perth encouraged the MacRuaidhris to take physical possession of their lands in the Uists and to establish a permanent presence on the island. There were no settlements on the island of the size and complexity of Bornais at this time, and it seems quite likely that a high-status MacRuaidhri family member was the principal occupant of mound 2 in the late thirteenth century. The abandonment of the large Late Norse house in the early fourteenth century could have been due to the construction of Borve Castle in Benbecula, which is traditionally linked with Amie MacRuaidhri.

Notes

1 Wilson 1851, 561.
2 A detailed consideration of the various accounts of the discovery, and the possible location of the hoard is provided in Stratford 1997 and Caldwell *et al.* 2009. A recent volume (Caldwell and Hall 2014) provides a valuable contextual discussion of the hoard, the chessmen and the game of chess.
3 Walrus ivory was not as good a raw material as elephant ivory; it has a core of secondary dentine with a granular texture and brown colour which detracts from the carving if exposed.
4 See Caldwell *et al.* 2009, 191 for detailed descriptions of clothing and equipment.
5 Interestingly there was no place for ships in the symbolism of the chess pieces. This acknowledged the origin of chess in essentially landlocked countries (India and the Middle East), where sea warfare was of secondary importance, but it perhaps also acknowledged the transition that had taken place in Scandinavia; seaborne raiding of the Viking period had been replaced by organised warfare between land armies.

6 A descendent of Somerled and early member of the Clan McDonald.
7 This is a translation of the Gaelic poem published by Clancy 1998, 288.
8 The complexities of this period are covered in detail by Duncan and Brown 1957 and Sellar 2000.
9 A full description of this house is available in Sharples 2020, chapter 7.
10 The coins from the Bornais excavations are discussed in detail by Gareth Williams in Sharples 2021, 103.
11 Changes in the ceramic forms over time were discussed by Harding and Sharples in Sharples 2020, 544.
12 The presence of the animals was indicated by the identification of hoof prints that depressed the surface of the infilling brown sand. The hoof prints were subsequently infilled with white windblown sand, which showed up very clearly when first exposed, but which was relatively quickly blown away.
13 A full description of House 5 on Bornais mound 3 is provided in Sharples 2005 and for the Cille Pheadair house see Parker Pearson *et al.* 2018, chapter 10.
14 See Sharples 2020, chapter 8.
15 The antler-working was originally published in Sharples and Dennis 2016. A considerable amount of analysis was undertaken as part of an undergraduate dissertation at Cardiff University by Rachel Smith (see Smith and Sharples in Sharples 2021, 29). Much of the discussion in this chapter is indebted to the observations of Ian Dennis.
16 Most of the combs found on the site in the phases prior to this Late Norse period were quite different. They were single-sided, and two distinctive types appear to have been fashionable in the eleventh and twelfth centuries. Both of these comb types were common on the Atlantic seaboard, and it is generally believed that they were being made in the Irish Sea area in the eleventh century (Ashby 2006).
17 See Clarke and Heald 2002 for an interesting discussion of the possible symbolic importance of these combs.
18 Small fragments of copper alloy sheet were found with the antler debris in the comb-maker's workshop on mound 2A, and these could have been used to make the distinctive rivets found in these 'fish-tailed' combs.
19 For an interesting account of the spread of chess and its importance in Medieval Europe see Yalom 2004.
20 See Mulville in Sharples 2020 for a discussion of the red deer at Bornais and Mulville 2016 for a general discussion of Norse interactions with red deer.
21 Unfortunately, the oil in flax seeds means they were more likely to totally combust than become carbonised, so these seeds only occasionally survive deposition on the hearth, and the quantities present at Bornais cannot be directly compared with the other plant remains.
22 Ingrem in Sharples 2021, 439–441.
23 Best in Sharples 2020, 573.
24 John of Fordun was one of the earliest historians of Scotland, writing in the latter half of the fourteenth century.

CHAPTER SIX

The origin of the clans

Introduction

One of the most spectacular monuments in the Western Isles is to be found in the church of St Clements in the southwest corner of the Isle of Harris. The church is literally at the end of the road adjacent to a small harbour and at the end of a narrow fertile valley. It is cruciform in plan with a choir and sanctuary at the east end and a large nave with two transepts which probably acted as chapels. There is a prominent tower at the west end, built onto a rocky outcrop. The tower and the transepts are exceptional features unparalleled in other churches in the Western Isles. This is the largest ecclesiastical building in the region and is only exceeded by the abbey at Iona in size and significance.

It was built in the sixteenth century under the patronage of Alasdair or Alexander 'Crotach', chief of the MacLeods of Dunvegan (Skye) and Harris, who was one of the more successful and long-lived clan chiefs in the islands. His tomb was built into the south side of the choir, and is one of the artistic treasures of late Medieval Scotland (Fig. 6.1). The tomb is placed under an arch and is sealed by a representation of Alasdair in plate armour clutching a large broadsword, clearly expressing his status as the military leader of the clan. The recess behind the burial is elaborately decorated in a highly symbolic fashion. There are three rows of panels, each containing a carefully carved scene which conveys both the religious and secular aspects of life.

The significance of religion in the life of the inhabitants is expressed by the central panels which depict the virgin Mary, flanked by two bishops, one of whom is named as St Clement. These are flanked by two important secular symbols of power and prestige: on the left is a castle, perhaps a representation of Dunvegan, the seat of this branch of the Clan MacLeod; on the right is a birlinn or West Highland galley, one of the most important weapons of war that a chief possessed. The more agreeable aspect of a chief's role is depicted in the panels on the bottom left where a hunting scene is depicted (Fig. 6.2); three stags are being chased by an important individual dressed in a long coat with a pointed hat or helmet and holding a long-handled axe or halberd, he is accompanied by two gillies with their dogs. Next to this scene is a more threatening depiction of St Michael and Satan weighing the souls of the dead, which is next to the inscription recording that the tomb was prepared by Alexander (Alasdair) in 1528, well before his death in AD 1545–7. At the top of these scenes is a panel depicting the sun flanked by two angels blowing horns, and the two adjacent panels show another two angels carrying candles.

FIGURE 6.1. A general view of the tomb of Alasdair Crotach in the church at Rodel, Harris. © Crown Copyright: HES.

FIGURE 6.2. A detail showing the castle, bishop and hunting scene in the tomb of Alasdair Crotach. © Crown Copyright: HES.

The arch that encloses the tomb is framed by a moulded pediment in dark schist, which suggests the gable end of a house. At the apex of this scheme is a panel containing a depiction of God holding Christ on the cross. He is flanked by eight panels depicting the symbols of the four evangelists and the 12 apostles.

Altogether, this is one of the most impressive tombs of its period in Scotland, and shows the sculptural abilities of the island stone masons only hinted at in the other monumental sculptures of the period. There are no comparable tombs with anything like this complexity in the rest of the Western Isles. A large armorial stone of Clan Ranald was present in the church at Howmore, South Uist until very recently, and is now in the museum at Cill Donnain. It may have originally been part of a similarly impressive tomb that was dismantled during the disruption that characterised the Reformation in Scotland.

The history

In 1354, John of Islay was powerful enough to declare himself Lord of the Isles, *Rí Innse Gall*, and, for the subsequent 150 years, John and his descendants dominated the social and political life of the islands until the title was abolished by King James IV in 1493. John had been an increasingly influential figure during the latter stages of the Wars of Independence, due to skilful manipulation of his relationship with both David II and Edward Balliol. In 1337 he made a strategic marriage to Amie MacRuaidhri that resulted in the acquisition of the Lordship of Garmoran in 1346, when Amie inherited the territory after the murder of her brother Ranald MacRuaidhri by the Earl of Ross.[1] This was effectively the end of the MacRuaidhri line of the family of Somerled.

John of Islay had further ambitions, and in 1350 his marriage to Amie was annulled to allow him to marry Robert Stewart's daughter, Margaret Stewart; Robert Stewert was then Regent of Scotland, and he became King in 1371. This marriage brought Kintyre and areas of mainland Argyll, that had previously been controlled by the MacDougalls, into the Lordship of the Isles, and allied John with the most powerful man in Scotland. On the death of John of Islay in 1386, the title of Lord of the Isles passed to Donald, his eldest son by Margaret Stewart. The Lordship of Garmoran, however, was inherited by Ami's son, Reginald, who became the founder of the MacDonalds of Clan Ranald. The Uists were separated out for Gofraid, Ranald's younger brother. During the latter part of the fourteenth century, the Lord of the Isles was closely involved in political manoeuvring within Scotland, and it has been argued that the territory 'was by far the largest and most powerful province of Scotland'.[2]

In the fifteenth century there was considerable conflict over the succession to the Earldom of Ross, and this was the major focus of attention for John's son, Donald, and then in turn, for his son, Alexander. The arguments over the inheritance of the Earldom of Ross eventually led to the Battle of Harlaw in Aberdeenshire in 1411. This was reputedly one of the bloodiest battles on Scottish soil, and one which pitted a large force of Gaels against the lowland Scots. The battle was arguably won by Donald, but he withdrew and eventually, in the following year, renounced his claim to Ross. Control of the Earldom of Ross continued to be disputed throughout the middle of the fifteenth century, as the Lord of the Isles moved in and out of favour with King James I and his successors. By the end of Alexander's life, the situation appeared relatively stable; as Lord of the Isles, he controlled most of the north and west of Scotland and was based in Dingwall. The significance of Ross to the Lords of the Isles was emphasised when Alexander died in 1449, and was buried in the cathedral at Fortrose in Easter Ross, not Iona, the ancestral burial place of the Clan Donald.

The position of Lord of the Isles was eventually forfeited in 1493 by John II, the son of Alexander. The decisive event was the signing of the Treaty of Ardtornish in 1462 with the King of England. This treaty proposed the overthrow of King James III of Scotland, and the partitioning of the Kingdom between King Edward IV of England and the Lord of the Isles. Signing this Treaty was a politically disastrous decision by John II, as it triggered a civil war with his illegitimate son Angus Og which eventually led to the forfeiture of most of the mainland territories of the lordship in 1476. Angus Og won a substantial victory over John II at the battle of Bloody Bay off the coast of Mull in the early 1480s, after which he effectively controlled the Hebrides until he was murdered in 1490. John lived on in exile in southern Scotland until 1503 when he died and was buried at Scone. Attempts were made to maintain the lordship through the first half of the sixteenth century, but the position could not be maintained after the death of Donald Dubh, the son of Angus Og, in 1545.

During the fourteenth and fifteenth centuries, a variety of families or clans established themselves in the isles and became powerful landowners and allies of the Lords of the Isles. These clans, and the bloody feuds that characterised their relationships, dominated the later history of the Outer Hebrides. The main clans in the south were the MacNeils of Barra, and the MacDonalds of Clan Ranald in the Uists. In the north were the two Macleod clans of Dunvegan and Harris (the Siol Thormoid), and of Lewis (the Siol Thorcaill). There were various dependent clans, such as the Nicholsons, the Morisons and the Mackenzies, whose significance rose and fell during the fifteenth and sixteenth centuries.

The settlement evidence

One of the most noticeable features of the settlement history of the islands of South Uist and Benbecula is the distinction between the contemporary settlement patterns and the archaeological settlement patterns. Contemporary settlements are located inland, away from the coastal plain, in areas characterised by bedrock outcrops, lochs and peat. In contrast, the archaeological evidence reveals that the main areas of settlement for most of the islands' population in the period from the end of the second millennium BC to the middle of the second millennium AD was the machair plain of the west coast.

This division is not such an obvious feature of the landscape in the northern part of the Western Isles, as in Lewis the machair is more limited in its distribution and does not create such a clear-cut divide in the landscape. In the Northern Isles (Orkney and Shetland), the evidence suggests that Viking and Norse settlements were located close to or underneath the historic farms on these islands.[3]

It is clear that sometime in the middle of the second millennium AD the inhabitants of the Uists chose to relocate their settlements inland away from the coastal plain. The physical distance between the two areas may have been quite small; at Bornais the suggested replacement settlement (Beinn na Mhic Aongheis) is only 800 m from the original settlement. Nevertheless, it is clear that this was a dramatic transformation of the settlement pattern; there had previously been nearly two thousand years of persistent living on the machair plain. During this time, there had been some relocation and reorganisation of habitation, but it was essentially a continuous period of occupation.

These inhabited landscapes, though spatially close, are radically different. The landscape surrounding the modern settlements consists of isolated rock outcrops with thin acidic soils, surrounded by low lying ground covered either in deposits of thick peat, seasonally flooded marshlands or lochs. The amount of land available for drainage and cultivation is strictly limited, and the acidic peaty soils, though not infertile, require careful management and favour different crops to those growing on the machair.

This relocation of settlement is only one aspect of the pattern of landscape occupation. Contemporary, and recent historical, agriculture depend on the exploitation of the machair plain for cereals and as a grazing resource. Individual crofts have a strip of blackland around the house occupied by the crofter, plus a strip on the machair plain. Depending on the geography of the township, these two strips could be linked or completely detached. The machair is normally cultivated on rotation; in the Uists cereals are cultivated for two years then grazed by cattle for two years. It is possible therefore that the settlement displacement observed in the archaeological record did not represent a complete abandonment of the machair, but was restricted to a relocation of the domestic space.

The timing of this realignment was prolonged and spread over several centuries, although we can examine with some degree of precision the chronology and nature of the abandonment of the excavated settlements of Cille Pheadair and Bornais. There are also some broad conclusions that can be derived from the machair survey undertaken by Mike Parker Pearson and from early maps of the islands. All these sources provide some information on the process of settlement movement from machair to blackland. This process in the Western Isles has to be put in the broader context of change that was taking place across Britain in the late Medieval period as large numbers of deserted settlements have been found in many different regions of Britain.[4] The situation in the Western Isles may have been part of a much wider phenomenon, though local factors need to be carefully considered and would have affected the particular character of the process.

At Cille Pheadair the last house built on the settlement was House 007 discussed in Chapter 5. This house had two small structures built inside it, one in the north end and one in the southwest corner (Fig. 6.3). These structures were built using the original house revetment walls but with additional walls cutting across the interior of the abandoned house. The new walls were minimalist constructions; a single faced revetment of large boulders with a turf and sand backing to provide support and insulation. The floor layers were thin and ephemeral, and suggest that occupation was short lived. Rebuilds were visible and there were several occupation layers separated by windblown sand layers.

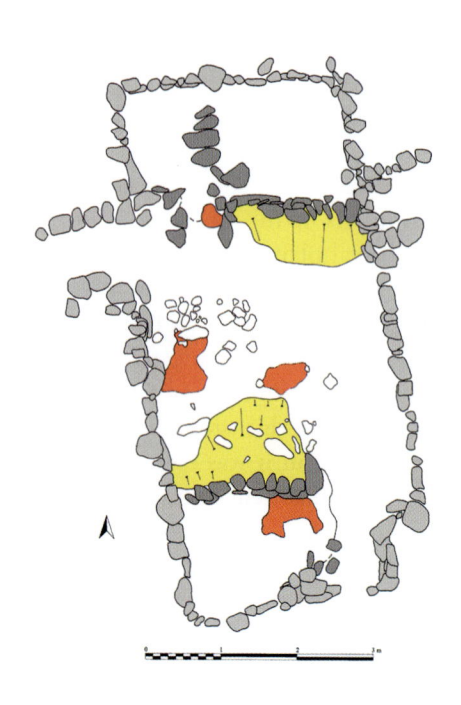

FIGURE 6.3. A plan of the final house at Cille Pheadair showing the later shelters built into the northeast and southwest corners of the house. © Mike Parker Pearson.

There appears to have been a difference between the occupation of the two structures; the southern structure had several peat ash layers which indicated the presence of hearths providing warmth and the potential for cooking. These ash layers were not found in the northern structure, but this produced a lot more finds, including a small, heavily fragmented ceramic assemblage. These structures may have been roughly contemporary but with different functions: one for sleeping and storage, and the other for cooking and inhabitation. A couple of radiocarbon dates and an English coin minted in Norwich in the period AD 1180–1247 suggest they were occupied in the early decades of the thirteenth century. This was not long after the abandonment of the original house, and may represent intermittent seasonal occupation of the settlement in the decades after abandonment. The location was eventually completely covered by windblown sand several metres thick that rendered the settlement remains invisible.

The abandonment sequence at Bornais varied from mound to mound but there were some related patterns. Late Norse House 3 was the last of the large high-status houses built on mound 2 and the final abandonment of this building is complex, well preserved and informative. The final occupation of the Late Norse house extended into the first decades of the fourteenth century, and it was probably systematically dismantled at the end of its life as it would have contained a lot of re-usable structural timber. After the house was dismantled there was a brief period when it was occupied by cattle, which left hoof prints impressed in the abandoned floor layer. These were only visible because they had been filled with a thin layer of white windblown

FIGURE 6.4. The impressions of cattle hoof prints pressed into the abandoned floor of House 3 and filled with white windblown sand.

sand (Fig. 6.4). On top of this, an ancillary structure was constructed at the south end of the house. This was a neat, well-built rectangular building comparable to the small structures at Cille Pheadair and to others at Bornais (Figs 6.5 and 6.6). The internal area was 2.7 m by 4.6 m; it had an entrance facing north, a well-defined floor with a hearth defined by a spread of peat ash, and a partitioned sleeping area on the west side. It was clearly designed to provide short term accommodation for one or two individuals and would probably have been quite comfortable. However, the absence of any substantial quantities of finds suggest it was not used for lengthy spells of occupation. There were several floor layers above the primary floor but none of them were rich in finds, and analysis of the soils suggested that animals rather than humans often used this structure for shelter in its later years. The radiocarbon dates unfortunately do not really help to date this activity, but it probably occurred within 60 years of the abandonment of the Late Norse house (3), sometime in the second half of the fourteenth century.

At least one other structure was constructed inside the Late Norse house on mound 2, though this was

FIGURE 6.5. A view of the shelter built into the south end of Bornais House 3 after it had been abandoned.

FIGURE 6.6. A plan of the shelter at the south end of Bornais House 3 showing the ashy floor layer extending out of the entrance.

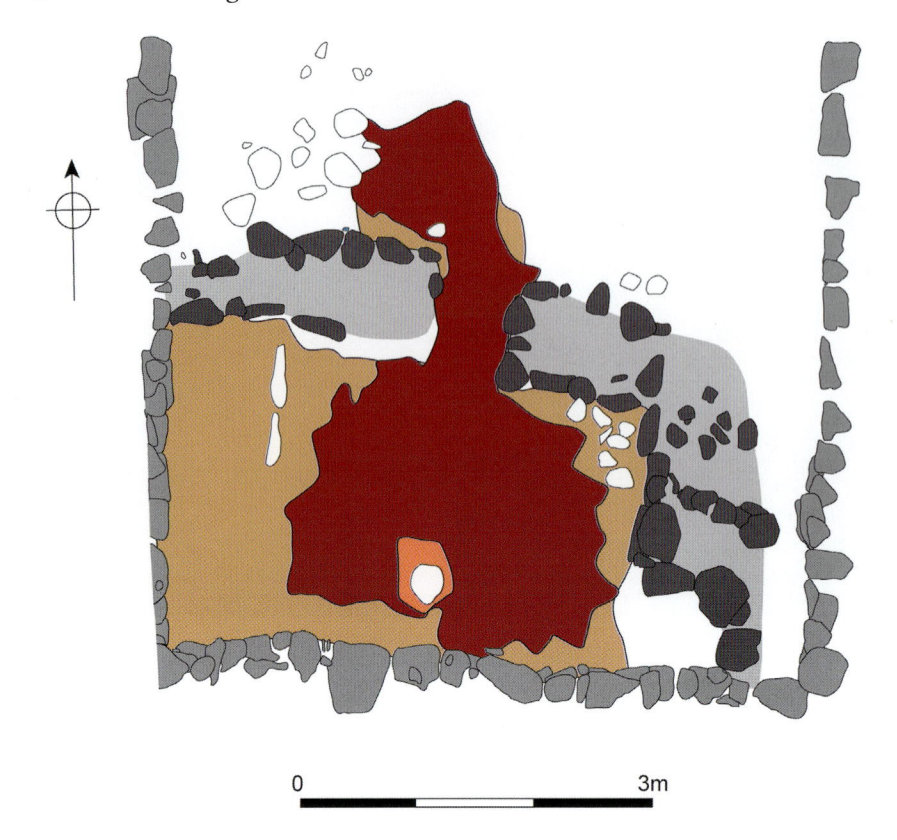

very insubstantial, comprising little more than a horseshoe shaped setting of boulders built in front of a large slab pulled off the west wall (Fig. 6.7). There were also dumps of stone slabs (and limpet shells) in the northern half of the house, suggesting people were collecting suitable stone in anticipation of building another structure inside the house. However, it seems this project was abandoned, and the slabs were covered by a sterile windblown sand that filled the house.

Mound 2 was a large mound, and it is impossible to be certain that occupation did not carry on into the fifteenth century in its other unexcavated areas. Nevertheless, in terms of what we found, the occupation of this mound seems to have ended by the end of the fourteenth century and it was only after this period that substantial deposits of windblown sand filled the structures.

Our exploration of mound 2A focused on the northern end of the settlement mound, which contained ancillary structures and midden deposits. The final construction in this area was a house abandoned around the middle of the fourteenth century. In its northeast corner was a construction similar to those found on the Cille Pheadair house and Bornais mound 2. However, this corner structure was tiny, approximately 30 cm in diameter (Fig. 6.7). This was clearly not a shelter, as it would not have protected anything bigger

FIGURE 6.7. Two of the smaller shelters built after the settlement had been largely abandoned, that on the left was built against the west wall of Bornais House 3, that on the right is built in the northeast corner of the final house in mound 2A.

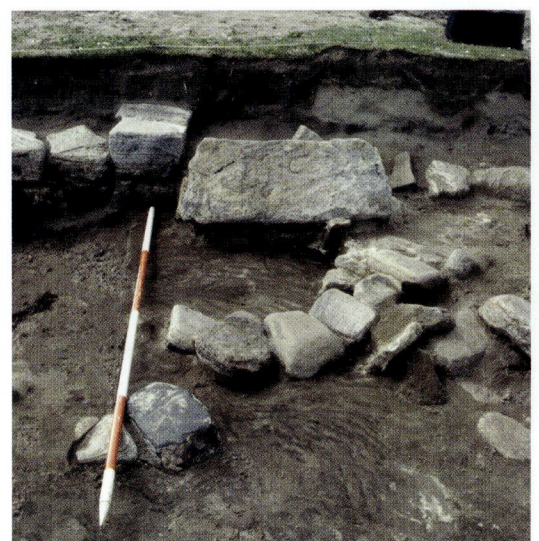

than a chicken and so raises questions as to how we should interpret these corner structures.

The house at the north end of mound 2A was probably not the last house built on this mound. Partial exploration of the south end suggested this area was the domestic focus for this mound. The last in a sequence of houses in this area closely resembled the Late Norse house (5) on mound 3, and could extend the occupation of this mound into the second half of the fourteenth century. This house was damaged by a later, possibly specialist, structure which was only partially observed at the edge of the excavation trench.[5] This structure was infilled with a thick layer of sterile windblown sand similar to that observed in the kiln on mound 3.

On mound 3, radiocarbon dates indicated that the final house was abandoned around the first two decades of the fifteenth century. There was no sign that any ancillary structures had been constructed in the abandoned house. The deposits filling the interior of the building instead suggest that after abandonment, the roof and the timber superstructure of the house were removed, and the enclosing turf walls were allowed to gradually decay to eventually fill the interior. A slight hollow was all that survived of the house, and this was eventually covered by windblown sand.

The kiln that lay immediately to the southwest of this house had a very different history of abandonment. Radiocarbon dates reveal that the final occupation of this structure was a little later than the adjacent house, and it continued to be used until the middle of the fifteenth century. This structure was dug into the settlement mound, and had an internal revetment wall up to a metre high. The final floor was covered by a thick layer of clean white windblown sand, the result of a catastrophic event that had completely infilled the structure.

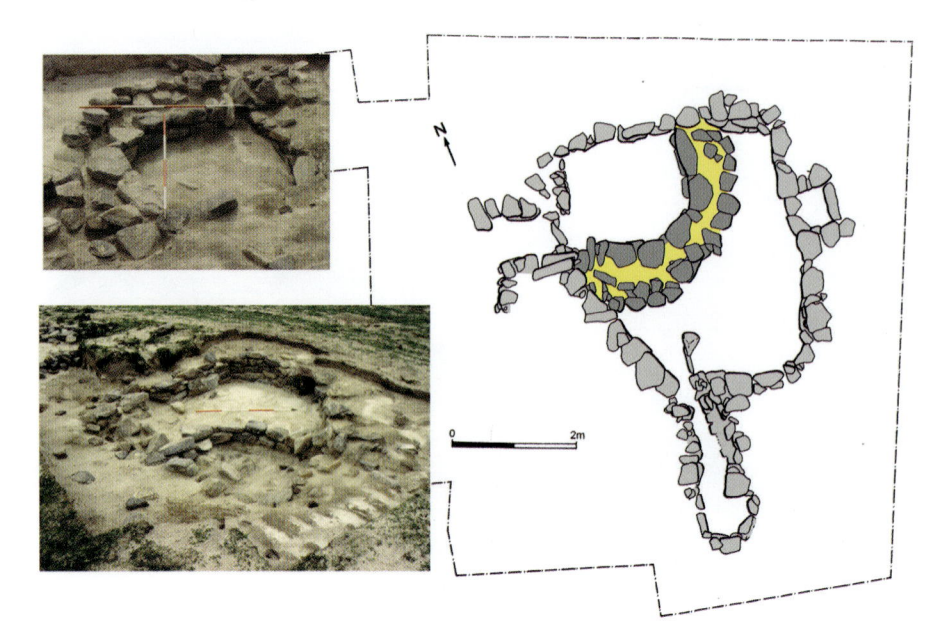

FIGURE 6.8. A plan and two views of the shelter built into the northwest corner of the kiln on Bornais mound 3. It was built as the kiln filled up with windblown sand.

Sometime during this period of infilling, a small ancillary structure, 3.0 m by 2.8 m, was built into the northwest corner of the kiln (Fig. 6.8). This structure was carefully constructed with a well-built wall, and was accessed through the original western entrance to the kiln. However, it does not appear to have been used as no floor layer was identifiable, and it was also covered by the blown sand that completely filled the kiln.

The evidence from mound 3 suggests that this part of the settlement was partially abandoned in the early fifteenth century, although the specialised grain-drying kiln continued to be used until the middle of the fifteenth century. This was then abandoned, probably as a result of a period of machair destabilisation which led to deep deposits of windblown sand burying the settlement. It appears that an unsuccessful attempt was made to create a shelter in the ruins of the kiln, but this had to be abandoned due to the quantities of sand accumulating at this time.

The evidence from the Udal contrasts with the sequences at Bornais and Cille Pheadair, as this settlement was occupied up to the end of the seventeenth century or into the early part of the eighteenth century, although information about the nature of this occupation is negligible. Mike Parker Pearson's survey of the machair settlement mounds on South Uist confirmed that most of these settlements were abandoned at the end of the Medieval period, but he identified four that survived into the post-Medieval period, after 1500. At the north end of South Uist, Machair Mheadhanach mounds 137 and 138 produced diagnostic post-Medieval pottery and were marked as settlements on the Blaue map of 1654. In the middle of the island, Staoinebrig mound 33 and Aisgernis mound 96 also produced post-Medieval pottery, and their occupation into the fifteenth and sixteenth centuries was confirmed by excavation.[6] The settlement of Baghasdail at the south end of the island was a substantial mound complex that included a nineteenth-century cemetery, and this settlement appeared on all the historic maps, including the Bold map of 1805. This machair settlement seems only to have been abandoned in the middle of the nineteenth century.

This brief survey of the settlement evidence suggested that the abandonment of the machair settlements at Cille Pheadair and Bornais preceded a major influx of windblown sand in the fifteenth century. There was some movement of sand in the fourteenth century, and this may have already been causing problems. However, it could be argued that the presence of windblown sand was an indication and not the cause of the abandonment of the settlements. Blown sand was a constant feature of the occupation of the machair plain, and the cleaning and maintenance of these settlements would have routinely involved its clearance. This cleaning would have ceased when the houses were abandoned. On the machair plain, any hollows, such as those formed in abandoned houses, would gradually fill with sand caught in the hollows sheltered from the constant winds. The natural (unproblematic) movement of sand blown in from the cultivated fields would, however, only gradually infill an abandoned house, and this slow incremental infilling would be clearly marked by relic soil horizons. None of these were visible in the infilling of the kiln on mound 3, or in the latest structures on mound 2 and 2A, which suggests larger than usual quantities of windblown sand were being deposited in the fifteenth century. This sand had to come from somewhere, and suggests that large deposits of machair were destabilised and forming unstable dunes at this time.

Climate and plague

The influence of climate change on human settlement has been a topic of considerable interest in recent years as the world responds to the climate emergency caused by global warming. The presence of a Little Ice Age has been well documented,[7] and the general consensus of opinion is that this started at the beginning of the fifteenth century and lasted well into the nineteenth century (Fig. 6.9). However, the historian Richard Oram has recently argued[8] that the optimum conditions for the Norse settlement of the North Atlantic were already

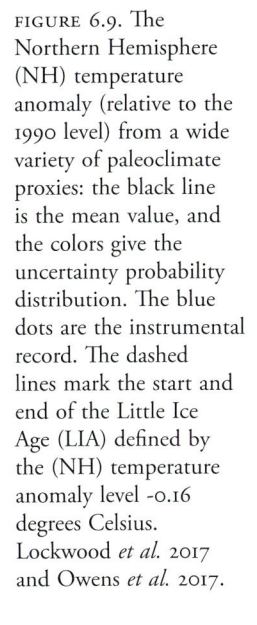

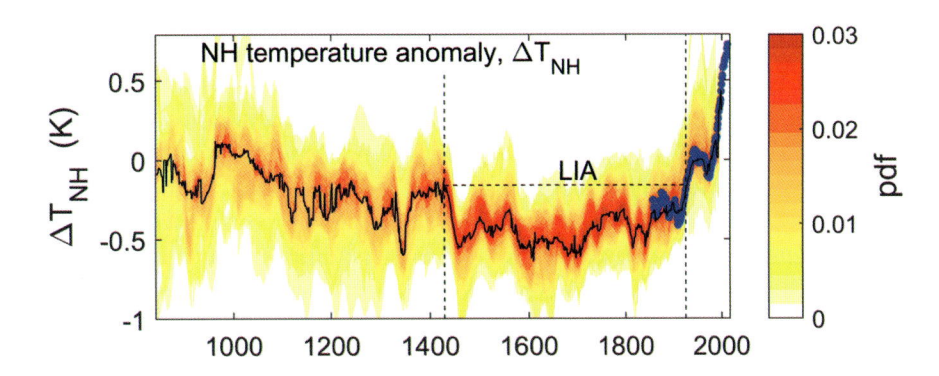

FIGURE 6.9. The Northern Hemisphere (NH) temperature anomaly (relative to the 1990 level) from a wide variety of paleoclimate proxies: the black line is the mean value, and the colors give the uncertainty probability distribution. The blue dots are the instrumental record. The dashed lines mark the start and end of the Little Ice Age (LIA) defined by the (NH) temperature anomaly level -0.16 degrees Celsius. Lockwood *et al.* 2017 and Owens *et al.* 2017.

being challenged by intermittent periods of severe weather from the middle of the thirteenth century. The scientific evidence for temperature variations and increasingly stormy conditions comes from Artic ice cores, dendrochronology and ocean sediment cores. From 1308, the pattern was set for 'harsh and bitterly cold winters; delayed and relatively cool springs; and warm wet autumns'.[9] The weather declined further in the winter of 1314/15, and generally conditions were very poor throughout the fourteenth century, with more regular, violent and prolonged winter storms due to the circulation of cold water from the polar regions.

Coinciding with this period of climatic decline was the appearance of virulent and deadly diseases in both the human and animal populations. Bubonic plague made its first devastating appearance in 1349, but there were further outbreaks in AD 1362–1363, 1380 and 1401. The first couple of epidemics are thought to have killed around one third of the contemporary population. The relationship of these diseases to the deteriorating climate is disputed, but the general lack of grain and the poor condition of the animals created by the successive years of bad weather would surely have left a severely debilitated community that would have easily succumbed to relatively mild outbreaks of plague, dysentery, and other infectious diseases. The devastating effects of infectious disease can be observed in an epidemic that swept St Kilda in 1727. It is estimated that 80–90% of the island's population died that year as the result of an epidemic of either smallpox or chickenpox. Only 'nine men, ten women, fifteen boys and eight girls remained alive on the island'.[10] Clearly, events such as these had the potential to devastate Hebridean communities and could lead to the abandonment of any settlement affected.

It is difficult to know exactly how climatic deterioration would have impacted the marginal landscapes of the Western Isles. The islands are subject to the full force of the Atlantic, so any increase in storms would have restricted seafaring; possibly jeopardising routine trading relationships with Ireland and seasonal fishing off the west coast. It is difficult to comment on the severity of this impact as this would require the excavation of settlements from the fifteenth and sixteenth centuries to acquire data directly comparable to that recovered from Bornais and Cille Pheadair.[11]

The environmental conditions most likely to cause extensive and cataclysmic erosion of the machair plain would have started with a period of very dry weather that killed the grasses and wildflowers that help to stabilise the thin soils of the machair plain. If this drought was followed by severe gales, then large patches of bare sand would be exposed. Once this happens, sand would move around for years if not decades. The severity of this destabilisation could have varied from township to township, depending on the precise nature of the underlying water table and the integrity of the surface vegetation, but erosion and sand deposition could have been sufficiently severe to have completely destroyed the economic viability of a settlement. Just such conditions were recorded in the 1480s and 1490s in Orkney[12] and it is possible that the fifteenth-century sand-blows at Bornais were due to the same period of distinctive climatic conditions.

The abandonment of the machair plain seems to have been a protracted affair that lasted a century or more. It is possible that the gradual abandonment of the different settlements was a response to the long-term impact of poor weather conditions making life ever more precarious. In addition, the effects of the plague from the middle of the fourteenth century must have dramatically accelerated this decline, and it seems highly likely that many of these settlements were now simply unviable due to the decline in population. Abandonment of these settlements may have contributed to the cataclysmic sand-blows that occurred in the fifteenth century. Successful agricultural regimes would have involved middening and manuring that maintained the stability of the machair soils. If this had not been undertaken because the settlements were abandoned, then fertility would decline as the soils became thinner, making them increasingly vulnerable to erosion.

It is unlikely that the abandonment of the settlement landscape represented the complete abandonment of the machair. The archaeological record suggests the occupants of Bornais tried to maintain a connection to the old machair settlement, and the shelters within the final buildings must indicate people visited to build and to occupy these shelters. The economic significance of these constructions and the visits they document is open to question. Some could have acted as shelters to protect visitors to Bornais from settlements some distance from the machair, though it seems unlikely they would have needed them if they were living in the Beinn na Mhic Aongheis, less than a kilometre away. They could have visited to restart cultivation in fields that had stabilised, or they could have been using pockets of stabilised, grassed-over dunes as pasture. Pasturing animals on the sand would have helped stabilise the machair, as manure was good for creating and improving the soils needed to stabilise the sand. However, some of these structures were clearly not practical: the corner structure on mound 2A in particular was far too small to be used. It seems more likely that this structure was created to memorialise the connection between the original occupants of the settlement and subsequent visitors, who must have regarded themselves as their descendants. Both the visits and these structures may have acted as a mechanism to maintain inheritance rights to the different settlement mounds and the land they were associated with.

Castle and church

The movement away from the machair coincided broadly with other significant changes in the settlement record, which included the construction or reoccupation of defensive structures throughout the islands.

Borve may be the only castle to have been built in the fourteenth century before the forfeiture of the Lords of the Isles, but there were a number of small towers and associated enclosures scattered around the coast and on islands in the inland lochs that probably date to the fifteenth and sixteenth centuries. The only example that has seen modern excavation is Dùn Èistean in Ness, at the northern tip of the Isle of Lewis, and this was not a typical structure,

FIGURE 6.10. A view of the tower in Dùn Èistean at Ness, Lewis. © Rachel Barrowman.

because it was made from unmortared stone. In its completed state it was a stone tower 7 m by 4.5 m that must have stood at least 2 m high, and had been rebuilt at least once (Fig. 6.10). It probably acted as a lookout point that monitored the surrounding coast and sea routes. Similar small towers were known in coastal locations at Caisteal Calabhaigh at the mouth of Loch Boisdale in South Uist, and Caisteal a'Bhreabhair, a sea stack south of the Isle of Eriskay in the Sound of Barra. There were similar small towers on inland lochs at Caisteal Bheagram to the north of Howmore in South Uist, and Dun MhicLeoid in Loch Tangusdale, Barra. Most of these towers were set within defended enclosures with subsidiary buildings, which included substantial halls, at Calabhaigh and Bheagram.

The tower on Dùn Èistean was located on a large sea stack adjacent to the coastal cliff edge of the Point of Ness, and had a substantial enclosure wall on the landward side of the stack, facing the cliff edge (Fig. 6.11). Several agglomerated clusters of small turf and stone built structures occupied the interior of the stack, and a corn drying kiln was found in an isolated rectangular building. Excavations reveal that the site was a defensive stronghold occupied only intermittently at the end of the sixteenth century; history suggests this was the stronghold of the Morisons, the hereditary brieves[13] of the MacDonalds. It was probably the stronghold referred to in the *Ewill Trowbles of the Lewis* written by a MacLeod in the early seventeenth century.

> After the death of Torq[uil] Dow the Breiwe and hiss kinn returned into The Lewes and strengthened themselves Within a fort in the Iland called ness Bot Neall MacLeiold the bastard brother of Torq[uil] Dow persewed them killed diverse of them and constrained them to leave the fort of Neise.[14]

FIGURE 6.11. A plan of the buildings on the stack at Dùn Èistean, Ness, Lewis. © Rachel Barrowman.

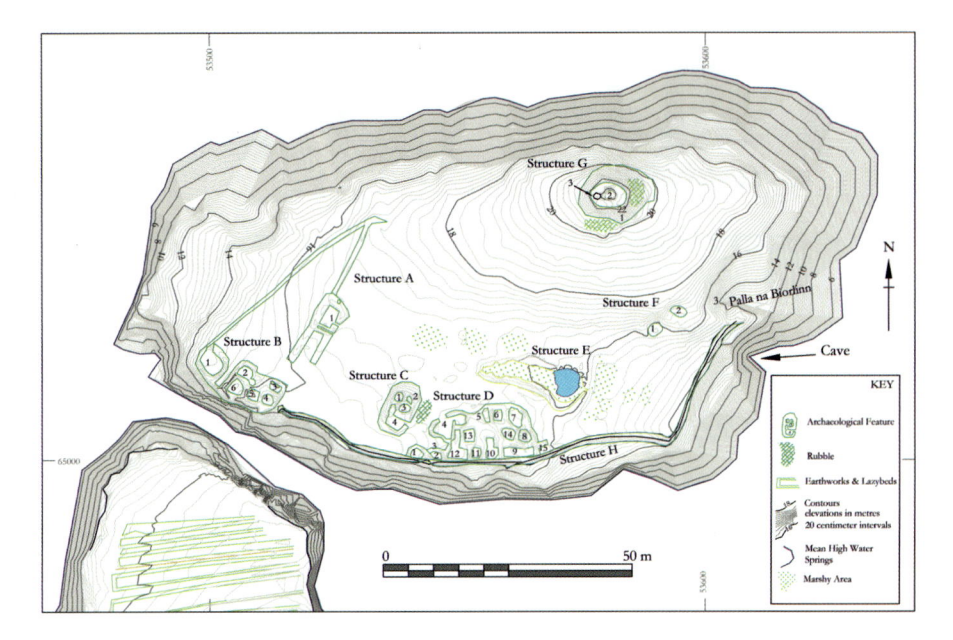

In this period, islands in lochs reemerged as attractive locations for high-status residences. There was some variation in the nature of the different structures that emerged during this period, and it is possible these might reflect subtle chronological changes that we cannot yet appreciate due to the lack of archaeological excavations of these structures.

A range of unusual and distinctive unmortared stone 'castles' were built on artificial islands. Dun Raouill in Loch Druidibeg on South Uist (Fig. 6.13), and Dun Ban in Loch Carabhat on North Uist were effectively large hall houses with attached curtain walls that created an adjacent courtyard.[15] They were built some distance from the shore and could only have been accessed by boat, a contrast with the earlier tradition of broch building when similarly enhanced artificial islands were connected to the mainland by a stone causeway.

A more common practice in the Western Isles was to reoccupy an abandoned broch and modify it to conform to contemporary tastes. In most cases, this involved the construction of a rectangular hall inside the broch tower. A good example of this was Dun an Sticar in North Uist (Fig. 6.14). This was a substantial stone walled hall, 9.9 m long and 4.9 m wide, which involved significant modification to the original broch where a large portion of the northern wall was removed to accommodate a new door and a window. Impressive stone causeways were constructed that were much wider than the original Iron Age causeway.

Other brochs show evidence of similar modifications, and many of these were referenced in the clan histories and appear to have been central to the identity of the clans that emerged in the fifteenth and sixteenth centuries. Unfortunately,

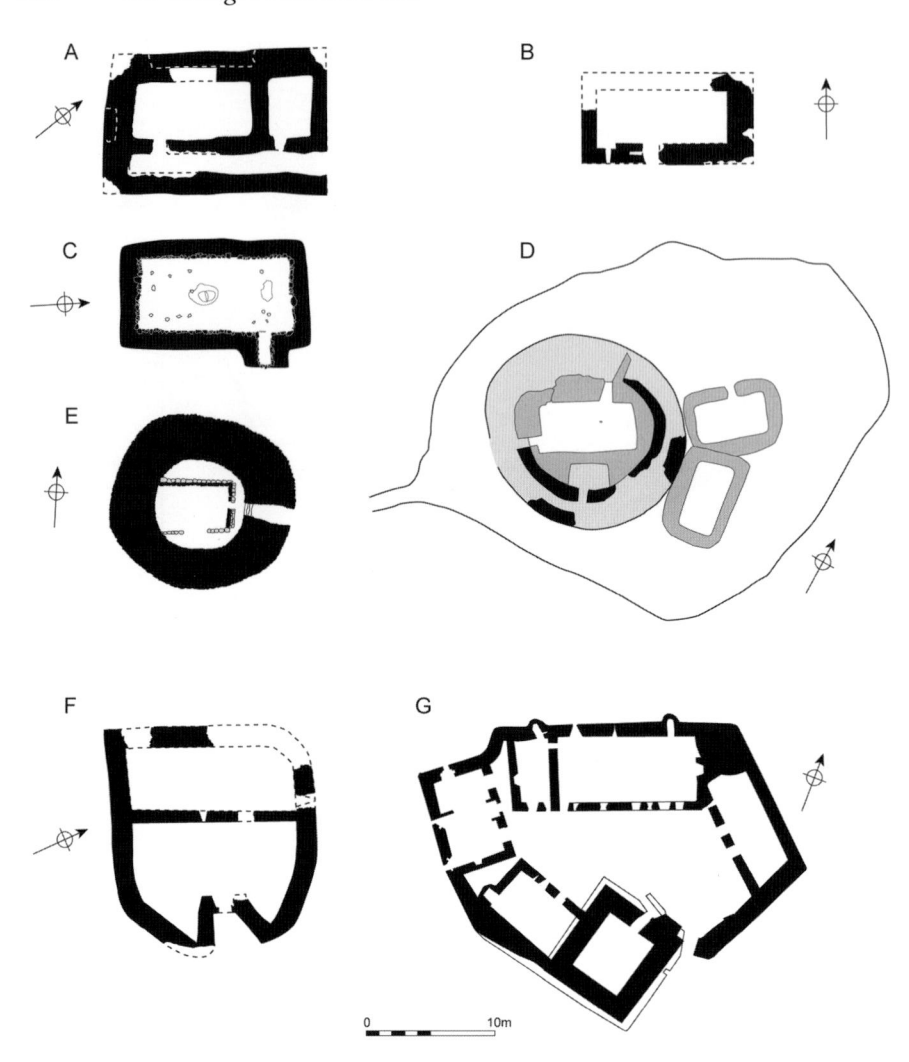

FIGURE 6.12. Plans of a variety of unusual castles and modified duns probably built in the fifteenth and sixteenth centuries.

the chronology of these reoccupations and fortifications is currently unknown, as none have been excavated and their dating is impossible.[16] The reoccupation of the island fortifications is more likely to have occurred in the fifteenth and sixteenth centuries, when warfare and endemic violence appear to have blighted the islands.

The only other substantial buildings with mortared walls that may have been built in this period are the churches. The historically significant churches on the islands are those associated with the burial places of the later clan chiefs: Cille Bharra on Barra is associated with the MacNeills; Howmore on South Uist with Clan Ranald; Teampill na Trionaid at Carinais, North Uist with Clan MacVicar; St Clements Church, Rodel, Harris with the Macleods of Dunvegan and Harris (Fig. 6.15), and Eoglais na h-Aoidhe at Aignish, Lewis with the Macleods of Lewis. Many of these churches have elaborately decorated sixteenth-century tombstones depicting armoured warriors, weapons,

FIGURE 6.13. The unmortared stone castle of Dun Raouill in Loch Druidibeg, South Uist, an isolated building only accessible by boat. © Crown Copyright: HES.

castles, and galleys, which indicate the importance of warfare to these societies. The tomb at Rodel in Harris is the most spectacular of these elaborate tombs (as discussed at the beginning of this chapter).

Conclusion

The fifteenth and sixteenth centuries marked a decisive end to a relatively stable period lasting 400 years when the islands were controlled by individuals descended from the Viking invaders of the ninth and tenth centuries. Even the MacDonald Lords of the Isles, who achieved overlordship in the fourteenth century, had Norse ancestry through Somerled which was only superficially obscured by the resurgent Gaelic ethnicity they promoted. The disruption of the fifteenth and sixteenth-centuries had many underlying causes. The effect of climate change may have been one of the most significant, with animals dying and crops destroyed by wind, windblown sand and rain. There was also every likelihood that major epidemics swept through the islands in this period.

FIGURE 6.14. Dun an Sticar in North Uist showing the substantial stone causeway leading out to the dun.

FIGURE 6.15. The church at Rodel, Harris. © Denys Pringle.

This was likely to have undermined the existing political structures, and made any resistance to the King of Scotland's abolition of the lordship difficult to sustain and support. The abolition of the lordship appears to have exacerbated existing tensions between the subservient clans, and led to increased hostility within the islands. Prior to this period, the clans had been able to direct their aggression towards external parties, most notably the Irish. This had been advantageous in providing a source of wealth for the competing clans, and allowed an outlet for the aggression of the young men that had been trained in warfare from an early age. Increasingly rough seas and shortages of basic subsistence may have made complex adventures overseas difficult and led to increased competition for the scant resources within the islands. The fortifications of this period certainly support the idea that internal feuding was increasingly common, and that resources needed to be defended.

Despite the disruption there were some notable continuities that can be documented. The size and shape of the houses used by the bulk of the population remained remarkably similar in the Uists, and the turf walled houses discussed in Chapter 5 were remarkably similar to those excavated at Beinn na Mhic Aongheis, and were at least structurally comparable to buildings standing in the 1930s and 1940s. There was evolution in the organisation of interior space, but this seems to have had little effect on the basic structure other than a shift in the entrance from close to the house gable to the middle of the long side of the house. The evolution of the grain drying kilns also clearly demonstrated elements of continuity, as those excavated on settlements cleared in the nineteenth century clearly evolved from the structures present on mound 3 in the fourteenth and fifteenth centuries.

This evidence for continuity across this period suggests that despite the endemic violence alluded to, the general population remained largely the same Norse-Gaelic ethnicity throughout the period. This was despite the attempt to 'civilise' the Isle of Lewis contrived by King James VI and some noblemen from Fife at the end of the sixteenth century. This was the first of many attempts to 'improve' the productivity of the islands, which culminated in the upheavals of the nineteenth century known as the Clearances, when many of the traditional clan chiefs sold their land and the new owners introduced radical approaches to land management that transformed the agricultural landscape. Large areas of land were completely cleared of people and what had been cultivated was given over to pasture for sheep. The current landscape of townships and fields was created in this period of flux, as were the fishing towns of the sheltered east coast.

Notes

1. See Oram 2004, 124 and Bannerman 2016, 335 for a full account of this event.
2. Bannerman 2016, 299.
3. Many of the excavated Norse settlements on Orkney have been discovered during work on contemporary farms i.e. Skaill and Orphir on mainland; Quoygrew on Westray (Barrett 2012) and Pool on Sanday are adjacent to recently abandoned farms.
4. Archaeologists actually established a research group known as the Deserted Medieval Village Research Group specifically to consider this distinctive phenomenon.
5. This structure is referred to as Ancillary Structure 3 (GEI) in Sharples 2020.
6. Raven 2005.
7. Fagan 2000.
8. Oram 2014.
9. Oram 2014, 227.
10. Gannon and Geddes 2015, 76.
11. This is problematic, as the blackland settlements that dominate the archaeological record for these centuries are in locales that do not preserve the material recovered from the machair settlements; mammal and fish bones. It highlights the importance of the four machair settlements that survived through the post-Medieval period. These are the only locations that could document the changes caused by the Little Ice Age.
12. Thomson 1987, 130.
13. It is unclear exactly how they operated, but essentially it is thought they were brought to disputes to recite and explain the law, but had no role in enforcing it (McConnich in Barrowman 2015).
14. This quote from 'The Evil Troubles' is reproduced by MacCoinnach in Barrowman 2015, illus 3.4 and he also provides a detailed history of the Morisons of Ness.
15. Dun Raouill has a hall 9.3 m by 4.8 m, but there is contiguous room at the north end of the hall. At Dun Ban the hall is 13.1 m by 5.3 m. Both sites are most fully described in the RCAHMS 1928 volume on the Hebrides.
16. John Raven (Raven 2005) has argued that the reoccupation of the Iron Age brochs began in the twelfth century, however, the author finds no evidence for this early chronology in the Outer Hebrides. The development of fortifications at this early date seems to be incompatible with the open nature of the settlements at Bornais and Cille Pheadair.

Bibliography

Angus, S. (1997) *The Outer Hebrides. The shaping of the islands*. Cambridge, The White Horse Press.

Angus, S. (2001) *The Outer Hebrides. Moor and machair*. Cambridge, The White Horse Press.

Armit, I. (1992) *The Later Prehistory of the Western Isles of Scotland*. Oxford, British Archaeological Reports (British Series 221).

Armit, I. (1996) *The Archaeology of Skye and the Western Isles*. Edinburgh, Edinburgh University Press.

Armit, I. (1997) Cultural landscapes and identities: a case study in the Scottish Iron Age. In Gwilt, A. and Haselgrove, C. (eds) *Reconstructing Iron Age Societies*. Oxford, Oxbow Books, 248–53.

Armit, I. (2005) The Atlantic roundhouse: a beginner's guide. In Turner, V., Nicholson, R.A., Dockrill, S.J. and Bond, J.M. (eds) *Tall Stories? 2 Millennia of Brochs*. Lerwick, Shetland Amenity Trust, 5–10.

Armit, I. (2006) *Anatomy of an Iron Age Roundhouse. The Cnip wheelhouse excavations, Lewis*. Edinburgh, Society of Antiquaries of Scotland.

Armit, I., Campbell, E. and Dunwell, A. (2009) Excavation of an Iron Age, Early Historic and medieval settlement and metalworking site at Eilean Olabhat, North Uist. *Proceedings of the Society of Antiquaries of Scotland* 138, 27–104.

Ashby, S. (2006) *Time, trade and identity: bone and antler combs in northern Britain c. AD 700–1400*. Unpublished PhD thesis, University of York.

Bannerman, J.W.M. (2016) The Lordship of the Isles (2): historical background. In Bannerman, J.W.M. *Kingship, Church and Culture: collected essays and studies*. Edinburgh: John Donald, 330–53.

Barrett, J.H. (1997) Fish trade in Norse Orkney and Caithness: a zooarchaeological approach. *Antiquity* 71, 616–38.

Barrett, J.H. (2012) *Being an islander. Production and identity at Quoygrew, Orkney, AD 900–1600*. Cambridge, McDonald Institute for Archaeological Research, University of Cambridge.

Barrett, J.H. and Richards, M.P. (2004) Identity, gender, religion and economy: new isotope and radiocarbon evidence for marine resource intensification in Early Historic Orkney, Scotland, UK. *European Journal of Archaeology* 7, 249–271.

Barrett, J.H., Beukens, R.P. and Nicholson, R.A. (2001) Diet and ethnicity during the Viking colonisation of northern Scotland: evidence from fish bones and stable carbon isotopes. *Antiquity* 75, 145–54.

Barrowman, R.C. (2015) *Dun Eistean, Ness. The excavation of a clan stronghold*. Stornoway: Acair Books.

Barrowman, R.C. (2023) 'Remember the days of old, consider the years of many generations': chapel-sites in the Isle of Lewis. *Proceedings of the Society of Antiquaries of Scotland* 152, 147–191.

Baug, I., Skre, D., Heldal, T. and Jansen, O.J. (2019) The Beginning of the Viking Age in the West. *Journal of Maritime Archaeology* 14, 43–80.

Best, J. (2014) *Living in Liminality: an Osteoarchaeological Investigation into the Use of Avian Resources in North Atlantic Island Environments*. Unpublished PhD thesis, Cardiff University.

Best, J. and Mulville, J. (2016) Birds from the water: reconstructing avian resource use and contribution to diet in prehistoric Scottish Island environments. *Journal of Archaeological Science Reports* 6, 654–664.

Boyd, J.M. and Boyd, I.L. (1990) *The Hebrides: A Natural History*. London, Collins.

Branigan, K. (2005) *From Clan to Clearance. History and archaeology on the Isle of Barra c. 850–1850 AD*. Oxford, Oxbow Books.

Branigan, K. (2010) *The Last of the Clan. General Roderick MacNeil of Barra 41st Chief of the Clan MacNeil*. Oxford, Oxbow Books.

Branigan, K. and Foster, P. (1995) *Barra: Archaeology on Ben Tangaval*. Sheffield, Sheffield Academic Press.

Branigan, K. and Foster, P. (2000) *From Barra to Berneray*. Sheffield, Sheffield Academic Press.

Broderick, G. (trans.) (1988) *Chronicles of the kings of Man and the Isles: their manuscript and history*. Ramsay, Celtic League.

Broderick, G. (2013) Some Island Names in the Former 'Kingdom of the Isles': a reappraisal. *The Journal of Scottish Name Studies* 7.

Buteux, S. (1997) *Settlements at Skaill, Deerness, Orkney. Excavations by Peter Gelling of the Prehistoric, Pictish, Viking and Later Periods, 1963–1981*. Oxford, Archaeopress.

Caldwell, D. (2010) *Finlaggan, Islay. The centre of the Lordship of the Isles. Excavations and fieldwork 1989–1998.* Edinburgh, National Museums of Scotland.

Caldwell, D. and Hall, M.A. (2014) *The Lewis Chessmen. New Perspectives.* Edinburgh, National Museums Scotland.

Caldwell, D., Hall, M.A. and Wilkinson, C.M. (2009) The Lewis Hoard of Gaming Pieces. A Re-examination of their Context, Meanings, Discovery and Manufacture. *Medieval Archaeology* 53, 155–203.

Campbell, E. (1991) Excavations of a wheelhouse and other Iron Age structures at Sollas, North Uist, by R J C Atkinson in 1957. *Proceedings of the Society of Antiquaries of Scotland* 121, 117–73.

Campbell, E. (2002) The Western Isles pottery sequence In Ballin-Smith, B. and Banks, I. (eds.) *In the Shadow of the Brochs: The Iron Age in Scotland.* Stroud, Tempus, 139–144.

Carver, M. (2016) *Portmahomack: Monastery of the Picts.* Edinburgh, Edinburgh University Press.

Carver, M. Garner-Lahire, J. and Spall, C. (2016) *Portmahomack on Tarbet Ness. Changing ideologies in north east Scotland sixth to sixteenth century AD.* Edinburgh, Society of Antiquaries of Scotland.

Cavers, G. (2022) *Clachtoll: An Iron Age Broch Settlement in Assynt, North-west Scotland.* Oxford, Oxbow Books.

Church, M.J., Arge, S.V., Brewington, S., McGovern, T.H., Woollett, J.M., Perdikaris, S., Lawson, I.T., Cook, G.T., Amundsen, C., Harrison, R., Krivogorskaya, Y. and Dunbar, E. (2005) Puffins, Pigs, Cod and Barley: Palaeoeconomy at Undir Junkarinsfløtti, Sandoy, Faroe Islands. *Environmental Archaeology* 10, 179–197.

Clancy, T.O. (1998) *The Triumph Tree. Scotland's Earliest Poetry AD 550–1350.* Edinburgh, Canongate.

Clancy, T.O. (2018) Hebridean connections: in Ibdone Insula, Ibdaig, Eboudai, Uist. *Journal of Scottish Name Studies* 12, 27–40.

Clarke, D.V. (1970) Bone dice and the Scottish Iron Age. *Proceedings of the Prehistoric Society* 36, 214–32.

Clarke, D.V. and Heald, A. (2002) Beyond Typology: Combs, Economics, Symbolism and Regional Identity in Late Norse Scotland. *Norwegian Archaeological Review* 35.2, 81–93.

Comeau, R. Seaman, A. and Bloxam, A. (2023) Plague, Climate and Faith in Early Medieval Western Britain: Investigating Narratives of Change. *Medieval Archaeology* 67:1, 1–28.

Cormack, W.F. (1989) Two recent finds of exotic porphyry in Galloway. *Transactions of the Dumfries and Galloway Natural History and Antiquarian Society* 54, 43–7.

Cowie, T. and MacLeod Rivet, M. (2015) Machair Bharbhais: a landscape through time. *Journal of the North Atlantic Special Volume* 9, 99–107.

Cox, R.A.V. (2002) *The Gaelic Place-Names of Carloway, Lewis: Their Structure and Significance.* Dublin, Dublin Institute for Advanced Studies.

Coyle McClung, L. and Plunkett, G. (2020) Cultural change and the climate record in final prehistoric and early medieval Ireland. *Proceedings of the Royal Irish Academy: Section C, Archaeology, Celtic Studies, History, Linguistics, Literature* 120C, 129–158.

Cramp, L.J.E., Whelton, H., Sharples, N., Mulville, J. and Evershed, R.P. (2015) Contrasting patterns of resource exploitation on the Western and Northern Isles during the Late Iron Age and Norse period revealed through organic residues in pottery. *Journal of the North Atlantic Special Volume* 9, 134–151.

Cramp, L.J.E., Jones, J., Sheridan, A., Smyth, J., Whelton, H., Mulville, J., Sharples, N. and Evershed, R.P. (2014) Immediate replacement of fishing with dairying by the earliest farmers of the northeast Atlantic archipelagos. *Proceedings of the Royal Society B*, dx.doi.org/10.1098/rspb.2013.2372.

Crawford, B.E. (1987) *Scandinavian Scotland.* Leicester, Leicester University Press.

Crawford, I.A. (1975) Scot (?), Norseman and Gael. *Scottish Archaeological Forum* 6, 1–16.

Crawford, I.A. (1981) War or peace – Viking colonization in the Northern and Western Isles of Scotland reviewed. In Bekker-Nielson, H., Foote, P. and Olsen, O. (eds) *Proceedings of the Eighth Viking Congress, Aarhus, 24–31 August 1977.* Odense, Odense University Press 259–69.

Crawford, I.A. (1986) *The West Highlands and Islands: a view of 50 centuries: The Udal (North Uist) evidence.* Cambridge, The Great Auk Press.

Crawford, I.A. (1988) Structural discontinuity and associable evidence for settlement disruption: five crucial episodes in a continuous occupation 250–1689 (the Udal evidence). In R. Mason (ed.) *Settlement and Society in Scotland: migration, colonisation and integration.* Glasgow, Association of Scottish Historical Studies, 1–34.

Crawford, I.A. and Switsur, R. (1977) Sandscaping and C14: the Udal, N. Uist. *Antiquity* 51, 124–36.

Dockrill, S.J., Bond, J.M., Turner, V.E., Brown, L.D., Bushford, D.J., Cussons, J.E. and Nicholson, R.A. (2010) *Excavations at Old Scatness, Shetland. Vol. 1: The Pictish Village and Viking Settlement.* Lerwick, Shetland Heritage Publications.

Dockrill, S.J., Bond, J.M., Turner, V.E., Brown, L.D., Bashford, D.J., Cussans, J.E.M. and Nicholson, R.A. (2015) *Excavations at Old Scatness, Shetland, Vol. 2: The Broch and Iron Age Village.* Lerwick: Shetland Heritage Publications.

Duncan, A.A.M. and Brown, A.L. (1957) Argyll and the Isles in the earlier Middle Ages. *Proceedings of the Society of Antiquaries of Scotland* 90, 192–220.

Dunwell, A.J., Cowie, T.G., Bruce, M.F., Neighbour, T. and Rees, A.R. (1995) A Viking Age cemetery at Cnip, Uig, Isle of Lewis. *Proceedings of the Society of Antiquaries of Scotland* 125, 719–52.

Einarsson, B.F. (1995) *The Settlement of Iceland: A Critical Approach.* Reykjavik, Hið íslenska bókmenntafélag.

Etchingham, C. (2001) North Wales, Ireland and the Isles: The Insular Viking Zone. *Peritia* 15, 145–87.

Fagan, B. (2000) *The Little Ice Age. How Climate made History 1300–1850.* New York, Basic Books.

Fisher, I. (2001) *Early Medieval Sculpture in the West Highlands and Islands.* Edinburgh, Royal Commission on the Ancient and Historical Monuments of Scotland.

Fleming, A. and Woolf, A. (1992) Cille Donnain: a late Norse church in South Uist. *Proceedings of the Society of Antiquaries of Scotland* 122, 329–350.

Fojut, N., Pringle, D. and Walker, B. (1994) *The Ancient Monuments of the Western Isles.* Edinburgh, The Stationary Office.

Forsyth, K. (2007) An ogham-inscribed plaque from Bornais, South Uist. In Smith, B.B., Taylor, S. and Williams, G. (eds) *West over Sea. Studies in Scandinavian sea-borne expansion and settlement before 1300.* Leiden, Brill, 461–478.

Forte, A.D.M, Oram, R.D. and Pederson. F. (2005) *Viking Empires.* Cambridge, Cambridge University Press.

Fuglesang, S.H. (1980) *Some aspects of the Ringerike Style: A phase of eleventh century Scandinavian art.* Odense, Odense University Press.

Gannon, A. and Geddes, G. (2015) *St Kilda. The Last and Outmost Isle.* Edinburgh, Historic Environment Scotland.

Gibbon, S.J. (2006) *The Origins and Early Development of the Parochial System in the Orkney Earldom.* Unpublished PhD Thesis, Orkney College/University of the Highlands and Islands.

Gilbertson, D. Kent, M. and Gratton, J. (1997) *The Outer Hebrides. The last 12,000 years.* Sheffield, Sheffield Academic Press.

Graham-Campbell, J. (1995) *The Viking-Age gold and silver of Scotland (AD 850–1100).* Edinburgh, National Museums of Scotland.

Graham-Campbell, J. (2020) *Viking Art.* London, Thames and Hudson.

Graham-Campbell, J.A. and Batey, C.E. (1998) *Vikings in Scotland. An archaeological survey.* Edinburgh, Edinburgh University Press.

Griffiths, D., Harrison J. and Athanson, M. (2019) *Beside the Ocean: Coastal Landscapes at the Bay of Skaill, Marwick and Birsay Bay, Orkney. Archaeological Research 2003–18.* Oxford, Oxbow Books.

Haansen, G. and Storemyr, P. (eds) (2017) *Soapstone in the North: Quarries, Products and People 7000 BC – AD 1700.* Bergen, University of Bergen.

Hall, M.A. (2007) *Playtime in Pictland: the material culture of gaming in early medieval Scotland.* Rosemarkie, Groam House Museum Trust.

Harding, D.W. and Gilmour, S.M.D. (2000) *The Iron Age Settlement at Beirgh, Riof, Isle of Lewis: Excavations, 1985–95. Vol. 1: The Structures and Stratigraphy.* Edinburgh, University of Edinburgh Department of Archaeology (Calanais Research Series 1).

Harrison, J. (2013) Building mounds, longhouses, coastal mounds and cultural connections: Norway and the Northern Isles, c. AD 800–1200. *Medieval Archaeology* 57, 35–60.

Henderson, G. and Henderson, I. (2004) *The Art of the Picts. Sculpture and Metalwork in Early Medieval Scotland.* London, Thames and Hudson.

Jennings, A. and Kruse, A. (2009) One coast three peoples: names and ethnicity in the Scottish west during the early Viking period. In Woolf, A. (ed.), *Scandinavian Scotland Twenty Years After* St Andrews, University of St Andrews Committee for Dark Age Studies, 75–102.

Jennings, A. and Kruse, A. (2009) From Dál Riata to the Gall-Gaidheil. *Viking and Medieval Scandinavia* 5, 123–49.

Kruse, A. (2005) Explorers, raiders and settlers. The Norse impact upon Hebridean placenames. In Gammeltoft, P., Hough, C. and Waugh, D. (eds) *Cultural Contacts in the North Atlantic Region. The Evidence of the Names.* Lerwick, NORNA, 141–56.

Lane, A. (1990) Hebridean pottery; problems of definition, chronology, presence and absence. In Armit, I. (ed.) *Beyond the Brochs: Changing Perspectives on* the Later Iron Age in Atlantic Scotland. Edinburgh, Edinburgh University Press, 108–30.

Lane, A. (2005) Viking-Age and Norse pottery in the Hebrides. In Sheehan, J. and Corráin, D.O. (eds) *The Viking Age: Ireland and the West. Proceedings of the 15th Viking Congress, Cork, 2005.* Dublin, Four Courts Press, 204–16.

Lethbridge, T.C. (1952) Excavations at Kilpheder, South Uist, and the problem of brochs and wheelhouses. *Proceedings of the Prehistoric Society* 18, 176–93.

Lockwood, M., Owens, M.J., Hawkins, E., Jones, G.S. and Usoskin, I.G. (2017) Frost fairs, sunspots and the Little Ice Age. *Astronomy and Geophysics* 58.2, 2.17–2.23.

Loe, L., Boyle, A., Webb, H. and Score, D. (2014) *'Given to the Ground': A Viking Mass Grave on Ridgeway Hill, Weymouth.* Dorchester, Dorset Natural History & Archaeological Society.

MacLaren, A. (1974) A Norse house on Drimore machair, South Uist. *Glasgow Archaeological Journal* 3, 9–18.

Mainland, I. and Batey, C. (2019) The nature of the feast: commensality and the politics of consumption in Viking Age and Early Medieval Northern Europe. *World Archaeology*, 50.5, 1–23.

Maldonado, A. (2013) Burial in Early Medieval Scotland: New Questions. *Medieval Archaeology* 57.1, 1–34.

McDonald, R.A. (1997) *The Kingdom of the Isles: Scotland's western seaboard, c. 1100 – c. 1336.* East Linton, Tuckwell Press.

McDonald, R.A. (2019) *The Sea Kings: The Late Norse Kingdom of Man and the Isles, c. 1066–1275.* Edinburgh, John Donald.

Milek, K.B. (2006) *Houses and households in early Icelandic society: geoarchaeology and the interpretation of social space.* Unpublished Ph. D. thesis, University of Cambridge.

Mitchell, J., Cook, M., Dunbar, L., Ives, R. and Noble, G. (2020) Monumental Cemeteries of Pictland. Excavation and dating evidence from Greshop, Moray and Bankhead of Kinloch, Perthshire. *Tayside and Fife Archaeological Journal* 26, 21–34.

Montgomery, J., Evans, J.A. and Neighbour, T. (2003) Sr isotope evidence for population movement within the Hebridean Norse community of NW Scotland. *Journal of the Geological Society* 160.5, 649–53.

Montgomery, J., Grimes, V., Buckberry, J., Evans, J.A., Richards, M.P. and Barrett, J.H. (2014) Finding Vikings with isotope analysis: The view from wet and windy isles. *Journal of the North Atlantic* 2.1, 51–9.

Moreland, J.F. (2019) AD536 – Back to nature? *Acta Archaeologica* 89.1, 91–111.

Morris, C.D. (2021) *The Birsay Bay Project Volume 3: The Brough of Birsay, Orkney: Investigations 1954–2014.* Oxford, Oxbow Books.

Mulville, J. (2002) The role of cetacea in prehistoric and historic Atlantic Scotland. *International Journal of Osteoarchaeology* 12, 34–48.

Mulville, J. (2010) Red deer on Scottish islands. In O'Connor, T. and Sykes, N. (eds) *Extinctions and Invasions: a social history of British fauna.* Oxford, Oxbow Books.

Mulville, J. (2016) Dealing with deer: Norse responses to Scottish Isles Cervids. In Barrett, J. and Gibbon, S.J. (eds) *Maritime societies of the Viking and Medieval World.* Leeds, Maney Publishing, 289–307.

Neighbour, T., Knott, C., Bruce, M.F. and Kerr, N.W. (2000) Excavation of two burials at Galson, Isle of Lewis, 1993 and 1996. *Proceedings of the Society of Antiquaries of Scotland* 130, 567–74.

Noble, G. and Evans, N. (2022) *Picts: Scourge of Rome Rulers of the North.* Edinburgh, Birlinn.

O'Grady, O.J.T. (2008) *The setting and practice of open-air judicial assemblies in medieval Scotland: a multidisciplinary study.* Unpublished PhD thesis, University of Glasgow.

Oram, R. (2004) The Lordship of the Isles: 1336–1545. In Omand, D. (ed.) *The Argyll Book.* Edinburgh: Birlinn, 123–39.

Oram, R. (2014) 'The worst disaster suffered by the people of Scotland in recorded history': climate change, dearth and pathogens in the long 14th century. *Proceedings of the Society of Antiquaries of Scotland* 144, 223–244.

Owen, O. (2023) Revisiting Tuckquoy – Still Full of Surprises. In Horne, T., Pierce, E. and Barrowman, R. (eds) *The Viking Age in Scotland.* Edinburgh, Edinburgh University Press.

Owen, O. and Lowe, C. (1999) *Kebister: The Four-thousand-year-old Story of one Shetland Township.* Edinburgh, Society of Antiquaries of Scotland (Monograph 14).

Owens, M.J., Lockwood, M., Hawkins, E., Usoskin, I.G. Jones, G.S., Barnard, L.A., Schurer, A. and Fasullo, J. (2017) The Maunder Minimum and the Little Ice Age: An update from recent reconstructions and climate simulations. *Journal of Space Weather and Space Climate* 7, A33.

Paulson, H. and Edwards, P. (trans.) (1981) *Orkneyinga saga: the history of the Earls of Orkney.* London, Penguin.

Parker Pearson, M. (ed.) (2012) *From Machair to Mountains: archaeological survey and excavation in South Uist.* SEARCH volume 4. Oxford, Oxbow.

Parker Pearson, M. and Sharples, N. M. (1999) *Between Land and Sea: Excavations at Dun Vulan, South Uist.* Sheffield, Sheffield Academic Press.

Parker Pearson, M. and Zvelibil, M. (2014) *Excavations at Cill Donnain. A Bronze Age settlement and Iron Age wheelhouse in South Uist.* Oxford, Oxbow Books.

Parker Pearson, M., Sharples, N. and Symonds, J. (2004) *South Uist. Archaeology and History of a Hebridean Island.* Tempus, Stroud.

Parker Pearson, M., Brennand, M., Mulville, J. and Smith, H. (2018) *Cille Pheadair. A Norse Farmstead and Pictish Burial Cairn in South Uist.* Oxford, Oxbow Books.

Parker Pearson, M., Mulville, J., Smith, H. and Marshall, P. (2021) *Cladh Hallan: Roundhouses and the dead in the Hebridean Bronze Age and Iron Age, Part I: stratigraphy, spatial organisation and chronology.* Oxford, Oxbow Books.

Raven, J. (2005) *Medieval Landscapes and Lordship in South Uist.* Unpublished PhD thesis, University of Glasgow.

RCAHMS (1928) *The Outer Hebrides, Skye and the Small Isles.* Edinburgh, H.M.S.O.

Richards, M.P. and Mellars, P.A. (1998) Stable isotopes and the seasonality of the Oronsay Middens. *Antiquity* 72, 178–84.

Ritchie, W. (1966) The post-glacial rise in sea level and coastal changes in the Uists. *Transactions of the Institute of British Geographers* 39, 76–86.

Ritchie, W. (1967) The machair of South Uist. *Scottish Geographical Magazine* 83, 161–73.

Ritchie, W. (1979) Machair development and chronology in the Uists and adjacent islands. *Proceedings of the Royal Society of Edinburgh* 77B, 107–122.

Ritchie, W., Whittington, G. and Edwards, K.J. (2001) Holocene changes in the physiography and vegetation of the Atlantic littoral of the Uists, Outer Hebrides. Scotland. *Transaction of the Royal Society of Edinburgh: Earth Sciences* 92, 121–36.

Selkirk, A. (1996) The Udal. *Current Archaeology* 13.3, 84–94.

Sellar, W.D.H. (1966) The origins and ancestry of Somerled. *Scottish Historical Review* 45, 123–42.

Sellar, W.D.H. (2000) Hebridean Sea Kings: the successors of Somerled. In Cowan, E.J. and MacDonald, R.A. (eds) *Alba: Celtic Scotland in the Medieval Era.* East Linton, Tuckwell Press.

Semple, S., Sanmark, A., Mehler, N. and Iverson, F. (2020) *Negotiating the North: Meeting places in the Middle Ages in the North Sea Zone.* London, Routledge.

Sharples, N. (2005) *A Norse Farmstead in the Outer Hebrides. Excavations at Mound 3, Bornais, South Uist.* Oxford, Oxbow Books.

Sharples, N. (2012) *A Late Iron Age Farmstead in the Outer Hebrides. Excavations at Mound 1, Bornais, South Uist.* Oxford, Oxbow Books.

Sharples, N.M. (2019) Monumentalising the domestic: House societies in Atlantic Scotland. In Currás, B.X. and Sastre, I. (eds) *Alternative Iron Ages. Social theory from archaeological analysis.* London, Routledge, 284–306.

Sharples, N. (2020) *A Norse Settlement in the Outer Hebrides. Excavations on Mounds 2 and 2A, Bornais, South Uist.* Oxford, Oxbow Books.

Sharples, N. (2021) *The Economy of a Norse Settlement in the Outer Hebrides. Excavations at Mounds 2 and 2A, Bornais, South Uist.* Oxford, Oxbow Books.

Sharples, N.M. and Dennis, I. (2016) Combs and comb production in the Western Isles during the Norse period. In Hunter, F. and Sheridan, A. (eds) *Ancient Lives: objects, people and place in early Scotland. Essays for David V. Clarke on his 70th birthday.* Leiden, Sidestone Press, 331–58.

Sharples, N.M. and Parker Pearson, M. (1999) Norse settlement in the Outer Hebrides. *Norwegian Archaeological Review* 32.1, 41–62.

Smith, B.B. and Banks, I. (2002) *In the Shadow of the Brochs.* Stroud, Tempus.

Smith, H. and J. Mulville. (2004) Resource management in the Outer Hebrides: an assessment of the faunal and floral evidence from archaeological investigations. In Housley, R.A. and Coles, G. (eds.) *Atlantic Connections and adaptations. Economies, environmental and subsistence in lands bordering the North Atlantic.* Oxford, Oxbow Books, 48–65.

Stratford, N. (1997) *The Lewis Chessmen and the enigma of the hoard.* London, British Museum Press.

Tesch, S. (2016) Royal Site and Christian Town and the Regional Perspective, c. 980–1100. Holmquist, L. Kalmring, S. and Hedenstierna-Jonson, C. (eds.) *New Aspects on Viking-age Urbanism c. AD 750–1100.* Stockholm, Stockholm University.

Thacker, M. (2016) *Constructing Lordship in North Atlantic Europe: the archaeology of masonry mortars in the medieval and later buildings of the Scottish North Atlantic.* Unpublished PhD thesis, University of Edinburgh.

Thomas, F.W.L. (1876) Did the Norsemen Extirpate the inhabitants of the Hebrides in the Ninth Century? *Proceedings of the Society of Antiquaries of Scotland* 11, 472–507.

Thomson, W.P. (1987) *History of Orkney*. Edinburgh, The Mercat Press.

Vesteinsson, O., McGovern, T.H. and Keller, C. (2002) Enduring impacts: social and environmental aspects of Viking Age settlement in Iceland and Greenland. *Archaeologia Islandica* 2, 98–136.

Welander, R.D.E., Batey, C. and Cowie, T.G. (1987) A Viking burial from Kneep, Uig, Isle of Lewis. *Proceedings of the Society of Antiquaries of Scotland* 117, 149–74.

Wilson, D. (1851) *The Archaeology and Prehistoric Annals of Scotland*. Edinburgh, Sutherland and Knox.

Wilson, D. and Klindt Jensen, O. (1966) *Viking Art*. London, Allen and Unwin Ltd.

Woolf, A. (2003) The Diocese of the Sudreyar. In Imsen, S. (ed) *Søkelys på Nidaroskirkens og Nidarosprovinsens historie*. Trondheim, Ecclesia Nidrosiensis 1153–1537.

Woolf, A. (2005) The origins and ancestry of Somerled: Gofraid mac Fergusa and 'The Annals of the Four Masters'. *Mediaeval Scandinavia* 15, 199–213.

Woolf, A. (2007) *From Pictland to Alba 789–1070*. Edinburgh, Edinburgh University Press.

Woolf, A. (2015) The early history of the diocese of Sodor. In Duffy, S. and Mytum, H. (eds.), *A New History of the Isle of Man volume III: The Medieval Period, 1000–1406*. Liverpool, Liverpool University Press, 329–348.

Wyatt, D. (2009) *Slaves and warriors in Medieval Britain and Ireland, 800–1200*. Boston, Brill Academic Publishers.

Yalom, M. (2004) *Birth of the Chess Queen. A History*. New York, Harper Collins.

Index

A'Cheardach Bheag, South Uist 45–6, 56, 61–2
A'Cheardach Mhor, South Uist 45–6, 56, 61–2
Ackergill, Caithness 77
Aðalstræti, Iceland 140–2, 161–2, 180
Æthelræd II, king of England 143
Alexander, Lord of the Isles 3, 225–6
Alexander II, King of Scotland 187
Alexander III, King of Scotland 187–8
Allasdale Dunes, Barra 45, 48, 62
Allt Chrisal, Barra 9, 45, 48
Altar, portable 3–4
Amie MacRuaidhrí 174, 188, 219, 221, 225
Amlaib Cuaran, King of Dublin 89
Anglo-Saxon
    assemblies 176
    cemeteries 70
    chronicle 86
    coins 114
    invasion 71
    kingdoms 71, 89, 131
Angus Mor MacDomhnaill 186
Angus Og 226
Aoineart, Loch, South Uist 27–8
ard marks 106–7
Ardchatten Priory, Argyll 173
Ardnamurchan 75, 132, 176
Ardtornish castle, Morvern 171, 218–9
Armagh, Ulster 4, 6
Aros, castle, Isle of Mull 218–9
astragalus, decorated 52–3
Aud the Deep-minded 89

Baghasdail, South Uist 168, 233
Balliol, Edward 225
Barra, Isle of 9, 20, 27–8, 72, 75, 79, 114–6, 132, 187, 217, 226, 243
Barrett, James 34, 125, 180, 243
Barvas, Lewis 6, 8, 22, 110, 112, 173
Bayesian statistics 16, 106
Beinn Mhor, South Uist 27, 199
Beinn na Mhic Aongheis 235, 240
Beirgh, Lewis 66, 68, 80, 245
Belmont, Shetland 6, 170
Benbecula, Isle of 20, 22, 25, 132, 174, 187, 218–9, 226
Bergen, Norway 184, 187, 209
Berneray, Isle of 27, 32
Best, Julia 34, 222, 243
Beveridge, Erskine 113
birds, bird bones 15, 31–2, 34, 154, 217, 243
Birsay, Orkney 6, 139, 170–1, 178, 180, 245–6
bishop 3, 132, 134, 173, 176, 181, 185, 223
Bloody Bay, battle of 226
Bold, map of South Uist 233
Bornais
    abandonment 228–33
    ancillary structures 14–5, 95, 109, 169, 198, 203–4, 229–32, 241

chronology
    radiocarbon 16, 33, 35, 38, 96, 104, 106–7, 110, 134, 159–60, 227–9, 231
    structure 15–19
excavation history 9–15
geophysical survey 12, 105, 168–9
house (3), Late Norse
    abandonment 198, 228–30
    occupation of 193–8, 217
    structure 14, 18, 189–193, 198, 208, 219–22
landscape 24–7
longhouse (1), Early Norse
    chronology 104, 110, 112
    occupation of 101–5, 117–8, 120–1, 123
    re-use 134–8
    structure 14, 15, 18, 98–101, 124, 164, 169, 178, 190
longhouse (2), Middle Norse
    deposition 127, 129–30, 138–54, 162, 165, 178, 217
    economy 154–6
    living in 155–60, 202, 220
    structure 11, 13–5, 18–19, 134–8, 177–9, 190, 221
mound 2A, houses 14, 105, 163, 169, 204, 216–7, 230–1
mound 3, house 5 13, 169, 199–202, 215–6, 220–2, 231
settlement size 168–72
Borve, castle, Benbecula 218–9, 221, 235
Bostaidh, Lewis 6, 17, 64–6, 80, 110, 119
Bridei, King of the Picts 71
Bristol, England 153, 178
brochs
    character 48–50
    chronology 16
    controversies 80
    location 10, 47, 50–1, 176, 237
    occupation 51–52
    reoccupation 237–8
    symbolism 52, 57
Bruce, Edward 188
Burray, Orkney 113
Butt of Lewis 9, 32

Caldwell, David 172, 180, 221, 244
Canna, Isle of 75, 132, 134
Cardiff University 35, 139, 153, 204, 222
Carmichael, Alexander 114
castle 8, 181, 189, 217–9, 221, 223–4, 235–9
cattle
    agricultural economy 120–1, 125, 216–7, 220
    bone artefacts 52, 97
    hearth metapodials 54–6
    Iron Age 51
    Neolithic 30
    special deposits 100, 112
ceramics (pottery)
    Beaker 47
    Late Iron Age 63–4, 68–9, 79, 244

lipids 31, 34, 118, 125, 244
   Minty ware 153
   Norse 11, 64, 93–5, 102–4, 110, 123–4, 132–3, 151–4, 156, 159, 164, 180, 197–8, 222, 228, 245–6
      platter 132, 153–4, 159, 197–8
   post-medieval 232
chess, chessmen 147, 183–6, 209–10, 221–2, 244, 247–8
Christian(ity) 3, 4, 72–6, 102, 114, 116, 132, 143, 164
Chronicles of Iona 75
Chronicles of the Kings of Man and the Isles 9, 243
church, chapel
   Columban 9, 72–75
   organisation 132–3, 173–5, 189
   Reformed orders 173
   remains 8–9, 114, 170–2, 174–7, 178, 181, 223, 238–40
Cille Bharra, Barra
   church 8, 219, 238
   cross slab 114–16
Cill(e) Donnain
   church 9, 174–7, 245
   museum 225
   wheelhouse 9, 58, 247
Cille Pheadair (see also Kilpheder), South Uist
   ancillary buildings 202–3, 228–9
   archaeobotony 125, 216
   bones 34, 119, 120, 125
   burial, Late Iron Age 17, 75–8, 81
   chronology 15–7, 19, 33, 233
   church 174, 176
   erosion 24, 94
   excavation history 5, 7, 9, 13, 15, 19, 32–3, 134, 247
   finds 92, 108, 114, 143, 153, 178, 195
   houses 7, 19, 109–10, 136, 141, 163–5, 169, 178–9, 199, 201–3, 220, 222, 228–30
   settlement 96, 134, 177, 188–9, 227, 234
Clachtoll, Sutherland 80, 244
Cladh Hallan, South Uist 31, 33, 247
Clan Donald 171, 176, 225–6
Clan Ranald 174, 176, 219, 225–6, 238
Clarke, David 79, 222, 244
Clearances 10, 19, 241
climate change 62, 69–70, 233–5, 239, 244–6
clinker 96, 106, 167, 214
Clontarf, Battle of 89
Cnip, Lewis
   burial 7–8, 17, 33, 83–6, 92, 104, 112, 123, 145, 150, 245, 248
   wheelhouse 39, 45–6, 61, 80, 243
Cnut, King of Denmark and England 129
cod 119–20, 123
coins 8, 15–6, 96, 98, 112–4, 124, 143, 179, 195, 222, 228
comb, composite
   discoveries 11, 95, 104, 107–8, 110, 122, 143–6, 156–7, 159, 164, 178–9, 197
   fashions 143–5, 217, 222
   fish-tailed 207, 209–10, 222
   in burials 83, 85, 92
   Late Iron Age 63–4, 66–7, 101
   making 204–7, 209, 212, 247
   pendant 145–6, 148
   trade 209, 217, 243
   use 69, 72
   workshop 14, 204, 207–8, 211–2, 222
comb, Iron Age 42–4, 60–1
comb, whale bone 96–7, 194–5
coprolite 44, 165
Cork, Ireland 88, 124, 178

Cormack, William 3, 33, 244
crab 42, 154–55
Cramp, Lucy 34, 125, 244
Crawford, Barbara 180, 244
Crawford, Ian 5, 33, 80, 93, 95, 122, 124, 244
croft/crofting 12, 48, 213, 227
crops, carbonised plant remains
   agricultural economy 116–8, 122, 166–8, 201, 215–6, 220, 227
   assemblages 11, 116–8, 154, 156, 167–8
   barley 25, 30, 51, 116–8, 122, 156, 168, 214–6
   damage/failure 31, 79, 212, 239
   drying kilns 118, 166–8, 204, 212–6, 240
   emmer wheat 30
   flax 96–7, 116–7, 122, 156, 215–6, 222
   Neolithic 30
   oats 25, 30, 116–8, 122, 156, 167–8, 215–6
   processing 108, 117–8, 156, 166–8, 216
   rye 25, 30, 116–7, 122, 156, 166–8, 215–6
cross-slab, stone 8, 72–4, 81, 114–6
Cumbria 102, 173

David II, King of Scotland 225
deer, red 30–1, 34, 56, 121, 155, 211–2, 222, 246
Dibidale, Lewis, silver hoard 8, 112, 184
die/dice 36–7, 52–3, 57, 79, 164, 209, 244
dog 44, 51, 66, 165, 223
dogfish skin 205
dog-toothed moulding 219
Donald Monro, Dean of the Isles 176
Dorset Ridgeway, burial 90–1
driftwood 39–40
Drimore, South Uist 6, 110–11, 142, 246
drinking horn 146–7, 179, 185
Dublin, Ireland 86–90, 129, 131, 144, 153, 178
Dun an Sticar, North Uist 237, 239
Dun Ban, Loch Carabhat, North Uist 237, 241
Dun Bharabhat, Lewis 56
Dun Carloway, Lewis 48–50
Dun Cueir, Barra 35, 66
Dùn Èistean, Lewis 235–7, 243
Dun MhicLeoid, Barra 236
Dun Raouill, South Uist 237, 239, 241
Dun Torcuil, North Uist 51
Dun Vulan, South Uist 9–11, 47, 50, 66, 247
Dunbar, East Lothian 92
Duns Scotus 174
Dunstaffnage, Argyll 181
Dunvegan, Isle of Skye 223, 226, 238

Ecgfrith, King of Northumbria 71
Edward IV, King of England 226
Edward the Elder 113
eggs, eggshell 32, 42, 154–5, 217
Eidsborg schist 107, 148–9
Eigg, Isle of 75, 132
England 3, 4, 9, 19, 28, 35, 57, 71, 77, 86, 89–90, 92–3, 129, 131, 153, 169, 178, 195, 209, 226
Eogánán, King of Picts 88
Eoglais na h-Aoidhe, Aignish, Lewis 219, 238
Epiphany, battle of 132
erosion, coastal 10, 13, 38, 46, 79, 84, 94, 109, 234–5
Fincharn, Church, Argyll 174

finds
   cauldron 151
   cobble tools 41–2

copper alloy 15, 107–8, 144, 150, 157, 159, 207
cross, amber 143
cross, bone 164, 178
cross, lead 102, 114, 164
finger-rings 8, 57–8, 112–5
flint 15, 159
glass 15, 104, 107–8, 143, 195, 197
knife, knives 83, 146–8, 156–8, 162, 179, 194, 197
lead 15, 102, 114, 143, 148–9, 159, 164
loom, loom weights 108, 150, 161–2
mail 197
needle cases 83, 85, 150
needles 61, 85, 102, 108, 148, 150, 156–8
pins 42, 57, 63, 66, 68, 69, 85, 92, 95, 104, 107–8, 110, 122, 130, 143–4, 156–7, 164, 197
rivets, boat 145–6, 197, 207, 222
spindle whorl 101, 104, 108, 148–9, 156–8, 162, 197
spoon 146–7, 179
steatite (soapstone) 15, 96, 101–3, 107, 110, 122–4, 153
tine decorated 146, 157, 179
whetstones 83, 102, 107–8, 147–9, 156–8, 162, 197
Finlaggan, Islay 171–2, 176, 244
fish bones, fishing
  assemblages 15, 42, 96, 119, 125, 154–5, 159, 194, 196–7, 217, 220, 241
  consumption 31–2, 34, 118–20, 123
  cooking 34, 151
Fisher, Ian 81, 116, 124, 245
Fordun, John of 219, 222
Forsyth, Katherine 97, 124, 245
Fortriu 71
Fortrose, cathedral, Ross 226
Freswick, Caithness 6, 209
Furness Abbey 173

Gaelic language 20, 114, 121, 180, 188, 222, 244
Galson, Lewis 75, 246
games, gaming 35–6, 186, 209–11, 221
Garmoran, Lordship of 132, 188, 225
Godfrey (Gudrodr) Haroldsson 89
Gofraid Crobán 19, 131–2, 172–3
gold 8, 15, 113, 143, 179
Gosemer Kirke, Denmark 4
Govan, Glasgow 116, 176
Graham-Campbell, James 33, 124, 179, 245
Granastaðir, Iceland 140–2, 160, 162, 180
Great Host 89, 114
Greece 1, 2, 33, 143
Greenland 89, 184, 248
Gudmund, bishop elect of Holar 134
Guðrøðr Óláfsson, King of Man and the Isles 132, 187

Haakon Haakonsson, King of Norway 9, 187–8, 217
Hadrian's Wall 71
Hagia Sofia, Constantinople 3
Hall, Mark 79
Hamar, Shetland 6, 170
Harlow, battle of 225
Harold Fairhair, King of Norway 124
Harold Godwinsson 90, 131
Harold Hardrada, King of Norway 90, 131
Harris, Isle of
  archaeology 19, 79
  Christianity 72, 173, 223–4, 238
  control of 187, 223, 226
  geology 20–1

landscape 9, 20–23, 31
Sound of 22–3, 94, 96
Harry Potter and the Philosopher's Stone 184
Hastings, battle of 90, 130
Heggen Church, Norway 128
Henry, III, king of England 195
herring 120, 123, 217
history 86–90, 130–2, 187–8, 225–6
Hordaland, Norway 87
Howmore, South Uist 8, 168, 174, 176–7, 189, 219, 225, 236, 238

Iceland 3, 4, 9, 85, 89, 105, 120, 121, 134, 169, 211
  houses 139–42, 160–1, 203
identities
  Gaelic/Norse 85, 132, 187–8, 198, 239, 241
  gendered 17, 84–6, 156–8, 162, 179, 202, 216
  personal 17, 66–69, 79, 209
  regional 19, 71, 237
Inchmarnock, Bute, Hostage Stone 88
Ingrem, Clare 34, 125
Inverness-shire 22, 77
Iona 4, 72, 86, 89, 173–4, 176, 223, 226
Ireland 3, 4, 9 70, 72, 77–8, 85–90, 98, 112, 114, 123–4, 131–2, 153, 169, 176, 178, 187–8, 218, 220, 245
Irish annals 71, 86, 248,
Islay, Island of 72, 116, 131, 171–2, 176, 178, 188, 225
Isotopes 33–4, 77, 86, 91, 118, 123, 125, 151, 243, 246–7
ivory, walrus 184, 209, 221
ivory, elephant 184, 221

James, I, King of Scotland 226
James, III, King of Scotland 226
James, IV, King of Scotland 225
James, VI, King of Scotland 241
Jarlshof, Shetland 6, 39, 61, 146, 150, 170–1, 209
Jarrow, England 4, 6
John, King of England 195
John of Islay, Lord of the Isles 219, 225
John II, Lord of the Isles 226

Kerrera, Argyll 187
Ketil Fletnose 89
Kilpheder 46, 58, 61–2, 80, 174, 246
Kisimul Castle, Barra 217–8
Krokees, Greece 2

Lane, Alan 93, 124, 132, 180, 245–6
Largs, battle of 188
Lethbridge, Tom 46, 80, 246
Lewis, Isle of
  archaeology 8, 19, 79, 110, 112, 183
  Christianity 72–3, 81, 173, 219, 238, 243
  control of 187–8, 226, 241
  'Evil Troubles of' 236
  landscape 21–2, 31, 83, 226–7
  name 20
  place names 34, 75, 244
  vegetation 28–9
Lewisian gneiss 20–1
Limerick, Ireland 88
limpets 42, 230
Lindisfarne, Northumbria 4, 6, 86
Little Ice Age 69–70, 80, 233–5, 241, 244, 246
Lochboisdale, South Uist 27–8
Lǫgmaðr, prince of Uist 131

Index

London, England 129
Lord of the Isles 5, 17, 132, 171–2, 176, 198, 218–9, 225–6, 235, 239–40, 243–4, 246
Lowe, Chris 33, 246
Lundin Links, Fife 77

MacAlpin, Cineád 88
MacDougall, clan 173, 181, 188, 225
machair
    agriculture 116–8, 121–2, 134, 167–8, 215
    archaeology 37, 40, 44, 83, 95, 99, 137–8, 167, 184, 241
    birds 32
    definition 10, 34, 247
    destabilisation and abandonment 232–5, 234–5
    landscapes 22, 24–8, 72, 79, 83, 134, 243
    settlement location 19, 46–8, 50–1, 62, 80, 110, 132, 168, 176–7, 218, 226–7, 232–3, 247
Machair Mheadhanach, South Uist 168, 232
MacLeod, Alexander of Dunvegan 223
MacLeod, clan 176, 223, 226, 236, 238
MacLeod, Malcolm 183
MacLeod, Roderick of Lewis 3
MacNeill of Barra 114, 176, 238
MacRuaidhri, clan 132, 187–8, 221
Maelrubha 75
Magnus Óláfsson berfoettr (Barelegs), King of Norway 95, 131, 172
Magnus, the Lawmender, King of Norway 188
Man, Isle of 19, 115, 131, 172–4, 176, 178
Man and the Isles, Kingdom of 2, 5, 9, 17, 19, 131–2, 134, 172–3, 177, 178, 180, 187, 195, 243, 246
Marshall, Peter 16, 33
Mesolithic 10, 29
Milek, Karen 161–2, 180, 246
Minch 9, 20, 22, 28, 30, 119
Mingulay, Isle of 27–8, 32
Morisons 226, 236, 241
Morris, Chris 180, 246
Mousa, Shetland 48, 50
Mulville, Jacqui 34, 125, 222, 243–4, 246–7
mythology 131, 184

Nechtansmere, battle of 71
Neolithic 30–1, 34, 70, 94, 103, 118
Ness, Lewis 32, 173, 236, 241
Ness, River, Inverness-shire 71
Newark, Orkney 118
Nidaros, Norway 173
Niðri á Toft, Faroes 141–2
Noggin the Nog 184
North Rona 9, 72–4
Northumbria 71, 89, 114, 241
Norway 3, 19, 34, 87–8, 96, 107, 124, 134, 148–9, 153, 173, 184, 186–8, 211
Norwick, Shetland 150

ogham inscription 96–7, 176, 178, 245
Olabhat, Loch, Lewis 68, 80, 243
Olaf of Dublin 88–9
Olaf Kyrre, king of Norway 98, 143
Óláfr Guðrøðarson king of Norway 131, 173
Old Scatness, Shetland 39, 72, 80, 245
Oma, Norway 141, 160, 162
Oram, Richard 233, 241, 245–6
Orkney 71–2, 89, 91–2, 113, 139, 165, 170, 172, 175, 178, 188, 203, 227, 241
    Earls of 89, 90, 124, 174–5, 178

Orkneyinga Saga 9, 175, 246
Oronsay, gold rings 8, 112–3
Orphir, Orkney 6, 121, 241

Pabbay, Isle of 72, 74
Papar 74–5, 81
Parker Pearson, Mike 5, 10–11, 13, 33–4, 80–1, 93, 109, 122, 124–5, 168, 179–80, 201, 222, 227–8, 232, 247
peat 21–2, 25, 27–9, 50–1, 83, 112, 226–7
peat ash 38, 54, 101, 106, 139, 141, 152, 164, 193, 198, 200, 204, 213, 228
phyllite, purple 107–8, 148–9, 180
Picts/Pictish 70–75
    archaeology 71, 75, 79–80, 177, 245–6
    art 71–2, 80, 92, 245
    burial 75–8
    church 73–75
    historical development 70–2, 79, 88, 111, 124, 248
    house 64–5
    language 20
    Viking interaction 88, 91–2, 122–3, 177
pig
    agricultural economy 120–1
    bone artefacts 105
    consumption 121–2, 155, 217
    Neolithic 30
pits
    hearth 96, 204
    house construction 37, 59, 98–9, 101, 137, 156
    structured activity 96, 98–101, 104, 109–110, 138–40, 191–3, 196–7
plague 70, 79–80, 131, 233–4, 244
pollen 28–9
Pool, Orkney 6, 241
porphyry, green 1–4, 33, 130, 143, 156, 178, 244
Portmahomack 6, 91, 92, 244
Portland, Isle of, England 86
pottery, see ceramics
Preston, Jennie 35
Ptolemy 71

Ragnall, King of Dublin 89
Raven, John 76, 133, 180, 219, 247
Reformation 225
Rhum, Isle of 30, 132
ring money 8, 112
Ringerike style 127–30, 134, 143, 148, 156, 178–9, 245
Ritchie, William 34, 247
Romanesque art 184
Rome/Roman 2, 3, 31, 35, 58, 71, 85, 118, 184
Ross, Earldom of 225–6
Rubha Ardvule, South Uist 24, 40–1
runic inscription 8, 114–5
Rushen Abbey, Isle of Man 173

Saddell Abbey, Argyll 173
St Clements, Rodel, Isle of Harris 173, 223–5, 238–40
St Columba 71–5
St Donnain of Eigg 75
St Germans, Peel, Isle of Man 173
St Kilda 23, 32, 234, 245
St Peters, Rome 3
saithe 31 119
Sandwick, Shetland 6, 77, 170
Scalloway, Shetland 35
sea level rise 25, 247
Seaforth, Loch, Lewis 21

Sheep
    bone artefacts 35, 150
    clearances 241
    Iron Age 51
    Neolithic 30
    Norse economy 120–1, 125, 216, 220
    pen 12
    special deposits 99
Shetland 72, 92, 102, 123, 153, 165, 170, 172, 176, 178, 227
Shiant Isles 9, 32
Ship 28, 87, 90, 105, 134, 186, 151, 221
    Birlinn 22, 223
Sigtuna, Sweden 4
Sigurd, the mighty, Earl of Orkney 89
Sigurd, the stout, Earl of Orkney 89
Skaill, Bay of, Orkney 139, 180, 241, 245
Skaill, Deerness, Orkney 170, 243
Skaill, silver hoard 113–4
Skuldelev 2, longship 151
Skye, Isle of 9, 20, 30, 71–2, 75, 77, 86, 113–4, 223, 247
Smith, Andrea 58
Smith, Rachel 222
Sodor, Diocese and Bishop of 132, 173, 180, 248
Sollas, North Uist 45, 62, 101, 244
Somerled 132, 173–4, 180, 187–8, 220, 222, 225, 239, 247–8
Stamford Bridge, battle of 19, 90, 130–1
Staoinebrig, South Uist 232
Stewart, Margaret 225
Stewart, Robert, King of Scotland 225
Stornoway Castle, silver hoard 8, 112, 184
Stornoway, Lewis 20–21, 75
Storr, Rock, Skye, silver hoard 113–4
Strathclyde, Kingdom of 88
Strome Shunamul, Benbecula 72–3
Sula Sgeir, Island of 32
Swedish memorial stones 128–9

Taransay, Isle of 72
Tax 66, 131–2, 134, 186
Teampull na Trionaid, Carinais 173–4, 177, 219, 238
textile production 61, 96–7, 108, 114, 122, 148, 157–8, 161–2, 195, 202, 216
Thacker, Mark 181, 219
Thing 173, 176–8
Thomas, Capt W.F.L. 121, 125, 248
Thorfinn, Earl of Orkney 89
Thorstein the Red 89
Tingwall, Shetland 176
Tioram, castle, Lochaber 218
tir unga 132
Treaty of Ardtornish 226
Treaty of Perth 19, 187, 188–9, 220–1
Trondheim, Norway 173, 184, 209
Tuckquoy, Orkney 6, 170, 246
Tynwald, Isle of Man 131–2, 172, 176, 178

Queen 147, 185–6, 248
Quoygrew, Orkney 6, 139, 165, 180, 241, 243

Udal, North Uist
    combs 66–7, 207, 209
    excavation history 5, 33, 93–4, 124, 244, 247
    fish 119
    Late Iron Age settlement 11, 63–4, 66, 80
    Norse house 95, 163, 165–6
    post-medieval settlement 232
    pottery 93, 132
    Viking settlement 17, 92, 95–6
    wheelhouse 44–5
Uig, Lewis 83, 147, 183–4, 186
Uist
    archaeology 44, 50, 79, 176–7, 179, 198
    architecture 8, 165, 176, 179, 198, 220, 240
    control of 132, 187–8, 221, 225–6
    destroyed 131
    landscape 20, 24, 27, 31, 39, 116
    machair 10, 19, 62, 227
    name 20
    wildlife 32, 165, 211–2
Uist, North
    colonisation 17
    excavations 8
    finds 8
    landscape 20, 22, 25, 94
Uist, South
    excavations 5, 9, 13, 32, 110
    finds 153
    landscape 20, 22, 24–8, 116, 121, 215
    machair 10, 116–7, 121
    settlement distribution 10, 19, 37, 48, 52, 132–3, 168–9, 178, 189, 226–7, 232
Underhoull, Shetland 6, 170
Uspak 187

Vatersay, Isle of 28
Viking
    art 85, 127–30, 179, 245, 248
    burials 6–8, 17, 83–6, 92–3
    colonisation and raiding 5, 9, 17, 32, 66, 78, 86–90, 102, 108, 111, 117–9, 121–3, 134, 148, 151, 177, 211, 243–4
    definition 17
    houses 95, 160–3, 191, 203
    metalwork hoards 8, 12–4, 184

Wales, Welsh 78, 102, 131
Wars of Independence 188, 225
Waterford, Ireland 88, 144, 146, 178
Wessex 86, 89
whale, whale bone 31, 40–1, 96–7, 100–1, 108, 184, 194–5, 207, 209, 212
wheelhouse
    Bornais 36–44, 79–80, 96
    chronology 16
    construction 40, 99, 138
    definition 37, 79–80
    destruction 58–62, 90
    destruction of roof 38–40, 52–3
    monumentality 78
    occupation 40–44, 52–3
    reconstruction 53–8,
    secondary hearth 53–6
    settlement patterns 47–48, 50–2, 79,
    Western Isles 44–48, 80, 94, 101
Whithorn 4, 144, 173
Wilson, Daniel 183, 221, 248
winkles 42, 193, 197, 217, 196
Woolf, Alex 124, 131, 173, 175, 179–81, 245, 248

York, England 89, 130, 146, 173